THE KILLING
of
SS Obergruppenführer
REINHARD HEYDRICH

ALSO BY CALLUM MACDONALD
Korea: The War Before Vietnam   *(1987)*

THE KILLING
of
SS Obergruppenführer
REINHARD HEYDRICH

◨

Callum MacDonald

COLLIER BOOKS
Macmillan Publishing Company
New York

Maxwell Macmillan International
New York   Oxford   Singapore   Sydney

Collier Books
Macmillan Publishing Company
866 Third Avenue, New York, NY 10022

Collier Macmillan Canada, Inc.
1200 Eglinton Avenue East, Suite 200
Don Mills, Ontario M3C 3N1

Library of Congress Cataloging-in-Publication Data

MacDonald, C. A.
 The killing of SS Obergruppenführer Reinhard Heydrich / Callum
MacDonald.—1st Collier Books ed.
  p. cm.
 Previously published: New York: Macmillan Pub. Co., 1989.
 Includes bibliographical references and index.
 ISBN 0-02-034505-4
 1. Heydrich, Reinhard, 1904–1942—Assassination. 2. World
War, 1939–1945—Underground movements—Czechoslovakia.
3. National socialists—Biography. 4. Nationalsozialistische
Deutsche Arbeiterpartei. Schutzstaffel—Biography. 5. Germany—
Politics and government—1933–1945. I. Title.
DD247.H42M33   1990   90-39946   CIP
943.086′092—dc20   [B]

Macmillan books are available at special discounts for bulk purchases for
sales promotions, premiums, fund-raising, or educational use. For
details, contact:

 Special Sales Director
 Macmillan Publishing Company
 866 Third Avenue
 New York, NY 10022

First Collier Books Edition 1990

10 9 8 7 6 5 4 3 2 1

The Killing of SS Obergruppenführer Reinhard Heydrich is published in a
hardcover edition by The Free Press, a division of Macmillan, Inc.

Printed in the United States of America

Contents

Introduction

In the unlikely setting of a park in a small Midland town, a simple monument commemorates one of the most daring secret operations of the Second World War – ANTHROPOID – the assassination of SS Obergruppenführer Reinhard Heydrich. Heydrich, the head of the Nazi security police and governor of occupied Bohemia–Moravia, was one of the most powerful men in the Third Reich. An ambitious, ruthless and intelligent personality, he was regarded by some as Hitler's most likely successor. When he was killed in the early summer of 1942, the Führer compared his death to a lost battle. Heydrich was buried as a Nazi martyr, his final resting place designed as a shrine to inspire future generations of SS men. The grave has now vanished, lost amidst the mines and barbed wire of the killing zone behind the Berlin Wall. Heydrich was the only prominent Nazi to be assassinated during the war by agents trained in Britain, and the operation has been the subject of speculation and debate ever since. According to one account, he was killed by the British Secret Service because he was about to arrest a prominent German traitor who had been supplying vital intelligence to London. According to another, Heydrich was assassinated to prevent the extermination of the European Jews, the 'Final Solution' for which he had been made responsible in 1941. On the wilder shores of the imagination, it was even claimed that the British had Heydrich removed because he knew too much about the treasonable activities of the Duke of Windsor in the summer of 1940. The real story is different but no less dramatic. It is one of heroism and self-sacrifice, but also of political expediency, betrayal and death. In this drama, the British Secret Service was not the principal actor. The operation was rooted in the political requirements of the Czech exile President, Eduard Beneš, and planned by Czech military intelligence with the assistance of the British Special Operations Executive, SOE.

This account attempts to set ANTHROPOID in its proper context, using previously unpublished evidence from the files of the Foreign Office and the Special Operations Executive as well as the recollections of former Czechoslovak intelligence officers. Any book on the assassination of Heydrich owes a debt to the memoirs of Colonel František Moravek and to the research carried out by the Czech journalist Miroslav Ivanov, who, twenty years ago, tracked down many surviving resistance workers involved in the operation. It would also have been impossible to write without the assistance of a series of people, some of whom must remain anonymous. I would particularly like to thank Stanislav Berton, of Roseville, New South Wales, who was more than generous with material from his archive on the wartime occupation of Czechoslovakia, and Mr C. M. Woods, the SOE Adviser at the Foreign Office. I am also grateful to Major M. F. Kašpar of the Association of Czechoslovak Legionaries, Josef Süsser, a former radio officer with Czech military intelligence, and Sir Peter Wilkinson, the former head of the Czech Section in SOE. Gustav Kay of Warwick supplied background material on the experiences of the Czechoslovak army during the war, while Ron Hockey, formerly of the RAF special duties squadron, provided many details about the ANTHROPOID drop. Professor Edward Táborský, who served as wartime secretary to President Beneš, called my attention to a diary entry relating to the operation. Professor M. R. D. Foot backed the research with good practical advice. Peter Hinchliffe of Brew Technical Translation Services translated the Czech documents. Early drafts of the book benefited from the constructive criticism of my colleague, Robin Okey, and my editor at Macmillan, Adam Sisman. I owe special thanks to my agent, Gill Coleridge, for her encouragement at every stage of the book. The research was facilitated by a grant from the British Academy. I am grateful to the following individuals and organisations for permission to quote: HM Stationery Office, the Public Record Office, the BBC Written Archives Centre, the National Archives of the United States, Stanislav Berton, Ron Hockey, and Professor Táborský.

Callum MacDonald
Warwick 1988

THE KILLING
of
SS Obergruppenführer
REINHARD HEYDRICH

The Target

1

Funeral in Berlin

On 9 June 1942 the body of SS Obergruppenführer Reinhard Heydrich, head of the Nazi security police, was laid to rest in the most elaborate funeral ceremony ever staged by the Third Reich. His coffin lay in state in the Mosaic Hall of the new Reich Chancellery surrounded by banks of flowers, while a steel-helmeted guard of honour kept a vigil over the bier. The streets of Berlin were draped with black and throughout Germany flags flew at half-mast. At 3 p.m., as the Berlin Philharmonic Orchestra played the death march from Wagner's Gotterdämmerung, the final act began. Before an audience consisting of Hitler and the leading figures of the Third Reich, the head of the SS, Heinrich Himmler, delivered a long eulogy on Heydrich's life and work, describing him as a Nazi martyr, 'an ideal always to be emulated, but perhaps never again to be achieved'. According to Himmler, Heydrich was 'one of the battalions of dead SS men who are still fighting for us. It is our holy duty to avenge him and to destroy the enemies of our fatherland.' He was followed by Hitler who, visibly moved, gave a brief address which praised Heydrich as the best of Nazis: 'He was one of the greatest defenders of our greater German concept . . . one of the bitterest foes of all enemies of the Reich.' The Führer then laid a wreath on the coffin and pinned to the black velvet cushion displaying Heydrich's decorations the highest grade of the German order, an honour specially created for those who had rendered exceptional service to party and fatherland. He patted the cheeks of Heydrich's small sons absent-mindedly, muttered 'Heydrich, he was a man with a heart of iron' and withdrew from the ceremony. The coffin, covered by a swastika flag, was placed on a gun carriage drawn by six black horses. Preceded by a company of Waffen SS and followed by a retinue of mourners from the Nazi party and the high command, the body was conveyed at a slow march to the Invaliden cemetery, where it was buried with full military honours near the Scharnhorst memorial amongst the heroes of Germany's previous wars.

This spectacle was carefully stage-managed by a commission under the Propaganda Minister, Josef Goebbels, to portray Heydrich as the ideal Nazi, a heroic martyr whose qualities offered an example to all Germans. The cult of Heydrich was particularly strong in the SS, where it was deliberately encouraged by Himmler. A bronze death-mask was sent to the SS officer school at Bad Tölz with a photo album of the funeral and a copy of Himmler's eulogy to inspire the cadets. As one of them later recalled, Heydrich was venerated at Bad Tölz as a 'blond god . . . almost a mystic figure. There was hardly a room in the cadet school without his picture.' A similar death-mask adorned Himmler's office and the Reichsführer SS spent weeks selecting a suitable design for Heydrich's gravestone. The windy rhetoric in the Mosaic Hall and the splendour of the state funeral, however, concealed the fact that few in the Third Reich really mourned Heydrich's passing. Even Himmler was ambiguous about the removal of a figure who had started as a protégé but was developing into a threat. Secret policemen always know too much for the comfort of their colleagues and Heydrich was no exception: 'The decisive thing for him was always to know more than others, to know everything about everyone, whether it touched on the political, professional, or most intimate personal aspects of their lives. . . . He liked to remain in the background and pull strings.' In life his presence was enough to throw a chill into any gathering. It was rumoured that his personal safe contained bulging dossiers on his fellow Nazis whose disclosure could prove embarrassing. When Heydrich died Himmler's first act was to seize the key to this blackmailer's hoard, which he appropriated for his own exclusive use.

Those who met Heydrich were impressed by his ambition, ruthlessness and duplicity. Eugen Dollman, his interpreter on a trip to Italy in 1938, recalled: 'Of all the "great" men with whom I came into contact, he was the only one I instinctively feared,' a judgement shared by the head of the Italian Secret Service, who remarked: 'In Himmler's place, I would never tolerate such a man near me.' Even within the twilight world of the Nazi security police Heydrich was feared rather than loved. His own protégé, Walter Schellenberg, who later rose to head the German intelligence service, found his very appearance sinister:

He was a tall, impressive figure with a broad, unusually high forehead, small restless eyes as crafty as an animal's and of uncanny power, and a wide full-lipped mouth. His hands were slender and rather too long – they made one think of the legs of a spider. His splendid figure was marred by the breadth of his hips, a disturbingly feminine effect which made him appear even more sinister. His voice was much too high for so large a man and his speech was nervous and staccato.

Schellenberg described his chief as a born intriguer with 'an incredibly acute perception of the moral, human, professional and political weaknesses of others. . . . His unusual intellect was matched by the ever watchful instincts of a predatory animal. . . . He was inordinately ambitious. It seemed as if, in a pack of ferocious wolves, he must always prove himself the strongest and assume the leadership.' Wilhelm Hoettl, another member of the Nazi security service, remembered Heydrich as a man without a moral code: 'Truth and goodness had no intrinsic meaning for him; they were instruments to be used for the gaining of more and more power. . . . Politics too were . . . merely stepping stones for the seizing and holding of power. To debate whether any action was of itself right appeared so stupid to him that it was certainly a question he never asked himself.' His was 'a cruel, brave and cold intelligence' and his life 'an unbroken chain of murders'. According to Pierre Huss, an American journalist who knew him well, Heydrich 'had a mind and mentality something like an adding machine, never forgetting or lapsing into the sentimental. . . . Nobody ever got a break or considerations of mercy.' He disliked criticism and reacted badly to the enquiries of foreign pressmen: 'A single evening of him on his best behaviour was enough to convince every one of us that he was a bad one to deal with if you were on the wrong side of the fence.' These traits served Heydrich well in the jungle of Nazi Germany where the weakest went to the wall and political predators flourished. When he died at the early age of thirty-eight, he had killed thousands but was regarded as a success in the murderous game of Nazi politics. Within the security police it was assumed that he was destined for the highest office and that ultimately he aimed at nothing less than succeeding Hitler as Führer of the thousand-year Reich.

This ruthless and amoral figure was born into a Catholic family in the provincial town of Halle an der Salle on 7 March 1904. He was the second of three Heydrich children, with an older sister Maria and a younger brother, Heinz Siegfried. His father, Bruno Heydrich, was a self-made man, a singer and minor composer who had risen into the middle classes by hard work and a fortunate marriage to Elizabeth

Kranz, the daughter of a prosperous musical family from Dresden. In 1899 the Heydrichs opened a conservatory in Halle which provided a musical education for the children of the aspiring middle classes. There is little doubt that they planned a musical career for their eldest son. Before he left school, Reinhard had developed into a talented violinist and he displayed a continuing love of music for the rest of his life. Although the family enjoyed a comfortable income from the academy, it suffered from unfulfilled ambitions. Elizabeth always regarded Halle as second best and planned that she and her husband should eventually take over the prestigious Dresden conservatory, owned by her parents. This move was blocked by her brothers and she was forced instead to endure provincial life. As for Bruno, he was a deeply frustrated man. His early career as an opera singer was a failure and he never achieved the recognition which he craved as a composer. His Wagnerian productions received some critical acclaim in Cologne and Leipzig but were never staged by the Berlin Court Opera. Nor was he granted the prestigious title of professor by the state authorities, despite numerous applications.

Bruno's professional problems reflected more than a simple lack of talent. There was a question mark over the status of the Heydrichs, who were never fully accepted by polite society in Halle. Bruno's humble origins undoubtedly counted against him in the Kaiser's Germany, where class barriers were strong and it was usual to 'deny social recognition to those who had succeeded in acquiring the material prerequisites of entry into the higher class'. Nor was the family helped by being Catholic in a mainly Protestant society. Bruno's lack of advancement, however, also owed something to the persistent rumour that he was Jewish. As one former resident of Halle recalled, 'most of the inhabitants . . . had not the slightest doubt about his Jewish origin.' In fact the story was completely baseless. After the death of his father, Bruno's mother had taken a second husband, a locksmith called Gustav Süss. As a result the family name was sometimes recorded as Heydrich-Süss, and Bruno was listed under this heading in the *Musical Directory* published in 1916, an entry which was changed in subsequent editions after he had complained to the publisher. Süss was not Jewish and bore no direct relationship to Bruno, but the fact that many Jewish families had the same name encouraged speculation. While Bruno tried to joke about the story, it counted against him. Anti-Semitism was common in imperial Germany, particularly amongst certain sections of the middle classes who felt threatened by rapid industrialisation and social change. These groups rejected the capitalist order of the late nineteenth century and demanded the restoration of a mythical *Volksgemeinschaft*, a folk community based on bonds of blood and culture where class conflict would be abolished and social harmony restored on the basis of race. Such ideas were accompanied by an extreme nationalism which emphasised the exalted destiny of the German people, and they were common currency amongst groups like the Pan-German League which advocated an imperialist foreign policy. In this *völkisch* ideology, the Jew was the symbol of the hated modern world, the agent of change which had produced trade unions, socialism and large industrial combines. It was influenced equally by the romantic vision of the German past conjured up by Wagner and by a crude Darwinism which emphasised racial struggle as the iron law of history. These strands were combined and popularised by writers such as Houston Stewart Chamberlain, whose racist classic, *Grundlagen des Neunzehnten Jahrhunderts* (*Foundations of the Nineteenth Century*), enjoyed a great vogue after its publication in 1899, going through eight editions and 100,000 copies by 1914. Politically, anti-Semitism was at its peak during the economic depression of the 1890s and seemed to lose ground with the return of prosperity in the first decade of the new century. Socially, however, *völkisch* ideas penetrated a wide section of the German middle class.

It was Bruno Heydrich's misfortune to live in a region where anti-Semitism was well established. He was an ironic victim of prejudice for he was a strong proponent of *völkisch* ideology, who compensated for his social frustrations by extreme nationalism and loyalty to the Kaiser. Although his wife was a practising Catholic, he never seems to have taken religion very seriously, preferring instead a secular philosophy based on racism and struggle. The maddening rumour about his ancestry did nothing to change his ideas. On the contrary, he embraced them more fiercely as a means of denying the story and gaining social acceptance. Bruno Heydrich was a fervent admirer of Wagner, whose style he copied in his own operas, and he fondly recalled a brief period of study with the master's widow, Cosima, at Bayreuth in the summer of 1890. Like Wagner, he was a convinced anti-Semite who regarded the Jews as a danger to Germany. Bruno also drew inspiration from the work of Houston Stewart Chamberlain, who acknowledged his own debt to Wagner and married the composer's daughter Eva in 1908. According to Chamberlain, nothing was more important than race. History was shaped by racial struggle, which dictated the life or death of nations. In this Darwinian system, the Germans were best fitted to succeed and rule. It was a philosophy that Bruno Heydrich inculcated in his children, particularly his favourite, Reinhard, whose fair hair and blue eyes fitted the stereotype of the Nordic hero. Despite Bruno's reputation as a nationalist, the rumour about his Jewish origins continued to embarrass the family. It directly affected his sons, who were taunted at school, and probably accounted for the marked inferiority complex displayed by Reinhard Heydrich for the rest of his life. It is possible that he was never fully convinced that the story was baseless and remained permanently uncertain about his own identity. One acquaintance later recalled that, as an adolescent, Reinhard told tall stories about his background: 'He was either scared to be taken for a Jew or actually was in doubt himself as to whether he was one.' While his younger brother, Heinz, resorted to violence, drawing a knife in the playground and threatening his tormentors, Reinhard avoided direct confrontation. He became a moody loner who tried to prove his superiority to his fellows by excelling them in the classroom and on the sports field. As a schoolboy, he was already displaying the ferocious energy and will to succeed which were later to carry him upwards in the hierarchy of the Third Reich.

Reinhard Heydrich was ten when the First World War broke out and it shaped his early adolescence. He accepted without question his father's belief in ultimate victory, despite the stalemate on the western front and the growing shortages caused by the British blockade. The abdication of the Kaiser and the armistice of 1918 thus came as a terrible blow. As Germany was humiliated by the peace of Versailles and shaken by social unrest, the bottom fell out of his world. Like many Germans, his family denied that their country had been defeated on the battlefield and blamed the internal enemy, the Jews, who had conspired with the allies to undermine the home front. In the anarchy which followed the armistice, the Heydrichs rallied behind the paramilitary forces of the right, the Freikorps, former soldiers dedicated to crushing revolution and restoring order. At the age of fifteen, Reinhard Heydrich joined one of the most notorious of these groups, the Märacker Freikorps, which fought a particularly bloody campaign against revolutionary elements in Halle, Magdeburg and Dresden in the spring of 1919. He later claimed to have served as a runner, although his duties probably extended to the denunciation of local 'reds', his first experience of intelligence work. When the Freikorps moved on, Reinhard and his father enlisted in a home defence force, the Halle volunteers, armed and trained by Märacker's troops. At this time also, Reinhard Heydrich joined the Deutscher Schutz und Truzbund, a violently nationalist and anti-Semitic organisation. Its symbol, a blue cornflower and swastika, was prominently displayed on his bedroom wall along with its slogan 'We are the Lords of the Earth.' According to some accounts, he explained his membership of this body as an attempt to remove the skeleton from the family cupboard: 'Old Heydrich can't be a Jew if his son is such a wild anti-Semite.' At the same time, however, it was more than protective camouflage and represented a natural step for someone raised in *völkisch* ideas. There is no evidence that as a teenager Reinhard Heydrich ever rebelled against his father's philosophy. On the contrary, it was his mother's faith which he abandoned, ceasing to make any pretence of being a practising Catholic. The experience of defeat and revolution merely confirmed the prejudices he had imbibed as a boy and completed the creation of an extreme nationalist.

Although the threat of communist revolution was averted, the Heydrich family, like the rest of the political right, took little pride in the Weimar Republic which succeeded the Kaiser. It was democratic and liberal, the very antithesis of the ideal *völkisch* community, and was regarded as the creation of Jews and socialists, the 'November traitors' who had stabbed the army in the back. It was further damned by its association with the hated treaty of Versailles, which handed over large tracts of German soil to 'inferior races' like the Poles. For the Heydrichs, these prejudices were reinforced by the practical consequences of change. The rise of the working class threatened the social position of the family, while the inflation of the early post-war period destroyed its savings. Bruno was reduced to begging a subsidy from the town council, pointing out the role of his music academy in the cultural life of Halle and emphatically denying that he was a Jew whose efforts had been 'animated by personal enrichment'. His application was rejected, the final blow by an establishment which had never quite accepted him. The experience of revolution and financial uncertainty directly influenced Reinhard Heydrich's choice of career. There was little future in the practically bankrupt conservatory, and chemistry, which he also considered, required a university education which his parents could no longer afford. On 30 March 1922, at the age of eighteen, he reported for duty at the gates of Kiel naval dockyard as an officer cadet.

This was not as strange a choice as it might at first appear. The navy had always enjoyed a special status with the middle classes of imperial Germany, which regarded it as a truly national entity, the authentic expression of German unity and claims to world power. It was a technological service, offering a career open to talent where an educated middle-class youth could serve his country. The construction of the high-seas fleet under Admiral Tirpitz at the beginning of the century enjoyed widespread popular support which was deliberately encouraged by the naval high command. As a boy, Reinhard Heydrich had been impressed by the warships glimpsed on a rare seaside holiday at Swinemünde, and during the First World War the walls of his room were plastered with pictures of battleships and naval heroes. After the armistice, Count Felix von Lückner, a famous commerce raider, was a frequent visitor at the Heydrich house and held the boys spellbound with tales of his exploits. The prestige of the navy was damaged in 1918 when the great mutinies signalled the beginning of the German collapse. It regained its honour on 31 January 1920, however, when the Hochseeflotte scuttled itself in British captivity at Scapa Flow, an act of defiance greeted enthusiastically by the German right. The crews became popular heroes and were repatriated to a triumphant reception. It is hardly surprising, then, that the navy attracted the young Heydrich. It promised him a firm identity as an officer and a gentleman which contrasted starkly with an uncertain future as a civilian in Halle. The navy was impeccably nationalist and fiercely selective, accepting neither Jews nor members of the lower classes as cadets. As one of his schoolfriends later recalled: 'His complex about his alleged Jewish origins must . . . be taken into account. He always wanted to be more "Nordic" than anyone else. Hence his attraction to the "Nordic" navy.'

In other ways, also, a naval career appealed to someone with Heydrich's background and ideology. Although severely restricted by the treaty of Versailles, the navy of the 1920s was regarded by its commander, Admiral Erich Raeder, as the nucleus of a future high-seas fleet. The officer corps played a key role in his plans. Raeder's officers were a self-conscious elite, with a code of behaviour which set them apart from civilian society and the Weimar system. His aim was to create a navy style: 'The implementing of this style, which reflected Raeder's patriarchal and conservative background, extended to all aspects of the officer's life – his dress, religion, family and even his wife, who was expected to adhere to Raeder's code of conduct. Raeder expected the naval officer to set an example for all Germany, especially the youth.' At a time of national humiliation, his men were to uphold the vision of a rearmed Germany with a powerful fleet which would again command the admiration and respect of the world. This navy style was maintained by courts of honour which enforced the unwritten rules and dealt severely with offenders. The navy prided itself on producing not only officers but gentlemen. Although supposedly apolitical, it had little respect for the liberal republic it ostensibly served. Many officers had been active in the Freikorps after the armistice and yearned for the imposition of an authoritarian political system under which Germany would rearm and gain its rightful place in the sun. It was to this organisation that the young Heydrich, already an extreme nationalist, turned for refuge from a civilian world which he neither liked nor understood. The navy was to mould and shape him for the next eight years, teaching him lessons he was later to use in a new and more sinister career.

The tall, awkward adolescent, who arrived in Kiel carrying a violin, the parting gift of his father, rapidly became the odd man out in his training squad. Heydrich had little in common with his fellow cadets who viewed with suspicion his pretensions to culture. His high-pitched voice earned him the nickname of 'billy-goat' and he was bullied by the instructors, senior petty officers who were not averse to making life difficult for their future superiors. One of them regularly routed him from his quarters to play the Toselli serenade on the violin, a ritual humiliation which gave him a lifelong aversion to the piece. The rumour about his Jewish origins, which had plagued him at school, pursued Heydrich into the navy. As a member of his cadet squad recalled: 'In our year Heydrich was considered more or less a Jew, because another member of the group from Halle told us that the family had formerly been called Süss.' It was not long before he was known to his fellows as 'blond Moses'. Although he passed his initial training and was soon promoted, Heydrich remained an introvert and a loner. He attempted to excel in his duties as a means of overcoming his social difficulties, displaying an aptitude for the technical side of the navy. In 1926 he became a wireless officer and remained in signals for the rest of his career at sea. He developed his skills in modern languages, passing examinations in English, French and Russian, but he despised foreign cultures. As a young officer, he dreamed about the overthrow of the Weimar Republic and its replacement by a regime which would harness German economic strength and technical ingenuity to a drive for world power. He was a strict disciplinarian, unpopular with the lower deck because he drove his men hard to prepare them for the coming struggle.

Heydrich's professional qualities were soon noticed by his superiors and he received good efficiency reports. He also sought distinction through sports, becoming an excellent small-boat sailor, swimmer, fencer and rider. He was selected for the naval pentathlon team and attended the military sports school at Wunsdorf where he broke his nose twice in riding accidents. For Heydrich, athletics was a means of proving his superiority rather than a mere pastime and reflected the belief in struggle with which he had been raised. He threw himself ferociously into competition and played to win. He hated to be beaten and often indulged in petulant and ungentlemanly behaviour. When he was eliminated from the German officers' fencing tournament at Dresden in the preliminary rounds, he hurled his sabre to the floor in a fit of rage and frustration, earning himself a rebuke from the umpires. It was later claimed that his only real recreations in the navy were music and spy thrillers, which he read avidly. It is untrue, however, that he was an apolitical figure. The thrillers merely confirmed his suspicion that Germany was riddled with foreign agents dedicated to maintaining the shackles of Versailles, an assumption common in the wardrooms of Raeder's navy. Moreover, he was also interested in political literature and regarded the radical right as the future saviours of Germany. Even at this early stage he was aware of the Nazi movement. His godfather, Count Ernst von Eberstein, had a son called Friedrich Karl who was ten years older than Heydrich and had graduated from the Freikorps to Hitler's headquarters in Munich. The two corresponded while Heydrich was in the navy and the connexion was to have important repercussions on Heydrich's future career. At this stage also, he first met Wilhelm Canaris, the first officer of the cruiser *Berlin* on which he served in 1923–4. Canaris was both a war hero and a man with a political reputation. He was suspected of complicity in the murder of the communist leaders Karl Liebknecht and Rosa Luxemburg by right-wing extremists in 1919 and of sympathy with the Kapp putsch, which attempted to overthrow the republic in 1920. He was naturally admired by Heydrich and quickly took the lonely young midshipman under his wing. Canaris shared with his awkward junior a rejection of the Weimar system and a love of music. Heydrich soon found himself a frequent guest in his superior's home where he accompanied Canaris' wife, Erika, herself a talented cellist, on his violin. The friendship of a senior officer with Canaris' nationalist credentials flattered the socially insecure young officer, who later recalled that for the first time he felt accepted by the navy. Within a few years the paths of the two men were to cross again under very different circumstances.

After six years at sea, Heydrich was promoted to first lieutenant and posted to the communications section of the naval staff in Kiel. It was an important step which displayed the confidence of his superiors in his political reliability and technical proficiency. Nothing is known of his activities at this stage although it is unlikely that he was simply a signals officer. The official Nazi version was that between 1928 and 1931, Heydrich was attached to naval intelligence. Although firm evidence has never emerged to back this claim, it is not implausible. The top-secret B-Dienst was based at Kiel while Heydrich was posted there. This was a signals interception and codebreaking unit which had served Germany well during the First World War and had survived clandestinely after the armistice in defiance of Versailles. Its mission was to gain intelligence on Germany's most probable enemies by monitoring and deciphering their radio communications, a task carried out under cover of the Inspectorate of Mines and Torpedoes. Heydrich's technical background and language qualifications made him a candidate for such a unit. Moreover his mentor, Canaris, had a long association with naval intelligence and may have recommended a posting to some form of secret work. Whatever the nature of his duties, Heydrich cannot have been unaware that since the great mutinies of 1918 the navy had kept a wary eye on political subversion and anti-militarism, an activity in which Canaris had once been closely involved. It was a role he was later to perfect as the secret police chief of the Third Reich. In 1931, however, Heydrich seemed destined for a life in the navy and regarded his staff attachment as the path to further promotion. As a young lieutenant, he dreamed of becoming an admiral, the ultimate symbol of professional status. He had little doubt that his career would reach this apotheosis in war. As the economic depression gathered strength after 1929, the Weimar Republic was shaken to its foundations. In the elections of September 1930, the Nazis made their first breakthrough into national politics, gaining 6.4 million votes and 107 seats in the Reichstag, an achievement which stunned observers. Heydrich hoped that Weimar would soon be discredited and replaced by an authoritarian system prepared to harness German resources to a bid for world leadership. A national revolution would crush the internal enemy, the Jews and their Marxist allies, and break the shackles of Versailles. As he remarked to one of his acquaintances when he heard the election results in 1930: 'Now there will be nothing else for [President] Hindenburg to do but name Hitler Chancellor. Then our hour will come.' Heydrich miscalculated this development by three years and, when it occurred, he was no longer a naval officer.

The ambitious young Lieutenant had one weakness which brought him into conflict with his superiors, an insatiable sexual appetite. In his relations with women, as on the sports field, he was never quite a gentleman, a failing which offended against the naval code of honour. By 1928 the gawky adolescent had filled out into a handsome young man of twenty-four, whose Nordic good looks were marred only by a broken nose and a voice which remained curiously high-pitched. Heydrich capitalised on his appearance and the prestige of his uniform to become a notorious womaniser. This aspect of his character, like his obsession with sport, was based on the need to conquer and dominate in order to prove his own superiority, part of the philosophy of struggle in which he had been raised. As in other areas of life, Heydrich could not bear to be thwarted, a trait which had already threatened to involve him in controversy during a naval visit to the Mediterranean. As a fellow officer recalled: 'We were guests of the German Club in Barcelona. The entire German colony turned out. . . . Heydrich got to know a young lady of impeccable social background and went for a stroll with her in the Club Gardens . . . [where] he behaved in such a manner that the girl slapped him in the face. Red with anger, he came to me to complain. . . . When I told him, "You deserved it," he left the party. . . . The lady in question lodged a complaint, and the following day Heydrich had to make an apology.' On this occasion, Heydrich escaped a court of honour, but his luck eventually ran out. In December 1930, at a dance in Kiel, he met Lina von Osten, a boarder at a teacher-training college in the town. After only four dates, he asked her to marry him. Part of her attraction was her Nordic appearance, which reinforced Heydrich's deep-seated drive to assert his own identity and deny the rumours of his Jewish ancestry. Her family background also counted. Although her father was a humble schoolmaster on the Baltic island of Fehmarn, the family could claim an aristocratic ancestry, a fact not without appeal for someone with Heydrich's inferiority complex. As for Lina, a naval officer was a considerable catch, offering the prestige and status which she believed her family deserved. She had no qualms about the authoritarian sympathies expected of her as a navy wife. The von Osten family were themselves extreme nationalists and anti-Semites. Both Lina and her brother were early members of the Nazi party, regarding Hitler as the only man who could save Germany and restore it to greatness.

At Christmas 1930, Heydrich and Lina travelled to Fehmarn and won her father's consent to their marriage. Heydrich returned to duty, leaving Lina to complete her holiday with the family. The announcement of his engagement in January 1931 proved to be the prelude to the sudden termination of his naval career. When Lina arrived in Kiel for the beginning of the new term, she was met at the station by an agitated Heydrich who informed her that something dreadful had happened. He was to be brought before a naval court of honour by a previous girlfriend who claimed breach of promise. According to Heydrich, he had met this girl at a ball after the Kiel regatta. She had subsequently appeared at his rooms one evening, asking for lodging for the night. Nothing had occurred between them, but the girl's father was demanding that Heydrich preserve her honour by marriage. Not without difficulty, Lina was persuaded that Heydrich was innocent of misconduct but asked if such an incident was enough to constitute a betrothal. Her fiancé replied bitterly: 'You don't know the navy.' The court of honour heard a different story and, unlike Lina, was not persuaded by Heydrich's version. The evidence suggested that Heydrich himself had invited the girl to Kiel and proposed that she spend the night with him because hotels were too expensive: 'Out of necessity she complied, but managed to resist Heydrich's advances.' The case was made worse by the fact that the girl was well connected. Her father was the superintendent of Kiel naval dockyard and a personal friend of Admiral Raeder. Since Raeder's opinions were narrow, inflexible and well known, Heydrich had every reason to fear the result of the court of honour. His behaviour at the hearing did not improve matters. He attempted to make light of the situation, displaying an arrogant disregard for the naval code of conduct which alienated the court. It concluded that Heydrich's behaviour called into question 'the possibility of such an officer remaining in the navy', a finding which was confirmed by Admiral Raeder. In April 1931, Lieutenant Reinhard Heydrich was discharged from the German navy. It was the height of the depression and he found himself on the beach, neither an officer nor a gentleman, one of over 5 million unemployed.

Heydrich returned to his home in Halle, where he broke down and locked himself weeping in his room. As Lina later recalled: 'Discharge from the navy was the heaviest blow of his life. . . . It was not the lost earning power which weighed on him, but the fact that with every fibre of his being he had clung to his career as an officer.' His mother blamed his fiancée for the disaster and their relations were always to remain chilly. As for the von Ostens, they had second thoughts about Heydrich as a prospective husband. A cashiered naval officer was a different proposition from a serving lieutenant with a guaranteed future. Although Lina refused to break the engagement, marriage was impossible until Heydrich found another job. At first he hoped for reinstatement, but an appeal against the findings of the court of honour failed, forcing him to face the future as a civilian. He investigated the possibility of the merchant marine, but there were few openings because of the depression, and his discharge from the navy counted against him. The Hanseatic Yacht School was prepared to employ him as an instructor at a respectable salary but he found the prospect unattractive. He continued to yearn for his lost officer status and disliked the idea of becoming a mere employee, paid to teach the children of the rich. His nostalgia for military life was soon satisfied in the ranks of the Nazi party, which was becoming increasingly powerful as the depression continued to undermine the Weimar Republic. Not only were Lina and her brother already enthusiastic Nazis, but Heydrich also had connexions with Hitler's movement in the shape of Karl von Eberstein, with whom he had corresponded while in the navy. Hitler's crude anti-Semitism and philosophy of struggle echoed the prejudices with which Heydrich had been raised, and as early as 1930 he had expressed his approval of the Nazi leader. It was to Hitler that Heydrich now turned, not only to save Germany but also to retrieve his own career, requesting his friend von Eberstein to pull strings at party headquarters in Munich on his behalf.

While Heydrich was serving on the naval staff in Kiel, von Eberstein had been leader of the Nazi Sturmabteilung or SA, in Munich and upper Bavaria. The SA provided Hitler's movement with muscle, its brownshirted thugs specialising in street battles and the intimidation of political opponents in the style of the earlier Freikorps. In 1931, however, von Eberstein joined another organisation, the Schützstaffel or SS. Although subordinate to the SA, the SS, founded in 1925 as Hitler's bodyguard, already looked upon itself as an elite organisation. Its ethos was largely shaped by Heinrich Himmler, the twenty-nine-year-old son of a Munich schoolteacher, who became Reichsführer SS in January 1929 and began a process of rapid expansion. Himmler's mild manner and pudgy bespectacled face hid a ruthless ambition and will to power. He dreamed of turning the SS into a Teutonic aristocracy, a race of Nordic supermen who would provide the leadership of a new and racially pure Germany, purged of Jewish and Marxist influence. He saw the SS as an Aryan order, set self-consciously apart by its ancestry, appearance, discipline and bearing. According to Himmler, his men were to become the imperial guard of the new Nazi Germany. To this end, the conduct of the individual SS man was regulated by a code of behaviour which extended beyond his official duties into his off-duty conduct and family affairs. Even his choice of wife was not wholly his own. The moral and racial purity of prospective brides was personally vetted by the Reichsführer SS. On the recommendation of von Eberstein, now an officer on Himmler's staff, Heydrich became a member of the Nazi party, number 544,916, in

June 1931. He joined the SA in Hamburg and was soon involved in bloody street battles against the communists and other opponents of the Nazis. He took this step on the understanding that his association with the beerhall brawlers was to be purely temporary and that von Eberstein would use his influence to secure a speedy transfer to the SS. It is not difficult to see the attraction of this elite organisation for Heydrich, a failure in the eyes of his own social class. Himmler's black order offered both a means to power and an instrument of revenge against a society which had rejected Heydrich as it had rejected his father. Through the SS, he could become a member of a new aristocracy, an alternative to the naval officer corps which had expelled him. Moreover the SS emphasised the creation of a racially pure Germany, laying to rest the ghost of Gustav Süss and offering a vision which had engaged Heydrich since his school days in Halle. For the rest of his life, Heydrich was to be identified with the ruthless struggle for power by the SS, first within Germany and subsequently throughout Europe. The organisation was perfectly matched with the man.

The expansion of the SS under Himmler was supported by Hitler, who regarded the organisation as a means of keeping tabs on potential rivals within the party who aspired either to control or to replace him. In addition to this police duty, the SS also reported on the activities of groups opposed to the Nazis such as the communists and socialists. Until 1931, the work was amateur, haphazard and poorly co-ordinated, a state of affairs which Himmler was determined to remedy. He was already looking towards a future in which Hitler controlled Germany. Knowledge was power and, if the SS was to establish itself not only within the party but also within the state, it required a proper intelligence service. He therefore began to look for someone capable of organising the SS intelligence service on a professional basis and was handed Heydrich's file by von Eberstein. Himmler was impressed by Heydrich's Nordic good looks, which fully met his ideal of an SS man, and by his naval background. He shortlisted the former officer, along with a second candidate, an ex-army captain named Horninger. Heydrich was informed that he was being considered for an important position in the SS and ordered to report to Nazi headquarters in Munich. At the last minute, however, while Lina was packing his bags for the trip, von Eberstein sent a telegram to say that Himmler had a bad cold. The interview was indefinitely postponed. This news threw Heydrich into a panic but Lina insisted that he must go ahead and force the issue. A telegram was sent to warn von Eberstein and Heydrich caught the night express from Hamburg.

His friend was less than pleased to see him on the platform at Munich the following morning, but agreed to telephone Himmler at his chicken farm outside the city and request an appointment. Although plainly irritated to find Heydrich on his doorstep, Himmler was persuaded to grant an audience. When the importunate candidate arrived at the house, the Reichsführer SS wasted no time on social preliminaries. In an abrupt manner, he informed Heydrich that he had twenty minutes to sketch out his plans for an SS intelligence service. Heydrich, who was unaware of the purpose of the interview, was taken aback but quickly rose to the occasion. Whether or not he had ever worked for naval intelligence, as Himmler apparently believed, his knowledge of military organisation made his task relatively easy. He quickly drafted a short memorandum which so impressed Himmler, who was totally ignorant on the subject, that Heydrich was hired on the spot. His hasty scribblings became the basis of the Sicherheitsdienst (SD), which grew into 'National Socialism's greatest informer organisation'. Although he did not know it, Himmler had made a fortunate choice. The rival candidate, Horninger, was an agent of the Bavarian political police.

In August 1931, Heydrich began his new work in Munich. He was to serve the SS well and to offer Himmler unswerving obedience at odds with his usual devious conduct. The reasons were not far to seek. Without the Reichsführer SS and his elite organisation, Heydrich was just another of the anonymous unemployed, an ex-officer without a future. He remained embarrassed by his expulsion from the navy and, in an attempt to curry favour with the 'old fighters' of the party, gave out the story that he had been dismissed for Nazi activities. His SS file omitted the painful details, noting only that he had been dismissed 'on non-service grounds' against the advice of his 'immediate superiors'. Heydrich's rise through the ranks was rapid and by July 1932 he had been promoted to Standartenführer or colonel. Although his pay was small and irregular, he was able to marry Lina von Osten at Christmas 1931 in a Protestant ceremony, conducted by a Nazi pastor. The church was decorated with a swastika and the organ played the Horst Wessel Lied, the anti-Semitic marching song of the SA. Heydrich had long since lost his faith and his Catholic baptism proved no barrier to the marriage. Lina joined her husband in Munich where she threw herself into the role of model Nazi wife and mother. As a newcomer to national socialism, Heydrich was anxious to gain the approval of his superiors. He was privately contemptuous of Himmler, who imagined himself the reincarnation of the medieval king, Henry the Fowler, and joked with his wife about his chief's 'crazed mysticism', but their public relationship was correct and formal. Heydrich addressed Himmler in the most obsequious terms and attempted to make himself indispensable, applying what he had learned in the navy about the art of pleasing a difficult senior officer. For his part, the Reichsführer SS was impressed with the abilities of his new subordinate and realised that he had picked the right man for the job. According to Himmler, Heydrich was a born intelligence officer, 'a living card index, a brain which held all the threads and wove them altogether'. The information he supplied aided Himmler's own intrigues and provided the basis of a partnership which was to carry both men ever higher in the Nazi hierarchy. Lina later claimed that her husband was the real driving force behind the colourless Himmler, bulldozing him relentlessly forward. It is more likely that each exploited the other, Heydrich's knowledge and organisational skills complementing Himmler's own ambitions and established position in the party. He pursued a less formal relationship with Ernst Röhm, the head of the SA, who became, along with Himmler, the godfather of Heydrich's first child, Klaus, in July 1933. Heydrich had private reservations about Röhm, a notorious homosexual, but regarded a connexion with the powerful stormtroop leader as a means of personal advancement. Röhm was Hitler's closest friend and the head of the organisation to which the SS was still subordinate. His friendship could prove important to a man whom many of the Nazi old guard despised as an upstart. When the political situation changed after Hitler came to power, Heydrich was to have no qualms about conniving at Röhm's murder.

The main threat to Heydrich's progress in these early years was the old rumour about his family, which again surfaced to plague him. As his wife later recalled: 'In February 1932, just a couple of months after the wedding, Reinhard's previous associates in the navy, on learning that he had a position with the SS . . . testified to the Gauleiter in Halle that Heydrich was not really Heydrich but Süss and was a Jew.' This denunciation was evidence of his continued unpopularity amongst his former shipmates which had been firmly established since his earliest days as a cadet. The Nazi official immediately reported the matter to party headquarters in Munich, which launched an exhaustive investigation into the racial background of the Heydrich family. This concluded that Heydrich and his father were 'free from any coloured or Jewish blood' but failed to kill the rumour completely. It continued to circulate within the Nazi establishment and was common knowledge amongst foreign journalists in Berlin. In 1935 and 1937, Heydrich was forced to threaten legal action against people who declared that he was of Jewish origin. As late as 1940, someone from Halle was jailed for repeating that 'Heydrich and his father were not of Aryan ancestry.' By that stage, however, it was either a brave or foolish man who risked Heydrich's wrath by publicly digging up the past. Those who tried were liable to disappear without trace into the totalitarian police apparatus which he had created.

Heydrich spent the two years before Hitler came to power building up the SD, uncovering spies in the party apparatus and evading the unwelcome attentions of the Bavarian political police. It was a dangerous and uncertain period. Murderous street battles between the Nazis and their opponents were common and there was much talk of civil war. At times the SA and the SS were proscribed and Heydrich was forced to work underground. His salary remained irregular and he and his staff were often reduced to living off a thin soup prepared by Lina. None of this, however, deterred Heydrich. He was prepared to work tirelessly for a Nazi victory, regarding his own salvation and that of Germany as inextricably bound up with the triumph of Adolf Hitler. From the beginning, Heydrich displayed a natural ability for intelligence work. He created a central card index of potential opponents and toured Germany to recruit a corps of full-time agents, which included his brother, Heinz, now a journalist in Berlin. His aim was to create a service staffed with professionals as a separate elite within the SS. He was confident enough to surround himself with clever young men, but kept a wary eye on his subordinates, never letting them know the complete picture or allowing them independent access to higher authority. He withdrew his network of agents from local SS units and established his staff in a secluded house on the outskirts of Munich, well away from Nazi headquarters, where too many people could pry into its work. His aim was to build up the SD as a separate organisation within the SS, answerable only to himself. It was to have its own mystique, an SD style as exclusive as that of the naval officer corps which had expelled him. Heydrich's model was the British Secret Intelligence Service (SIS), an example he had encountered only in the pages of the spy fiction which he devoured in the navy. Like many Nazis, he was fascinated by the British Empire and attributed its success to the cunning of British intelligence. He believed that the British treated spying as an honourable profession, a calling fit for gentlemen and patriots. According to Heydrich, every decent Englishman was 'ready to aid the Secret Service, regarding it as his obvious duty. . . . British power was really based on the Secret Service for the best-informed have a great advantage over others. That was true both of commercial competition and of politics – and in England the two were very much the same thing. . . . The SS had adopted as its ideal this English view of intelligence work as a matter for gentlemen.' British agents were the cream of the establishment, an elite within an elite. Heydrich set himself to copy this pattern, concentrating on recruiting middle-class young men with an academic background like his later protégé, Walter Schellenberg, a lawyer who joined the SS in 1934 because it contained 'the better type of people'. According to Heydrich, SD agents were to be 'trusted people who acted purely from the best of motives and enjoyed the respect of the community by virtue of their achievements, their professional ability and their objective and sober judgement'. It was even said that he chose to call himself 'C' because this was the traditional cover name for the head of SIS. In fact it is doubtful if Heydrich possessed this piece of information in the early days of the SD and he probably found his example nearer home. It cannot have escaped his notice that amongst old Nazis Hitler was known as 'Der Chef' (the Boss), or 'C'. His adoption of the term was a symbol both of a desire to identify with the Führer and of the lust for power which shaped his entire personality.

Despite his emphasis on the British model, Heydrich created an organisation in his own image. The SD was staffed with the sons of the German middle classes, who shared his alienation from Weimar society, 'spiritually rootless' young men, 'uninhibited by any of the generally accepted norms of conduct'. It would be a mistake, however, to regard Heydrich as a mere technician, an amoral opportunist who offered his skills to the SS to escape the consequences of dismissal from the navy. His cold exterior concealed powerful ideological and emotional drives which made Heydrich a truly dangerous man. The SD was deliberately designed by him as the tool of Hitler's national revolution. Once the Nazis had gained power, it would root out Jews and Marxists, crushing the enemy on the domestic front as the preliminary to a war of conquest which would reverse the verdict of Versailles and usher in a thousand-year Reich. In this final cataclysmic struggle for German living space, there was to be no stab in the back such as had occurred in 1918. Nor were Jews and Marxists his only targets. In Heydrich, the urge towards power was fuelled by a primitive desire for revenge, not only against the 'November traitors', but also against the symbols of the old imperial Germany. His contempt for the symbols of this Germany – the officer corps, the bureaucracy, the Churches – was absolute and he was to seek their destruction throughout his career. The accumulation of power in the name of security would allow Heydrich to punish a conservative establishment which had humiliated his family and expelled him from the navy. What he could not join, he would sweep away and replace with a new Aryan aristocracy, the SS. This remained a distant goal during the early days in Munich. Before Hitler came to power, the SD was a tiny organisation with a headquarters staff of seven and only forty full-time agents scattered throughout Germany. It was not even the sole intelligence organisation of the Nazi party. Heydrich, however, was already dreaming of becoming Hitler's secret policeman. He envisaged the SD as the nucleus of a Nazi security system which he could shape and control, a vehicle for his own exalted ambitions. He was astute enough to realise that 'in a modern totalitarian system of government, there is no limit to the principle of state security, so that anyone who is in charge of it is bound to acquire almost unrestricted power.'

2

Hitler's Secret Policeman

Hitler's appointment as chancellor in 1933 opened a legal path to power and removed politics from the streets. The state would not be overthrown by the Nazis but infiltrated and seized from the inside. Himmler and Heydrich rapidly realised that in the new situation created by Hitler's appointment the SS and SD alone were too small and weak to serve their ambitions. The future depended on seizing and holding an outpost in the state bureaucracy which could then be shaped to serve their own purposes. As the SS always had a police role in the party, it was natural that their efforts should focus on the police and in particular upon the political police: 'There was good reason for this – of all public institutions the political police was the one providing the greatest scope . . . for secret processes, unauthorised executive measures and deviation from normal rules.' In Weimar Germany there was no national police force and control was exercised by the various provincial governments. Himmler and Heydrich planned to centralise this system and fuse it with the SS to create a new state protection corps which would act as the instrument of the Führer's will. It would be directly responsible to Hitler and free of either legal or political restraints. This security empire would guarantee the SS a leading role in the new Germany and could be turned against rivals inside and outside the party. In January 1933, Heydrich temporarily abandoned his position as head of the SD to serve on Himmler's staff with direct responsibility for implementing this plan. The small intelligence organisation was pushed into the background while its creators concentrated on seizing the levers of state power.

There were many obstacles to overcome before the SS controlled the entire German police. After January 1933, the focus of Nazi activity shifted from Munich to Berlin as Hitler manoeuvred to consolidate his position at the expense of the traditional conservative politicians who had made him chancellor. Himmler and Heydrich were relegated to the margins of this struggle. Not yet in the front rank of the party, they were left to kick their heels in Munich while the political action occurred elsewhere. Bavaria did not have a Nazi administration but Hitler hesitated to remove its provincial government until his own position was more secure. The Bavarian premier threatened to resist any attempt to topple his regime and his political police continued to harry the Nazis. As long as this situation continued, the SS plan was doomed to frustration. The only official appointment offered to Heydrich in early 1933 was the post of 'security expert' on the German delegation to the international disarmament conference in Geneva. He fitted badly into the world of formal diplomacy, which aroused all his savage resentments against the old Germany, and he rejected the whole concept of disarmament as a tool to maintain the shackles of Versailles. As far as he was concerned, negotiation was the tactic of weaklings and unworthy of a true German. He made no secret of his contempt for the diplomats with their 'shabby compromises' and his studied insolence offended everyone. His outrageous conduct in the bars and nightclubs of the Swiss capital was soon notorious. Heydrich's appointment came to an abrupt and undignified end when he was recalled at the request of the Ambassador for hauling down the Weimar flag and hoisting a gigantic swastika over his hotel, in defiance of the Swiss manager.

The political importance of Himmler and Heydrich lasted until after the elections of March 1933 when the Reichstag passed an enabling act dismantling the last remnants of parliamentary government and grant-ing almost total power to Hitler. Only then did the new führer feel secure enough to dismiss the Bavarian state government in Munich and install a Nazi commissioner. In his anxiety to ensure delivery of the official telegram from Berlin, Heydrich raided the central post office and seized the vital message at pistol-point. A convoy of black cars full of armed Nazis then roared off to occupy the government buildings, including the headquarters of the Munich police, which fell without a fight. The security system in Bavaria was rapidly reorganised. Himmler became chief of the political police with Heydrich as his deputy. From the beginning, Heydrich was uninterested in the ideological purity of his officers, many of whom had persecuted the Nazis on behalf of the previous regime. Instead of initiating a drastic purge he continued to employ competent professionals, who were to serve him well. Amongst these men was Heinrich Müller, a member of the Bavarian political police who had expected the worst from the Nazis only to be retained by Heydrich and to gain later notoriety as head of the Gestapo. Heydrich was astute enough to realise that self-interest guaranteed the loyalty of these new subordinates who faced a grim future without the protection of the SS. The new force created by Heydrich was employed by Himmler to smash and overawe all sources of opposition to the consolidation of Nazi power in Bavaria. The police became an instrument of administrative terror unrestrained by the courts. The leadership of the political parties, trade unions and the Jewish community were arrested and consigned to a newly created detention camp at Dachau on the outskirts of Munich. By the end of 1933 over 16,000 people had suffered beatings and humiliation behind its barbed wire. The majority were conditionally released after a short stay in order to spread the word about the fate which awaited opponents of the Nazis. Himmler was careful to maintain his own control over this coercive apparatus by a policy of divide and rule. Heydrich was denied jurisdiction over Dachau, which was run by SS Oberführer Theodore Eicke, a former policeman. 'Papa' Eicke made his own brutal rules, encouraging a virulent hatred of the prisoners and warning his guards that pity for an enemy of the state was unworthy of an SS man.

From their position in Bavaria, Himmler and Heydrich were able to take over the police of the smaller German states. Prussia, however, the largest of the provinces, remained outside their jurisdiction despite a series of intrigues. Until Prussia fell, the dream of a totalitarian police system controlled by the SS remained incomplete. Power in Prussia was held by Hermann Göring, first as Minister of the Interior and subsequently as premier. While Heydrich was engaged in his Swiss escapade, Göring was consolidating his position in the front rank of the Nazi party through his control of the Prussian police. Indeed he seemed likely to foreclose on the SS scheme by adopting it himself. The uniformed police was reinforced with Nazi auxiliaries and anti-Nazi officials were dismissed. In April 1933, the Prussian political police was removed from legal control and consolidated into an independent force, the Gestapo, with its headquarters in a converted art school on the Prinz Albrechtstrasse in Berlin. Göring openly boasted that his security forces were above the law and would be employed to crush any opposition. Himmler's representative in Berlin, Obergruppenführer Kurt Daluege, threw in his lot with Göring, hoping to replace Himmler as Reichsführer SS by attaching himself to someone with real power. When Heydrich visited Daluege in March 1933 to assert Himmler's control, he was refused an interview and was ignominiously expelled from Prussia. According to Göring, Himmler and Heydrich would 'never get to Berlin'.

The perennial power struggle amongst the Nazi leaders, however, soon offered them their opportunity. Although Hitler crushed the political opposition and the trade unions in 1933, he was reluctant to challenge other centres of power, most notably the officer corps, which was capable of overthrowing his regime if its privileges were threatened. Hitler's caution did not suit everyone in the party, and in particular his temporising alienated Ernst Röhm, the head of the SA, who called for a thorough purge of the old order. A brutal anarchist, without the bureaucratic skills of Himmler and Heydrich, Röhm demanded a 'second revolution' from which his swaggering brown-shirts would emerge supreme. Röhm made no secret of his desire to take control of the armed forces and to abolish the traditional power of the German officer corps. He dismissed the generals as 'old clods' and lobbied Hitler to appoint him Minister of War. His contempt was fully reciprocated by the military leaders, who regarded the SA as a rabble of 'peculators, drunkards and homosexuals'. Röhm's activities were increasingly unwelcome to Hitler, who had exploited the revolutionary threat of the stormtroopers in the struggle for power but now found their demands politically embarrassing: 'Henceforth he was the State, and it was undignified to have to play up to old comrades whose only recollections were of fighting in the streets and bashing policemen on the heads.' In the bitter quarrel between the SA and the army, Göring sided with the generals. He had his own eyes on the War Ministry and viewed Röhm as a dangerous rival. It was a situation which could be exploited by Himmler and Heydrich to improve their own position. In April 1934 Göring reluctantly surrendered control of the Gestapo to Himmler in return for SS support in his feud with Röhm. Neither side had any doubts about the real meaning of this bargain, which aimed at nothing less than the murder of the entire SA leadership.

Göring and Himmler delegated the details of their conspiracy to Heydrich, who acted with his usual combination of cynicism and efficiency. Apparently he had no qualms about planning the death of a man who only months before had acted as godfather to his eldest child. Heydrich's task was to exploit the growing tension between the army and the SA to force Hitler into drastic action against his erstwhile comrade. His men were soon hard at work, manufacturing evidence that Röhm was planning a coup and planting rumours calculated to inflame the situation. Heydrich found willing accomplices in the generals who were prepared to accept any ally in order to bring Röhm down. The head of the Armed Forces Office at the War Ministry, General Walther von Reichenau, was a frequent visitor at Gestapo headquarters: 'He . . . found Heydrich a congenial partner . . . [and later] provided barracks, weapons and transport for the great coup.' The army intended to hold itself aloof from the purge while the SS did the dirty work. At first Hitler hesitated to deal with Röhm but on 30 June 1934 he finally launched the so-called 'blood purge' which destroyed the political power of the SA. Whether or not he seriously believed that Röhm was planning a coup, it was clear that the officer corps would not allow the situation to continue and that without the support of the army the regime could not survive. Heydrich's efforts provided Hitler with a convenient pretext for what had become a political necessity. While the soldiers remained in their barracks, the SS death squads went into action. Röhm was arrested by Hitler at his holiday retreat in Bavaria and executed at the Stadelheim prison in Munich along with the rest of his staff. Meanwhile, in Berlin, Heydrich's men fanned out through the capital acting on the basis of death-lists compiled long before the supposed emergency. The SA leadership in the city was rounded up without a fight and shot by firing squad at the SS barracks in Lichterfelde. The Gestapo not only hunted down prominent SA men but settled scores with others who were considered a danger to the regime. One of Heydrich's targets was Franz von Papen, Hitler's Vice-Chancellor, a conservative member of the Catholic centre party. Von Papen was one of those who had attempted to manipulate Hitler, only to realise his mistake. Under the influence of his assistants he had begun to take the risk of criticising the Nazis in public. On 30 June the SS smashed down the doors of his office, shot his press secretary dead and arrested the rest of his staff. The safes were blown open and their contents seized. Only the intervention of Göring saved von Papen from an SS bullet. Others were not so lucky. Another conservative Catholic, Dr Erich Klausner, Director of the Reich Ministry of Transport, was shot dead by a Gestapo agent who was ordered by Heydrich to cover up the crime by faking a suicide.

The blood purge represented the victory of technocrats over the mindless activism of the streets. Unlike Himmler and Heydrich, Röhm failed to grasp the importance of infiltrating the state and paid the price. Hitler had favoured Himmler even before 30 June by making the SD the sole intelligence agency of the Nazi party, a symbol of the importance he attached to the SS as the ultimate guarantor of his authority within the movement. After the purge the SS made further

important gains. The SA was handed over to Viktor Lutze, a political
nonentity, and banished to the margins of power. The SS was freed
from subordination to the discredited brownshirts and became an
independent organisation responsible only to Hitler. In the wake of
these changes, Himmler and Heydrich pressed ahead with the construction of their security empire. The Gestapo was reorganised with
the assistance of men like Müller, who were transferred from Bavaria,
and its authority extended throughout Germany. Simultaneously the
SS fought off attempts by the Nazi Minister of the Interior, the
colourless Wilhelm Frick, to subordinate its expanding machinery of
repression to his own authority. Nor was the Ministry of Justice allowed
to intrude on the closed world of the security police. Lawyers, even
Nazi ones, were anathema to the political soldiers of the SS, who
recognised no authority but the Führer's will. The creation of this
autonomous system was formally recognised in June 1936 when
Himmler was appointed chief of the German police, a position he
combined with his party office as Reichsführer SS. Heydrich became
head of the security police or SIPO, which included the Gestapo and
the criminal police, while his former rival Kurt Daluege was given
control of the uniformed police or ORPO. The personnel of both
SIPO and ORPO was gradually absorbed into the SS to create a force
which was responsible neither to the state nor to the party but to Hitler
alone. The SD was not formally integrated into SIPO although their
functions overlapped and there was friction between ambitious young
SD intellectuals like Walter Schellenberg and professional policemen
like 'Gestapo' Müller. Although Heydrich considered amalgamating
the party intelligence agency with the political police, he found it useful
to maintain the independent status of the SD, so a complete merger
never took place. In September 1939 both were directly subordinated
to a new security office, the Reichssicherheitshauptamt. The RSHA,
essentially an umbrella organisation for the various agencies controlled
by Heydrich, was a jungle of competing jurisdictions and petty
intrigues whose only unity lay in the person of its head. Heydrich found
this situation useful, however, for controlling his subordinates and
ensuring that he retained ultimate control.

From the beginning Himmler and Heydrich regarded the police as
an instrument of political struggle. Himmler defined the mission of the
police, led by the SS, as 'the internal defence of the people', a role
capable of indefinite extension. According to Heydrich the old enemies
of the movement had not been eradicated by the Nazi seizure of power.
They had simply gone underground where they continued to plot the

destruction of the new Germany in league with international Jewry. There must be ceaseless vigilance to unmask and root out all sources of potential opposition. He was the surgeon who would save the nation by ruthlessly excising any trace of ideological or moral infection. In pursuit of these doctrines, the Gestapo was removed from the last vestiges of legal control and became an autonomous body. It had the power of detention without trial and could commit its prisoners directly to the growing SS concentration camp empire under Theodore Eicke. It was not only potential political opponents who suffered under this system. Heydrich's security police also attempted to rid Germany of 'anti-social malefactors' such as habitual criminals, homosexuals, drunkards and the 'work shy'. People in these categories were simply rounded up and consigned to the camps on no other basis than their past record. In the security police, Heydrich had an instrument of tyranny unparalleled in German history but his thirst for power remained unsatisfied. He intrigued constantly to take over the concentration camps and thus to gain control of the entire machinery of repression. The brutal 'Papa' Eicke, however, was protected by Himmler, who was wary of granting his energetic subordinate such unlimited powers: 'Eicke and his empire continued to constitute a tiresome gap in Heydrich's web.'

The Jews occupied a special place in Heydrich's attempt to purge Germany of 'anti-social' elements. In Nazi mythology, the Jews were *the* enemy, the agents of a malign international conspiracy against the Aryan race. From the beginning, Jewish organisations were closely monitored by the security police and by 1939 the SS had assumed a leading role in the 'Jewish question'. For Himmler and Heydrich, the solution was simple. The Jews had no place in the new Germany and must be removed by a combination of expropriation and deportation. In this process, rich Jews must be forced to pay for the emigration of their poorer brethren. The approach was first pioneered on a large scale by an obscure young SD officer named Adolf Eichmann in Vienna after the Nazi seizure of Austria in March 1938. He perfected a centralised bureaucracy for robbing and expelling the Austrian Jews, placing modern management skills at the service of the irrational anti-Semitism which defined national socialism. In January 1939, the system was extended to the rest of the Reich as the result of a directive establishing a Central Office for Jewish Emigration under Heydrich's direction, a task he delegated first to Gestapo Müller and subsequently to Eichmann. The directive, which cut across competing state and party jurisdictions, symbolised the final supremacy of the SS in the struggle to control Jewish policy. Nor was this surprising. The Jewish question was defined from the beginning as a matter of national security concerning the racial defence of the German people and thus the natural business of the security police. For the SS, as for Hitler, the 'racial cleansing' of the Reich, like rearmament, was designed to prepare Germany for war, the ultimate aim of the Nazi state. Before the inevitable struggle for living-space began, the country was to be purged of the internal enemy. The German people must never again be robbed of their imperial destiny by the 'stab in the back' which had betrayed the army in 1918.

The police were not only an instrument of repression but also a weapon in the byzantine politics of the Third Reich. Himmler aimed at the elimination of all competitors inside and outside the party and the ultimate creation of a Nazi state dominated by the SS. A start had been made with the murder of Röhm but many barriers remained, in particular the continued influence of the old elites in the early years of Hitler's government. Unlike Röhm, Himmler did not seek an open quarrel with the establishment but proceeded indirectly, chipping away at its position by a stream of intrigues and smears. In this campaign, Heydrich's security organisation played a leading role. In mounting an attack on the remnants of the old order, Himmler could not have chosen a better subordinate. From the beginning Heydrich betrayed a deep personal hatred for the old Germany and sought not only to discredit but to humiliate its representatives, often by sexual scandals either real or invented. One target of the SS was organised religion and in particular the Roman Catholic Church. Himmler was suspicious of an institution which attempted to maintain an independent existence within the Nazi state and which owed its ultimate allegiance to Rome. He saw it as an ideological challenge to the SS, the Jesuits of the new Aryan order, and regarded its influence on youth as pernicious. Heydrich pursued the SS vendetta against the Church with relentless venom. While he was contemptuous of the archaic Teutonic mysticism which absorbed Himmler, he also despised Christianity as the religion of the weak, the antithesis of the philosophy of war and struggle which alone could make Germany great. He regarded the Catholics as a particular danger because they owed moral allegiance to the Pope, thus threatening the vision of a German racial community united behind the Führer. It was no accident that the SS singled out prominent Catholic politicians such as von Papen and Klausner during the Röhm purge, since it was committed to the eradication of the political power enjoyed by the Church under the Weimar Republic. Heydrich could not forgive himself for missing von Papen on that occasion and continued to hound him after he became Ambassador to Vienna in 1934. One member of his staff was accused of homosexuality and forced into exile. A second vanished when the Nazis annexed Austria in March 1938 and his mutilated body was found floating in the Danube. Von Papen had no doubts that the Gestapo was responsible and went in fear of his own life as long as Heydrich remained alive.

The ultimate aims of the SS went beyond the eradication of political Catholicism to the destruction of the Church itself as a centre of power and moral authority. Heydrich attempted to discredit the clergy by engineering a number of show trials based on accusations of currency smuggling and sexual misconduct by priests and nuns which were given wide publicity in the SS journal, *Das Schwarze Korps*. He later developed a more elaborate plan to speed the decline and disintegration of organised religion. According to the SD agent Wilhelm Hoettl, Heydrich intended to disrupt the Church from the inside by sending his own men to the theological seminaries for training as priests: 'Within ten or fifteen years his emissaries would have attained . . . positions [in the hierarchy] from which it would be possible for them to begin their deadly work of destruction.' A similar scheme was to be directed against the Protestant Churches. This ambition was never realised since Hitler decided to postpone a final reckoning with Christianity until after the war and in 1941 Heydrich was forced to curb his campaign. His attacks on the clergy led to a break with his mother, who remained a strict Catholic despite her Nazi sympathies. She was never reconciled with her eldest son, although he continued to support her financially from his SS salary.

Another object of SS attack was the German officer corps, which had connived at the Röhm purge. In assisting Himmler to cut the SA down to size, the generals found that they had created a new and more dangerous rival. The traditional position of the army as the sole bearer of arms in the German nation conflicted with Himmler's desire to found SS military formations. As a reward for his services to Hitler during the Röhm affair, Himmler was allowed to raise three infantry regiments in order to carry out 'the special internal tasks' allocated to the SS by the Führer. These SS military formations were to be political shock troops directly available to Hitler for the suppression of civil disorder, the imperial guard of the new Nazi state. The decision was unpopular with the army commander, General Werner von Fritsch, a monocled representative of Prussian tradition, who was determined to block the further expansion of Himmler's military empire. As a result, he soon became the target of Heydrich's sordid intrigues. In pursuing the SS dispute with the army, Heydrich was working off a personal grudge which dated back to his ignominious dismissal from the navy in 1931. The officer corps represented a tradition which had expelled and humiliated him and on which he wished to be revenged. Moreover the general staff was a rival in his chosen field of intelligence. There was growing friction between Heydrich's expanding police system and the military espionage and counter-espionage organisation, the Abwehr, particularly when the SD began to trespass into the field of foreign intelligence after 1933. The professionals of the Abwehr regarded Heydrich's brash young men as blundering amateurs, often with reason for the early foreign operations of the SD were anything but subtle. In 1934 Heydrich attempted to kidnap Rudolf Formis, a German radio engineer and member of the dissident Nazi organisation, the Black Front, who was broadcasting anti-Hitler propaganda from a secret wireless station just over the Czech border. The affair was entrusted to a small team under SS Sturmbahnführer Alfred Naujocks, a character more noted for brawn than intelligence. Instead of masterminding a quiet abduction, Naujocks became involved in a gun battle with Formis in a Czech hotel room. The SD man was wounded in the affray and Formis killed. While a second agent rounded up the hotel staff at gun-point, Naujocks destroyed the transmitter with a thermite bomb, burning himself badly in the process. The two then fled across the border leaving a trail of obvious clues for the Czech police, including their car, which they abandoned at the frontier. The affair had to be hushed up at governmental level and Heydrich raged at his unfortunate subordinates, whose blunders reflected badly on the authority and prestige of the SD.

Heydrich intrigued constantly to discredit and undermine the Abwehr. By the end of 1934 the situation had become serious enough for the War Minister, General Blomberg, to remove the head of military intelligence, an unimaginative naval captain named Patzig. His replacement was Wilhelm Canaris, an officer who seemed the ideal candidate to resolve the tension. He had worked in naval intelligence during the First World War and was a convinced right-wing nationalist with a record of support for the Freikorps after the armistice. Moreover Heydrich had been his protégé and admirer as a young naval officer, a fact which might smooth over the rivalry between Abwehr and SD. On the surface a cordial relationship soon developed between the little white-haired Admiral and his former subordinate. The two families lived near each other in a respectable Berlin suburb and joined together for picnics, croquet matches and musical evenings which revived memories of the old days in Kiel. Every morning the two intelligence chiefs went riding in the Tiergarten. This friendship seemed to be reflected at the professional level. In 1935 a compromise was reached between Heydrich and Canaris which defined the jurisdiction of the SD and the Abwehr. The so-called ten commandments, however, were breached almost as soon as they were signed. The Heydrich–Canaris relationship concealed the continuation of a bitter power struggle. Whatever the face he chose to put on in public, Heydrich did not trust the 'levantine' Canaris or the 'shady barons' of the general staff. In the summer of 1935 bugs were discovered in the telephones of both the War Ministry and the Abwehr, which had undoubtedly been placed there by Heydrich's agents. For his part, Canaris attempted to collect evidence on Heydrich's supposed Jewish ancestry which might prove useful in the underground struggle between army and SS.

This wider dispute rapidly centred on the person of Werner von Fritsch, the leading military critic of the SS. Himmler and Heydrich made a series of attempts to discredit the army commander. In 1935–6 Heydrich's agents spread rumours that he was planning a military coup against Hitler in an attempt to force his dismissal. A covert campaign also began to involve von Fritsch, an austere bachelor, in a sex scandal. The General was unwise enough to offer accommodation to an unemployed member of the Hitler Youth who was planted on him by the Gestapo in an attempt to find evidence of homosexuality, an offence against both German criminal law and the military code of honour. Although this ploy proved unsuccessful, Heydrich was able to find a professional blackmailer, a petty criminal named Schmidt, who was prepared to testify that he had witnessed von Fritsch commit a homosexual act with a youth picked up at a Berlin railway station. Neither the planted rumours of a coup, nor the dossier on von Fritsch's supposed sex life, however, could move Hitler to action. The Führer remained unwilling to alienate the officer corps, whose support he required for the rearmament programme. When Himmler produced the file based on Schmidt's testimony in August 1936 he was ordered by Hitler to burn 'this muck'. Heydrich, however, did not give up. The file was not destroyed but saved for a more propitious occasion and when von Fritsch visited Egypt on leave in 1937 he was discreetly trailed by SD agents in the hope that he would sample the carnal delights of Cairo. Since the army commander was merely seeking a cure for bronchial catarrh, the SS bloodhounds were once again disappointed.

The SS feud with the general staff was behind Heydrich's involvement in the Tukachevsky affair of 1937, one of the most controversial foreign operations launched by the SD before the outbreak of war. Through contacts in the Russian émigré community in Paris, Heydrich learned that the Soviet army commander, Marshal Tukachevsky, was planning a coup against Stalin with the encouragement of prominent German generals. This fantastic tale was probably planted by the Russians as part of their preparations for the great purge of the Red Army which occurred in the summer of 1937. Heydrich's informant was a double agent who derived an income from both the SD and the Soviet NKVD. It is likely that Heydrich was aware of this but saw the possibility of using the information to his own advantage. As he informed his protégé, Walter Schellenberg: 'We can show that these contacts have as their purpose a double military putsch, in Moscow to get rid of Stalin, in Berlin to get rid of Hitler. We can kill two birds with one stone.' While providing Stalin with an excuse to purge his general staff, the SS could also eliminate those German officers it considered unreliable. It would not be difficult to produce a dossier containing evidence of treason in both Moscow and Berlin. After the First World War the German army had co-operated closely with the Russians in order to evade the disarmament provisions of the Versailles treaty, a covert programme cancelled by Hitler on ideological grounds. It was only necessary to combine edited material from this period with documents provided by the SD forgery department to demonstrate the existence of a conspiracy. It is likely that von Fritsch was again one of Heydrich's main targets. As the German army commander he was the natural candidate for the role of co-conspirator with his Soviet opposite number. Moreover in the 1920s he had been an ardent champion of the secret co-operation with Russia terminated by the Nazis.

According to Schellenberg, Heydrich's plans for a double blow against the Russian and German military elites ran into opposition from Hitler. When Himmler raised the subject, the Führer insisted that the operation be strictly limited to incriminating Soviet generals. Decapitating Stalin's armed forces was one thing, backing the SS against the German army quite another. Heydrich was forced to curb his ambitions and accept this restriction. His dossier on the Tukachevsky conspiracy was handed over to the Russians in May 1937 for a cash payment of 3 million roubles by the hero of the Formis affair, Alfred Naujocks, posing as a corrupt SD agent. It is doubtful if the NKVD was taken in by this transparent ruse, particularly since it was probably behind the original story of a Soviet military plot. In keeping with the cynicism of the whole affair, the Russians paid for Heydrich's masterpiece with forged currency, which proved unfortunate for SD agents in the Soviet Union who later tried to pass the notes. It is unclear what role the dossier played in the subsequent arrest and execution of Tukachevsky and his fellow officers but Heydrich was quick to take the credit. It was immaterial to him whether or not he had been used by Stalin. What mattered was the way the affair was perceived in Germany, where it was portrayed as a shrewd blow against the Red enemy by the master plotters of the SD. Canaris, who learned about Heydrich's role only after the execution of Tukachevsky, was shocked. For him it displayed not only the scope of Heydrich's ambitions in the intelligence field, but the depths of cynicism to which he could sink. From that moment he was under no illusions about the SS. As he complained to his predecessor Patzig in October 1937, they were 'all criminals from top to bottom, and bent on ruining Germany'. In the following years Canaris became involved in a series of military plots against Hitler. While he never took a leading role in these affairs, he allowed the Abwehr to harbour a group of committed anti-Nazi officers, most notably his deputy, Colonel Hans Oster. It is hardly surprising that Heydrich, who soon had wind of these developments, regarded military intelligence as a nest of traitors, another item in the reckoning against the 'shady barons' of the general staff.

As long as Hitler resisted pressure to purge the officer corps, SS plots against the army were doomed to frustration. By the end of 1937, however, relations between the Führer and his military leaders were starting to fray. While the generals supported rearmament, they had increasing reservations about Hitler's plans for armed expansion, which they feared would plunge Germany into a war for which it was still unprepared. It was a situation which Himmler and Heydrich hoped to turn to their own advantage. Matters were brought to a head, not by the SS but by Göring. In January 1938 the War Minister, General Werner Blomberg, married a young secretary in a quiet ceremony which was honoured by the attendance of Hitler. Unfortunately for Blomberg, his wife was a lady with a past. Her mother had run a massage parlour in the red-light district of Berlin and she herself had posed for obscene photographs which were in the files of the criminal police. The Gestapo was well aware of the situation and had been watching her since the discreet affair with Blomberg began in 1935. Nevertheless Himmler and Heydrich allowed the marriage to go ahead in the hope of starting a second time-bomb ticking under the general staff. This plot came to fruition prematurely when Göring acquired the compromising photographs early in the new year. He immediately took the evidence to Hitler, hoping to start a scandal which would provoke the removal of Blomberg and his own appointment as War Minister, a post he had coveted since 1933. Himmler and Heydrich exploited these premature revelations about Blomberg to pursue their own feud with the army. The old dossier on von Fritsch was immediately revived and presented to Hitler as further evidence of moral corruption amongst the top military leaders. The SS hoped to humiliate the officer corps, using the real evidence against Frau Blomberg to lend credence to the false charges against von Fritsch. The army, trapped by Prussian tradition, would be unable to resist. Its rigid code of honour could never tolerate a prostitute as a general's wife and a homosexual as a commander. The situation must have given Heydrich particular satisfaction as he recalled the circumstances of his own dismissal in 1931.

In reviving the charges against von Fritsch, Himmler and Heydrich nearly overreached themselves. Hitler seized on the double scandal to reorganise the high command, removing his critics and assuming personal control of the War Ministry. At the same time, he was careful not to push the army too far and conceded an investigation of the charges against von Fritsch by a military court of honour, a development unforeseen by Heydrich. It was soon clear that the evidence against the army commander had been wholly manufactured to support the ambitions of the SS. Canaris exploited this situation in an attempt to discredit a dangerous rival, lobbying senior commanders to demand the dismissal of Himmler, Heydrich and the entire leadership of the security police for attacking the honour of the German army. For a time the situation hung in the balance and Berlin was swept by rumours of an impending military coup. Heydrich was well aware of the dangers and displayed an agitation at odds with his usual appearance of icy calm. Preparations were made to defend Gestapo headquarters against the Berlin garrison and Schellenberg, a crack shot, found himself invited to supper in his chief's office with instructions to bring his pistol and plenty of ammunition. The crisis was defused by the Nazi seizure of Austria on 12 March 1938 which delayed the trial of von Fritsch. When the court reconvened three weeks later, it was rapidly proved that the Gestapo case rested on perjured evidence and von Fritsch was acquitted. The army, however, demanded neither his reinstatement nor the dismissal of Himmler and Heydrich. In the wake of the Austrian operation, few officers were prepared to confront a triumphant Führer. Von Fritsch was pensioned off and the power struggle between army and SS, Abwehr and SD, remained unresolved. The real winner was Hitler, who consolidated his power over the officer corps and removed a possible obstacle to his expansionist military plans. Von Fritsch never recovered from his ordeal. In 1939 he deliberately sought an honourable death on the battlefield, falling to a sniper's bullet at the siege of Warsaw. Heydrich greeted the news with a typically sneering remark about the old man's suicide.

On 1 September 1939, Hitler invaded Poland, beginning the struggle for 'living-space' for which Heydrich had longed since his days as a young naval cadet. Forty-eight hours later, Britain and France declared war on Nazi Germany. Hitler had originally intended to postpone a showdown with the western powers until a later date and tried to offer them an excuse for evading their obligations to their Polish ally. To this end, Heydrich was ordered to engineer a series of frontier incidents which would place the blame for the German invasion 'on other shoulders', an operation codenamed TANNENBERG. Heydrich's plan called for a series of fake Polish attacks across the German frontier on the eve of the Nazi invasion. The destruction of Poland could then be presented to the world as a legitimate response to unbearable provocation. As Heydrich emphasised, 'actual proof' of Polish attack was essential 'both for the foreign press and for German propaganda'. Bodies dressed in Polish uniforms must therefore be found at the site of the incidents and displayed to the press. These were to be provided by condemned prisoners from the concentration camp at Sachsenhausen, a task entrusted to Gestapo Müller under the macabre codename, CANNED GOODS. By the middle of August 1939, the preparations for TANNENBERG were complete. In strict secrecy, a special SD squad was assembled at the police school in Bernau and issued with Polish uniforms, weapons and papers. It was assigned three targets in Silesia, personally selected by Heydrich – the German customs house at Hochlinden, the forestry school at Pitschen and the local radio station at Gleiwitz.

The radio station at Gleiwitz was considered the most important objective, since it was intended to provide immediate public evidence of Polish aggression. The transmitter was to be seized while on the air and the noise of shooting, followed by an impassioned tirade in Polish, relayed throughout Germany on the national network. Heydrich assigned this part of the operation to Alfred Naujocks, the SD thug who specialised in strongarm tactics. Naujocks spent several days in the Gleiwitz area with a small team of six men, reconnoitring the target and awaiting the code words from Berlin which would launch the raid: 'Grandmama dead'. They came on the evening of 31 August as the German army prepared to invade Poland at dawn the following day. Naujocks and his men drove in two cars to a wood near the transmitter, where they changed into Polish uniforms. At 8 p.m., they broke down the doors of the radio station and burst into the foyer, firing pistols in the air and yelling in Polish. The staff were beaten up and handcuffed while a Polish-speaking agent prepared to read his prepared text into the microphone. At this stage, things began to go wrong, for Naujocks and his men could not find the switch which would relay the broadcast to the transmitter at Breslau and thus on to the national radio network. With time running out, they abandoned the effort, and the speech was hastily gabbled out on the local wavelength before the attackers fled. As Naujocks left the building, he stumbled over a corpse which had been dumped at the entrance. Unlike the bodies which were being simultaneously deposited at the scenes of the other attacks, this one did not come from a concentration camp. It was the corpse of a well-known nationalist from the Polish minority in the area who had been murdered on Heydrich's orders to lend the Gleiwitz attack added credibility.

Although Operation TANNENBERG failed to prevent an Anglo-French declaration of war, Heydrich had no regrets about the affair. Nor had he any qualms about the cold-blooded murder of concentration-camp prisoners. As far as Heydrich was concerned, the victims were expendable in the interests of the Nazi state. His war, which began with the killings involved in TANNENBERG, rapidly involved him in larger programmes of mass murder. The racial cleansing which he had supervised in Germany was extended to the occupied territories and became by 1941 a programme of deliberate genocide which swallowed up Jews, gypsies, Slavs and other 'undesirables', who were ruthlessly extirpated to clear the way for an Aryan empire. This grisly process began with the occupation of Poland. On 22 August 1939, Hitler informed Himmler that Poland was to be 'wiped off the map'. The ruling class was to be exterminated and the population reduced to slavery. This political task was unsuitable for the regular armed forces and the Führer looked to the SS to do what was required. Himmler delegated the task of murder to special units of Heydrich's security police, the notorious Einsatzgruppen, which rapidly imposed a reign of terror behind the front. As Heydrich coarsely remarked: 'We'll spare the little men, but the aristocrats, priests and Jews must be killed.' Within three weeks of the invasion he was able to boast that only three per cent of the Polish ruling class remained alive. The scale of these atrocities caused new friction with the army, which questioned the legality of Heydrich's murderous campaign. Military representatives at Führer headquarters refused to shake hands with SS officers and there were protests to Hitler. This atmosphere was exploited by Canaris, who hoped that pressure from the generals would curb the growing power of the SS. There was fresh talk of a military coup and an Abwehr agent was sent to the Vatican to explore the possibilities of a compromise peace with the allies. In the end, however, the generals backed away. The army was diverted by the triumphant campaign in the west which ended with the fall of France in June 1940, and Poland was left at the mercy of the SS and the Nazi party. Heydrich, who had picked up rumours of Canaris' activities, filed the information away as yet another count against the Abwehr.

The Polish massacres proved to be merely the preliminary to a vaster piece of macabre social engineering, the 'Final Solution of the Jewish Question' for which Heydrich became the executive agent in the summer of 1941. Despite the activities of the Einsatzgruppen in Poland, the approach favoured by the security police at first remained forced emigration. In the summer of 1940, after the fall of France, Eichmann began working on a plan to transform the island of Madagascar into a 'Jewish reserve' controlled and exploited by the SS, an idea which came to nothing when Britain failed to surrender and the continent remained blockaded. As emigration routes were cut by the extension of hostilities and increasing numbers of foreign Jews began to fall under the sway of the thousand-year Reich, a more radical approach evolved. This applied the cold bureaucratic technique perfected by Eichmann, not to emigration but to deportation and mass murder under the camouflage offered by total war. It is unclear when the policy of genocide received final approval but it certainly developed from Operation BARBAROSSA, the Nazi invasion of the Soviet Union in June 1941. This was envisaged by Hitler as a racial war for living-space, the final cataclysmic battle in the eternal conflict between German and Slav. In this struggle, the 'Jewish–Bolshevik intelligent-sia' was to be eliminated. Hitler made it clear to his generals that the normal rules of war were to be suspended and that communist officials were to be shot out of hand, a decision communicated to army group commanders in the notorious 'commissar order'.

The 'special tasks' involved in this war of annihilation were assigned to the SS. Einsatzgruppen were once again formed from Heydrich's security police to follow behind the advancing armies, imposing order in the rear areas and combing the POW camps for communist officials. Heydrich was anxious to avoid the military interference which had hampered police operations during the Polish campaign and was careful to work out in advance the exact relationship between his murder squads and the army. The agreement which he secured assigned to his units 'particular tasks of security policy' behind the front and authorised 'executive measures . . . against the civilian population', a form of words broad enough to allow his commandos to 'commit every crime known to God or man, so long as they were a mile or two from the firing line'. Nevertheless, Heydrich was careful not to define the full meaning of his mission. This was only revealed to the Einsatzgruppen commanders in an oral briefing just before BAR-BAROSSA. In these secret instructions, Heydrich ordered his death squads to go beyond enforcement of the commissar order and to murder every Jew in their operational areas: 'Judaism in the east' was 'the source of Bolshevism and must therefore be wiped out'. Heydrich's men were to 'sweep the steppes clean'. In the first weeks of the invasion, Einsatzgruppen reports camouflaged mass murder as anti-partisan activity, a sign of Heydrich's continued concern about possible military complaints. Only when it became clear that the army, fully committed to Hitler's version of total war in the east, would raise no objections was this ruse abandoned and the extermination of the Russian Jews as a people openly admitted.

The massacre of Soviet Jewry left untouched the Jewish population of Germany and occupied Europe. On 31 July 1941, while the Einsatzgruppen were pursuing their murderous campaign behind the Russian front, Heydrich was ordered by Göring to 'carry out all the necessary preparations with regard to organisational and financial matters for bringing about a complete solution of the Jewish question in the German sphere of influence in Europe'. The full meaning of this directive was never spelt out but that autumn the SS began to construct extermination camps at Belzec and Chelmno in Poland, and in September the first experimental gassings were carried out at Auschwitz. Heydrich had no part in this aspect of the 'Final Solution'. His task was to co-ordinate the deportation of the European Jews eastwards to meet their fate, a role which would undoubtedly have earned him a death sentence at Nuremberg had he survived the war. Such a vast task required meticulous preparation. As a first step, Heydrich had to secure the co-operation of the various bureaucracies needed to implement the 'Final Solution', from the railways which would provide the deportation trains to the Foreign Office which would arrange for the surrender of Jews from satellite countries such as Hungary and Slovakia. In November 1941, he summoned representatives of the relevant state and party offices to a conference in the pleasant Berlin suburb of Wannsee. The guests were informed that drinks and lunch would be provided to see them through the rigours of the day. The meeting was twice postponed and did not finally occur until 20 January 1942, when Heydrich outlined to the assembled bureaucrats his thoughts on the 'Final Solution'. According to Heydrich, Europe was to be 'combed through from west to east for Jews', who would be held in temporary transit ghettos before being transported further east where the able-bodied would be formed into work gangs to build roads for the Reich. A large number would 'doubtless drop out through natural wastage' and the survivors, the fittest of their race, would have to be 'treated accordingly'. He said nothing of the fate of those originally unfit to work. Adolf Eichmann, his 'Jewish expert', who kept the minutes, had no doubts about what was being proposed. As he recalled at the trial in Jerusalem which sentenced him to death, behind the bureaucratic language, the participants were knowingly discussing mass murder. Nobody raised a moral objection to the proposed annihilation of 11 million people. The conference was wholly concerned with the practical details involved in transporting the Jewish population of Europe to its death.

Eichmann, who was in considerable awe of his chief, recalled that after the meeting Heydrich relaxed beside an open fire with brandy and cigars for a cosy chat with his staff. He had just colluded in mass murder and yet could find satisfaction in having co-ordinated the various agencies required to implement the 'Final Solution'. As a result of Wannsee, what had been 'tentative, fragmentary and spasmodic was to become formal, comprehensive and efficient. The technical services such as the railways, the bureaucracy and the diplomats would work in harmony towards a single goal.' According to Schellenberg, Heydrich had private reservations about the 'Final Solution', remarking that it was 'sheer madness to have created this Jewish question'. Schellenberg's account, however, is supported by no other evidence. On the contrary, Heydrich carried out his orders with a merciless efficiency which allowed for no exceptions. On one occasion he flew all the way from Berlin to Minsk to deliver a personal reprimand to an official who had attempted to withhold certain categories of German Jew from execution. The war had transformed Heydrich from a convinced anti-Semite into a mass murderer. He was intoxicated by Hitler's vision of an Aryan empire which would last for a thousand years and regarded the annihilation of the Jewish race as a necessary step towards this end. In this respect, he echoed the views of Hitler, who proclaimed to the Reichstag only ten days after the Wannsee meeting that the Jews were the implacable enemies of the German race. Either one or the other must go to the wall. According to Hitler, the war would not end with the 'uprooting of the Aryans' but with 'the complete annihilation of the Jews'. This was all the justification that Heydrich required. To those who complained about his activities, he replied that 'neither he nor the RSHA had prompted these liquidations but that it was Adolf Hitler's personal command'.

The services rendered by Heydrich in the occupied east confirmed his image as the ideal SS man, a role he had always coveted. His blond good looks already gave him a start on the bespectacled Himmler, who despite his uniform and imposing titles always appeared like a displaced headmaster. Moreover he displayed to the full the qualities of physical and moral hardness expected of the new Nazi man. As a former SS officer cadet later recalled: 'I cannot repeat all the qualities attributed to him but one was outstanding – his hardness. . . . It is significant that, almost without exception, his pictures showed him as the winner of the Reich route march.' Heydrich believed that the SS must display physical toughness to show its superiority to the old ruling classes and to offer an example to German youth. As in the navy, he threw himself into sports with an absolute determination to succeed. He was often pictured as the captain of the SS fencing team and persuaded Himmler that all senior SS officers should be compelled to practise with the sabre. Unwilling to be a mere desk warrior, he learned to fly and bought his own stunt plane, overcoming Himmler's protests that his life was too valuable to risk in this way. At the beginning of the Polish campaign, he joined the Luftwaffe as a reserve officer and flew as a turret gunner in a bomber squadron. In 1940 he flew fighters over Norway and France to the acute distress of Himmler, who was awed by the determination of his subordinate to put himself deliberately in harm's way. His flying career came to an end only when he was shot down near Bersina in the early weeks of BARBAROSSA and had to be rescued by German troops. This was too much for Himmler and he was grounded. He had reached the rank of major and earned himself the iron cross first and second class and the front-line flyer's badge in bronze and silver. Combat flying reflected Heydrich's obsession with competition. It became the ultimate sport in which he staked his life on his personal skills. It also displayed his continued determination to prove the superiority of the SS. He wanted to show his military critics that the SS was not a bunch of asphalt soldiers who lurked behind the front, but a warrior elite worthy of a leading role in the thousand-year Reich.

Heydrich's physical hardness was combined with emotional hardness, the quality most prized by the SS. As Himmler informed SS officers after the Polish campaign: 'We have had to be hard. We have had to shoot thousands of leading Poles to show how hard we can be. I must proclaim aloud that it is much easier to advance against the enemy in battle than to master an enemy population of inferior race, to shoot, to deport, to hunt down shrieking and weeping women.' Heydrich had already proved himself in this area as head of the security police and his wartime activities in the occupied east provided any confirmation that was needed. SS officers were meant to combine physical and moral hardness with a sense of German decency. As Himmler later argued: 'One principle must be absolute for the SS man: We must be honest, decent, loyal and comradely to members of our own blood and to no one else.' SS officers must be able to commit acts of extreme brutality for the Reich and yet in their private lives show an example of clean Aryan living to the German people. Heydrich fulfilled this role by posing as a good husband and father, devoted to the 'dear intimacy of the family circle'. In a letter to his wife on the eve of the Polish campaign, which she was to open in the event of his death, he wrote: 'I may have faults ... but you are infinitely dear to me and I love my children equally. Please think of our life together with respect and love and, when time has done its healing work, give the children a father again – but he must be a real man, like the one I wanted to be.' Lina was urged to raise their sons in the SS creed to be 'kind and generous towards their own people and ruthless against our enemies at home and abroad'. At his funeral in 1942 his marriage was hailed as a glowing example of Nazi family life, a political statement as well as a personal commitment.

The private life of this ruthless paragon of Nazi virtue failed to live up to the public image. In reality, Heydrich was a profoundly divided personality. The sportsman, pilot and father of official propaganda was a familiar figure in the red-light district of Berlin. He would often compel his subordinates to accompany him on epic binges in the bars and brothels of the capital, occasions dreaded by his staff since he was dangerously unstable when drunk and displayed a strong sadistic streak. They came to fear the afternoon phone call from their chief, the leering voice and the suggestion that they join him for dinner and then 'go places'. Heydrich remained a compulsive womaniser but regarded sex as an expression of power in which he had to dominate and humiliate his partners. This gave him a bad reputation amongst Berlin prostitutes and his adjutants had to pimp for him: 'Even the most pitiful little whore would not want him a second time and would have preferred any other customer to Heydrich.' Eugen Dollman, the SS officer who translated for Heydrich on an official visit to Italy, found himself witnessing a bizarre spectacle in a Naples brothel. Before his astonished gaze, Heydrich assembled the entire staff in the grand salon and with a dramatic gesture emptied a purse of gold coins on to the marble floor, inviting them to fight for the coins: 'A Walpurgisnacht orgy ensued. Fat and thin, ponderous and agile, [the girls] scrambled madly across the salotto on all fours. . . . Even the old cashier lowered herself painfully on to her hands and knees, and only the yellow tom-cat, spitting satanically in one corner, declined to join in.' The touching letter to his wife, penned on the eve of war, was typically written after an evening in the bars and brothels of Breslau to celebrate his clearance to fly with the Luftwaffe. It is hardly surprising that his marriage was not a happy one. His wife resented his long absences while he suspected her of a series of affairs, including one with his subordinate, Walter Schellenberg, and had her watched by the security police. The truth was that Heydrich neither liked nor trusted anyone: 'He lived in a world populated by the self-created chimeras of a hostile distrust, scented behind everything treachery, intrigue or the snares of hidden enmity, and thought only in terms of dependence.' His energies, abilities and intellect were harnessed to a character which lacked a coherent moral centre. The only realities he recognised were power and the struggle for power, traits which accurately reflected the real nature of the movement he had served since his expulsion from the navy in 1931.

3

The Czech Connexion

As Hitler began to implement his plans for European domination, the power struggle between Abwehr and SD, army and SS, spilled over the German border. Nowhere was this clearer than in Czechoslovakia, which became an early victim of Nazi expansion. The Czech state, founded on the ruins of the Habsburg Empire, contained a substantial German-speaking minority which lived just beyond the frontier of Hitler's Reich. In 1938 the grievances of these Sudeten Germans provided the Führer with a convenient excuse for the assertion of Nazi power in central Europe. Czechoslovakia, with its well-equipped army and modern industrial base, was a strategic threat which had to be eradicated in advance of the great war which Hitler already contemplated. Moreover he regarded the Czech lands as an historical part of German living-space foolishly lost by the Habsburgs. Bohemia had once been German and would be German again. The Czech state must be ruthlessly crushed. As Hitler announced to senior military commanders in May 1938: 'It is my unalterable decision to smash Czechoslovakia by military action in the near future.' Himmler and Heydrich were his willing tools in this task of destruction. They dreamed of transforming the conquered Czech lands into an SS state, a totalitarian model which would one day be applied to the Reich itself.

The leader of the Sudeten Germans was Konrad Henlein, a bespectacled gym teacher of no particular intelligence who was thrust into prominence when the economic depression of the early 1930s brought Sudeten grievances to a head. Henlein's aim was to secure a wide measure of autonomy from the government in Prague which would allow the Sudetens to run their own affairs. Although his movement was secular and nationalist, Henlein was backed by the Kameradschaftbund, a shadowy secret society much influenced by the model of Austrian clerical fascism and the ideas of the Austrian Catholic philosopher, Othmar Spann. The Kameradschaftbund aimed at transforming the Sudetenland into a spiritual commonwealth run by an intellectual elite, at once German, Catholic and authoritarian. The presence of this group in the leadership of the Sudeten movement did not please the more radical of Henlein's followers and created tensions which were later exploited by the SS. While Henlein willingly accepted a subsidy from the Nazis, he also sought other means of bringing pressure to bear on Prague. Through contacts in the Sudeten German landed aristocracy, he established links with the British Foreign Office and was invited to London in 1935 and 1937. Henlein hoped to play off the rising power of Nazi Germany against Britain's fear of war to realise his own dreams for the Sudeten Germans. It was a dangerous game and one which earned him the lasting enmity of the SS. Heydrich regarded Henlein as a compromiser who might sell out to the Czechs. He was deeply suspicious of his contacts with Britain and even more of his backers in the Kameradschaftbund, whom he regarded as tools of Rome, purveying a fascist model at odds with the ideology and interests of the greater German Reich. Accordingly Heydrich set himself to undermine the Sudeten leader and reduce his movement to a reliable tool of Nazi expansion.

In pursuit of this goal, Heydrich established contacts with the radical wing of Henlein's movement, which stood for union with the Reich and the assertion of German racial supremacy in the Czech lands. This was led by a one-eyed bookseller from Karlovy Vary named Karl Hermann Frank, whose name was to be closely associated with Heydrich's throughout his career. Frank, like his master, was a profoundly damaged personality who combined ability and intelligence with a wholly negative addiction to destruction and revenge. For him it was not enough to assert a Sudeten–German identity. The Czechs were to be humiliated and ultimately destroyed as a people, an ambition which was to make him the natural agent of SS plans. As one critic later recalled: 'Frank united in his person a perverse hatred of everything Czech with a degree of duplicity which I have never seen either before or since.' While establishing links with Frank's group, Heydrich attempted to discredit Henlein and his friends in the Kameradschaftbund. He denounced Henlein as an agent of British intelligence and encouraged radical plots against his leadership. As the head of the SD foreign espionage section, Oberführer Heinz Jost, later recalled: 'Himmler and Heydrich discharged volleys of abuse on the leader of the Sudeten Fatherland Front [and] I received an order to maintain a constant watch on Henlein.' An SD office was established in Dresden for this purpose, linked to Berlin by special telephone and teletype links. In November 1937, Heinz Rutha, one of Henlein's closest advisers, was arrested by Czech police and charged with homosexual offences. Two weeks later he hanged himself in his prison cell. Heydrich always found accusations of homosexuality a useful way of smearing his opponents and it is likely that the material on Rutha was leaked to the Czechs by the SD. When Austria was seized in March 1938, the spiritual father of the Kameradschaftbund, Othmar Spann, was arrested by the Gestapo and sent to a concentration camp. He was soon to be followed by his Sudeten disciples.

While Heydrich intrigued with Karl Herman Frank, Henlein was backed by Canaris and the Abwehr. Canaris supported self-determination for the Sudetens and their incorporation into the Reich, but not at the price of war. The Admiral wished to curb the SS and feared that an alliance between Heydrich and the Sudeten radicals might plunge Germany into a disastrous conflict for which it was unprepared. He therefore tried to strengthen Henlein's position against his anti-Semitic, anti-Catholic rivals. This task was assigned to Abwehr Abteilung 2 (Minorities and Sabotage) under Major Helmut Groscurth, a conservative nationalist who shared his chief's opinions about the criminal nature of the SS and was active in a series of military conspiracies against Hitler before he was captured at Stalingrad in 1943. Groscurth's mission was an ambiguous one. His military task was to prepare a Sudeten fifth column to co-operate with an invading German army. In this capacity he established secret arms dumps, collected intelligence on Czech defences and trained sabotage groups. At the same time he tried to strengthen Henlein and encourage a negotiated solution to the Sudeten problem, something which caused endless friction with Heydrich's SD and police network. Groscurth enjoyed some limited success in bolstering the Sudeten moderates against SD intrigues but by the beginning of 1938 the balance was shifting towards Heydrich. Under pressure from the radicals and impressed by Hitler's triumph in Austria, Henlein capitulated and agreed to act as Hitler's tool. As Jost later recalled: 'What was he to do? Withdraw from the political scene and hand over to Karl Hermann Frank or remain and try to save what could still be saved? He gave in.' At a meeting with Hitler in March 1938 he agreed to magnify Sudeten grievances to isolate the Czechs from their allies and give the Führer a pretext for war. This surrender led to a temporary suspension of Heydrich's intrigues against Henlein but as events were to show he had forgotten and forgiven nothing.

Czechoslovakia faced the Nazi threat under its second president, Eduard Beneš. The son of a small farmer from Bohemia, Beneš had been active in the independence movement against the Habsburg Empire before the First World War. A natural radical, he was influenced as a young student by the figure who became the spokesman of the Czech national revival, Tomáš Masaryk, a professor of philosophy at Prague University, and the two men became closely associated. In 1914 both agreed that the war spelt the end of the Habsburgs and offered a unique opportunity for the cause of national liberation. While Masaryk went into exile to work towards this goal, Beneš remained in Prague to maintain links between the home resistance, nicknamed the 'Maffia', and the émigrés. In 1915, Beneš too was forced to flee abroad on a false passport barely one step ahead of the police. He had to abandon his wife, who spent four years in an Austrian jail before she saw her husband again. Beneš escaped through Switzerland to France and spent the remainder of the war lobbying the allies in favour of independence. He maintained close contact with the home resistance, which provided a stream of valuable political and military intelligence for the émigré politicians. This material was passed on to the allied high command and helped Beneš obtain a hearing for the Czech cause in Paris and London. By the end of the war, Britain, France and the United States had endorsed the creation of an independent Czechoslovakia on the ruins of the Habsburg Empire, an outcome that owed much to his dedication and astute diplomacy. His experiences in the liberation struggle reinforced the aloof and secretive side of Beneš' personality and left him with a taste for intrigue. As he later remarked: 'There has never been a revolution without espionage and conspiracy.' It also left him with the conviction that Czechoslovakia must pursue an active foreign policy if it wished to maintain an independent existence.

In the post-war period Beneš served permanently as the Czech Foreign Minister and tried to cultivate a role which was above domestic politics. Governments might come and go, but Beneš remained. A lonely, austere figure, he had no intimate friends and lived only for his country. He hated social gatherings and neither smoked nor drank. As even his admirers admitted, Beneš lacked the human warmth of Tomáš Masaryk. According to Robert Bruce Lockhart, he was 'a difficult man to know well' for his mind was 'machine-like in its compact tidiness and his reserve . . . almost impenetrable'. His conversation was 'factual and entirely unemotional. Each point was marshalled in its proper place and, when dealt with, was marked off on his fingers'. His tendency to deliver tedious lectures was remarked upon by the British diplomat, Harold Nicolson, who dealt with him at Versailles. Nevertheless, Nicolson considered Beneš 'a plausible little man with broad views' and remarked upon his 'intelligent eyes, rather like Keynes's' and his fine forehead. Others were less impressed and in some circles, particularly in the British Foreign Office, Beneš gained a reputation for being too clever, which was to harm him during the Munich crisis. Despite his chilly personality and dry precise manner, Beneš was a natural optimist with a strong nineteenth-century belief in the inevitability of progress. As he later argued: 'In the most difficult position I have never despaired. In politics I always behave as though I were playing tennis. When my opponent is "forty" and I am "love" and the next ball may be the last, I am still convinced that I can win the game'. His only personal conceit concerned his appearance. A short man, just over five feet tall, he was always well dressed and insisted that photographers take their pictures from angles which concealed his lack of inches. According to his biographer, Compton Mackenzie: 'It would be absurd to call him a dandy, but his ties and his shirts and his suit always appeared to have been chosen deliberately to get on with one another. He used to remind me of a well preened chaffinch.'

Beneš' record as the friend and collaborator of Masaryk made him the natural choice to succeed the father of the republic as president when the old man was forced by ill-health to retire in 1935. His appointment coincided with the growing crisis in the Sudetenland and its exploitation by the Nazis. In addressing the problem, Beneš stood by the vision of a unified state of Czechs and Slovaks. He was unwilling to concede autonomy to the Sudetens or to the other minorities lest this begin a process that would end with the dissolution of the Czechoslovak republic. He was similarly distrustful of the demands of many Slovaks for home rule. Beneš, like Masaryk, was prepared to recognise a Slovak identity but only within a unitary state. It is clear that while he articulated Czechoslovak nationalism, he feared that the country created in 1919 was a fragile one, liable to fly apart under the conflicting demands of its constituent peoples and fall victim to its larger neighbours. In defending it, he was determined to remain true to the vision of Tomáš Masaryk. This was not always easy for the prosaic Beneš, who lacked his predecessor's charismatic personality and claims to greatness. While sometimes admired, he was never loved and often criticised. As a result, he experienced strong inner tensions, which were sometimes reflected in devious conduct and an intolerance of opposition. His dry academic manner concealed a sense of mission which, like de Gaulle's, bordered on the Messianic. Throughout his life, Beneš clung to the idea that as Masaryk's disciple he knew better than anyone else what was best for his country.

Faced with the Sudeten problem, Beneš attempted to strengthen the international position of Czechoslovakia, an effort in which intelligence played a key role. Intelligence material had gained the Czechs a hearing in allied capitals during the First World War and was now employed to guarantee the continued independence of the country. In 1935 Czech military intelligence was headed by Lieutenant-Colonel František Moravec, a balding professional officer who, like Beneš, was a former student of Tomáš Masaryk. Moravec had deserted to the Russians from the Habsburg army in 1916 and during the revolution had fought the Bolsheviks as a member of the Czech legion, a group which was to have a powerful influence in post-war Czechoslovakia. Like Beneš, Moravec had known hardship and exile. He shared with his president a talent for intrigue and an absolute commitment to the national cause which overrode the personal claims of family and politics. The greatest day in his life was when the Czech legion entered Prague, the capital of the newly created republic, in 1919: 'It was an experience given to few men. It was to help mould the character of a generation. I have often thought that there was about the men who marched into Prague with Masaryk the same dedication as gripped the followers of Garibaldi, Bolivar and Washington. A country had been fought for and won. I believe that some of the fervour of that day stayed always with the founding generation.' It was to be Moravec's tragedy to fight for the Czech cause in two world wars and to die in exile far from the country that he loved.

When Moravec was appointed to the intelligence section of the general staff in March 1934 he found a moribund organisation obsessed with the former imperial power Austria rather than with the danger of a rearming Germany. Its principal network in Vienna regularly delivered 'detailed information . . . about the private life and love affairs of former archdukes . . . which read like the libretto of a Lehar operetta'. As one senior officer complained: 'I have no idea of the battle order of even the peacetime German divisions, but they tell me which Austrian archduke has slept with whom. . . . I think our intelligence service must be the worst in the world.' Clearly this dismal situation could not be allowed to continue and Moravec set himself to reform the system. He secured an increased budget, employed a new group of young, enthusiastic officers and concentrated the Czech intelligence effort on Nazi Germany, whose contacts with Henlein were already causing concern. These changes were part of a wider reform of the general staff which was accompanied by a massive increase in military spending and the construction of modern defences along the German frontier. Within two years, Moravec was beginning to produce results. As he later recalled: 'Although our recruitment of agents inside the Reich began from scratch we soon discovered that even a brutal police state like Hitler's could be penetrated. We were to find, in fact, that the tight Gestapo-backed security of the Third Reich could be completely riddled.' While this was an exaggeration it was nevertheless soon widely recognised that Beneš possessed one of the best intelligence organisations in Europe, a fact which was to have a powerful influence on subsequent events.

Beneš hoped to convince the major powers that supporting Czechoslovakia was in their own best interests. The Czechs already had a security pact with France but in May 1935 Beneš sought additional insurance in a new treaty with the Soviet Union. This committed the Russians to defend Czechoslovakia against aggression, although only if the French first fulfilled their military obligations. The pact reflected his conviction that Czechoslovakia could survive only within a European security system which included both east and west. He saw no advantage in excluding the Russians and believed that Czechoslovakia could balance between communism and capitalism, incorporating the best of both sides. Intelligence played an important role in military co-operation with Paris and Moscow. Moravec maintained a close association with the representative of the Deuxième Bureau in Prague, Major Henri Gayou, an amiable but limited individual nicknamed 'Smidra' because of his resemblance to the bumbling village policeman in Czech folk tales. He also had regular meetings with the head of the Deuxième Bureau, Colonel Fauché and other French intelligence chiefs. Through these channels the Czechs were able to pass on information about the progress of German rearmament and Hitler's military plans. Despite this flow of high-grade material, Moravec found the French distinctly cool. They refused to co-ordinate a joint intelligence effort against the Nazis and absorbed everything which the Czechs had to give without conceding anything in return. This attitude was paralleled in the military sphere where the French refused to draw up a joint operations plan for use in the event of war. By the beginning of 1938, Moravec was losing faith in France. He detected a curious mixture of complacency and defeatism in Paris and privately concluded that, in the event of a crisis, the French would not fight. Despite his growing sense of alarm, he had little choice but to maintain contact with the Deuxième Bureau and hope for the best.

Intelligence co-operation with the Soviet Union was never as close but followed a similar pattern. Moravec, who had fought the Bolsheviks in 1917, was more sceptical than Beneš about the desirability of links with Moscow but obeyed orders like a good soldier. As he later remarked, the rise of Hitler made him view the Soviet Union from a different angle. In the summer of 1936 Moravec and the leading experts on his staff were despatched to Moscow for talks with the Russians. His team received a cordial welcome and spent two weeks in discussions with General Uritsky of Soviet military intelligence and other high-ranking officers. It was soon evident to Moravec that the relationship would be one-sided: 'We were well prepared for the conference and gave our Soviet colleagues a series of reports which provided a picture of all the basic units of the German armed forces. . . . The Russians listened carefully and, without any display of reaction, made copious notes. . . . only the data brought by our side were discussed and analysed. The Russians produced very little of their own.' Moravec concluded that this stemmed less from the Soviet mania for secrecy than from the fact that they possessed practically no information about events in Germany. The destruction of the German communist party by the Gestapo had blinded them. Uritsky himself admitted difficulties in running agents into the Reich. He asked the Czechs to help him establish new networks which would be directed by a large Soviet intelligence mission based in Prague. Moravec baulked at the idea of giving the Russians free range in Czechoslovakia and in the end Uritsky accepted a more modest proposal. Soviet intelligence was allowed to establish a resident in Prague but he was to work under the control of Moravec. All operations were to be cleared with the Czechs and any information produced by the Russian networks was to be shared. On this basis intelligence co-operation began.

A Soviet representative appeared shortly after Moravec's return from Moscow. He was a charming regular soldier named Captain Kuznetzov, who was given the cover name of Rudolf One and reported to Moscow through a controller in the Russian Consulate. Kuznetzov did not last long and was recalled to Moscow within months where he disappeared in the great purges. His successor, Rudolf Two, proved to be anything but an asset. He was a drunken boor obviously selected more for political reliability than brains. According to Moravec his operations were dismal failures and he spent most of his time in bars

The man with the heart of iron. Reinhard Heydrich, Hitler's ideal Nazi.

The ideal Nazi family. Heydrich, his wife Lina and their first son.

The Butcher of Prague. Hitler's viceroy raises the SS flag over the city on his arrival.

The best of friends. Heydrich and his Gestapo chief, Karl Hermann Frank.

Defeated but still proud, the remnants of the Czech army arrive at Cholmondeley Park, near Chester in England, after the fall of France.

Czech President Beneš inspects his troops in Britain. The men are still wearing their French uniforms, which they had been given by the French army after Czechoslovakia had been overrun. This was the only platoon that the French had allowed to retain its weapons.

Beneš and Churchill inspect the Czech Brigade at Edgehill in Warwickshire. Beneš seized the opportunity to impress the Prime Minister with his knowledge of German plans to invade the Soviet Union.

SOE takes a hand. Hugh Dalton, the Minister of Economic Warfare, with Czech troops on manoeuvres.

Beneš with his intelligence staff at the radio station provided by SIS at Woldingham, summer 1940. Left to right: *Colonel Emil Strankmuller, unknown, Moravec, Beneš, General Ingr, the Czech Defence Minister, and Jaromir Smutný, the head of Beneš's chancery.*

Operation ANTHROPOID *begins. Colonel Palaček* (centre), *the officer responsible for selecting agents, with Sergeant Anton Svoboda* (on his left), *one of the original assassins.*

Sergeant Josef Valčík, 'SILVER A'. Valčík acted as the look-out man.

Sergeant Jan Kubiš, 'ANTHROPOID'. It was Kubiš's bomb that killed Heydrich.

Lieutenant Adolf Opálka, 'OUT DISTANCE'. Opálka made a last-ditch attempt to halt the operation because of the reprisals he anticipated, and the danger to the other parachutists in hiding.

Sergeant Josef Gabčík, 'ANTHROPOID'. Gabčík commanded the assassination team, pursuing his target with single-minded intensity. To his frustration, his sten-gun jammed at the vital moment.

Himmler visits his protégé in Prague.
He expressed concern about Heydrich's
contempt for elementary security.

Heydrich and his wife at a concert of
his father's music on the night before
the assassination. He was to fly to
Berlin the next day for an important
meeting with Hitler on Nazi
occupation policy.

'where his primitive dissipation at times approached bestiality. My office several times had to hush up unsavoury scandals resulting from his amorous activities.' This behaviour was perhaps understandable given what was happening in the Soviet Union. During the purges any form of contact with foreigners was considered suspicious and a posting abroad was often the preliminary to a death sentence. Despite these problems Moravec continued to work with the Russians to the limited extent possible. Czech intelligence facilitated the transit of Russian soldiers to fight in Spain during the civil war and passed on information about German rearmament and military plans. Co-operation, however, remained largely a one-way street. The Russians, like the French, were prepared to take but not to give. Czechoslovakia, a small power fighting for its independence, had little choice but to accept these unfavourable terms. The alternative was isolation and destruction.

Although Czechoslovakia had no military pact with Britain, Moravec also worked closely with the SIS. Beneš recognised that Britain could play a key role in any crisis over the Sudetenland. If London showed its determination to resist aggression, Hitler would be deterred and France and Russia encouraged to stand firm in their commitment to the Czechs. If Britain remained aloof, Czechoslovakia was likely to be abandoned by its erstwhile allies. It was therefore vital to mould British perceptions of Nazi Germany, a mission which was entrusted to Czech military intelligence. Information from Moravec's networks was used to convince London of the German danger and to neutralise the favourable impression made by Henlein in certain high political circles. By 1936 a good working relationship had been established with the SIS station chief in Prague, Major Harold 'Gibby' Gibson, who operated from the legation under the threadbare cover of Passport Control Officer, a post notorious throughout Europe as synonymous with spying. He was an old SIS hand who spoke fluent Russian and had operated against the Soviet Union from Istanbul, Bucharest and Riga before his posting to Prague in 1933. His background and experience reflected the obsession with communism which had dominated SIS since the 1920s and had produced a service dependent on a network of Russian émigrés which was thoroughly unreliable and penetrated by the Soviet security services. The year after his arrival in Czechoslovakia, however, Germany was defined as the ultimate potential enemy, a move which reflected growing unease in London about the Nazis, and priorities changed. Gibson began to run agents into the Reich but their contribution was soon overtaken by the high-grade intelligence supplied by Moravec. This was welcome both to Gibson and to his superiors, who experienced difficulties establishing their own networks and remained under tight financial constraints. Although the Treasury increased the SIS budget in 1936, the organisation was hampered by lack of funds until the beginning of the war: 'Until 1939 it was unable even to afford wireless sets for its agents.' Moravec was thus subsidising the British intelligence effort and, as with the French and the Russians, was forced to give more than he received. In the long term, however, his co-operation with Gibson was to have unforeseen consequences which ensured the survival of Czech military intelligence after the country it served had been swallowed up by Hitler.

The Czech reputation in the intelligence field rested largely on one particular agent, codenamed A–54. It was information from this source which attracted attention in Paris, Moscow and London and made co-operation with Moravec worth while. Although he boasted about his success in penetrating Heydrich's security screen after 1934, Moravec did not find his most successful recruit; A–54 found *him*. The leading Czech agent was a 'walk-in', one of the most ambiguous categories in the shadowy world of intelligence. His association with the Czechs began in March 1937 when Moravec received a personal letter containing details of German mobilisation plans and offering further information in return for cash. By his own admission, Moravec found this approach almost too good to be true and his assistants unanimously concluded that the whole thing was a Nazi plant. Nevertheless, Moravec decided to take the risk, starting an association with A–54 which was to produce increasing quantities of high-grade material both before and during the war. The real motivation of A–54 has remained a mystery and even his identity was unknown to Czech intelligence for some time after he began to pass information. He was in fact a member of the Abwehr based in Dresden called Paul Thümmel. Since Dresden was the main base of operations against Czechoslovakia, Thümmel was well placed to inform Moravec about German military plans and links with Henlein. His importance, however, went beyond that. Thümmel was an old Nazi, a holder of the coveted gold party badge, and a personal friend of many important figures from the days of political struggle, including Heinrich Himmler. This gave him access to information which he might not otherwise have had and allowed him to straddle the worlds of the party and the army in a way open to few others. The question remains why such a figure should have offered his services to the Czechs. Although he was paid, he was never given enough to compensate for the risks he was taking and he continued to work for Moravec after Hitler had extinguished the Czech state. This leaves open the possibility that he was a double agent, something which was sometimes suspected by Beneš, but there are problems about such a conclusion. Some of the information which Thümmel supplied was unlikely to have been deliberately leaked by the Germans even as part of a cover and deception plan. It was simply too important. The most likely explanation is that Thümmel, like Canaris, was a conservative nationalist who broke with Hitler because he feared that the Nazis would plunge Germany into a disastrous war. His first approaches to the Czechs coincided with increasing alarm in military circles over Hitler's war plans and the growing influence of the SS. Whether he was working with the opposition group which Canaris protected in the Abwehr or was acting on his own, however, remains a mystery. Whatever his true role, A–54 was to prove a bankable asset for Moravec until he was uncovered and arrested in 1942.

Despite his best efforts, Beneš was unable to mobilise international support for Czechoslovakia when Hitler engineered the Munich crisis in 1938. Neville Chamberlain refused to commit Britain to the support of France in the event of war and instead attempted to secure a negotiated settlement of the Sudeten question. The French used this as an excuse for not fighting. Since France would not go to war, Soviet treaty obligations became a dead letter and Czechoslovakia was isolated. Beneš, who had represented the new Czech state at Versailles in 1919, found himself excluded from the Munich conference of September 1938 when Britain, France, Germany and Italy agreed to the cession of the Sudetenland over his head. It was a bitter moment for Beneš as it was for all Czechs. He was under great pressure from the army to reject Chamberlain's mediation and to fight Germany alone but decided that this would simply mean the annihilation of his country. It was a controversial decision and one which many held against him ever afterwards, for in handing over the Sudetenland with its frontier defences Beneš left Prague at the mercy of Hitler. The Führer was not long in asserting his power. In the immediate aftermath of Munich, the Germans made it clear that they would not deal with the rump Czech state as long as Beneš remained president. Hitler hated him and identified him correctly with the spirit of Czech nationalism which he was determined to crush. Beneš was forced to resign and was succeeded by Emil Hácha, an ageing ex-bureaucrat who was already a sick man when he was appointed. At the age of fifty-four Beneš had once more to contemplate exile, for it was clear that his life would be in

danger if he remained. At the end of October he flew to London for
medical treatment, arriving unannounced at Croydon airport where
only weeks before Chamberlain had returned from Munich promising
cheering crowds 'peace for our time'. Early in the new year he sailed for
the United States where he had been offered the professorship of
sociology at the University of Chicago. Beneš, however, had not
abandoned politics for the life of a scholar. As he explained to a group
of friends before he left his country, Hitler would one day go too far and
provoke a European war. The international coalition which had failed
at Munich might yet emerge to defeat Germany. When that happened
he hoped to become the spokesman of the Czech cause as he had been
in an earlier conflict. The shame of Munich would be wiped out and
Czechoslovakia restored as a member of a triumphant anti-Nazi
alliance. For Beneš the reversal of Munich became both a national
crusade and a personal obsession. As he later recalled: 'From September 1938, sleeping and waking, I was continually thinking of this
objective – living for it, suffering on its account and working for it in
every one of my political actions.'

The new government, abandoned by its allies, hastened to make the
best deal that it could with Berlin. Czech policy was subordinated to the
Nazis. The Soviet pact was denounced and the communist party
banned. The army, the symbol of the nation, was hastily demobilised.
Pictures of Masaryk and Beneš disappeared from the schools. Hitler
was even invited to nominate a German as a member of the cabinet.
Slovakia was granted autonomy, a situation which was soon to be
exploited by the Nazis, and Czechoslovakia became Czecho-Slovakia,
signifying the retreat from the unitary principles on which the state had
been founded. As for the Germans who still remained within the
reduced territory of the republic, they were granted extensive privileges under pressure from Berlin and defined themselves as part of
a national socialist community led by Adolf Hitler. The attempt to
placate the Führer had an immediate effect on Moravec, who was
ordered to cease operations against the Reich. The efforts of his
counter-espionage service in the Sudetenland had made him an
unpopular figure with Henlein's supporters and there was pressure for
his dismissal and arrest. He was constantly watched by SD agents, who
made no secret of their presence in Prague, and it was clear that his life
was in danger. Under these circumstances, Moravec came to a
dramatic decision. He would transfer the operations of Czech military
intelligence abroad, outside the murderous reach of Heydrich's
Gestapo. Like many army officers he disapproved of the Munich

agreement and believed that Czechoslovakia should have gone down fighting rather than surrendering to Anglo-French pressure. The events of September 1938 were not an end but a beginning. Whatever the policies of his government, Moravec had declared war on Hitler. But where to establish a new base? Moravec, like most Czechs, could not forgive the French for backing down during the Munich crisis. A profound sense of bitterness and disillusion ruled out moving to Paris. The Russians had emerged from the events of September with more credit. Stalin was not a party to the infamous deal over the Sudetenland and could not be blamed for avoiding war while France pursued a policy of appeasement. Whatever the popularity of the Russians in Czechoslovakia, however, Moravec did not want to join the Czech communist leader, Klement Gottwald, in Moscow. He remained suspicious of Stalin and was unwilling to evade one dictator only to fall into the grip of another. This left Britain, perhaps a strange choice in the light of Neville Chamberlain's conduct at Munich. Whatever the British role on that occasion, however, London had broken no solemn treaty obligation and thus avoided the scorn and contempt visited on Paris by the Czechs. It was therefore to his friend Gibson that Moravec turned for assistance with his plan of escape.

In his dealings with the British, Moravec had one trump card, his control of A–54. He had expected his key agent to vanish in the aftermath of Hitler's triumph. As he later argued, A–54 had the opportunity open to few spies of simply disappearing to live on his earnings rather than running further risks on behalf of a beaten and humiliated country. Instead Thümmel contacted his control officer, Captain Fryc, at the new frontier and made it clear that he was prepared to continue working for the Czechs. SIS was anxious to guarantee access to what A–54 produced. In the autumn of 1938 all kinds of alarming tales about Hitler's war plans were emerging from Germany. As one British intelligence officer later recalled: 'There were so many authentic rumours . . . that whatever happened, *someone* could say "I told you so".' The head of SIS, Admiral Sir Hugh Sinclair, was under pressure to supply the government with information and was often embarrassed by what he had to provide. In these circumstances it was important to guarantee access to a well-established source. Moreover, if Hitler did break loose, British strategy and the reputation of SIS might depend on the kind of information which A–54 could provide. The Czechs were not the only foreign intelligence service exploited by SIS. In January 1939 at a meeting in Paris between British, French and Polish intelligence officers, the first steps were taken towards co-operation in the field of cryptology. This gave SIS access to Polish research on the Enigma coding machine employed by the German armed forces and later provided the basis for the greatest intelligence coup of the war, the cracking of Nazi ciphers or ULTRA which reduced the value of old-fashioned agents like Thümmel. In the early stages, however, ULTRA remained scrappy and puzzling. While this situation continued, the Czechs could exploit their possession of the mysterious A–54. According to Moravec, he did not have to make the first move in the conspiracy with SIS. It was Gibson who approached him that winter with the offer of a plane to carry the head of Czech military intelligence and his senior officers to Britain. Whatever the truth of this version, it is clear that Thümmel was the key to the negotiations. By the beginning of 1939, the groundwork for Moravec's daring plan had been established. He had devolved operations on a series of out-stations in foreign capitals, transferred secret funds abroad, and drawn up a list of the personnel who would accompany him into exile. SIS had agreed in principle to provide him with a refuge. Only the timing of the last act remained to be decided. In the event this was dictated by Hitler and only a warning from A–54 prevented Moravec's scheme from being overtaken by events.

The ink was scarcely dry on the Munich agreement before the German army swept through the abandoned Czech defences into the Sudetenland. In the wake of the advancing columns came Heydrich's special security commandos. As the Nazi party newspaper, *Völkischer Beobachter*, proudly announced on 1 October: 'In the security police field Gestapo men working in close co-operation with the troops immediately commenced combing out Marxists, traitors and other enemies of the state in the liberated territory.' As Major Groscurth rapidly discovered on a tour of the area, these definitions were wide ones and included many of Henlein's closest associates. Heydrich was using the opportunity to resume the feud temporarily suspended on Hitler's orders in the spring. Henlein's wife was terrified that her husband would be murdered. As she complained to Groscurth: 'They are doing all they can to get rid of him. He has as many enemies in the Gestapo as among the Czechs. Heydrich hates him.' The behaviour of the SD squads and of the Waffen SS units which accompanied the regular army confirmed Groscurth's prejudice against the SS 'swine'. The Abwehr tried to protect the Sudeten leader and his associates but with little success. Henlein had played too great a role in Nazi propaganda to be physically eliminated but he found himself pensioned off as gauleiter of the Sudetenland, a post with little real power. His associates in the Kameradschaftbund were not so lucky. After months of harassment by the Gestapo they were arrested early in 1939 along with several hundred members of the Sudeten youth league and charged with homosexual offences. Condemned as enemies of the state, they were consigned to a concentration camp where they remained until 1945. The real winner amongst the Sudetens was not Henlein but Karl Herman Frank, who was soon to reap the rewards of his loyalty to the SS.

Despite his triumph at Munich, Hitler felt cheated by Chamberlain's intervention. In October 1938 he was already planning to eradicate the rump Czech state and he assigned a key role in this process to Himmler, Heydrich and the SS. As he explained to senior military commanders during an inspection tour of the Sudetenland: 'We don't need the army to take over Bohemia and Moravia. . . . all the preparatory work will be done by political means. All I ask of you is that you have the armed forces ready to march. No mobilisation. No unnecessary expense. The Czechs may squeal, but we will have our hands on their throats before they can shout. And anyway, who will come to help them?' Hitler planned to destroy Czechoslovakia by a combination of internal intrigue and external military pressure. The Slovak provincial government would be encouraged to declare independence and ask Berlin for protection. German troops would then enter the Czech lands of Bohemia–Moravia to preserve order and the area would become a permanent part of Nazi living-space. In January 1939, Hitler held a secret meeting in Berlin with Himmler and Heydrich to arrange for the subversion of Slovakia. As he explained to his listeners, after that it would be 'quite easy . . . to deal with the remaining Czech portion of the Republic'. The mission was assigned to the man who had bungled the kidnapping of Rudolf Formis from Czechoslovakia in 1934, Alfred Naujocks, who was soon busy contacting separatist politicians and smuggling arms to Slovak fascist organisations. At the beginning of March, the German army was ordered to prepare for a 'pacification operation' in Bohemia–Moravia, co-ordinated with the SD plot. The generals were informed that Czech resistance was not expected.

As soon as Thümmel learned of the impending invasion, he crossed the Czech border and contacted Captain Fryc. He brought with him details of the German military plan which called for the advance of four German divisions at dawn on 15 March and the occupation of Prague by 9 a.m. The troops would be accompanied by special squads of security police with orders to hunt down members of Czech intelligence and interrogate them with 'special severity' to discover their sources in Germany. Thümmel was not unnaturally anxious about this prospect but was assured that the Czechs had contingency plans. Satisfied on this point, he agreed to continue his activities and was given contact addresses in Holland and Switzerland for use after the seizure of Prague. Moravec had now to decide what to do with the explosive information which had just landed in his lap. As a loyal officer his first instinct was to warn the government, however much he disapproved of its pro-German line since Munich. His warnings were not taken seriously. Ministers could not believe that Hitler would launch such a flagrant act of aggression against the already subservient Czech state. Moreover Moravec was identified with the discredited policies of Beneš and had made no secret of his anti-Nazi leanings. He was suspected of engineering a provocation to disrupt relations between Prague and Berlin. Called before a meeting of the cabinet on 11 March, he recommended that the government go into exile after destroying all stores of military equipment, blowing up the War Ministry and sabotaging key munitions plants. This drastic prescription was sneeringly dismissed. Moravec was told to calm down and 'bring us better news in future'. It was the most humiliating moment of his life.

Moravec had planned to request official permission to transfer his operations abroad as part of this wider strategy of denying resources to the enemy. Now he had to act on his own, justifying his position on the grounds that the government had betrayed the nation and lost any claim to moral authority. Time was short and he turned to his colleague Gibson for assistance. Late at night on 13 March, a vehicle from the British Embassy entered the underground car park of the War Ministry, where it was loaded with Moravec's most important files. These were later smuggled out of the country in the British diplomatic bag. The next morning Moravec left home as usual without informing his wife and two children of the dramatic events which were about to occur. As he later recalled: 'I merely said that I was going on an overnight trip to Moravia and asked my wife to pack a couple of shirts and a toothbrush.' When he arrived at the War Ministry he summoned his eleven best officers and exploded his bombshell. That afternoon they would accompany him to London on an unscheduled KLM flight diverted to Prague by Gibson. They were not allowed to say goodbye to their families. With the capital swarming with Nazi spies and the government determined to demonstrate its loyalty to the Reich, the slightest leak could prove fatal. The men listened to Moravec in silence. Nobody complained. He had rightly judged that none of his chosen companions would put personal considerations before their duty to the nation. In the afternoon, Moravec emptied the safes and made arrangements for the destruction of his remaining secret files while his officers left the War Ministry in ones and twos to avoid the attention of watching Gestapo agents. At the airport sympathetic customs officers looked the other way while Moravec and his staff boarded their KLM flight in the midst of a blinding snowstorm which had grounded all other aircraft. The contrast between this sur-reptitious escape and the victorious entry of the Czech legion into Prague in 1919 was bitter but unavoidable. As Moravec later recalled: 'While sitting in the Dutch plane flying towards England . . . I found myself suddenly swept by black thoughts. The bitter struggle of the past years, the blood and sweat of so many, what had it all amounted to? The republic of Masaryk was dead. For the second time in my life I was an exile. My wife and children were lost to me, abandoned in the stricken country below, somewhere under the swirling flakes, left to the mercies of the invaders. Bitterness welled within me. As our plane passed over the frontier mountains of Czechoslovakia, I put my head in my hands and cried.'

While the British press speculated next day about the arrival of a secret flight with eleven mysterious passengers at Croydon airport, the last vestiges of Czech independence were being suppressed by the Nazis. On 14 March, under strong German pressure, Slovakia declared its independence. Later that evening an ailing Hácha boarded a train for Berlin where he hoped to persuade the Führer to uphold the authority of the Prague government. Instead Hácha found him-self faced with the blunt announcement that German troops would occupy Bohemia–Moravia the following day. If any resistance was encountered, the Luftwaffe would bomb Prague into rubble. He must place his people under the protection of the Nazi Reich. After hours of browbeating, during which he fainted and had to be revived with an injection, a weeping Hácha signed the proffered document in the early hours of the morning. Waffen SS troops had already crossed the Munich frontiers which had endured for just over four months. Skidding and sliding in the snow, the first units of the Wehrmacht entered Prague, watched by a stunned population: 'Some of the onlookers broke down and wept; some abandoned themselves to impotent rage; some rushed shouting abuse at the German troops.' The Czech army, demoralised and broken, remained in its barracks. Only the Eighth Silesian Regiment at Mistek disobeyed orders and put up a brief but hopeless resistance. In the wake of the troops came the Gestapo, which launched an immediate round-up of German émigrés, communists and other subversives. In the first week of the occupation 1600 were arrested in Aktion GITTER (Operation FENCE), a figure which soon grew to 4639 as Heydrich's men tightened their grip on the Czech police. The failure of the government to act on Moravec's warning netted Hitler not only the great Skoda armaments works at Plzeň but also the complete equipment of the Czech army and air force including 600 tanks and 1000 aircraft, material which proved useful in the French and Russian campaigns. In addition to this booty the Nazis laid hands on stockpiles of Czech raw materials and the entire gold reserves of the National Bank. Only in the area of intelligence were the Germans thwarted. When a special Abwehr unit arrived at the War Ministry to carry off Moravec's precious files before they could be seized by the Gestapo, it found nothing but powdered ashes blowing forlornly amongst the trampled snow.

On the evening of his bloodless coup, Hitler arrived in Prague and was greeted at the Hradčany castle, the official presidential residence, by an SS guard of honour. He preceded Hácha whose train had been deliberately delayed. When the old man finally reached the castle which he had left as the head of an independent state only the day before, he was forced to use the servants' entrance. It was a symbol of the status which the Czechs were to be accorded by their new masters. The future of the area was rapidly settled. On 16 March Hitler proclaimed Bohemia–Moravia a Nazi protectorate, avoiding outright annexation to the disappointment of party officials in the Sudetenland and other neighbouring provinces who had hoped to extend their own authority. The Czechs were allowed to retain an 'autonomous government', shorn of responsibility for defence and foreign affairs, supervised by a Reichsprotektor appointed by Berlin. For this post, the Führer selected Konstantin von Neurath, a career diplomat and former Foreign Minister, dismissed in 1938 because he lacked enthusiasm for Hitler's expansionist plans. It was a totally cynical move, dictated by a desire to win international respectability. As Hitler explained to Goebbels, who had pressed for the appointment of a Nazi fanatic, Neurath was the best man for the job: 'In the Anglo-Saxon world he is considered a man of distinction. The international effect of his appointment will be reassuring because people will see in it my decision not to deprive the Czechs of their racial and national life.' Hitler's long-term aims, however, had not really changed and were revealed in the appointment of Heydrich's creature Karl Hermann

Frank, now an SS Brigadeführer (Brigadier-General), as state secretary of the new protectorate. Frank, whose hatred of the Czechs and their culture was notorious, was placed in control of the police and in this capacity answered not to the 'respectable' Neurath but to Heydrich and Himmler in Berlin. The situation could hardly have seemed more hopeless for a country which had enjoyed only twenty brief years of independence. But even at this dark moment an exile movement was forming, dedicated to the destruction of the Nazis and the restoration of the Czech state. It was a development which was to prove fatal for Heydrich, who had done so much to destroy the republic of Masaryk and Beneš.

The Plan

4

Exiles

Moravec's 'first eleven' was installed by SIS in Rosendale Road, West Dulwich, where it operated under the cover of a radio shop run by a British agent named Reg Adams. By the terms of the unwritten agreement which had brought it to London, the Czech intelligence group worked almost exclusively with SIS. When Major Gayou of the Deuxième Bureau proposed close collaboration, he was politely frozen off by Moravec who had neither forgiven nor forgotten the French betrayal at Munich. The Russians received a similar response and all contact ceased when Stalin signed the notorious Nazi–Soviet pact in August 1939. Moravec, however, was never simply a mercenary at the command of British intelligence. He was a nationalist determined to place his organisation at the disposal of a Czech authority dedicated to the restoration of independence. He would work *with* the British, not *for* them. Moravec believed that only one figure was capable of leading and inspiring an exile government, Eduard Beneš. As he later recalled: 'I wrote to Beneš at once, informing him of our arrival and placing myself and my staff at his disposal as the natural leader of any nascent liberation movement.' The former President had already broken his self-imposed silence and resumed the role of national spokesman abdicated since Munich. From his exile in the United States, he condemned the Nazi occupation of Prague and swore vengeance on its authors. According to Beneš, 'the independence of Czechoslovakia was not crushed; it continues, it lives, it exists.' He quickly accepted Moravec's offer and announced his intention of joining him in London. At the end of July 1939 Beneš established himself in a cramped suburban villa on Gwendolen Avenue, Putney. It was a far cry from the splendour of the presidential apartments in the Hradčany castle, now occupied by the Reichsprotektor of Bohemia–Moravia, but

Beneš was buoyed up by his perpetual optimism. He was no stranger to hardship and hoped that the European war which was looming that summer would result in the defeat of Hitler and the liberation of his country. As during the First World War, he was determined to promote the Czech cause amongst the allies and guarantee himself a seat at the peace conference.

Beneš faced a hard struggle which tested even his considerable diplomatic skills. He took the view that Hitler's aggression in March 1939 had abolished Munich. That agreement and everything which followed had neither legal nor moral validity. The Czechoslovak republic continued to exist within its pre-Munich frontiers and Beneš remained president despite his resignation in October 1938 under Nazi pressure. These sweeping claims found little favour with the governments of Britain and France, on which the restoration of Czech independence depended. The close working relationship developed between Moravec and SIS was not reflected at a political level in either London or Paris, where Beneš' attempts to organise an exile movement were greeted with a daunting combination of icy non-cooperation and outright obstruction. Britain and France refused to recognise the legality of Hitler's action in March 1939 but would neither repudiate Munich nor endorse Beneš, who was allowed to live in London only on condition that he refrained from political activity. This ban was lifted at the outbreak of war and the Czechs were allowed to organise an army. Since the Nazi occupation of Prague, young men had been leaving the protectorate to fight abroad for their country, often with the connivance of sympathetic police and customs officers who looked the other way. Some crossed by night into Poland. Others posed as Sudeten Germans, procured travel documents for Austria and made their way through the mountains into Yugoslavia. Most ended up in France, where they joined the Foreign Legion. In October, they were transferred to a new Czech army, based in a former refugee camp at Sète on the Mediterranean coast. A Czech military staff under General Ingr was created in Paris. The treatment of the Czech army, however, was symbolic of the political position of the exiles. The French high command seemed to know little and care less about the welfare of its Czech allies. The troops lost their smart Foreign Legion uniforms and were issued with kit which had probably first done service with French recruits in 1914. Weapons were few and antiquated. There were no boots and the soldiers had to wear wooden clogs. There was increasing frustration and bitterness with the situation amongst men who had travelled across Europe at great personal risk to fight, only to find themselves relegated to the margins of the allied war effort. As one later recalled, at Sète they were treated worse than dogs. It was an experience shared by the political leadership during the seemingly endless months of the phoney war.

At the end of December 1939 a National Council, headed by Beneš, was recognised by the allies as the representative of the Czechoslovak peoples, an ambiguous formula which avoided any commitment to the unity of the republic and left the Czechs far behind the Poles, who were the heroes of the hour and had a government-in-exile. It was a struggle even to achieve this inferior position since the French tried for months to exclude Beneš and promote their own candidate. The situation merely encouraged an atmosphere of recrimination and intrigue. As one refugee complained, amongst the exiles it was a war of 'all against all'. Contact between Beneš and the Foreign Office was provided by Robert Bruce Lockhart, a former diplomat and journalist, best known for his well-publicised activities in Russia during the revolution. Lockhart had lived and worked in Prague, knew Beneš well and was sympathetic to his cause. He was, however, denied access to the inner circle at the Foreign Office, which was notoriously suspicious of outsiders, particularly flamboyant ones like Lockhart who embraced unfashionable causes. He was rarely able to see important officials and was dismissed as being 'more Czech than the Czechs'. As he later recalled, the job was 'the most difficult of my career . . . and put a severe strain on my reserves of patience, obstinacy and restraint'. Beneš and his Foreign Minister, Jan Masaryk, the son of the first President, chafed at their inferior status. As Masaryk, who had resigned as ambassador to London after Munich, complained: 'I am only a former envoy. How can a private individual negotiate with the Foreign Office?' The exiles pressed for recognition as at least a provisional government, believing that this would motivate the army and consolidate their authority at home. In March 1940, Beneš complained that continued delay might lead his people to turn to Moscow, despite the Nazi–Soviet pact and the defeatist propaganda of the Czech communists, who condemned the war as an imperialist quarrel. As he complained to a high Foreign Office official, how could he 'prevent his countrymen displaying hatred towards the West, which betrayed them and now would not even regard them as equals in adversity. . . ? Why should they join the army and how could the rise of the Communist movement at home be prevented?' While the phoney war continued, these appeals fell on deaf ears. Beneš was informed that recognition would be granted only when his authority on the National Committee had been unequivocally established. Since the French were still backing his rivals and Beneš needed recognition precisely to secure unequivocal authority, the result was deadlock.

It is hardly surprising that in this situation Beneš distrusted the French and had little faith in Chamberlain. He traced his troubles to the lingering hope in Paris and London of a compromise peace, an outcome which would have meant the shipwreck of all his hopes. Wherever he looked, he saw the possibility of betrayal. The atmosphere in London and Paris was chilly. Across the Atlantic the US President, Franklin Roosevelt, pledged himself privately to Czech independence but made no public moves. America remained neutral. As for the Russians, they had signed a pact with Hitler, closed the Czech Embassy and recognised the 'independence' of Slovakia. While Beneš continued to hope for a speedy Nazi collapse, his perennial optimism was balanced by what his closest associates called a 'Munich complex'. Czechoslovakia had been sacrificed once to great power self-interest and might well be sold again. Throughout the war he was haunted by the nightmare of a new deal with Germany at Czech expense. As his friend Lockhart noted in November 1940: 'What he would like . . . is some dramatic statement (to which Roosevelt would also subscribe) that we shall never make peace with Hitler and Naziism. . . . What he fears . . . is that at one fine moment or another we shall make a compromise peace with Germany and leave Central and South-eastern Europe in the lurch.'

Beneš possessed assets even at this dark stage in his career. The most important was the redoubtable Colonel Moravec, whose intelligence organisation served Beneš in a number of different ways. Through the transmitters supplied by Moravec's friends in SIS, Beneš was able to establish contact with the 'Maffia', the underground resistance movement which began to emerge after the Nazi occupation of Prague. The support of the home Czechs, demonstrated through these channels, provided Beneš with a legitimacy which might otherwise have been lacking. As Moravec later recalled: 'This contact with home was exclusively at the disposal of President Beneš, who well understood its political importance and guarded it jealously in order that it should not, as he always put it, "get into the wrong hands".' Moravec was also useful in the political struggles within the exile community. Beneš coldbloodedly exploited the close links between Moravec and the British intelligence services to harass and discredit his rivals. Moreover part of a loan from the SIS secret fund to Moravec, negotiated in early 1940, was quietly diverted to Beneš' own political purposes. Lastly there was the vital asset of A–54, who re-established contact with the Czechs at The Hague in June 1939 and passed on a stream of information about Hitler's intentions during the phoney war, guaranteeing the continued support of SIS. From an early stage, Beneš established the habit of dealing with Moravec alone. Since knowledge was power, he wanted it concentrated in his own hands. As he once remarked, his colleagues joked that Moravec was the Czech Himmler: 'They wonder why I talk to him every day. They do not understand that politics requires intelligence and without it nothing gets done.' These secretive methods persisted even after the consolidation of a government-in-exile which accepted Beneš' authority. The plain fact was that he did not trust the judgement of his ministers, even Jan Masaryk, the nearest thing to a friend he ever had. Beneš was convinced of his own abilities and his unique mission. Ultimately, like de Gaulle, he believed that nobody else truly represented the spirit of the nation. As a result many decisions, particularly in the intelligence field, were reached by Beneš and Moravec alone. Nothing was ever recorded except in the minds of two men who were natural conspirators.

Beneš exploited his control over intelligence to promote the Czech cause with the allies. This was true of the information provided by A–54, which was manipulated to suit the political purposes of the exile movement. Whatever the value of Paul Thümmel, there were always lingering doubts in the mind of Beneš about his real status, although these were never divulged to SIS. As Beneš later informed an assistant, he did not think that A–54 'was consciously working for us with the approval of the German General Staff [i.e. as a double agent], although he did not rule this out. He checks all the information from this source and only uses it as long as it suits the line, the policy which he himself wants to support. . . . It is not always a matter of whether a report is true, but of what use is made of it.' In other words, what mattered was not the truth of Thümmel's reports but the impression they made on SIS and the British government. The existence of a home army under the control of the exiles was similarly exploited. There is little doubt that Beneš deliberately exaggerated the strength of the underground to improve his bargaining position with his reluctant allies. In the spring of 1940, Lockhart claimed that passive resistance and unattributable sabotage had reduced Nazi war production in the Protectorate by twenty-five per cent, a wild and unverifiable figure. Beneš was attempting not only to win favour with the allies but also to show that the nation rejected German rule. His emphasis on a strong and united home army was insurance against a compromise peace which would leave Hitler in possession of Bohemia–Moravia.

The existence of a possible fifth column in the German rear attracted British attention even during the stagnant period of the phoney war. Lockhart was greatly impressed by the potential of the Czechs, which he called to the attention of his superiors. According to Lockhart: 'Action inside the Protectorate will be of far greater military value than the action of the Czechoslovak army abroad. . . . if the proper encouragement is given, the military effort of the home Czechs not only will be effective but can also be controlled by the Allied Governments and, within reason, launched at any moment they may desire.' Others had a more professional interest. One was Section D of SIS, established in 1938 to investigate the possibilities of sabotage and subversion. As early as March 1939 it was authorised to begin a campaign in Austria and the Czech borderlands in which Moravec, with his established links to SIS, must inevitably have played a role. Another was MI(R), a section of military intelligence also established in 1938 to consider covert warfare. In October 1939 a section of this office under its deputy head, Colonel Colin Gubbins, was established in Paris as Number 4 Military Mission. Its duty, which was not disclosed to the French, was to work through General Ingr with the Czech home army. A similar function was performed in London by another officer of MI(R), Captain Peter Wilkinson, who dealt directly with Moravec. Through these channels Czech intelligence kept the War Office 'generally informed' about the operational plans of the underground, passed on requests for weapons and received tactful British military advice. Gubbins, a wiry Scotsman with an established interest in covert action and paramilitary warfare, was later to prove an important friend to the Czechs and was affectionately known among the exiles as 'Moravec's Englishman'. Until the strategic situation changed, however, interest in a Czech fifth column was limited. Only when the British found themselves with their backs to the wall did the home army become a negotiable asset.

The dramatic events of 1940 which culminated in June with the fall of France, transformed the position of the exiles. With the United States neutral and the Nazi–Soviet pact still in force, Britain stood alone against a triumphant Hitler. In this situation any ally became valuable and secret armies assumed an unpredicted importance. In May 1940, the Chiefs of Staff, foreseeing the collapse of France, 'strongly advocated the stimulation of revolt within the conquered territories as one of the best means of bringing about Germany's downfall' and recommended the creation of a special agency for sabotage and subversion which combined the functions of Section D and MI(R). In mid-July this new organisation took shape as SOE (the Special Operations Executive) under Hugh Dalton, a thrusting and ambitious Labour politician who became Minister of Economic Warfare in Churchill's coalition government. He was ordered by the Prime Minister to 'set Europe ablaze' as part of a general strategy which combined blockade, bombing and subversion to weaken Germany and pave the way for a British return to the continent. The ability of secret armies to change the situation was wildly overestimated but the British had nowhere else to turn pending a dramatic change in US or Soviet policy. Britain's ability to win by such means was a necessary fiction, the only source of hope in the darkest hour of the war. In this atmosphere Lockhart's arguments about the value of a Czech underground whose activities could be co-ordinated with British strategy by an exile government received a more sympathetic hearing. As one Foreign Office official cynically remarked, now that the British position had changed for the worse, it was necessary to view the Czechs in a new light. On 23 July, the day after the war cabinet approved the creation of SOE, Britain recognised the provisional government of Czechoslovakia. When Lockhart arrived in Putney to offer his congratulations, he found the normally unemotional Beneš almost moved to tears: 'When I came out, the ante-room was full of Czechoslovaks – new ministers waiting to be given office, ex-members of the Czechoslovak Parliament, civil servants and Dr Beneš's personal staff. The sun, shining through the windows, lit up a sea of smiles.'

The Blitz forced Beneš to evacuate the villa in Gwendolen Avenue and move to the safer rural setting of Aston Abbots, a small village near Woburn. He remained in constant touch with his administration in like London but preferred to work alone, never allowing any single minister to know too much. As before, he used his connexions with Moravec to reinforce his bargaining position with the British. Despite the recognition of the exiles as a provisional government, Beneš was far from satisfied. Provisional status still left the Czechs at the bottom of the exile league when compared with the Poles or the Dutch, who had fully recognised governments in London. At diplomatic receptions the Czechs were forced to trail in last, a humiliating position for someone like Beneš, who had been at Versailles in 1919 and considered himself a leading European statesman. Moreover Britain had not yet repudiated Munich, which was important for the credibility of the exiles at home. If Russia entered the war with this problem unresolved, the Czech people might abandon hope in the west and turn to the communists for salvation. This was a nightmare which haunted Beneš almost as much as the spectre of a compromise peace, since it would leave him high and dry when the war ended. Moreover, the repudiation of Munich was the necessary preliminary to a radical solution to the Sudeten problem involving the mass expulsion of the German minority from post-war Czechoslovakia, something which was demanded with increasing insistence by a home population suffering under the occupation. With Munich out of the way, the British might endorse such a move as part of the peace settlement. Beneš hoped to strengthen his hand in negotiations with the Foreign Office by demonstrating that Czechoslovakia was pulling its weight in the war effort, an approach which exploited Moravec's links with the secret world of wartime London.

In September 1940, the redoubtable Colonel was bombed out of his cover address in West Dulwich, which lay directly in the path of the great German daylight raids on the capital. The stick of high explosives which hit Rosendale Road demolished Reg Adams' radio shop with its precious communications equipment and almost destroyed the secret files smuggled out of Prague by 'Gibby' Gibson. Moravec himself had a narrow escape when a near-miss rocked his shelter on its foundations. After the raid his friends in SIS stepped in once more. A new communications section was established at Woldingham, just off the Pilgrims' Way near Redhill in Surrey. Although the radios were supplied by the British, the Czechs were given full operational control. Moravec's headquarters was transferred to two floors of a large building at Porchester Gate, now a hotel. In a typical clandestine touch, his personal suite could be entered by an outside staircase from the yard, a facility useful for someone in Moravec's business where it was inadvisable for all guests to use the front door. He was assigned three liaison officers by SIS, a colonel and two captains, who dealt either directly with him or with his deputy Major Emil Strankmuller. The main interest of SIS remained the material passed to the Czechs by A–54. Although ULTRA had begun to produce results, it was by no means as comprehensive as it became later in the war and its deficiencies could not be made good by British agent networks in Europe, most of which were rolled up in the wake of the French collapse. There was thus pressure on Moravec to produce increasing amounts of information from A–54 in the summer of 1940, particularly anything relating to Operation SEA LION, the Nazi invasion of Britain which was expected any day.

Moravec, however, had his own problems. With all of western

Europe except Sweden and Switzerland in Nazi hands, it was difficult to maintain contact with Thümmel. In this situation, Moravec decided to take a calculated risk and run A–54 through the Czech underground. Since Thümmel had just been posted by the Abwehr to Prague, with special responsibility for the Balkans and the Near East, there would be few problems about regular contact at a time when every scrap of intelligence might prove vital. On 20 June 1940 the assignment was given to the THREE KINGS, a circuit attached to the military resistance organisation, the ON, and run by three former officers, Colonel Balabán, Colonel Mašín and Captain Morávek, codename OTA, men whom the Czech intelligence chief could trust. Information from A–54 was relayed to Britain by the THREE KINGS over their transmitters Sparta 1 and Sparta 2, where it was deciphered by Major Strankmuller at Woldingham. It was then reviewed by Beneš before being passed to SIS through one of the British officers at Porchester Gate. The new system took time to establish and by early July headquarters was becoming desperate, perhaps because of the awful suspicion that Thümmel had bowed out under the impact of Hitler's recent victories. When contact was finally re-established, the underground was immediately ordered to ask Thümmel about SEA LION. In the next two months he was able to supply many details of the German plan, which were passed on to London over the Sparta transmitters or smuggled by courier to Czech intelligence officers in Stockholm and Geneva. On 23 September Beneš sent a message to Prague emphasising the importance of the intelligence link: 'Your work has had positive results here. The British appreciate us the more when they compare us with the Poles, the Dutch and even the French who have nothing equal to offer. You are contributing greatly to the good name of the whole nation.'

In the autumn of 1940, Moravec began to co-operate with a second British secret organisation, the newly created SOE, which was slowly taking shape after the decisions of the summer. The Czechs were highly recommended to Dalton by Lockhart, who was not only the Foreign Office representative with the provisional government but also a member of the propaganda section of SOE. After a talk with Beneš in October 1940, Lockhart sent Dalton an enthusiastic report on the home army, which he defined as the most 'formidible subversive movement now available to us in Europe'. By sabotage, passive resistance and an eventual rising, the Czech underground could do incalculable harm to the German war machine. Lockhart argued that SOE must assist the resistance movement with money and arms, combining maximum support with minimum interference. He was preaching to the converted, for like many Labour politicians Dalton was an opponent of Munich and sympathised with the Czechoslovak cause. As SOE policy evolved in the autumn of 1940, it followed Lockhart's general recommendations. The organisation was divided for operational purposes into several 'country sections', covering the nations of occupied Europe. The Czech section was run by Peter Wilkinson, who was absorbed into SOE from MI(R) after spending the summer assisting Gubbins to set up secret British guerrilla groups which were to be activated in the event of a Nazi invasion. Gubbins himself had been recruited into SOE that November as director of operations and training with the rank of brigadier, an appointment he owed to Dalton, who was impressed by his wide knowledge of eastern Europe. Gubbins became the driving force within SOE, determined to place subversion at the centre of British strategy as the fourth arm of warfare. He was an admirer of the Czechs and the Poles, regarding their underground organisations as models for the rest of Europe, and did what he could to assist both groups of exiles.

Wilkinson's task with the Czechs was very like the one he had already performed for MI(R). Unlike the other country sections of SOE, with the exception of the Poles, the Czech section did not run its own agents. The Czechs had their own functioning intelligence organisation and an underground movement whose existence predated the creation of SOE. They were used to controlling communications with the homeland, courtesy of SIS, and to running the show where the resistance was concerned. Since any interference with this established system would have been counter-productive, Wilkinson's job was one of tactful co-operation rather than direction. His mission was on the one hand to assist the Czechs with operations, arrange for the training and transport of agents and explain Czech needs to the British Chiefs of Staff, while on the other making the Czechs aware of the requirements of British strategy. It was a delicate task which demanded tolerance and diplomacy. Since SOE was thus dependent on Moravec for information about the home army, the Czechs enjoyed considerable freedom of manoeuvre. Moreover Moravec was quite capable of exploiting the rivalry between the fledgling SOE and the established SIS. Sir Stewart Menzies, who replaced Sinclair as 'C' in November 1939, and senior members of his staff never reconciled themselves to the new organisation, which they regarded as crassly amateur and likely to compromise SIS attempts to re-establish agent networks by drawing the unwelcome attention of the Nazi security forces. Resentment of SOE soon assumed the dimensions of a feud, which could be exploited by a figure like Moravec who had a foot in both camps.

Unknown to either SIS or SOE, the Czechs were also in touch with another secret organisation, Soviet military intelligence, codenamed UNCLE. Beneš had always believed that Russia would enter the war sooner or later despite the Nazi–Soviet pact. When the time came he wanted to make sure that Stalin backed the exile government and not the Czech communists. Since reaching London he had been careful to remain on good terms with the Soviet Ambassador, Ivan Maisky, and from time to time passed on information of interest to the Kremlin. It was the Russians, though, who made the running. Frozen off by Moravec in March 1939, they renewed their request for intelligence co-operation a year later, suggesting that Beneš send someone to Moscow to work out the details. Nothing came of this approach but in June 1940 Colonel Balabán of the THREE KINGS established direct contact with the Russians in Belgrade and arranged to pass information to an intelligence officer operating under the cover of the Soviet Consulate in Prague, a reversion to the pre-war system of co-operation. Beneš approved this arrangement but laid down strict conditions. He wanted to keep the main threads of the relationship with Moscow in his own hands and to deny the Russians an opportunity to penetrate the home army under the guise of co-operation. Balabán was authorised to pass on only information of a military–strategic nature, and was warned to allow his Soviet contacts no insight into the organisation of the underground or domestic politics. As Hitler's attention began to turn eastwards after the postponement of Operation SEA LION, the Czechs were able to provide Moscow with intelligence from A–54 about German military plans which Beneš hoped would drive a wedge into the Nazi–Soviet pact.

As the months passed by with no perceptible sign of a breach between Hitler and Stalin, Beneš began to have doubts about the prospects in the east and to place more faith in the early participation in the war of the United States. As late as 21 June, only one day before BARBAROSSA, he refused to believe Moravec's information that a German attack was imminent: 'I think they will make an agreement [and] there will be no war. I wish, if it had to happen, it would happen in the spring of next year, when the Russians will be more ready. I am afraid that now they shall be easily defeated. Germany will have successes again and in the end Russia will make a separate peace with her.' These doubts dictated his attitude to fresh Russian demands for closer co-operation with Czech intelligence. Although it was agreed in

January 1941 at a secret meeting with a senior officer of Soviet military intelligence (the GRU) in Istanbul that the Czechs would send a representative to Moscow, Beneš delayed until April before despatching Colonel Píka to the Soviet capital. He recognised the importance of such a connexion in the event of war but feared that the Germans and the Russians were playing a complex game of their own. If Hitler was merely bluffing to force Stalin into a more subservient relationship, he did not want Czech interests sacrificed as part of a new Nazi–Soviet pact. Caution demanded that the GRU should be allowed as little insight as possible into the Czech intelligence network and its links with the home army. Since the Russians for their part had no intention of annoying the Germans by flaunting their relationship with the exiles, Píka was able to do little but kick his heels in Moscow under strict police surveillance until the Nazi invasion. At the same time, Beneš took care to protect his relationship with the British against any Soviet betrayal. On 4 June when Gubbins visited Porchester Gate to discuss the latest news about Nazi plans, Moravec 'was able to tell him that we had officers in Russia. . . . The Englishman gulped and Moravec did not have to spell it out diplomatically. Intelligence was not even mentioned.'

Beneš' dealings with SIS, SOE and the Russians were underpinned by his control of the home resistance, which was vital to his relationship with all three secret organisations. After the fall of France, it was the underground which transmitted Thümmel's information to London for distribution to British and Soviet intelligence. The existence of a home army also allowed Beneš to claim, through SOE, that the Czechs were making a military contribution to the defeat of Hitler. Moreover the political support of the resistance, expressed through Moravec's radio centre at Woldingham, legitimised Beneš' claim to represent his country and was an important asset in dealing with the Foreign Office on the matter of full recognition. Beneš lost no opportunity to impress British officials with the strength of his support at home and the contribution of the underground to the allied war effort. In February 1941 Beneš and Masaryk lunched with Eden and Lockhart at Claridges. The British Foreign Secretary was impressed by the Czechs and made arrangements to meet Beneš regularly. He also recommended that Churchill dine with the exiled President. As he informed the Prime Minister, the 'little man' had 'an impressive story to tell of his organisations in his own country, and I think you would be interested.' Beneš found a ready audience in Churchill, who was fascinated by the secret world of intelligence: 'During his early adventures at the outposts of empire he had acquired a fascination for cloaks and daggers which never left him.' When Churchill visited the Czech forces at Edgehill in April 1941, Beneš impressed the British leader with the extent of his intelligence on Hitler's plans to invade the Soviet Union, taking care to conceal his own private fears that this might merely be part of an elaborate diplomatic bluff. He then presented Churchill with a memorandum on recognition, hoping that a direct appeal to the top would produce action. The ploy worked. Summoned to the Foreign Office the following day, Lockhart saw scrawled on the Czech memorandum in the Prime Minister's distinctive hand: 'I do not see why the Czechs should not be placed on the same footing as the other Allied Governments. They have deserved it.' Underneath Eden had written: 'I agree.' As Beneš later emphasised, the endless stream of military and political information from the underground was the key to progress: 'Without this permanent contact with our country . . . our Movement abroad would not have gained many of the successes which were granted to it.'

Although Beneš deliberately exaggerated the strength and activities of the 'Maffia' in conversations with British officials, the Czech underground – despite widespread Gestapo arrests in the first year of the war – was stronger and better organised than any in Europe in 1940–1, with the exception of the Poles. Its activities were co-ordinated by a shadowy central council, UVOD, which emerged in 1940, representing every anti-Nazi group except the communists. The influence of this central council reached all the way into the Protector-ate regime, which, while ostensibly co-operating with the German occupation, attempted to shield the resistance. The Prime Minister, General Alois Eliáš, was in regular contact with London and the state President, the ailing Hácha, secretly recognised Beneš' authority. Not without reason, Neurath complained that the exiles were as well informed about his dealings with Czech ministers as his superiors in Berlin. Beneš encouraged the Protectorate government to remain in office, both to protect the home army and to provide a Czech administration ready to take over in the event of a sudden German collapse. A power vacuum, he feared, would be exploited by the communists. The existence of the Hácha regime, however, was a double-edged weapon. As long as Beneš could demonstrate its loyalty to the exile government and its links with the resistance, it was an important factor in maintaining his credibility with the British. If it ever became a mere tool of the Nazis, however, a self-seeking group of quislings, it would weaken the exiles by tarring the Czechs with the brush of collaboration. Even more dangerously, such a development might be the first step towards a German peace offer to Britain which would leave Hitler in possession of the Protectorate. This might be attractive to certain circles in London who would argue that the Czechs were happy under Nazi rule. As Beneš warned UVOD in March 1941: 'At the time it has to start yielding, Germany will offer the evacuation of western European countries, but it will insist upon the incorporation of . . . Bohemia and Moravia and Austria into the Reich. . . . The moment will probably come when . . . you will be offered concessions. . . . I beg and insist that both threats and offers of any kind be resolutely rejected. . . . Upon our demand president Hácha and the government must be ready to resign their offices immediately.' In April Beneš received such a pledge from Hácha and Eliáš and was content for the time being to go along with their opportunist policies, which allowed the underground to survive and avoided the imposition of direct rule. As he informed Lockhart, it was important to maintain the Protectorate regime until the moment of revolt. If the Nazis ever tried to turn them into quislings, its ministers would resign on orders from London. In agreement with the exiles, the home army avoided dramatic acts of resistance liable to provoke Nazi reprisals and endanger the existence of a Protectorate government. As Beneš explained to Lockhart in October 1940, its efforts were concentrated in three areas – undetectable sabotage against German communications, passive resistance such as slow-downs in the factories, and the collection of intelligence. An open challenge was to be avoided until the Reich was on the verge of collapse. Then the underground would emerge into the streets, seize key positions and send flying columns to reoccupy the Sudetenland. These tactics were calculated to preserve the position of the exile regime, which might lose its moral authority by prematurely demanding dramatic sacrifices from the captive population at home. They also reflected an astute judgement about the internal politics of Nazi rule in the Protectorate which was characterised by a struggle for power between Karl Hermann Frank and the Reichsprotektor, Freiherr Konstantin von Neurath.

The German administration of the Protectorate reflected the existing rivalry within the Reich itself between the rising power of the SS and the older political, bureaucratic and military establishment. The Reichsprotektor, Neurath, was a representative of the old Germany, a conservative nationalist who had been sacked as Foreign Minister in 1938 for his doubts about Hitler's expansionist plans. He believed that Bohemia–Moravia was a natural part of German living-space but argued that the Czechs must be led rather than pushed into accepting a place in the greater Reich. Neurath opposed an open attack on Czech culture and autonomy, preferring to run the Protectorate with a 'weak hand and . . . loose reins'. A bureaucrat rather than a politician, he was content to leave everyday affairs in the hands of Eliáš, Hácha and the protectorate regime. From the beginning he and his staff attempted to limit the power of the SS, represented by the State Secretary, Karl Hermann Frank, an effort which was supported by the military commander of Bohemia–Moravia, General Frederici, and by the Abwehr. The traditional civil servants in Neurath's office made no attempt to hide their contempt for Frank, whom they regarded as a degenerate and a criminal. As for Frank, he intrigued ceaselessly against his nominal superior with the support of Himmler and Heydrich in Berlin. His control over the security police, which Neurath was unable to break, was employed as the entering wedge for SS power.

The SS scored several early victories in this struggle. In the autumn of 1939, Frank used Czech student demonstrations in Prague on national day, 28 October, as an opportunity to strike at the intelligentsia, regarded by the SS as the foundation of Czech nationalism. Police intervention caused trouble at an otherwise peaceful occasion and resulted in the death of one student. Two weeks later, when incidents occurred at the funeral, Frank persuaded Hitler that there was a threat to public order. The Führer flew into a rage and authorised drastic action. The following dawn, in a well-coordinated operation, the SS raided student residences throughout Prague. Those who resisted were shot on the spot and the others arrested, beaten and humiliated. The leaders of the student council were taken to the airport and executed by firing squad. Over 1000 others were transported to Oranienburg concentration camp, where they were held as hostages for Czech good behaviour. The citizens of Prague awoke to find the colleges ransacked and the bodies of students lying in pools of blood. In a proclamation in the controlled press Frank announced: 'A group of Czech intellectuals with the help of the fugitive ex-President Beneš has been attempting for some time to disturb the peace and order of the Protectorate of Bohemia and Moravia. . . . It was discovered that some of the perpetrators of these acts of resistance were to be found in the Czech Universities. Because on 28 October and 15 November these elements violently attacked individual Germans, all Czech Universities will be closed for three years.' As a final symbol to the people of where real power lay, the college of law in Prague was turned into an SS barracks. These events took place behind Neurath's back and were part of an elaborate conspiracy cooked up between Frank and the SS leadership in Berlin. While the Reichsprotektor deplored this crude demonstration, Himmler and Heydrich registered approval by promoting Frank to the rank of SS Gruppenführer. The whole experience taught the resistance and the exiles the importance of avoiding public challenges to Nazi rule, which were only exploited by the bitterest enemies of the Czech people.

The attack on the universities was followed by other repressive measures. On 2 December Frank issued a grim public threat to the Czechs: 'From today on, we will employ the sharpest means without any warning. Whoever is not with us is against us, and whoever is against us will be ground to pieces.' In February 1940 hundreds of members of the Czech gymnastic association, SOKOL, a traditional bastion of nationalism, were arrested. At the same time evidence began to accumulate of Eliáš' intrigues with London as the Gestapo penetrated and broke up several resistance networks which had been constructed with little regard for security. As one underground leader reported: 'Due to the clumsiness of our people, pogrom after pogrom has been directed against us with the result that now we remain merely a handful.' The material on Eliáš went into a growing Gestapo dossier for eventual use against the Protectorate Prime Minister and his sponsor, Neurath. In the right circumstances it could be used to prove that the Reichsprotektor was a bumbling incompetent whose softness had allowed the Czechs to plot against the Reich under his very nose. For his part, Neurath grumbled about the 'sledgehammer' tactics favoured by Frank and called for an end to the 'senseless arrests carried out by the SS'.

While Frank's control of the security police was exploited to undermine Neurath, it was also useful in other ways. By 1940 the SS had established a considerable economic presence in the Protectorate based on the property of sequestered Jews and anti-Nazis which was incorporated into Himmler's growing business empire. As later events were to show, his ultimate ambition was to control the output of the Skoda arms works for the benefit of the Waffen SS. Over Neurath's protests, Frank arrested the staff of the Czech Land Office and installed an SS officer, Oberführer Curt von Gottberg, who quickly extended his tentacles to control not only land resources but also the state forests. Gottberg's aim was to evict Czech farmers and replace them with Germans and he boasted openly that within ten years no Czech would be able to own land or property in Bohemia–Moravia.

Neurath was able to check the wilder ambitions of the SS, however, because while Hitler was determined to assert German power, he was equally anxious to avoid trouble as long as the outcome of the war remained uncertain. In 1940 Bohemia–Moravia was economically integrated into the Reich by the removal of customs barriers but drastic action against the Czech people and their culture was postponed. Poland was given priority in the Führer's grisly plans to Germanise the Slavs. As Hitler himself recognised, there were simply not enough Germans available to support a policy based on deportation and resettlement. Moreover Bohemia–Moravia contained the great arms factories at Brno and Plzeň besides other industries important to the war effort, all considerations which argued against a radical policy. As Goebbels noted in May 1941: 'The Führer has great praise for the work the Czechs have been doing in the armaments field. Not a single case of sabotage to date. And what they produce is good, serviceable and solid. The Czechs have proved themselves. They are hard-working and reliable. A valuable acquisition for us.' In these circumstances, Neurath was able to contain Frank by persuading Hitler to postpone a reckoning with the Czechs.

His greatest success came in the summer of 1940 when he found an unlikely ally in his baleful rival, although the two men continued to work towards incompatible goals. The fall of France led to pressure from local Nazi bosses for the liquidation of the Protectorate and the partition of Bohemia–Moravia amongst the neighbouring German provinces. This feeling was particularly strong amongst the Sudetens, who felt cheated of their proper share of the spoils in March 1939. These demands were resisted by both Neurath and Frank, who referred the matter to Hitler for a decision. The Reichsprotektor wished to avert drastic action against the Czechs while his ambitious subordinate regarded the Protectorate as the basis of his own personal power. One day he hoped to replace his despised superior and show the Czechs who was the real master of Bohemia–Moravia. Frank's sudden transformation into a stalwart defender of Czech autonomy drew a sarcastic comment from Heydrich, but his intentions were far from charitable. Both Neurath and Frank justified the maintenance of a special status for Bohemia–Moravia on the grounds that it offered the best route to ultimate Germanisation of the Czechs, a line with which Hitler agreed. At a meeting in Berlin in September 1940, he ordered that the Protectorate was to be maintained 'at least for the duration of the war, on the other hand preparations are to be made for the prospective Germanisation of the area and its inhabitants.' While the majority of the population might ultimately qualify for assimilation, 'Those . . . about whom there existed doubts from a racial point of view or who were antagonistic towards the Reich should be excluded. . . . This category should be exterminated.' Neurath probably did not understand the significance of the phrase used to indicate extermination, *Sonderbehandlung* or special treatment, although Frank undoubtedly did since it was standard SS language. From the Reichsprotektor's point of view, the vital thing about Hitler's decision was that it staved off radical action, which would increase the power of the SS. Until a later stage only the preliminary steps could be taken, and in October 1940 Himmler ordered Heydrich to start identifying possible candidates for Germanisation, using doctors' reports on school children and old conscription records. A similar caution was evident in Hitler's attitude towards the Czech underground. He rejected Frank's demand for the arrest of the Protectorate Prime Minister, General Eliáš, despite Gestapo evidence of his dealings with London, and ordered the postponement of trials involving resistance leaders arrested earlier in the year. According to Hitler, it was important not to create martyrs: 'The Government under Prime Minister Eliáš will continue to be tolerated; accounts will be settled with the resistance movement and Czech personalities who have compromised themselves, at a later stage.' Meanwhile Neurath would remain in office to keep the Czechs quiet until the moment came for drastic action.

These decisions created an uneasy equilibrium in Prague. Frank continued to intrigue against Neurath and the Protectorate regime but despite a fresh appeal to Himmler in February 1941 was unable to arrest Eliáš. Meanwhile the damning police file on the Prime Minister continued to grow and the Gestapo steadily penetrated the resistance networks painfully rebuilt since the spring of 1940. As long as Neurath remained though, Frank and his sinister masters in Berlin were unable to launch the smashing blow which would reduce the Czechs to subservience and transform Bohemia–Moravia into an SS state. While this deadlock continued, Beneš was able to exploit his links with the Protectorate to gain credibility in London and Moscow without plunging his small nation into a bloodbath. Hitler was containing the SS terror for his own reasons, nor was there any pressure from London or Moscow to disturb the delicate balance in Prague. SIS wanted intelligence from the home army and had no interest in stirring up trouble which might jeopardise its sources. 'C' and his staff were satisfied with the material from Thümmel relayed over the underground transmitters controlled by Moravec. As for SOE, while it remained true to the notion of setting Europe ablaze, that phase was relegated to the future when British armies were ready to return to the continent. Until then a direct challenge to Nazi power was to be avoided. As Dalton defined SOE strategy: 'The underground fighters should show sufficient active resistance to cause constant embarrassment to the occupying forces.... But they should keep their main organisations underground and avoid any attempt at large-scale risings or ambitious paramilitary operations which could only result in severe oppression and the loss of our key men. They should do all they can to prepare a widespread underground organisation ready to strike hard later, when we give the signal.' The Czechs were thus not asked to go beyond their established policy of preparation coupled with unattributable sabotage and passive resistance. The Russians, lurking in the wings while the Nazi–Soviet pact lasted, were, like SIS, interested in intelligence rather than subversion and made no demands for direct action by the home army. This favourable situation was not to last. In June 1941 Hitler launched Operation BARBAROSSA, opening a new and more bitter phase in the world conflict. As the German panzers raced across the Russian steppes that fateful summer, Beneš found himself facing difficult decisions which he had been able to avoid at an earlier stage in the war.

5

Time For Action

On a frosty day in October 1940, the 3000 men of the Czech Brigade arrived in Leamington Spa, near Warwick. Headquarters under General Miroslav was established in a large Victorian villa in the centre of the town while the various units of the brigade were dispersed to military installations and requisitioned country houses in the surrounding area, Milton Morell, Milton Paddox, Wellesbourne and Kineton. It had been a long and difficult journey from central Europe to the heart of England and as winter settled over the unfamiliar Warwickshire countryside nobody from general to private could know if he would ever see his home again. The brigade had landed in Britain three months earlier, bitter and demoralised. Rushed into battle inadequately trained and equipped in May 1940, the Czechs were rapidly caught up in the French military collapse. When France surrendered on 17 June, its former allies were left to shift for themselves. Many soldiers conscripted from the Slovak community in France simply deserted. The remainder, exiles who could not risk falling into the hands of the Gestapo, determined to escape to Britain and continue the fight. Under the command of General Ingr, these elements retreated towards the Mediterranean coast along roads clogged with refugees and the broken remnants of the French army while Beneš in London desperately lobbied the British authorities to secure evacuation ships. Despite his best efforts, the troops were nearly abandoned in the general confusion and the situation was only saved by Lockhart who pulled strings at the Admiralty to rescue the remnants of the Czech division. The men sailed without their heavy equipment but with a deep and abiding contempt for France which was held guilty of a double betrayal, first at Munich and again in the recent fighting when it had once more left its Czech allies in the lurch.

The troops were sent from Liverpool docks to Cholmondeley Park near Chester to re-equip and reorganise. As Beneš later admitted, the men had been badly shaken by their recent experiences. There was a sour atmosphere of disillusion and defeat which encouraged recrimination and a search for scapegoats. Political and ideological disputes arose which the officers were unable to contain. One group of soldiers blamed the political and military leadership for their predicament. They complained that the army was dominated by fascists and anti-Semites and demanded to be discharged. In all 480 men refused to obey orders. This alarming news rapidly reached the ears of MI5, which blenched at the thought of letting loose 480 disaffected aliens on the eve of a Nazi invasion. Colonel Moravec believed that communist elements were behind the incident, a view shared by the British security services, although Beneš was careful to avoid assigning blame. The culprits were temporarily interned at York and then drafted into the Pioneer Corps, which provided unskilled labour for the British army. Beneš was anxious to close the whole embarrassing incident, which reflected badly on his own claims to represent the Czechoslovak people, and asked for the move to be hushed up to avoid misunderstandings or the creation of an 'unfortunate precedent affecting the morale of the remaining Czechoslovak Military Forces'. In August 1940, the provisional government concluded a military agreement with the British and a liaison mission under Colonel Pollack was assigned to the Czech army, which was reorganised as a brigade on the British model. Morale rapidly improved after the incidents at Cholmondeley Park and Lockhart was soon able to report a new spirit amongst the troops. The Czech Brigade was not a crack unit like the Cossack guard of imperial Russia but it represented 'democracy on the march'. It was composed largely of volunteers, well-educated men who had sacrificed everything for their country. The rank and file were motivated by two burning emotions. The first was to create a better society in post-war Czechoslovakia. They were not fighting simply to restore the old republic. This was a sentiment of which Beneš was well aware and which he took into political account. The second was a bitter hatred of the Germans. The Czech troops wanted to fight and win to reverse the verdict of Munich and Prague. These emotions were partly fuelled by a haunting sense of guilt at being in a place of safety while the home population was at the mercy of Karl Hermann Frank and his brutal security police. The only way the army could return with pride was to fight its way back, sharing with the underground a common victory against the Nazis. As one British observer remarked, the soldiers could 'never hold up their heads in Prague unless they have been in actual combat with the Germans. It is true that a large proportion . . . were in the retreat across France but that is not considered sufficient and the men themselves realise full well that they will receive no welcome in their own country unless they have actually fought the Germans in the later stages of the war; and of course it is the urgent wish of every man in that Brigade to have a go. . . .' As the winter of 1940/1 turned to spring and the cherry trees began to blossom along the streets of Leamington, this seemed a distant prospect. For some of these men, though, an opportunity to hit back at the invader was to come sooner than they guessed.

In April 1941 a Humber staff car containing Moravec's deputy, Major Emil Strankmuller, arrived at brigade headquarters in Leamington Spa. A visit from a high-ranking member of the intelligence staff was unusual but Strankmuller had come with a special purpose. He wanted the brigade to supply the names of men suitable for special duty. His requirements were strict. The men selected were to be patriotic, brave and intelligent. They were to be capable of controlling their emotions under stress and of keeping secrets. He wanted nobody with a history of drinking or womanising. The nature of the unspecified special duties was immediately apparent to his listeners – Strankmuller was recruiting agents. By early May, after extensive enquiries by company officers, headquarters was able to supply the names of thirty-six soldiers who fulfilled his exacting requirements. The candidates were visited by Colonel Palaček, the Czech intelligence officer in charge of selecting agents and asked if they were willing to consider secret work at home. The voluntary nature of this decision was stressed since it was impossible to draft men for so dangerous a mission. By mid-May, Moravec was ready to send a group of twelve officers and twelve NCOs for initial parachute training and a Most Secret and Urgent order from the Czech Defence Ministry in London despatched the first batch of recruits to RAF Wilmslow, near Manchester. The plan to send teams of agents to the Protectorate had been worked out with SOE in the early spring and was primarily intended to improve communications with the home army. The War Diary of the Czech Defence Ministry noted on 30 April 1941: 'Received WO [War Office] authorization to send 4 officers and 5 non-commissioned officers for parachute training. Young officers and non-commissioned officers have been selected. . . . The WO intends to train this nucleus of parachutists in a total number of pupils amounting to about 14 officers and 22 non-commissioned officers. The commanding officer of the brigade and Staff-Colonel Moravec have been informed.' The agents were to be dropped into Bohemia–Moravia that autumn as three-man intelligence and radio teams, reinforcing the capacity of the home army in these two important areas. This scheme originated in the political requirements of Eduard Beneš. With Hitler apparently poised to invade the Soviet Union, it was important to guarantee his vital radio links with the home army. The flow of political and military information from A–54 and other sources must continue as the war entered a new and decisive stage, ensuring that Beneš was not left on the sidelines. Intelligence was essential to his credibility in the allied camp. With the communists likely to become active at home in the wake of a Nazi attack on Russia, it was also necessary to maintain control over the central resistance council, UVOD, allowing him to dictate the response of the underground to the new political situation in Bohemia–Moravia. Moreover, it is clear that Beneš hoped for substantial logistical backing from Britain for the Czech resistance which would strengthen it against the communists and improve the prospects of a national uprising when the time was ripe. If SOE was to send in large quantities of arms, a plan Gubbins was developing in the spring of 1941, it was necessary to establish an extensive communications network manned by trained military personnel to co-ordinate supply drops and provide a link with the British high command. The existing system had worked well since 1939, relaying thousands of messages, but it was clearly incapable of bearing these new burdens.

When Strankmuller visited the headquarters of the Czech Brigade on his recruiting mission, an attempt had already been made to land a radio agent in the Protectorate, codenamed Operation BENJAMIN. It had ended in disaster on 17 April 1941, when the man and his equipment were dropped over Austria because of a navigational error, common in the early days of long-distance night flying. Thereafter the long, clear nights of spring and summer made flights to the Protectorate impossible but Moravec was clearly anxious to have a pool of agents ready when the operational season began again in the closing months of 1941. The need to reinforce existing radio networks was already all too clear as the Germans tightened security precautions on the eve of BARBAROSSA. Whatever Neurath might think, Frank feared the reaction of the Czechs to an assault on their fellow Slavs to the east and was determined to stamp out resistance in advance. In February 1941 his security police arrested almost the entire central committee of the Czech communist party and destroyed its radio links with Moscow.

The home army also suffered losses, amongst them members of the THREE KINGS circuit which acted as Thümmel's contacts with London and the Soviet Consulate in Prague. On 22 April Balabán was arrested. Three weeks later, on 15 May, his comrades Mašín and Morávek were located by detector vans in the middle of a transmission. While Mašín defended the doorway with his pistol, Morávek escaped from a third-floor window by sliding down the thin steel radio aerial, severing a finger in the process. Mašín was captured, beaten up and dragged off to the cellars of Gestapo headquarters at the Peček Palace. From material captured at the scene, the Nazis suspected that a high-ranking German was in contact with the resistance, but although they tortured Mašín they were unable to identify the mysterious figure.

On 10 June, Frank reported his latest triumph to his masters in Berlin: 'We have successfully uncovered an intelligence ring – not communist . . . but serving the USSR, and we have confiscated several clandestine transmitters. Thanks to the intervention of the state police we can say that the organised resistance movement has been largely disposed of, although in its place there is a much smaller, but undoubtedly more dangerous organisation concentrating on espionage and sabotage.' The last part of this message was a renewed plea for the removal of the restraining hand of Neurath, whose influence, although weakening, was still sufficient to prevent the reign of terror advocated by Frank to break the Czechs. As a result of the Gestapo raid on the THREE KINGS' transmitter, Czech intelligence was cut off from A–54 on the very eve of BARBAROSSA, when accurate information was vital. The panic ended only when Morávek came on the air, using a transmitter borrowed from another group, and again began to relay information provided by Thümmel. The whole experience underlined the need to reinforce communications with the Protectorate. Without the underground radios, Beneš was blind and helpless, incapable of commanding the attention of the allies or of controlling the political situation at home.

Beneš had always believed that Czechoslovakia would be saved by the widening of the war, and he regarded the Nazi invasion of the Soviet Union as the beginning of the end for Hitler. With the United States already moving towards open hostilities after the Lend–Lease Act of March 1941, the Nazis faced an alignment of forces which his logical mind predicted they would be unable to defeat. If the Russians could hold out until the end of the summer, Beneš expected a rapid reversal in the fortunes of war and perhaps a German collapse as early as the second half of 1942, a piece of wishful thinking based on little but his characteristic optimism. There had been moments of anguish before BARBAROSSA when he doubted that Hitler would really launch an invasion despite the information from A–54, doubts which he was careful not to communicate to Moscow. His only fear when the operation finally began was that Britain would stand aside as Hitler drove eastwards, a fear which was set at rest in the first days of the fighting, when Churchill made plain his determination to extend full support to Stalin, regardless of ideology. For the first time Beneš was able to see a real prospect of victory and he displayed an excitement rare in so austere a man. As his private secretary, Edward Táborský, who was with Beneš when the first official news of the invasion was announced, later recalled: 'As I sat with him in his Aston Abbots study on that fateful Sunday celebrating the event and listening to the news bulletins . . . I could discern in his face . . . a satisfaction more serene and more intense than I had seen since the outbreak of war in September 1939.' The head of his chancery, Jaromir Smutný, was quite blunt about the reasons for Beneš' exultation which vindicated the strategy he had pursued since Munich: 'He has worked consciously and continuously to promote the war, since, if the whole of Europe did not go to war, Czechoslovakia would remain occupied by the Germans for centuries and the Czechoslovak nation would to all intents and purposes disappear again . . . and . . . suffer the same fate as the Polabian Slavs. Only war could save Czechoslovakia.'

Beneš' secret contacts with Moscow seemed to pay off in the weeks after the Nazi invasion of Russia. BARBAROSSA burst like a thunderbolt on the Soviet Union. Within two weeks of the attack, Hitler's panzers had reached the River Dnieper and nearly 600,000 prisoners had fallen into the hands of the Wehrmacht. Nothing seemed able to stop the blitzkrieg. The German generals regarded the war as practically won, an opinion shared by Hitler, who predicted that the fighting would end by mid-September with the Russians pushed behind the Urals. He was so confident of victory that he ordered a shift in the armaments programme away from the requirements of the army towards the production of submarines and aircraft necessary for a renewed attack on Britain. As Russia reeled under these stunning blows, Stalin was anxious to cultivate the Czechs. Like the British after Dunkirk, he needed all the allies he could find. It was a matter of national survival. The first fruits of the new Russian attitude came on 18 July, when the Soviet Union extended full diplomatic recognition to the London Czechs and confirmed that, for Moscow, Munich did not exist. The two countries pledged to assist each other 'in every way in the present war against Hitlerite Germany' and Czech volunteers, interned by the USSR after the fall of Poland, were released to fight as a national unit on the Russian front under their commander, Lieutenant-Colonel Svoboda.

These negotiations gave a new impetus to talks with the British on the issue of full recognition, which had stalled since the spring despite the goodwill of Churchill and Eden. Beneš used the Russian lever to hurry the Foreign Office along, arguing that if Moscow acted before London the result would strengthen the communists and undermine the position of his own pro-western regime. In the event the Russians won the race by several hours. At noon on 18 July, Masaryk signed the Czech–Soviet treaty. Three hours later, in the pouring rain, he drove with Lockhart to the Foreign Office to initial an agreement with Britain. As Eden wryly remarked, the Czechs were having a day of treaties. The British form of full recognition was more reserved than the Soviet since it made no commitment on post-war frontiers and thus left the issue of Munich and the Sudetenland unresolved. The British censor went so far as to remove a passage from a broadcast by Beneš to Czechoslovakia stating that the areas lost at Munich would be returned after the war. Beneš, although irritated, was convinced that he had passed a major hurdle and that the rest would eventually follow. For the first time his regime was the diplomatic equal of the other exile governments and was assigned a full ambassador by the Foreign Office in the shape of Philip Nichols. Lockhart, whose title 'British Representative' had been a galling symbol of the ambiguous status of the Czechs, went off to work full-time in propaganda, although he retained his strong personal interest in the fortunes of the exiles.

Beneš was too much of a realist to expect something for nothing and was well aware that he would have to pay for these diplomatic advances. If Czechoslovakia was to be supported by the allies, it must make a contribution to winning the war. As before BARBAROSSA, Beneš hoped to make this contribution chiefly in the field of intelligence, a fact reflected in the decision to reinforce radio communications with the Protectorate by dropping parachute groups. The Russians were quick to exploit their links with the Czechs in the weeks after the German invasion, which provided all the proof required that Moravec had access to a highly placed source with knowledge of Hitler's military plans. A new visitor soon joined the SIS officers at Porchester Gate, haunting the corridors in search of information. This was a Soviet officer named Cicajev, whom Moravec suspected represented the NKVD rather than military intelligence, a symbol of the importance attached by Moscow to information from A–54. As Moravec later recalled: 'He . . . began our co-operation in a suppliant mood. Russia was losing.' At a later stage in the war it was to be a different story. The Czech transmitters at Woldingham were soon bombarding the underground with questions for Thümmel which were clearly supplied by Moscow. Where were the main German reserves? What was the present position of Führer headquarters? What were the Germans planning in Turkey? The list was endless. As Kiev fell and the Nazis began to hammer on the gates of Leningrad, there was an air of desperate urgency about these Soviet approaches. As before Munich, Moravec received little intelligence in return, perhaps because the Russians had none to give. Beneš was indifferent to this imbalance. For him the aim of intelligence co-operation was political. His goal was to improve the bargaining power of the exile government with Moscow and the Czech communists. Moravec's sponsors in SIS, who had been deliberately kept in the dark when the intelligence link was first established, found his contacts with Moscow useful. By arrangement with Moravec, they began to channel material, which probably included some ULTRA intelligence, to Cicajev through the Czechs. The reasons for this are obscure although SIS perhaps suspected that Czech intelligence, with its long history of co-operation with Russia, enjoyed more credibility in Moscow than SIS with its firm anti-Soviet background.

It was soon clear, however, that for Moscow, mere intelligence co-operation was not enough. Fighting with their backs to the wall, the Russians demanded a military contribution from their allies which would relieve the pressure of the blitzkrieg on their tottering front. As early as 19 July Stalin wrote to Churchill suggesting a British landing in northern France to divert Hitler's forces from the east. The British, who were in no position to invade the continent, staved off this pressure, stressing that Britain was contributing to the allied cause by diverting arms to Russia and bombing German industrial centres. Beneš had fewer options. His only asset apart from intelligence was the home army and the Russians wanted him to use it. With thousands dying every day in the struggle against the invader and the very existence of the Soviet state at stake, arguments about the risk of bloodshed and Nazi reprisals cut no ice with Moscow. The Protectorate contained important arms factories which provided equipment for Hitler's panzer divisions. Over its railways rolled trains from southern Germany and Austria carrying supplies and reinforcements for the advancing Nazi forces. It was made clear to the London Czechs that the Russians wanted something done about this situation. As early as 24 June, the Soviet Military Attaché approached Moravec to propose a joint sabotage campaign and Moscow radio appealed to the Czech people to aid the USSR by rising against the Germans. Russian pressure intensified during the summer as the Red Army continued to retreat. On 17 August Moravec's transmitters at Woldingham informed UVOD that the Soviet general staff was pressing for action against petrol stores, oil-tank farms, aircraft factories and railways in Bohemia–Moravia. Such action was considered imperative in view of the critical situation at the front.

Beneš' initial reaction was to resist. His first messages to the Protectorate in the wake of BARBAROSSA ordered the home army to stay calm and await events. It should obey only its own leaders and not the siren voice of Moscow. As he explained to Lockhart, he was unwilling to expose the underground to German reprisals, which might well destroy it and leave a clear field for the communists. Nothing was to be done to endanger the prospects of a national uprising at a time chosen by the London Czechs and not by the Russians. It was for this that the underground was to continue to prepare and plan. Beneš complained about the tone of the Moscow broadcasts and persuaded the British to make similar representations. As Eden pointed out to the Soviet Ambassador, Ivan Maisky, nobody but the Germans would benefit from premature action in the Protectorate. At the same time, Beneš was sensitive to any suggestion that the home Czechs were doing nothing or, worse, aiding the Nazi cause. He reacted immediately when the puppet government of Slovakia declared war on Russia on 24 June and Hácha made a speech praising the German crusade against Bolshevism and urging the population to work for a Nazi victory. Such actions threatened to undermine the position of the exiles by raising questions about their control over the situation at home and creating the impression that only the communists were resisting the Nazis. Beneš feared that the next step might be the raising of volunteers in the Protectorate to fight alongside the Germans on the Russian front. On 24 June, he sent a strong message to Hácha and Eliáš, warning that they must be prepared to resign rather than give aid and comfort to the enemy: 'For the honour of the nation and its postwar unity, in the interest of avoiding bitter conflicts between ourselves immediately after the war and especially of not giving the Communists a pretext to take over power on the basis of the justified reproach that we helped Hitler, you . . . must not retreat in any way. There is a danger that by wanting in some way to defend the interests of the nation you could give the impression of helping the Nazis in the war against Russia.' Since Britain and the United States supported the Soviet Union, such an outcome might be disastrous for the post-war position of Czechoslovakia and the political prospects of the exile regime. The future of the country depended on maintaining a united front at home and commanding the continued support of the allies. Although Hácha replied that his speech was a final concession to the Germans and that he would resign if necessary, trust and confidence between the Protectorate regime and the exiles was clearly beginning to break down. While Hácha's priority remained to avert German reprisals, Beneš felt it imperative to maintain his standing with the allies and in particular with the USSR.

Despite these concerns Beneš had still not reached the point of risking bloodshed on the home front and attempted to bolster his position in the allied camp by other methods. He pressed the British to launch bombing raids against arms factories in the Protectorate, arguing that this would provide an opportunity for concealed sabotage and counter the propaganda of the communists who claimed that only the Russians were really fighting and that the nation must look to Moscow for its salvation. He claimed that the home army had stepped up unattributable sabotage and 'systematic passive resistance' in the wake of BARBAROSSA. As a result production in Bohemia–Moravia had declined by 33 per cent, a dramatic development in one of Hitler's main arsenals. SOE and presumably the Russians also were supplied with an extensive list of underground actions inside and outside the Protectorate which included a fire at the Reich Air Ministry and a bomb explosion at the Anhalter station in Berlin, supposedly aimed at Himmler's special train. The Russians remained unmoved and had an important weapon at their disposal to force Beneš to comply with their demands – the Czech communist party. Beneš was extremely sensitive to a possible challenge to his own authority from this quarter, which was one of his main reasons for cultivating Moscow. Russia was popular at home even during the period of the Nazi–Soviet pact because it was uncontaminated by Munich, and there was widespread public sympathy for Moscow when Hitler launched his invasion, coupled with the hope that national liberation would be aided by the Red Army. It was a feeling easily exploited by the communists, who rapidly adopted a militant anti-Nazi line. Within days of BARBAROSSA there was a wave of petty sabotage in the Protectorate which included the cutting of brake hoses on trains, the introduction of sand into the axle boxes of railway rolling stock and the cutting of military telephone lines. The danger existed that the communists might seize control of the national resistance if the home army sat idly by and did nothing to aid the Russians. Political developments at home would escape the control of the London Czechs and leave them high and dry when the war ended. Beneš was enough of a realist to know that whatever his formal promises, Stalin would have no interest in supporting the authority of the exile regime if it did not serve Soviet interests, and the Russian leader clearly wanted the home army to fight. On the other hand, a joint sabotage campaign by UVOD and the communists, with Anglo-Russian backing, might be kept within bounds which would not endanger the prospects of a national rising. This would appease Moscow and provide the basis for bringing the communists into a national political coalition where they could be tamed and controlled. As he informed UVOD on 12 August, the entry of the Soviet Union into the war had made the relationship between the home army and the communists a pressing issue. It would be best to draw them into co-operation as soon as possible, lest at a later stage their militancy appealed to the mass of the people and gave them the upper hand at a time when the Red Army was advancing.

By the middle of August, Beneš was feeling pressure for action not only from Moscow but also from London. On 29 August, UVOD was informed that SOE had expressed 'a great and pressing interest' in sabotage in the Sudetenland. There was a danger that, if the Czechs did not respond, the British would bring in Sudeten German refugees to do the job, a possibility fraught with unpleasant political consequences. Anything which redounded to the credit of the Sudeten exiles in London, over whom the British had consistently refused to grant Beneš authority, might complicate the final denunciation of Munich and interfere with post-war plans to expel the German population from the Sudetenland. It is unclear why SOE changed its line at this stage although the British Chiefs of Staff were clearly anxious to do what they could to relieve pressure on their new Soviet allies. The entry of Russia into the war made the British view the role of home armies in a different light. With a major new land power fighting the Germans, national uprisings were clearly less important to British strategy. After BARBAROSSA the emphasis gradually changed towards a sabotage role for the European underground coupled with a decision to use the small numbers of aircraft the RAF would release from the bomber campaign to build up resistance movements in the immediate area of an eventual British landing. This tilted the balance of SOE's efforts towards western Europe and particularly France. Gubbins' scheme to supply the Czech and Polish home armies by regular air drops was dismissed as an impossibility. Consciously or unconsciously, these countries were now assigned to the Soviet zone of operations, which implied the co-operation of the underground with Russian military plans. It was the beginning of a rapid decline in the share of resources which the Polish and Czech home armies, previously treated as models, could command from Britain. In the circumstances, it was natural that SOE should use its influence with the Czechs to do its Soviet ally a favour. Beneš himself was apparently unaware of the change until 1944 when he found London unwilling to drop supplies for the Slovak uprising without the consent of Moscow, a decision he took very badly.

By the end of the summer Beneš was prepared to capitulate to allied pressure. On 13 August his Defence Minister, General Ingr, informed the home army that during the long moonless nights of the coming autumn and winter the London Czechs intended to fly in teams of agents trained in intelligence, communications and sabotage. The resistance was ordered to locate dropping zones throughout the Protectorate and prepare ground parties to receive the parachutists and their equipment. The flights would be combined with bombing missions to distract the Germans and offer the underground the chance to launch its own sabotage attacks under cover of the raids. On 30 August Beneš spelt out the reasons for the new departure in a personal message to UVOD. According to Beneš it had been made plain by both London and Moscow that sabotage against war industries in the Protectorate coupled with regular disruption of railway traffic would have important effects on the strategic situation on the eastern front. The London Czechs, who were competing with other exile groups such as the Poles for influence in the allied camp, had little alternative but to launch a systematic sabotage campaign, although large-scale action likely to provoke massive German reprisals would still be avoided. Clearly anticipating objections from the home army, Beneš warned that 'our whole situation would definitely appear in an unfavourable light if we . . . did not at least keep up with the others.' Sabotage teams were already being trained for their missions in both Britain and the USSR. In the new strategic situation created by BARBAROSSA, it was necessary 'to pass from theoretical plans and preparations to deeds', which would maximise Czech influence in London and Moscow when Germany collapsed, perhaps as early as 1942.

This Most Secret message revealed that some kind of plan had recently been worked out with the Russians either by Moravec and

Cicajev in London or through Colonel Píka's intelligence mission in Moscow. The Soviet teams were drawn from Czech exiles in the USSR who were trained at an NKVD spy school in the Lenin Hills near the Russian capital. Their mission was to establish radio contact between the Czech communists and Moscow and to launch a campaign of sabotage in association with party members against targets like railway lines and electric power installations. As early as 31 August the first group of nine was dropped near Warsaw by the Red Air Force, which at that stage in the war did not possess planes with the necessary range to reach Bohemia–Moravia. The agents made their way through occupied Poland to the Protectorate and established radio contact with their Russian controllers. They were soon followed by a second group dropped on or about 10 September 1941. Meanwhile in Britain more soldiers were recruited from the Czech Brigade in Leamington and sent on courses at a network of special training schools (STSs) established by SOE that spring as the organisation geared itself up for its task of subversion. Although General Ingr informed the home army in August 1941 that the exiles were training 160 parachutists, the actual commitment was more modest than this figure suggests. These men were meant to provide a pool of trained manpower from which agents could be drawn as and when required.

Their training followed a rigorous pattern. The agents, or joes in SOE slang, were first sent to a paramilitary school near Mallaig in the Scottish Highlands for commando training. This included rock-climbing, firing exercises, elementary sabotage, unarmed combat and a course in silent killing with Captain Bill Sykes, formerly of the Shanghai Police. Those who failed this gruelling test were quietly returned to the brigade. The remainder, trained to the highest peak of physical fitness, were thrown into an intensive five-day parachute course at RAF Wilmslow without any rest or leave before being despatched to STS XVII, the SOE sabotage school at Brickendonbury Manor in Hertfordshire, run by Major George Rheam, a pioneer in the art of scientific destruction. Radio operators were sent to a separate school for instruction in the techniques of clandestine communication by one of Moravec's experts, Lieutenant Gold. Their training completed, the parachutists were either returned to the brigade until they were needed or sent directly to a holding centre at STS 2, the Villa Bellasis, a requisitioned country house in the home counties near Dorking. Although STS 2 was administered by a British officer and run by British auxiliary staff, the agents were commanded by Staff Captain Sustr of Czech intelligence, who prepared the joes for their specific operational tasks. This was perhaps the weakest part of the training and one over which SOE had no control. The Czechs had no first-hand experience of running agents into occupied Europe and underestimated the pervasive Nazi security system. The first parachutists were handicapped by the poor quality of their false documents and were shocked by the strong police controls which made many at home reluctant to offer them shelter. The experience sometimes caused total psychological collapse and on occasion voluntary surrender to the Gestapo. As late as August 1942 there were complaints that Moravec's agents were inadequately prepared for the dangers of life in the Protectorate. For the parachute teams, STS 2 was the last posting in Britain. From Bellasis they were taken to the RAF aircraft which were to drop them over the Protectorate, a homecoming few of them could have foreseen only months before. There was no escape plan. The agents would remain underground until they were either killed or captured or Czechoslovakia was liberated by an allied victory. At the time nobody predicted that the war would last another four years. Buoyed up by the official optimism encouraged by Beneš, the parachutists expected hostilities to end within eighteen months.

The Czechs who passed through these SOE training establishments in the summer of 1941 contained a high proportion of NCOs and relatively few officers. The NCOs of the Czech army were generally of a high calibre and, but for the fact that the brigade already had too many officers for a unit of its size, many would long since have been promoted. It was the NCOs who provided weapons and explosives instruction for the troops, and this experience, combined with their high motivation and intelligence, made them ideal material for sabotage missions. Long after the war they were still remembered by their SOE instructors as exemplary students. Two types of parachute team graduated from Bellasis. The first, composed of one officer and two NCOs, was designed for intelligence collection and communications. The work of these teams was co-ordinated by the officer and at least two members received special radio training before going into the field. This was intended to ensure that the death or capture of one member did not knock out the entire group. The second type consisted of two NCOs and was designed for sabotage, an activity easily learned by men accustomed to the daily handling of guns and explosives. The task of hiding and supporting both sorts of parachute team was assigned to the home army with which they were meant to co-operate. The selection of the personnel for an individual mission was a delicate matter. It was clearly dangerous to ask men who disliked each other to work underground where the daily risk of arrest stretched nerves to breaking point and exacerbated the smallest differences. The only basis on which the parachutists could work efficiently was mutual respect and trust, which would allow them to overcome the inevitable difficulties and dangers they would encounter in the Protectorate. Accordingly the instructors kept a close eye on the friendships that developed during training and tried to assign agents to their operational groups on this basis. Individual preferences were respected to the maximum and there was a large measure of self-selection.

Amongst the men at the commando school near Mallaig in September 1941 were two NCOs who played a key role in subsequent events, Josef Gabčík and Jan Kubiš. Wartime photographs of the two men show strong and determined young faces, Gabčík's picture in particular hinting at the brooding inner strength which he was later to display. Aged twenty-nine in 1941, Gabčík was a former locksmith from the Zilinia district of Slovakia. A short, powerfully built man, he had served in the Czech army from April 1932 to October 1938, reaching the rank of sergeant. Demobilised after the Munich crisis, he had worked as a storekeeper in a military chemical factory before escaping into Poland in March 1939. Before leaving, he had destroyed the stock of mustard gas in his care by pouring acid over it, rather than see the material fall into the hands of the Nazis. Evacuated to France with 435 others just before the outbreak of war, he had joined the French Foreign Legion before being transferred to the Czech division at Sète in October 1939. Gabčík had distinguished himself in action during the Battle of the Marne while serving with a machine-gun section and held both the French croix de guerre and the Czechoslovak war cross. By all accounts, he was popular with the men of his infantry company, which in late 1940 was billeted on an estate at Moreton Paddox, a small village between Leamington and Stratford-upon-Avon. He was a frank and open character, although capable of quick outbursts of anger. An English family whom he visited while off duty later recalled his volatile temperament: 'If Josef missed a bus, or knocked a drink over, or broke a bootlace . . . up he soared like a rocket, spurting rage . . . to burst effectively, briefly and brightly at a high altitude; then with a wry appraisal of his own ridiculousness, he would laugh himself . . . down to ground level again.'

Jan Kubiš was twenty-eight in 1941, the son of a peasant family from the Trebic district of Moravia. Kubiš, like Gabčík, had served as a sergeant in the Czech army for several years before Munich and had followed the same route through Poland to the French Foreign Legion and the Czech division at Sète in 1939. Before the fall of France he had been decorated with the Czechoslovak war cross for his part in a skirmish with a German patrol. When the Czech brigade was formed in Britain, he served as a senior NCO in the first infantry battalion under Major Krček, based at Moreton Paddox. Unlike Gabčík, Kubiš was a shy and softly spoken man who never lost his temper and often seemed to be brooding sadly on the homeland that he had lost. Both men were highly professional soldiers, nationalists who had endured the shame of demobilisation after Munich and had seen their country fall to the Nazis without a shot. It was a burning desire to reverse this verdict which had carried them across the frontier and preserved their spirit during the military débâcle in France. Both were anxious to seize the first available opportunity to hit back at the Nazis. In early 1941 Gabčík, who could see no immediate prospect of combat as a company sergeant-major, requested a transfer to the RAF, where Czech airmen had established a deadly reputation during the Battle of Britain. As his application argued: 'I have asked for my transfer because I think that I could make better use of my technical qualifications in the air force. I said to myself that I too should like to help the Czechoslovak cause as much as I could, to contribute to our victory and that of the Allies. In making this request I understand that my admission to the air force will mean the loss of all the advantages arising from my service in No. 3 company of the First Infantry battalion. . . . I should be glad if I could carry out the duties of gunner. For all these reasons I beg you to give my request a favourable reception.' Gabčík's application was overtaken by events. He was soon to have an opportunity to fight the enemy in a far more direct and personal way than by serving in the RAF.

When brigade headquarters asked the infantry units to nominate men for special duties, Gabčík and Kubiš were natural candidates. As one of their company officers, Lieutenant Kašpar, later recalled, they had all the qualities demanded by Czech intelligence. They were first-class soldiers, deeply patriotic and expert in the handling of guns and explosives. Their courage and patriotism had been proved to the full in France, where they were amongst the last to retreat when the Czech Division fell back from the Marne. Although aware of the difficulties and dangers of underground work, both men immediately volunteered when interviewed by a member of Moravec's staff. On 16 August 1941, Kubiš and Gabčík left Leamington for the last time as part of a new batch of joes, detached from their units by brigade order 324 and despatched northwards for special training at Wilmslow and the SOE commando school near Mallaig. The courses were designed to push men to their physical and psychological limits in order to weed out candidates who could not function under the crushing pressures they would face in the field. After six gruelling weeks in the Scottish Highlands, Gabčík and Kubiš passed out of STS highly recommended by their British instructors. Gabčík was described as a keen and disciplined soldier, less imaginative than his comrades. He was absolutely reliable, a first-class parachutist who displayed good qualities of leadership. Kubiš was considered slow but trustworthy and very popular with the other trainees. A steady and reliable candidate, he had proved particularly skilled in the handling of explosives. The stolid and unreflecting character of both men made them ideal candidates for underground work where a lively imagination was often a handicap. They could be trusted to obey their orders to the letter without dwelling too much on the consequences. Like the other NCOs of their group, Gabčík and Kubiš were destined for STS XVII, Brickendon-bury, and training as saboteurs. As things turned out, however, their mission was to be dramatically different, one which set them apart from their comrades and made them the leading actors in one of the most daring operations of the Second World War.

While the agents selected to spearhead his sabotage campaign were still in training, Beneš launched an initiative designed to impress London and Moscow with his control of the situation at home. On 14 September, the BBC Czech service called for a boycott of the Protectorate press which had long since become a tool of Nazi propaganda. In the next few days, newspaper sales declined by up to fifty per cent, as the population demonstrated its silent contempt for the Nazis. Beneš explained to his friend Lockhart that the boycott was designed to fulfil two purposes. The first was as a test mobilisation for an armed uprising which proved that events at home could be co-ordinated by orders from London. The second was as a demonstration to Moscow that the home population would obey the Czech service of the BBC rather than the strident voice of Moscow Radio. If Stalin wanted to influence the situation in Prague he would have to co-operate with the legal government of Beneš in London, rather than promote the communist exiles around Klement Gottwald in Moscow. It was all part of the strategy of impressing the allies and forcing the communists into a national political coalition under his own control. It fulfilled the additional function of sending a warning to the Protector-ate regime – its moral authority was dependent on the support of the London Czechs, which would be withdrawn if it took the path of open collaboration. If forced to choose between Beneš and Hácha, the people would follow Beneš. On 21 September, the exile government called off the boycott. In a message of congratulations to UVOD sent over Moravec's transmitters at Woldingham, Beneš informed the home army that the demonstration had served its purpose. It had shown the strength and determination of the Czech people and produced favourable comments in the British press and radio. To continue would be counter-productive and might provoke German reprisals.

As the press boycott ended, UVOD was warned to expect the first parachute mission from Britain, Operation PERCENTAGE, at the beginning of October. This consisted of a single agent, Corporal František Pavelka, carrying a radio, spare crystals and new codes for the home army. His arrival was to be the prelude to a series of drops in the autumn and winter carrying further communications and sabotage groups to reinforce the Czech underground and the political credibility of Eduard Beneš. With Soviet parachutists already on the soil of Bohemia–Moravia, the way seemed open to a new and more militant phase of resistance which would win the respect of the allies and put the London exiles in a position to influence the peace settlement in central Europe. Beneš' ambitious plans, however, were forestalled by dramatic developments in the Protectorate which dealt a crushing blow to the underground and the political prospects of the London Czechs. On 27 September 1941, the controlled press in Prague carried a stunning and unexpected announcement: 'The Reichsprotektor of Bohemia–Moravia, Herr Konstantin von Neurath, has had to suggest to the Führer that he be given leave on medical grounds. . . . Under the circumstances the Führer could not refuse . . . and has entrusted SS Obergruppenführer and General of Police Reinhard Heydrich with the performance of the duties of the Reichsprotektor for Bohemia–Moravia.' The news symbolised the triumph of the SS in the long struggle to dominate the Czech lands and spelled the doom of a home army which had provided Beneš with political credibility since the beginning of the war. As his plans began to collapse around him, he resorted to desperate measures which were to entangle the fate of two obscure NCOs, Josef Gabčík and Jan Kubiš, with that of Reinhard Heydrich, one of the most powerful figures in Hitler's Reich.

The Operation

6

The Butcher of Prague

Heydrich's appointment as acting Reichsprotektor, which began the final episode in his devious career, was the result of a conspiracy. It was a plot with two victims – Freiherr Konstantin von Neurath, long the object of SS intrigues, and Karl Hermann Frank, whose burning desire for supreme power in the Protectorate was used as a stalking horse for Heydrich's own ambitions. In the summer of 1941, as German panzers raced towards Moscow, Heydrich began to think of his future in a new Nazi empire stretching from the Atlantic to the Urals. For him it was no longer enough to be head of the security police. He wanted to be more than 'the dustbin of the Reich', the man who did the dirty work for others. As the day of victory dawned, Heydrich planned to emerge from Himmler's shadow and become a major figure in shaping the destiny of the new Europe. Bohemia–Moravia was to be the first step. If he proved capable of handling the Slavs of the Protectorate, new and more powerful positions might open up in the administration of the occupied east, the vast area of racial and economic empire which Hitler planned to wrest from a defeated Russia as the key to the future of the thousand-year Reich. In this respect Heydrich's personal ambitions coincided with the interests of the organisation which had created him, the SS. Himmler had been denied the total domination he craved in the Soviet eastern territories partly as a result of the intrigues of Hitler's secretary, Martin Bormann, who was already emerging as the power behind the throne in the Nazi party. If the Protectorate could be successfully converted into an SS state, it would vindicate SS claims in other areas and prove a valuable weapon in the struggle which was already beginning within the party for supreme power in Hitler's European empire.

In August 1941, Heydrich began to bombard Himmler with reports about the shortcomings of Neurath as Reichsprotektor and to put forward his own claims to the post. Himmler promised to raise the issue with Hitler but never seemed to find the right atmosphere at Führer headquarters. This dithering partly reflected the extent to which the Reichsführer SS had come to rely on the energy and administrative ability of his ambitious subordinate. On one level at least, Himmler genuinely regarded Heydrich as the ideal SS man and was reluctant to break the close association which had existed between them since 1931. At the same time, he had an acute political sense and hesitated to promote Heydrich to a post outside his own direct control, whatever the immediate advantages to the SS. In this situation Heydrich secured another and unlikely ally – Martin Bormann – like him an ambitious plotter determined to climb to the highest level. Bormann was to prove a key figure in supporting Heydrich's case although his reasons for doing so remain a matter for speculation. If Heydrich regarded the Protectorate as the first step towards political power and the strengthening of the SS in its emerging competition with the party, Bormann was anxious to break up the combination of Himmler and Heydrich. He hoped to distract Heydrich from intrigues against the party in the occupied east by tying him down in the administration of Bohemia–Moravia, far from the centres of power in Berlin and Führer headquarters. Unlike Himmler, therefore, Bormann encouraged Heydrich's ambitions, emphasising that an appointment to the Protectorate would open the way to new and more important posts. It is doubtful if Heydrich, the professional sceptic, was fooled by this show of cordiality which concealed the fact that two ambitious and cynical men had made a temporary alliance of convenience.

If Heydrich was to gain total power in Bohemia–Moravia, he had to convince Hitler of the need for drastic measures. Despite a series of SS intrigues, the Führer had consistently refused to remove Neurath and had insisted in 1940 that a final reckoning with the Czechs should be delayed until after the war. Nowhere in occupied Europe had he conceded unrestricted authority to the SS, preferring a system of divide and rule. If Heydrich was to realise his ambitions, he had to convince Hitler that the Protectorate was on the verge of open revolt. His technique was to exaggerate the scale of Czech resistance to suit his own political purposes, much as Beneš was doing for different reasons in London and Moscow. In October 1941, recalling the circumstances which led to his appointment, Heydrich claimed that the situation in the Protectorate had deteriorated to the point where 'the unity of the Reich was undoubtedly in danger'. Nazi rule was endangered by a large-scale resistance movement determined to stab Germany in the back by 'sabotage, terrorist . . . activities, destruction of the harvest [and] slowing down of work'. In fact neither the communists nor the home army contemplated a major rising at that stage of the war and Beneš in particular opposed spectacular actions which would provoke reprisals. Although the Abwehr reported 114 incidents of sabotage in September 1941, the data must be treated with caution since the Germans had no accepted definition of sabotage and often listed accidents under this heading. Moreover both the Abwehr and the Gestapo routinely inflated the figures to make their performance look more impressive. In fact the situation in Bohemia–Moravia was probably no worse than elsewhere in occupied Europe.

While Neurath conceded that opposition to Nazi rule had increased since BARBAROSSA, he did not consider it serious enough to warrant special measures. His position was undermined, however, by Heydrich using Karl Hermann Frank and the security police commander in Prague, Karl Böhme, a man regarded even by the Gestapo as an unscrupulous thug. Frank set out to prove that Neurath's complacency was creating a crisis in the Protectorate, an approach well calculated to rouse Hitler's fury. He not only exaggerated the threat of the resistance but also probably fabricated evidence with the help of his subordinate Karl Böhme. It was later suspected that the two most serious incidents of sabotage in August 1941, the destruction of a fuel dump containing 100,000 litres of petrol and a dynamite attack on a German children's home, were launched by neither the communists nor the home army but by agents of the Gestapo and SD. There was certainly no doubt amongst leading members of Neurath's staff that their boss had been the victim of a conspiracy cooked up by Frank. Nor did Frank seriously dispute the charge, admitting later that national security provided a useful excuse for the imposition of harsh measures against the Czechs. Frank's mistake was to believe that he was destined to succeed the discredited Neurath as ruler of the Protectorate, a position he had always craved. He was soon to discover that he had been merely a pawn in a larger conspiracy which had its origins not in Prague but in Berlin.

The alarming police reports which landed on Heydrich's desk in the late summer of 1941 were passed on to Himmler, Bormann and Hitler to create the right atmosphere in the proper quarters for a change in Prague. As a result Heydrich was in an excellent position to exploit the situation when Frank, perhaps acting on his orders, brought matters to a head in the middle of September. The boycott of the Protectorate press, called by Beneš on 14 September, provided Frank with his opportunity. In this respect, Beneš' attempt to demonstrate the strength of the home army both to the communists and to the allies was to prove expensive, playing into the hands of the most radical Nazi elements and setting the stage for SS rule. At a stormy meeting on 16 September, Frank confronted Neurath and demanded sweeping measures against the Czechs designed to crush all opposition. The Gestapo had long since penetrated the home army and possessed damning dossiers on the links between Beneš and the Prime Minister of the Protectorate regime, Alois Eliáš. Only Neurath's determination to work with and through the Czechs and Hitler's desire to avoid creating martyrs had so far prevented dramatic measures. Frank's demands were all too familiar to the Reichsprotektor and were refused. They would have meant the virtual repudiation of Neurath's policies and the concession of total power to the SS, an organisation he despised. The following day Frank met with his subordinate police commanders and decided to appeal directly to Hitler. When he left Prague airport on 20 September to keep his appointment at Führer headquarters, Frank carried a briefcase filled with complaints about Neurath's inaction in the face of an imminent national rising. As his Junkers–52 droned towards Hitler's gloomy bunker in the woods of East Prussia, Frank had no doubt that it would soon be carrying him back as the new Reichsprotektor. He was to be disappointed.

On the morning of 21 September Frank briefed Hitler and was accorded the honour of lunching with the Führer. He was not the only participant in the discussion of Czech affairs, however, for that afternoon Heydrich flew in from Berlin. He arrived with a dossier which described in exhaustive detail the structure of the home army and the links between Beneš and the Protectorate regime. The material had been supplied by Karl Böhme and was clearly intended to impress the Führer with Heydrich's grasp of the situation. In a crisp military manner, Heydrich briefed a fascinated Hitler, condemning Neurath as an appeaser, a weakling who had failed to control the Czechs. A new approach was necessary to preserve the integrity of the Reich. The question was taken up again the next day with Himmler adding his voice to demands for drastic action because he scented a clear advantage in the transformation of the Protectorate into an SS state. It was not Himmler, however, but Bormann who was the key figure in persuading Hitler to appoint Heydrich. This was not a difficult task. Hitler was furious with the Czechs, claiming that they had confused leniency with weakness. As he later complained, they regarded Neurath as an amiable old gentleman and took his goodwill for stupidity. They had to be taught a lesson. In this situation he naturally turned to Heydrich, the man who specialised in imposing order without regard for legal or moral restraints. Neither Frank nor Neurath were consulted about the new appointment. Summoned to Führer headquarters to explain himself on 21 September, Neurath was delayed for two days by bad weather. By the time he finally arrived at Hitler's bunker, his fate was sealed. In the presence of Frank, he was brusquely informed by the Führer that his policies had failed and that he was to take a vacation. Heydrich was to become acting Reichs-protektor in order to smash the resistance. The news stunned not only Neurath, but also Frank, the man who had done so much to bring him down. Both had fallen victim to Heydrich's intrigues.

Heydrich regarded his appointment as a victory over the old order. Hitler had replaced a representative of the traditional aristocracy with a figure who was already a symbol of the new Nazi elite, the SS. As the Führer's viceroy, Heydrich could now lord it over the military caste from which he had been ignominiously expelled in 1931. On one of his first trips to Prague, his staff witnessed a revealing act of self-assertion. Shortly before landing, Heydrich ordered them to remain in their seats when he left the aircraft to watch 'the sort of respectful and smart reception your chief gets from those conceited officers at the airport'. The disgraced naval Lieutenant had come a long way since 1931. His wife did not at first share his jubilation. When he phoned her with the good news from Hitler's bunker he received a frosty reception. The marriage had been under strain for years because of Heydrich's sexual philandering and long absences from home. His wife now suspected that she would see even less of him and complained bitterly. She was soon reconciled by Heydrich's promotion to Obergruppenführer with increased pay and allowances and his promise to take the whole family to Prague. For Lina Heydrich, always a snob and a social climber, the prospect of becoming first lady of the Protectorate had an irresistible appeal. At last she could attain through her husband the aristocratic status she had long craved. When Heydrich returned to Berlin the couple celebrated a new beginning, breaking out the champagne at a cosy family evening with the Schellenbergs. Even on this relaxed occasion, Heydrich's perennial suspicion did not desert him and he asked Schellenberg, a former law student, to examine the order appointing him to Prague for any clauses which could limit his power. He might despise the legal profession but it had its uses.

On 27 September Heydrich arrived in Prague. The following

morning he reviewed a guard of honour in front of the Hradčany castle and the black flag of the SS was raised over the turrets and spires of the city. The ceremony was watched by a thin line of German civilians: 'No Czech policeman, no Czech at all, could be seen on the occasion of this second occupation of Prague . . . within the space of two and a half years.' Four days later Heydrich set out his programme in a secret speech to Nazi officials. He left his listeners in no doubt that times had changed and that policy was now in the hands of the SS, Hitler's shock troops. According to Heydrich, he had two main aims. The first was to mobilise the area behind the German war effort, a task which involved a combination of toughness and concessions. The Czechs were to be shown who was the boss and opposition was to be ruthlessly crushed. At the same time the population was not to be pushed 'to the point of explosion and self-destruction'. It must be shown a way out by working loyally for the Reich. If full use was to be made of the Czech armaments industry, 'the Czech workers must be given their grub'. He had already arranged to raise the fat rations of armament workers by 400 grammes and would release this news at the proper psychological moment. Heydrich was under no illusion that he could make the Czechs love the Germans by this approach. He merely wished to convince them that it was in their interests to remain quiet until the outcome of the war was decided. There was a second and long-term aim, however, which was to remain a strict secret until the moment of victory. Heydrich set this in the context of the German racial mission to push back the Slavs. According to his view of history the Protectorate was German and the Czechs 'had no right to be here'. The area must ultimately be incorporated into the Reich. The good racial elements would be Germanised and those of inferior blood 'got rid of' by extermination or sterilisation. Good racial elements which resisted Germanisation would be deported to the Reich for re-education but if this did not work they would be 'put . . . against the wall'. They must not survive to form a new leadership class. Heydrich emphasised that achievement of his first aim would pave the way to this ultimate goal. As a preliminary the secret racial screening of the population would begin 'through various backdoors'. The whole address was delivered in a tone of icy determination which impressed even hardened members of the security police in Heydrich's audience.

When Heydrich spoke on 2 October, the first phase of his programme had already been in operation for several days. On the morning of 27 September martial law was proclaimed and a series of special courts established to impose summary justice on those accused of disturbing the political or economic security of the Protectorate. The tribunals were dominated by the security police and few prisoners were acquitted. The accused were either sentenced to death or handed over to the Gestapo to meet an anonymous end in a concentration camp. The SS terror burst without warning upon both the Czechs and the officials of the Reichsprotektor's office, which Neurath had staffed with traditional German bureaucrats. As one of them remarked in the privacy of his diary: 'None of us could guess or learn what Heydrich and his Gestapo intended for we had no links with them.' They only knew that their new master had arrived with his own SS staff and a long arrest list. The first victims were those already in detention for underground activities, some of whom had been held since 1940. They were followed by others swept up in the police dragnet which followed Heydrich's arrival. Of 404 people condemned to death by the special courts, 215 were charged with various forms of political resistance. Those executed contained a high proportion of ex-army officers and the nationalist intelligentsia. As part of his campaign against the underground Heydrich was trying to deprive the Czechs of their natural leaders in order to pave the way for his long-term aim of Germanisation.

The death sentences represented only a minute proportion of those arrested. For psychological reasons, Heydrich wished the number of executions to decline gradually, creating an impression that calm had been restored and encouraging the population to co-operate for the sake of a quiet life. In fact the wave of arrests which followed his arrival resulted in the detention of between 4000 and 5000 people by the end of November. On 17 October Heydrich informed his staff that 'there were so many cases that the intended slow but steady decrease in the number of those sentenced would not be achieved to the desired extent.' It was therefore up to the security police to propose 'how the shootings and executions which in spite of this are necessary could be carried out under cover – that is the possible transfer to a camp (Mauthausen, etc.) where people are shot during organised escapes'. The home army suffered more than the communists, who maintained their own separate clandestine organisation, from Heydrich's campaign. The Gestapo had better intelligence on the nationalist resistance and its ranks had been thoroughly penetrated by informers since 1939. Within days of Heydrich's arrival all radio links with London were severed, cutting off the flow of information from A–54. His contact Captain Morávek, cover name OTA, was a hunted man with the Gestapo hot on his heels. Corporal František Pavelka, dropped over the Protectorate on 4 October in Operation PERCENTAGE with new codes and crystals for the UVOD transmitters lasted only three weeks and was arrested when he went to an address under surveillance by the police. The first Soviet parachute group suffered the same fate and was executed in secret in December 1941. In a report to Bormann, Heydrich was able to boast that his massive police operations had destroyed the leadership structure of the resistance and smashed its clandestine radio network. By the end of the year the home army had practically ceased to exist as a coherent force.

The emergency measures were aimed not only against the underground but also against black marketeers, who were held responsible for the food shortages which plagued the Protectorate. Heydrich tried to capitalise on public resentment of the black market to discredit the resistance. The underground and the 'hyenas of the home front' were lumped together as the enemies of the Czech people. Of 404 death sentences handed down by the martial law courts, 189 were for economic crimes. In pursuit of illegal traders Heydrich executed Germans as well as Czechs. This apparent even-handedness concealed his real aim, which was to release Czech agricultural production for the Nazi war effort. The attack on the black market was accompanied by a recount of grain and livestock which relied on the impact of the terror to produce an accurate return. The peasants were promised amnesty for past evasion but faced death or eviction for relations with the Czech working class. Shortly after his arrival in Prague he ordered the distribution of confiscated black-market food to the canteens of the armaments factories. This was followed by a carefully orchestrated shop-floor campaign which encouraged the workers to voice their economic grievances. On 24 October Heydrich received a trade union delegation at the Hradčany castle and promised to improve living standards. In the following weeks fat and tobacco allowances were raised for certain categories of labour and 200,000 pairs of shoes distributed free through works councils. These moves further cheating. A similar interest in production dictated Heydrich's owed nothing to a belated sense of social justice on Heydrich's part. He was combining terror and bribery to produce more arms for the Reich. If the Czechs were to work, they had to eat. They would work all the harder if the alternative was withdrawal of the new economic concessions or a death sentence for sabotage. As he admitted to his staff, his aim was 'the depoliticisation of the Czech population', a policy which implied the concentration of the individual 'on his job and his material needs'.

The arrests which followed his arrival did not spare the Protectorate regime, long regarded by the SS as a nest of traitors. Heydrich's lesson to the Czechs began at the top with the Prime Minister, Alois Eliáš. Before he left Berlin, he arranged for the trial and condemnation of Eliáš by a special session of the Nazi people's court, brushing aside the doubts of officials at the Ministry of Justice. The Prime Minister was arrested within hours of Heydrich's arrival and sentenced to death on 1 October. The execution was subsequently postponed and Eliáš was held as a hostage for the good behaviour of the Czech people. His arrest demoralised his colleagues, who did not know who would be next. Heydrich deliberately encouraged this uncertainty by hinting that Eliáš' testimony might be required in further treason trials. Hácha, sick and ageing, was easily manipulated by Hitler's new viceroy. On the day of Eliáš' arrest he prepared a letter of resignation but it was never sent. Instead he embarked on a policy of collaboration, designed to spare the Czech people further bloodshed. This was exactly what Heydrich had intended. Hácha was to be led on by the gradual relaxation of the emergency measures which Heydrich claimed to have imposed 'with a bleeding heart'. In the next two months the state President was enlisted in a propaganda campaign which called on the Czechs to accept the logic of their position and blamed London and Moscow for provoking the SS terror by stirring up the 'fools of the resistance'. He called on his fellow citizens to fulfil their obligations to the Reich: 'At stake is no longer merely the fate of individuals but the fate of your children and of the whole nation.' Hácha's gestures of loyalty culminated on 4 December 1941 with a speech over Prague radio denouncing Beneš. The exiled President was accused of stirring up trouble with no thought of the consequences. He could not see wives and mothers weeping for children and husbands led astray by broadcasts from London. Heydrich congratulated himself that the state President had finally 'moved over to the German side'.

Heydrich kept Hitler informed about his progress with a series of reports specially printed in the large type which the Führer preferred. These were relayed through Bormann whose temporary alliance with Heydrich was still unbroken. While he had moved from under Himmler's shadow, Heydrich also maintained close links with the Reichsführer SS both by telephone and by regular personal visits to Berlin. If Bormann had hoped to remove him from the centre of affairs, he was to be disappointed. Heydrich kept his personal JU–52 on permanent stand-by and used a special train when the weather was too bad to fly.

With his usual ferocious energy, he combined his old tasks as head of the Reichsicherheitshauptamt with his new position, relying heavily on his deputy, Karl Hermann Frank, for the day-to-day running of Bohemia–Moravia. While bending the Czechs to his will, he also found time to complete the administrative arrangements for the 'Final Solution' and to plan further increases in the power of the security police at the expense of the party and the army. The fate of the Czech Jews was sealed even before the Wannsee conference. Heydrich was determined to impress Hitler with his efforts in this direction and emphasised on 17 October that the Jews were to be expelled with all possible speed. The enemies of the German race would not be tolerated in the SS state he was creating in Bohemia–Moravia. As an initial step a ghetto was to be established in the fortress town of Terezin (Theresienstadt): 'From there the Jews will be taken to the East. Agreement from Minsk and Riga to take over 50,000 Jews respectively has already been received. After the complete evacuation of all Jews, Theresienstadt will be settled by Germans in accordance with perfect planning and will become a centre of German life.' At the end of November the first transports of Czech Jews arrived in the new ghetto. For the majority it was a way station to the SS death factories further east. Of 93,942 Jews deported from the Protectorate, only 3371 survived the war.

Heydrich found respite from these labours on the estate of Panenské Břežany twelve miles outside Prague, which had been confiscated from a Jewish sugar magnate in 1939 to become the official residence of the Reichsprotektor. He often worked on his official papers there and even found time for an occasional evening of chamber music at which he played his violin. For his status-conscious wife, the château was a dream come true. She launched an extensive programme of improvements, installing new bathrooms and a large swimming pool with concentration-camp labour thoughtfully provided by Himmler. It was said that in this rebuilding Frau Heydrich 'spared neither the marks nor the Jews'. She also found a new hobby collecting antique German porcelain, as befitted a lady of the manor. At the insistence of Himmler, a company of SS was quartered in the village outside the walls. Heydrich grumbled constantly about the guards and always travelled without an escort, accompanied only by his driver Oberscharführer Klein, a strapping six-footer. His contempt for precautions worried visitors from the Reich such as Hitler's architect, Albert Speer, and departed from his normal practice:

Heydrich, whose entire house in Berlin was linked by alarm bells (even in the toilet) to the surrounding police stations, with the duty room of the bodyguard unit and with the Prinz Albrecht Strasse, whose . . . official cars before the war were equipped with replacement number plates, with pistols in front of each seat and sub-machine guns in front of those riding in the rear seats – this same Heydrich was travelling in contravention of the regulations he had himself drawn up for the protection of leading personalities of state and party.

As acting Reichsprotektor, however, Heydrich regarded his personal security as a political matter. He categorically refused an escort on the grounds that it would damage German prestige. The Czechs must never imagine that they were feared by Hitler's viceroy. As long as he retained the psychological initiative he would not be attacked. This arrogance was eventually to cost Heydrich dearly. While he was despatching thousands to their deaths in the autumn of 1941, plans were already being drawn up in London to end his grisly career.

The appointment of Heydrich and the wave of arrests and executions which followed took the exile government by surprise, but from the beginning nobody was under any illusions about the German objective. It was quickly agreed that Heydrich had been sent to Prague to smash the resistance and bind Bohemia–Moravia ever closer to the Reich. On 30 September Gubbins spoke to General Ingr, the Czech Minister of Defence, about the new situation. Ingr explained that Hitler was responding to the recent success of the home army. Undetectable sabotage had lowered industrial output 'by as much as 30% and was having a very adverse effect on the German war production programme'. The Gestapo had been pressing for months for 'the most extreme measures including wholesale arrest and indiscriminate punishment. This Neurath resolutely refused to do, insisting on evidence and some semblance of trial before conviction. As a consequence, he now found himself replaced by someone with fewer qualms of conscience. . . . he had no doubt that the reign of terror would continue . . . for many weeks as Heydrich was a very ruthless man.' A week later, speaking to a journalist from *The Times*, Beneš echoed Ingr, claiming that undetectable sabotage had cost the Germans enough equipment for three divisions. As a result Heydrich had been ordered to institute a reign of terror. His aim was to smash the resistance by executing 3000 key men. It was clear that this bloody campaign demanded an answer. The exile government could hardly stand on the sidelines wringing its hands while in Prague its best men were slaughtered. On 3 October the Czech Prime Minister, Jan

Šrámek, declared that the nation would never yield to 'Hitler's bestial rage. . . . All true Czechoslovaks swear over the graves of their inhumanly executed soldiers, workmen, artisans, peasants and intellectuals, that they will justly revenge their death and will endure in the struggle against the German oppressor until ultimate victory.'

Unknown to Šrámek, preparations were under way to back this threat with action. According to Moravec, the initiative came from Beneš himself, who suggested 'a spectacular action against the Nazis – an assassination carried out in complete secrecy by our trained paratroop commandos' and presented to the world as 'a spontaneous act of national desperation'. At this stage there was uncertainty about the target and the old enemy of the Czechs, Karl Hermann Frank, was considered as a candidate along with the newcomer Heydrich. He was saved by his relative obscurity. Whatever Frank's crimes, Heydrich was the bigger prize. As Hitler's representative and head of the Nazi security police, Heydrich's death would have the maximum propaganda impact at home and abroad. The plan which emerged in October 1941 was a closely guarded secret. Beneš consulted none of his ministers and knowledge of the operation was limited to Moravec and a few senior intelligence officers. Nor did he commit himself in writing. Moravec was given only oral orders and was content to act on that basis. Strict secrecy was a routine precaution in clandestine operations where the slightest leakage of information could prove disastrous. It was all the more vital in the world of exile politics which was notoriously gossipy and insecure. On occasion even Beneš was capable of giving intelligence officers nightmares by indiscreet boasting about resistance operations. But other considerations were also involved. Beneš, like politicians before and since, found it convenient to insulate himself from the secret world of intelligence, which often involved controversial operations and dirty tricks. By keeping his talks with Moravec off the record, Beneš ensured that nothing could ever be traced directly back to him. If politics required it, he could disown his subordinate. It was a game which both the President and his master of spies knew and understood. Moravec was to remain silent about Beneš' role in the affair until long after the war.

Beneš had always adopted a cautious approach to resistance, arguing against spectacular acts likely to stir up the Nazis, jeopardise the home army and endanger his links with the Protectorate regime. When he suggested an assassination, he knew the inevitable consequences. Assassinations always provoked severe reprisals against the local population. In October 1941, for example, the Nazis executed fifty French hostages in retaliation for an attack on the military commandant of Nantes. The SS terror in the Protectorate, however, removed the previous inhibitions against dramatic action. Heydrich was already smashing up the home army and killing civilians. Eliáš had been condemned to death and the Protectorate government was drifting towards open collaboration. In these circumstances fear of reprisals was overshadowed by the desire for revenge. This primitive sentiment was reinforced by powerful political factors. The collapse of the home army left Beneš without a bargaining position at a time when the allies were pressing for action. As Moravec later recalled: 'President Beneš ... told me that in his consultations with representatives of allied countries the subject of meaningful resistance to the enemy cropped up with humiliating insistence. The British and the Russians, hard-pressed on their own battlefields, kept pointing out to Beneš the urgent need for maximum effort from every country, including Czecho-slovakia.' In this situation, Beneš turned to his only remaining asset, the parachute groups trained that spring and summer by SOE to reinforce the home army. Beneš now felt forced to use these men as a substitute for the underground, no matter what the risks to their survival caused by the new situation in the Protectorate. ANTHROPOID was the most spectacular mission in a broader campaign of sabotage and subversion planned by the exiles to show the world that the Czechs were hitting back and had not surrendered to their Nazi oppressors.

If Beneš felt that his credibility in Moscow and London depended on dramatic evidence of Czech resistance, he also feared for his position at home as a result of Heydrich's police measures. The parachute groups were not only to impress the allies but also to act as a rallying point for the badly shaken underground. They would provide a framework around which the movement could reorganise and a means of communication between the exiles and the Protectorate. In this respect, Beneš was looking towards the post-war period. The decima-tion of the home army threatened to leave the communists with a clear field and increased the danger that Stalin would choose to deal with them rather than the exile government. If Beneš was to dominate the political scene and keep his rivals in check, he needed to reconstruct an organisation which took its orders from London and not from Moscow. According to Moravec, ANTHROPOID was to play a key role in this revival 'by providing a spark which would activate the mass of the people'. It is unclear precisely what was meant by this phrase, but Moravec implies that Beneš hoped Nazi reprisals would force the Czech people into the resistance. They would 'react to ... German pressure with counter-pressure'. As events were to prove, Beneš disastrously misjudged the impact of the assassination on the home front and later found it convenient to deny any role in the affair.

In proposing ANTHROPOID, Beneš feared that time was running out for Czechoslovakia. If Russia could hold out against the German attack until the winter it might prove the beginning of the end for Hitler – 1942 would be a decisive year and Nazi power would start to crumble. If the Czechs were to influence the post-war settlement, they had to make a contribution to this process, otherwise the great powers would concede them nothing. The President's optimism about the war was balanced by the haunting memory of Munich. The nearer Hitler came to defeat, the greater the danger of a German peace offer which would leave the British Empire intact in return for a free hand in east and central Europe. While Churchill had pledged full support to the Soviet Union, Beneš suspected that powerful elements outside the government still regarded Hitler as a barrier against Bolshevism, a sentiment which had encouraged the sacrifice of Czechoslovakia in 1938. In this respect ANTHROPOID was insurance against any settlement which left the Nazis in control of the Protectorate. The assassination of Heydrich would be a symbol of the Czech desire for freedom. It would appeal to public opinion, particularly in the United States, and thus check any possible British moves towards a compromise peace, a new Munich which ignored the interests of the exile government.

Beneš left the technical details of the operation in the professional hands of his intelligence chief. Moravec's first task was to recruit suitable assassins and he turned to the Czech soldiers who were being trained by SOE for men with the necessary skills. In early October he sent for the dossiers on the volunteers and checked them personally for suitable candidates. An exhaustive search turned up the names of two senior NCOs completing their parachute training at RAF Wilmslow. The first was Josef Gabčík, who was to remain with the operation until the end. The second was a sergeant from the Czech Brigade named Anton Svoboda, who was later to be replaced by Jan Kubiš. It seemed to Moravec that these two men possessed the qualities he needed. They were proficient soldiers, brave, patriotic and could be relied upon to obey their orders without question. These factors were reinforced by another consideration. Gabčík was a Slovak and Svoboda was a Czech, a combination which had not occurred by accident. The two men were to symbolise the nation founded by Tomáš Masaryk and Eduard Beneš. Moravec's assassins were to operate alone without the assistance of the home army, which was not informed about their mission. This decision was taken on security grounds even before radio

communications with UVOD were cut on 4/5 October. It was clear
from the scale of the Gestapo round-up that the resistance had been
thoroughly penetrated and its codes compromised. By consulting the
home army, Moravec might merely forewarn the Germans. For the
agents, however, this meant the most difficult possible start to their
mission, a night parachute drop without a reception committee.

On 2 October 1941 Colonel Palaček arrived at Tatton Park, the
mansion near Manchester which housed the Czech agents on the SOE
parachute course. He quietly removed Gabčík and Svoboda and drove
with them to Piccadilly station, where they caught the night train to
London. Palaček gave the two men no explanation for this sudden
journey and they knew better than to ask. The reasons became clear the
following morning when they were brought to Moravec's private office
at Porchester Gate for a personal briefing by the head of intelligence.
Moravec began with an emotional appeal which emphasised the terror
in the Protectorate:

> The radio and newspapers have told you about the insane, murderous
> slaughter that is going on at home, in our own houses. The Germans are
> killing the finest men we have. . . . our people have fought – now they are in
> a difficult position. It is our turn to help them from outside. . . . This
> October is the saddest October national holiday that our country has
> known since its independence – the holiday must be marked in a most
> outstanding fashion. It has been decided that it shall be done by a stroke
> that will go down in history in exactly the same way as the slaughter of our
> compatriots. In Prague there are two persons who are representative of the
> killing. They are K. H. Frank and the newcomer Heydrich. . . . in the
> opinion of our leaders, we must try to make one of them pay for all the rest,
> so as to prove that we return blow for blow. That, essentially, is the mission
> with which you are to be entrusted.

Moravec emphasised that once they were dropped from the aircraft
over Bohemia–Moravia Gabčík and Svoboda would be completely on
their own. 'For evident reasons' assistance from the home army was out
of the question. Finally he stressed the 'utmost historical importance'
of the assassination and asked the two men to think it over: 'If you still
have any doubts about what I have set out, you must say so.' Although it
was clear that their chances of surviving such a desperate operation
were slim, Gabčík and Svoboda volunteered without hesitation. That
afternoon they returned to Manchester to complete their parachute
training. They were to be dropped over the Protectorate in the first
suitable moon period, around 10 October, and the date of the
assassination was fixed for Czech national day, 28 October. This was to
prove an absurdly optimistic timetable.

The same day as he briefed his assassins, Moravec approached SOE for technical assistance. He mentioned 'an assassination' without specifying the target and gave no reason for the operation. According to an internal Czech Section minute dated 3 October 1941: 'The Home Organisation in the Protectorate is NOT being informed of this operation. At Czech HQ only Colonel M. Moravec and Major Str. Strankmüller know about it. The purpose is for the two men to carry out an assassination. They know that they cannot come out of the attempt alive. It is essential to carry it out during this month.' The team was to be dropped over Borek airfield near Plzeň, which was 'unused, unprotected and unwatched'. It was an 'essential condition' that Staff Captain Sustr, who commanded the Czech volunteers at STS 2, 'should accompany the flight as he knows the locality'. Sustr was to help the pilot identify the ridge which was a vital landmark on the final approach to the drop zone. Besides an aircraft, Moravec requested that SOE equip each of his agents with a revolver, three hand grenades, suicide tablets and one of 'any other weapon' which 'we would consider particularly suitable for the job'. The Czech Section did not enquire too closely about the purpose of the operation. The Czech exiles recruited, briefed and targeted their own agents, a process into which SOE was permitted little insight. If they wanted to kill a prominent Nazi, that was up to them. To demand more details might jeopardise security and cause political difficulties with the Czechs, who were notoriously touchy about their operational independence. Assassination was in any case well within the founding charter of SOE and raised no moral objections in the midst of a total war. Dalton's own memorandum to Churchill of 16 June 1940 which resulted in the creation of SOE mentioned fighting the Nazis by many different methods 'including industrial and military sabotage . . . terrorist acts against traitors and German leaders, boycotts and riots'. Moreover with Hitler beginning his final drive on Moscow, anything which stirred up trouble behind the German lines was worth encouraging. If Moravec can be believed, SOE had been pressing the Czechs for months to step up their activities. There was thus never any doubt about British support for the mission, which was given the codename ANTHROPOID.

While SOE supported the mission in principle, it considered the Czech timetable quite unrealistic. This was a familiar and delicate problem in SOE dealings with all the exile governments in London, who often wanted immediate action for their own political purposes without realising the limitations placed on SOE by factors such as training and the availability of aircraft. It was clear from the beginning that the ANTHROPOID team could not be dropped on 10 October because they could not finish their parachute course in time. Moreover they had to be trained for the specific purpose of assassination. It was not enough simply to drop them from a plane over the Protectorate armed with pistols and grenades and hope that somehow they would miraculously succeed in their mission. SOE seems to have persuaded Moravec of these realities for on 10 October the Czechs agreed that 'ANTHROPOID should be given further special training' separate from other Czech students. The same day, during a practice jump at RAF Wilmslow, Svoboda landed badly and suffered severe concussion, always a risk in parachuting. He was eventually returned to his unit and survived to become an old man in Prague. After consulting Gabčík, Moravec replaced the injured man with Jan Kubiš. As old friends the two could be relied upon to work smoothly together, something vital in underground work. Moreover Kubiš, like Svoboda, was a Czech, preserving the original structure of the group as a symbol of the nation.

By this stage Heydrich had definitely emerged as the target, a decision communicated to SOE at a series of meetings to consider the technical aspects of the assassination. This increased the attraction of the Czech plan for the British organisation. The spectacular killing of the man responsible for the Gestapo terror throughout occupied Europe would encourage resistance movements everywhere and disrupt the Nazi security machine which was SOE's main opponent. It would also provide SOE, which had yet to establish itself in the wartime bureaucracy, with the kind of success necessary to justify its existence. As Dalton complained in December 1941, so far such missions had been few and far between: 'Our last reports have been most bare, long tales of what has not been done. . . . I am particularly anxious for a successful operation or two.' It is possible that Moravec also notified SIS about the assassination plan but, contrary to later speculation, SIS had no part in either suggesting or facilitating the killing. Sir Stewart Menzies, 'C', may have hoped that his own operations would benefit from the disruption of the Nazi security services, but former members of his staff doubt that he was ever directly involved. SIS was not geared to this kind of operation and its interest in the Czech parachute teams focused on the radio and intelligence groups which were to restore the flow of information from A–54 disrupted by the arrival of Heydrich. On the British side, ANTHROPOID was entirely an SOE affair.

It was clear from the beginning that much must be left to the initiative of Gabčík and Kubiš once they had reached Prague.

ANTHROPOID was not the kind of operation which could be planned in meticulous detail. At the same time, in consultation with Moravec and experts from SOE, the agents agreed that the best way of killing Heydrich would be to attack his car. As an SOE account later noted: 'The special training in the UK was based on a plan that the attack on Heydrich should be made when he was travelling by car from where he lived to his office in Prague or to any known appointment and that it must be carried out at a corner where the car would have to slow down. Otherwise the choice of place and timing was left to the initiative of the ANTHROPOID team.' For such an attack, SOE recommended a combination of guns and grenades. The first assassin would be armed with a sten gun, a cheap mass-produced weapon considered ideal for clandestine operations. The sten was light, rugged and easily broken down into three pieces for concealment in a briefcase or shopping bag. At short range it was deadly, capable of spraying 550 rounds a minute from its stubby barrel. As a back-up, the second agent was to be armed with grenades. These were not standard British army issue but bombs specially created for the ANTHROPOID operation by Major Clarke, the SOE explosives expert. They were based upon a design developed for use against tanks in the Western Desert and looked rather like aerosol cans wrapped in tape. The thrower unscrewed a bakelite cap, set the fuse and tossed the bomb, taking care to avoid the powerful blast which followed. In mid-October a series of experiments took place at an SOE training school with the agents using these weapons against an old Austin which was rolled down a ramp and around a corner at various speeds. During the tests, Gabčík carried the sten and Kubiš the bombs, a choice dictated by Kubiš' expertise with explosives.

When the experiments ended in late October, Gabčík and Kubiš were sent to the Czech holding unit under Staff Captain Sustr at STS 2, Bellasis, where they joined twelve other agents destined for the Protectorate. This was an unwise move which endangered the ANTHROPOID operation. Although security at Bellasis was tight and no parachute group was allowed to know the mission assigned to the others, their companions soon realised that there was something special about Gabčík and Kubiš. Speculation grew that they had been trained for an assassination. Perhaps because of these rumours, the two were removed from STS 2 in the middle of December and brought to London, where they were held apart from the other parachutists at a safe house belonging to Czech intelligence in Stanhope Terrace while they waited for an aircraft to take them on the first stage of their mission. Gabčík and Kubiš occupied the first floor and their arms and explosives were stored in the cellar. At some stage during that month they were interviewed secretly by Beneš. His secretary, Táborský, later recalled that Moravec turned up one morning to see the President accompanied by two or three young men, an appointment unlisted in the official diary. According to the chief of intelligence, they were 'going on a long journey'. Táborský was struck by their quiet demeanour and their youth: 'One of them seemed to me more a boy than a soldier, let alone a parachutist, ready for anything and setting off right into the midst of that hell.' His account was confirmed by Moravec in his memoirs: 'The two men were received by President Beneš. He stressed the historical importance of what they were about to do. He knew this was a do-or-die mission and I could see that – like me – he was affected by the moving simplicity with which they accepted their lot. When he said goodbye to them, there were tears in his eyes.' Beneš was careful to keep no official account of the meeting, a symbol of his political caution as well as of the tight security which surrounded the entire plan. There was only one exception to this secrecy. While the details were still being worked out with SOE, Moravec's deputy, Major Strankmüller, informed the Russians about ANTHROPOID. His orders can only have come from Beneš, who had strong political reasons for wishing to impress his Soviet ally. Through Cicajev in London and Colonel Píka in Moscow, the Russians had been pressing for greater resistance activity since the beginning of BARBAROSSA. With the home army reeling under Heydrich's police measures, Beneš was in no position to oblige. He had to convince Stalin that the Czechs were playing a real part in the war, otherwise the Soviet Union might drop the exile regime and deal only with the communists. His anxiety was reinforced by the loss of communications with Prague which deprived him of the one thing the Russians had always valued, the flow of high-grade intelligence from A–54. The situation threatened Czech relations not only with the Russians but also with SIS.

The restoration of communications with Prague was thus a priority which ranked alongside the killing of Heydrich. While Gabčík and Kubiš were still in training, the first attempts were made to drop a radio group into Bohemia–Moravia, using the moon periods originally assigned to ANTHROPOID. This mission, codenamed SILVER A, consisted of three men, Lieutenant Alfred Bartoš, Sergeant Josef Valčik and the radio operator, Corporal Jiří Potuček. Its orders were to restore communications with UVOD, the central council of the Czech underground, organise an intelligence network and re-establish contact with Thümmel. It was also to perform other undefined special tasks which might be considered necessary by London. As events were to show, these included co-ordinating the reception of a wave of parachutists from England in the spring of 1942, aimed against the Czech industrial complex and the rail network, the kind of targets considered important by the Soviet general staff. Neither Beneš nor Moravec appears to have noticed the inherent contradiction in these tasks, a contradiction which was to haunt the entire parachute campaign. Intelligence work of the type entrusted to SILVER A was incompatible with the big bangs expected of the sabotage groups, which were likely to stir up the Germans. Both intelligence and sabotage would be endangered by the success of ANTHROPOID, which would jeopardise every parachutist in the Protectorate by provoking ferocious German repression. Far from rallying the population around a revived resistance movement, the killing was likely to destroy the remains of the underground along with parachute groups sent to revive it. Beneš never seems to have thought about these implications. Driven by the need to improve his position at home and abroad, he demanded too much of the parachute campaign, with unfortunate results for most of the agents involved.

It was one thing to prepare missions and quite another to deliver them to their targets. The only practicable route was by air and this was subject to many frustrating restrictions. Flights could take place only in the long winter nights which allowed aircraft to make the return journey to Bohemia–Moravia without being caught by the dawn over occupied Europe. Since the pilot identified the dropping zone visually, missions could be flown only on the five days each side of the new moon when the weather was suitable in *both* England and the Protectorate. Since a huge saucer of cloud hung over central Europe for most of the winter, the required combination of moon and weather was rarely available. Even then it was a matter of finding a plane. The RAF allocated SOE a special-duties squadron, No. 138, but starved it of aircraft. The air force put greater faith in the bombing offensive than in clandestine operations, which were given a low priority. Before 1943 there were never more than six long-range aircraft for special operations and the numbers were inevitably reduced in practice by the demands of maintenance and enemy action. In 1941, the only bomber available was the twin-engine Whitley which could just reach Bohemia–Moravia with a full fuel load and a light cargo. It had a poor reputation with both aircrew and joes, who referred to it unaffectionately as the 'flying coffin'. In October the RAF reluctantly made available three modern bombers, four-engine Halifaxes with a much longer range. These, however, had to be converted for parachuting by cutting a hatch in the fuselage floor and installing a winch to retrieve static lines, a process which took time. It was therefore with a Whitley that three attempts were made to land SILVER A, all of them failures. It was a situation which was increasingly frustrating for Beneš. As Christmas approached three vital missions were piled up in England awaiting transport – SILVER A, ANTHROPOID and SILVER B, a second radio group assigned the task of creating an intelligence network in the Svratka region of Bohemia and organising supply drops for the local resistance.

In desperation Beneš besieged the British for one of the new Halifaxes, an aircraft large enough to carry all three groups simultaneously. Despite the intervention of both Eden and Dalton, however, the Air Ministry remained unmoved. There could be no question of diverting further aircraft from the bomber offensive against Germany and the Czechs would have to take their place in the queue for one of the Halifaxes already assigned to special duties. In the end Beneš made a deal with the Poles, the other exile group with a claim on 138 Squadron's long-range aircraft, which gave the Czechs priority on the next flight. There was still a delay, however, caused by shortage of planes. The only operational Halifax crashed in Sweden during a return flight from Poland and the Czechs had to wait until a replacement was delivered. It was a frustrating time for Beneš whose political future depended on dropping agents into the homeland as soon as possible. The problem was not resolved until 28 December 1941. That morning Flight-Lieutenant Ron Hockey of 138 Squadron collected a new Halifax, modified for parachuting, from Northolt aerodrome. As he later recalled: 'I went into the Met Office about lunch time, and thought there was a slim chance of doing a Czech operation that night. In view of the number of outstanding operations, I decided to try all three which were in the queue. In order to save time, I alerted the Air Ministry Branch responsible, and arranged to land at Tangmere to load. This was the reason for using Tangmere – the three groups coming from near London.'

In the early afternoon a brief telephone call informed Moravec: 'It's on.' He immediately left his headquarters and drove to Stanhope Terrace where he collected Gabčík and Kubiš. Moravec decided to take the men for an informal farewell meal, designed to relieve the tension and prevent them from dwelling too much on the dangers they were about to face: 'They enjoyed the food, making simple little jokes and not mentioning one word about their mission or the fact that among the equipment just issued to them were two capsules of quick-acting poison to be used on themselves in the event of unbearable torture.' In the late afternoon Moravec left London and drove his agents through the gathering winter twilight to Tangmere aerodrome, where ANTHROPOID was joined by SILVER A and SILVER B, brought from STS 2 by Captain Sustr. The men were issued with their false papers and searched to ensure that they were carrying no scrap of evidence, even a bus ticket, which would connect them with Britain in the event of a Gestapo search. Before climbing into their heavy flying-suits they were warned against talking to each other during the flight or discussing their missions, a necessary security precaution. They were then driven across the tarmac to where Hockey's aircraft, NF–V L9613, was waiting, its engines idling. Before he climbed the ladder into the fuselage, Gabčík turned to Moravec and held out his hand: 'You can rely on us, Colonel. We shall fulfil our mission as ordered.' The hatch slammed, the chocks were pulled away and the Halifax roared down the flare path and vanished into the dark December sky.

Hockey's course took him over France and Germany. It was a tense flight because the plane was heavily loaded with fuel and sixteen men including the crew. This made evasive action difficult in the event of an attack. There was a brief scare over Darmstadt when the Halifax was trailed for twenty minutes by two nightfighters but the Germans lost the bomber in the dark and were unable to find it again despite dropping flares. After that the main problem was to find the dropping zones assigned to the three teams. This was far from easy, because of the weather. As Hockey's flight log remarked: 'Pinpointing became impossible owing to heavy snow which blotted out all roads, railways, rivers and small towns.' The situation was in fact more dangerous than this laconic remark implied. It was very difficult to judge height in these conditions especially descending out of clouds, but Hockey had to come down to 500 feet to drop his agents. There was thus a grave risk of flying into the ground and on the first attempt to establish its position the Halifax lost its trailing aerial in some trees. Captain Sustr, who accompanied the flight because of his personal knowledge of the countryside, was unable to identify any landmarks. In this situation it was decided to drop the agents at an approximate position rather than return to England with the ensuing danger to morale and the possibility of security leaks caused by gossip at the holding centre. The first group out of the hatch was ANTHROPOID, which according to the log was dropped east of Plzeň at 02.24 on 29 December. Before he jumped, Gabčík gripped Sustr by the hand and remarked: 'Remember, you will be hearing from us. We will do everything possible.' ANTHROPOID was soon followed into the night by SILVER A and SILVER B. His mission accomplished, Hockey turned the Halifax for home, pursued by sporadic flak over Plzeň. In his wake, Gabčík and Kubiš swung slowly downwards under their camouflaged parachutes towards the snow-covered soil of the Protectorate, where their target, Reinhard Heydrich, was scoring fresh triumphs in his bid for a leading role in the new Nazi Europe.

7

Return

While Beneš' agents were still kicking their heels in Britain the military situation changed dramatically. On 5 December the Russians launched a counter-attack in front of Moscow, forcing the Germans into a retreat which threatened for a time to become a rout. Simultaneously a major new enemy entered the struggle. On 7 December Japan attacked Pearl Harbor and four days later Hitler declared war on the United States. Denied a quick victory in the east, Germany had to mobilise new economic and human resources to knock the Russians out of the war before the Anglo-Americans could open a second front in the west. Hitler responded to the crisis by taking direct control of operations, firing senior officers left and right. From now on the generals were 'merely postmen purveying Hitler's orders'. The army was to be rebuilt by drafting workers from reserved occupations and replacing them with forced labour from the occupied territories. On 10 January 1942 Hitler ordered maximum production to re-equip his ground forces for the decisive battles in Russia, a move which was already long overdue. In 1941 German industry produced only 200 tanks a month, 400 short of the number required to replace the losses on the voracious battlefields of the east. When the Russian campaign began in June 1941 Heydrich scoffed at doubters who questioned the possibility of a quick victory. His opinions were confirmed in October when Hitler boasted that the Soviet enemy was on the brink of defeat and would never rise again. According to Heydrich the Russians would be driven behind the Urals and their territory settled by Nazi warrior peasants. Germans must become accustomed to thinking in terms of vast space, as befitted an imperial race. By the end of November, though, it was clear that all was not well with BARBAROSSA, a view confirmed by the events of early December.

While he did not abandon the SS vision of the future, he realised that it had been temporarily postponed. Well aware that his political prospects depended on impressing Hitler, Heydrich was quick to respond to the new situation. The Protectorate was to be geared up for a longer war by the complete reorganisation of the economy. This in turn required political reform. For the sake of efficiency Heydrich wanted the Czechs themselves to administer the necessary changes, allowing a reduction in the German staff of the Reichsprotektor's office who would be released for the front. Behind the façade of autonomy, Bohemia–Moravia was to be fully integrated into the war economy of the Nazi Reich.

The SS had always regarded the Protectorate regime as a dangerous relic of past independence which hindered the proper subordination of the Czech people to the master race. When he arrived in Prague, Heydrich ignored the Czech ministers, who were deliberately left confused and leaderless, fearing that they were about to share the fate of Eliáš. The Minister of Health, Ladislav Klumpar, was reduced to haunting the offices of German civil servants in a forlorn attempt to find out if his name appeared on an arrest list. Heydrich regarded this period of uncertainty as the necessary preliminary to political restructuring. As he informed Bormann on 16 November, the regime must be reorganised so as gradually to liquidate Czech autonomy from the inside. The catalyst was the situation on the eastern front. As BAR-BAROSSA ground to a halt in the snow before Moscow, Heydrich took action. The Protectorate government was transformed into an efficient instrument of Nazi policy, an executive council which merely responded to orders from the Hradčany castle. According to Heydrich it was no longer to be 'the supreme clearinghouse for Czech complaints against the Reich' but 'an extended arm of the Reichsprotektor'. As he later boasted, under the new system 'The Czech minister is actually no minister in our sense; we know quite well that he fulfils orders. . . . I can't put up with any Czech cabinet council deliberating *whether* my instruction should be carried out or not. The Czech ministers can only talk about *how* to carry it out.'

A key element in the reform was the creation of a Ministry of Labour and Economy under a German technocrat, Walter Bertsch, who acted as Heydrich's spy in the cabinet, preventing Czech ministers from conspiring against their Nazi masters. In deference to his presence, all discussions had to be in German, a reminder to his Czech colleagues of where power really lay in the new system. An important role was also assigned to the Ministry of Education and Propaganda under Emanuel

Moravec, an outspoken advocate of co-operation with the Nazis. Formerly a fierce nationalist and an advocate of resistance at Munich, Moravec had changed his position completely since 1939 and was regarded by Heydrich as a useful tool. His task was the psychological mobilisation of the Czech people behind the German war effort through a newly created office for public enlightenment and propaganda. At the same time he was to reform the educational system to break the hold of nationalist schoolteachers over the young and produce more compliant workers for German industry. A reluctant Hácha was bludgeoned into accepting these changes and the new cabinet was announced on 19 January 1942. At the inaugural ceremony Eliáš's replacement, Krejčí, pledged that his government would give its all 'for the final victory of Germany in Europe'. In return for these pledges of loyalty, Heydrich lifted martial law in Prague and Brno and released some Czech students from the concentration camps where they had been incarcerated since 1939. The Czechs were to be shown that collaboration paid.

In the following months Bertsch presided over a vast reorganisation of Czech industry. Companies unnecessary to the war economy were closed down and others were amalgamated with larger plants. More than 100,000 workers were removed from 'unsuitable' jobs and redirected by the Ministry of Labour in what amounted to a system of industrial conscription. From December 1941 Czechs could be called up for war work anywhere in Germany and between April and November 1942 around 79,000 surplus workers were recruited for service in the Reich. In February 1942 the work pattern in the Protectorate's war industries changed. The eight-hour day was suspended in favour of twelve-hour shifts designed to maximise production. The SS had a particular interest in this industrial reorganisation. Himmler had been expanding his economic empire in Bohemia–Moravia since 1939 under the benign eye of Karl Hermann Frank and the process accelerated with the arrival of Heydrich. SS firms in the pharmaceutical and wood-working industries were soon making healthy profits from German war contracts. In March 1942 Himmler went even further and with Hitler's approval attempted to divert the output of the vast Skoda arms factories to the Waffen SS. The Director-General of the complex, an honorary SS Standartenführer, was ordered to develop new lines of light and heavy weapons in systematic co-operation with the SS ordnance office. Himmler had chosen his time well, promoting SS interests in the armaments industry when Hitler was piqued with the army for its failure of nerve before Moscow.

The situation was an administrative nightmare for the new Minister of Armaments, Albert Speer, who was soon complaining that in economics as well as politics, the SS was treating Bohemia–Moravia as its own province.

In order to reduce the sting of longer hours without higher pay, Heydrich made some extra concessions to the working class. In April 1942 the Czech social security system was overhauled and benefits were raised by around thirty per cent to bring the Protectorate into line with Germany. Heydrich argued cynically that those who worked loyally for the Reich should share in its social achievements. May Day was proclaimed a public holiday and to celebrate the occasion 3000 armaments workers were offered free holidays in luxury hotels at fashionable resorts previously the exclusive preserve of the rich. For the others free football, theatre and cinema tickets were distributed through the trade unions. The official propaganda accompanying these measures portrayed Heydrich as the friend of the workers. According to the controlled press he was carrying out an unparalleled social reform which recognised the value of labour for the first time in Czech history. In fact Heydrich's measures were purely cosmetic and promoted solely in order to secure an increase in output for the war. Improved unemployment benefits meant little in a system of industrial conscription and better pensions were irrelevant given his post-war plans to deport or murder a large proportion of the population. As for the free holidays, they cost the Germans nothing. The hotels were requisitioned and the other costs were met by Czech employers and insurance companies.

While Bertsch mobilised the economy, Emanuel Moravec began an attack on the education system designed to create more labourers for Germany. The universities had been closed since November 1939 and the Nazis now turned their attack on the secondary schools. In his first press conference, the Minister of Propaganda dedicated himself to the elimination of the unproductive intelligentsia which was to be replaced by a new class capable of filling technical positions in industry. As part of this process Heydrich planned to reduce secondary education by two years and introduce compulsory youth service, modelled on the Hitler Youth and German Labour Corps. In this reorganisation Heydrich never lost sight of what he called his 'inner purpose', the secret Nazi plan for Germanisation, deportation and mass murder. As he explained in a secret speech on 4 February, Czech youth, removed from the influence of nationalist teachers, was to be trained as far as possible in Germany. Those considered fit for Germanisation would never return to Bohemia–Moravia. The others would be deported to the east, 'the ideal future homeland of the 11 million Jews from Europe', where they could act as foremen and supervisors of concentration-camp labour. For Heydrich resettlement was a synonym for extermination. The forty to sixty per cent of the Czech population whom he guessed would prove unfit for Germanisation was destined to share the fate of the Jews in the 'ideal future homeland' being prepared by the SS at Auschwitz and Treblinka. They would be replaced by Aryan settlers introduced by Himmler in his capacity as Reichskommissar for the strengthening of Germandom. According to Heydrich this would constitute 'the first stage in the slow Germanisation of the near East'.

As a first step Heydrich proceeded with a racial survey of the population, building on information already collected by the SS since 1940 from sources such as old conscription records. As he emphasised to his staff, using the chilling language of the SS social engineer, it was vital 'to obtain a definite cross-section of the national and tribal substance [of the Protectorate] and thus provide the basis for implementing the required measures'. In order not to alarm a population encouraged by propaganda to equate collaboration with survival, SS investigations were to be carried out by the security police in secret, camouflaged as something else. The medical screening of Czech youth during labour service was part of this process as was the introduction of a new identity card which required the head of each household to provide comprehensive information on his family and its antecedents. This survey not only facilitated labour mobilisation and population control but also provided the data required by the experts at the SS Race and Resettlement Office. As Heydrich reported to Bormann on 18 May: 'Camouflaged under the motto of the introduction of the German Kennkarte as a domestic passport, the national registration of the entire population of Bohemia and Moravia, which alone will produce a complete picture of the percentage of those who are fit for Germanisation, is proceeding according to age groups within the framework of a medical examination.' In support of these moves a special SS commando was despatched to the Protectorate that spring with five mobile X-ray units to subject the entire population to a systematic racial examination under the guise of a campaign against tuberculosis.

In the meantime Heydrich lost no chance of promoting German culture. As he informed Bormann, his aim was quietly to strengthen German influence in every possible way and deprive the Czech people of their national consciousness. German books and films flooded into the Protectorate and public servants were encouraged to learn German. As part of this re-education process Heydrich became interested in the past, raiding Czech history for examples to prove that the area had only enjoyed peace and prosperity when it aligned with Germany against the barbarian hordes of the east. One of these was Wenceslas, the patron saint of the Czechs, whom Heydrich claimed had turned his face against the Slav world and recognised 'the historical destiny of this area and its eternal involvement with the Reich'. Another was General Wallenstein, who had fought against the rebellious nobility of Bohemia–Moravia during the thirty years' war on behalf of the German Emperor. According to his wife, Heydrich became obsessed with Wallenstein, making numerous visits to historical sites associated with his name: 'Bohemia . . . was his problem. And Bohemia was Wallenstein's problem too. That was where he saw the similarity.' A second line of attack was mounted through an SS racial expert imported by Heydrich: 'In order to convince the Czechs . . . that they must be considered merely as a tribe and not as a nation. . . . His job . . . is to investigate the origin of well-known personalities and to prove that . . . these persons possess German blood. In exploiting these investigations from the point of view of publicity . . . the investigated persons are to be played up . . . as "Great Masters of this Space" so as to dilute . . . Czech national pride. . . .' Space was a word deliberately chosen to deny Czech nationhood and imply a cultural void waiting to be filled by Germany. Heydrich privately admitted that all this propaganda was completely cynical. It implied that his aim was 'gradually [to] educate the Czechs' to make them feel like Germans as a preliminary to incorporating the inhabitants of the Protectorate into the Reich. As he explained to his staff, he had to conceal his real aim because of the military situation: 'If I should at this moment resort to measures clearly showing that I do not intend to leave a part of the population in the country, we would shortly have a revolution on our hands which would cause us difficulties.'

While he attempted to undermine Czech culture and national identity, Heydrich emerged as a patron of the arts, an unusual role for a security policeman. Czech higher education was systematically attacked, but Heydrich built up the German university in Prague, endowing several new chairs and attempting to transform it from an educational backwater into a leading academic institution. He hoped that it would function as a tool of empire, providing ideas and surveys useful to the SS in the grisly task of creating a new Nazi civilisation in the Slav lands to the east. As a musician himself, Heydrich did not neglect this branch of the arts, although he employed it as a tool of German cultural supremacy. He became a patron of the German Philharmonic Orchestra, a congenial role in view of his father's difficulties with the musical establishment of Prussia, and reopened the German concert hall in Prague founded in the nineteenth century but converted at independence into the Czech Chamber of Deputies, something considered by Heydrich an act of desecration. As he remarked cuttingly at the reopening ceremony: 'The organ console at which Anton Bruckner . . . once sat . . . [was] smashed with an axe to make way for a bust of Masaryk.' This one sentence asserted German artistic superiority and dismissed Czech independence as a barbaric anomaly. A similar note was struck at the staging of Mozart week in December 1941, when Frank made a speech describing Prague as 'Mozart's second home', a cradle of German art and culture. To push the message home, Smetana square was renamed after the German composer. Heydrich's ultimate aim was to convert Prague into one of the leading cities of the Reich, the gateway to the new Nazi empire in the Balkans and the occupied east. He dreamed of transforming the city into a monument to his own greatness with the assistance of Hitler's architect Albert Speer, a figure Heydrich was eager to cultivate because of his friendship with the Führer. According to his wife he considered Speer's very agreement to visit the Protectorate and discuss the project as a sign of Hitler's special favour. Heydrich planned to rebuild Prague, like Berlin, in the Nazi imperial style, with a German opera house and a new government complex around the Hradčany castle. The city was to be encircled by a ring road and linked by autobahn to the rest of the Reich. This grandiose vision, which aped Hitler's plans for Berlin and other major cities, showed how far Heydrich had emerged from Himmler's shadow. He clearly now considered himself a candidate for the inner circle of Nazi power, a view confirmed by his enthusiastic reception at Führer headquarters in February 1942.

As Heydrich had intended, his energetic performance impressed his superiors and was compared favourably to the bungling and indecision of his predecessor. On 23 January, Hitler registered his approval of SS rule: 'Neurath let himself be completely diddled by the Czech nobility. Another six months of that regime and production would have fallen by 25 per cent. Of all the Slavs, the Czech is the most dangerous, because he's a worker. He has a sense of discipline, he's orderly . . . he knows how to hide his plans. Now they'll work for they know we're pitiless and brutal.' The following week, in the presence of Heydrich, Hitler boasted: 'We'll settle the Czechs' hash if we follow a consistent policy with them. . . . A great part of the Czechs are of Germanic origin and it's not impossible to re-Germanise them.' Nor was the Führer alone in his admiration. On 15 February Josef Goebbels, the Minister of Propaganda, had a long talk with Heydrich, who bragged about the impact of his latest moves. As Goebbels noted approvingly in his diary:

> Heydrich's measures are producing good results. . . . The danger to German security from Czech elements . . . has been completely overcome. Heydrich operates successfully. He plays cat and mouse with the Czechs and they swallow everything he places before them. . . . Slavs, he emphasised, cannot be educated as one educates a Germanic people. One must either break them or humble them constantly. At present he does the latter. Our task in the Protectorate is perfectly clear. Neurath completely misjudged it, which is why the crisis in Prague first arose.

According to Goebbels, Heydrich's policy was 'truly a model one. . . . As a result the Protectorate is now in the best of spirits, quite in contrast to other occupied or annexed areas.'

Heydrich's successful mobilisation of the economy and the creation of a government which openly collaborated with the Nazis increased the political pressures on the exiles in London. Beneš continued to believe that 1942 would be a decisive year, a view confirmed by the Soviet military successes outside Moscow and the entry of the United States into the war after Pearl Harbor. In a broadcast to the Czech people on the anniversary of the Nazi seizure of Prague, he announced that the Germans knew they could no longer win and that the war would come to a climax not later than the spring of 1943. It was essential to hold firm for the next eighteen months. His characteristic optimism was balanced by increasing concern about the prospects for Czechoslovakia whatever the outcome of the fighting. It was embarrassing to approach the Russians about the post-war structure of central Europe or the British about the future of the Sudeten Germans while Czech factories were grinding out weapons to kill allied soldiers and Hácha had enlisted in the crusade against Bolshevism. Beneš was haunted by the fear that the Protectorate, like Slovakia, would eventually declare war on the allies and send troops to the eastern front, putting the final nail in the coffin of Czech prospects at any peace conference. There was also the danger of a compromise peace to consider. Beneš remained convinced that once the balance of military power swung decisively against Germany either Hitler or his generals would make a peace offer. He regarded Heydrich's measures as the possible preliminary to proposals which would leave the Nazis in control of Bohemia–Moravia. It was thus more essential than ever to dispel the impression of the Czechs as a quisling nation, a view encouraged by every public statement from Emil Hácha and Emanuel Moravec.

In December 1941 the exile government took several calculated steps in the diplomatic sphere. Beneš formally broke with Hácha and for the first time since the beginning of the war launched an attack on the Protectorate regime over the BBC, claiming that since Heydrich's arrival there was 'neither a government nor a president in the so-called Protectorate'. It was quietly explained to the Foreign Office that senility had led the state President into collaboration with the Germans. The old man was completely gaga. In the week after Pearl Harbor, Masaryk announced that Czechoslovakia was in a state of war 'with all countries which are in a state of war with Great Britain and the United States', a move calculated to appeal to allied opinion and forestall any move towards belligerency by Hácha under Nazi influence. On 1 January 1942 the exile government subscribed to the declaration of the United Nations pledging all the allies to employ their full resources against Germany, Italy and Japan and never to conclude a separate peace with them. These were all symbolic gestures, however, unlikely to make much of an impact, particularly on the Russians locked in a death struggle with the Nazis on the eastern front. If the Czech national cause was to survive and flourish, words must be backed with actions by the summer of 1942, whatever the human cost. As during the First World War, Beneš looked to revolutionary activities at home, paid for by Czech blood, to thrust the cause of independence into the mainstream of world events. It was a cold and calculating decision by a man who, like de Gaulle, believed that he and no other represented the spirit of his nation.

As Beneš had recognised since October 1941, the destruction wrought on the home army by Heydrich made parachutists the key element in any campaign of political disruption and sabotage. In January 1942, when Heydrich's new course became clear, two further groups were added to the communications and sabotage teams already awaiting aircraft under Sustr at STS 2. On 24 January the Czechs asked SOE to train two squads for 'anti-personnel attacks on local Quislings' which were assigned the codenames IRON and TIN. IRON was later abandoned and its target is unrecorded in the available records, but it is probable that it was Hácha, who had betrayed Beneš by failing to resign in October and had lent himself to Heydrich's propaganda campaign against the exiles. Sergeants Cupal and Švarc of TIN were turned over to SOE for a course of instruction which included 'weapon training, throwng bombs, demolitions, special methods . . . PT and unarmed combat' – roughly the programme followed by their predecessors, Gabčík and Kubiš. The target assigned to TIN was Emanuel Moravec, the Minister of Propaganda and the main collaborator in the reorganised Protectorate government. ANTHROPOID was now part of a general terrorist attack on the political structure established by Heydrich in January 1942. The new operations were probably mounted under pressure from Soviet intelligence, which wanted Beneš to do something about the problem of collaboration.

Simultaneously the sabotage plan was extended. It was a source of permanent frustration to the exiles that Czech factories were churning out weapons for the Germans at a rate, according to Beneš' figures, which accounted for one-third of arms production in the occupied areas. Since most of these tanks and guns were bound for the eastern front, it was a cause of particular embarrassment in relations with Moscow. Beneš realised that his sabotage groups could not do sufficient damage on their own to affect the situation but believed that this problem would be overcome if he persuaded the RAF to bomb the Skoda works in co-operation with a parachute group. The exiles had been pressing for an attack since the spring of 1941 without result. On 15 March 1942, Beneš renewed his pressure on the Air Ministry with a memorandum arguing that Skoda represented the largest concentration of Nazi war industry outside the Ruhr. Its destruction would do more to please the Russians than the recent bombing of the Renault factory in Paris and improve morale in the Protectorate by demonstrating that the western powers were fighting for Czech liberation. Under cover of the bombing the workers could complete the wrecking of the plant. Nine days later, STEEL, one of the sabotage groups at STS 2, was renamed OUT DISTANCE and began training to plant a radio beacon to assist the British bombers to their target. This device, known as a Rebecca set, broadcast a signal capable of guiding an aircraft from a distance of twenty-five miles and had been developed by the RAF specifically for use in conjunction with agents. It could be carried in a suitcase disguised as a biscuit tin and was easily erected within a minute by one man. After consulting 'Bomber' Harris, the Air Ministry agreed to a raid on the Skoda factory that spring in co-operation with OUT DISTANCE, an operation codenamed CANONBURY.

SILVER A, dropped by Hockey with SILVER B and ANTHROPOID on the night of 28/29 December 1941, played a key role in these ambitous plans, since it would provide Beneš' only means of communication with the Protectorate in the first half of 1942. Bartoš made contact with the Czech radio centre at Woldingham on 15 January after several false starts caused by undetected damage to his receiver. SILVER A was lucky to survive beyond the first stage of the operation. It landed in the wrong place, Valčik was separated from his companions during the jump and the false papers provided by Czech intelligence proved worthless. It was luckier than SILVER B, however, which disbanded and went into hiding after its radio set was broken and the contact addresses it had been given by London turned out to be useless. With the help of local sympathisers, SILVER A was reunited in Pardubice, Bartoš' home town, where it was able to survive despite committing some elementary blunders. Bartoš visited his mother and allowed Potuček to do the same, starting inevitable rumours about the arrival of parachutists from England which fortunately never reached the ears of the Gestapo. With the connivance of a friendly Czech policeman, Potuček and the radio were installed in a deserted quarry outside the town, while Bartoš and Valčik began to establish intelligence networks to spy on troop movements towards the eastern front and identify targets for sabotage and bombing. Bartoš masqueraded as a travelling insurance agent, while Valčik secured a job as a waiter in a restaurant frequented by German officers. New papers and ration cards were provided by the local resistance.

From the beginning the men of SILVER A operated under severe psychological strains because Nazi security measures were much tougher than their instructors at STS 2 had led them to expect. On one occasion in February 1942 this tension erupted in a personal quarrel between Bartoš and Valčik over a woman, which had to be smoothed over before the group could work efficiently. It was also reflected in Bartoš' first messages to London, informing his superiors that while the underground continued to exist, its members had been forced to scatter and live under new names: 'The terror . . . is powerful and for everyone politically active there is a permanent Gestapo agent. For us . . . work is exceptionally difficult in spite of our contacts. Future workers . . . must be provided with every possible form of legitimation – birth certificate, regional papers etc.' Travel was dangerous because of the strict police controls on hotels and the railways were guarded by anti-sabotage groups from the local communities who were held personally responsible for the safety of their stretch of the line. As Lockhart remarked on reading this report, it showed 'not only the severity of the Heydrich regime but also the considerable measure of success achieved by this expert in terror tactics in hampering the activities of the Czech secret organisation'. In a later message on 16 February, Bartoš drew the obvious conclusion, advising Czech intelligence that in view of the pervasive German controls it would be best 'to make the utmost use of those [parachutists] who are here and limit the number of fresh arrivals to the lowest possible figure'. Although Beneš was delighted with the restoration of communications with the Protectorate through SILVER A and promoted Bartoš to the rank of captain as a sign of appreciation, he found this particular advice unwelcome. On 11 February SILVER A received a message emphasising the importance of stimulating resistance from abroad 'by all valid means. It was with this intention that we have sent and . . . shall continue to send groups of parachutists into the different regions of our country. . . . It will be necessary for you to take the required steps for establishing and maintaining these groups in order to send to London the results of their intelligence and resistance activities and . . . to convey our orders and instructions to them.' Unknown to Bartoš, Beneš was in fact adding to the missions to be dropped that spring and for political reasons had no intention of curtailing the programme whatever the dangers to the survival of his agents. The parachutists were expendable in the higher cause of national survival.

The message of 11 February warning Bartoš about Beneš' intentions also instructed him to find out what had happened to SILVER B and ANTHROPOID, neither of which had surfaced since vanishing from Hockey's bomber into the winter night six weeks before. Heydrich's recent successes made it particularly important to discover the fate of ANTHROPOID, which played a key role in Czech plans for political disruption. It was mistakenly believed in London that SILVER B had been betrayed to the Germans and that ANTHROPOID might have suffered a similar fate. If Gabčík and Kubiš had been killed or captured, replacements would have to be found. The operation was too important to cancel. As Colonel Moravec later recalled: 'By my calculations at least ten days must elapse before the men could make proper preparations. Two, then three weeks went by. When four weeks had elapsed and nothing happened, I began to worry. Had something gone wrong?' ANTHROPOID had no radio set and could not warn London if it ran into difficulties. In this situation Moravec decided to breach the strict security which had held ANTHROPOID apart from the other parachute groups and ask Bartoš to find his missing assassins. SILVER A was given the emergency addresses assigned to ANTHROPOID in Plzeň and the code words for making personal contact with the group: 'Miluska from station seventeen greets Vysocil' (the cover name of Josef Gabčík). Station seventeen was a reference to STS XVII, Brickendonbury Hall in Hertfordshire, where the Czech parachute groups had been trained in sabotage.

Colonel Moravec's worst fears proved to be unfounded but ANTHROPOID had indeed hovered on the brink of disaster and was lucky to survive its first few hours on Czech soil. As Gabčík floated down out of the winter night under his parachute canopy, he misjudged his height and landed heavily, injuring his left foot on the frozen ground. As a result he was unable to walk without the aid of his companion. To make matters worse, the two agents found themselves in an unfamiliar countryside of bare fields without the woods and hills which they had counted on for cover. In the cloud and darkness the Halifax had dropped them not over Borek aerodrome near Plzeň but over the village of Nehvizdy, twenty miles from Prague. It was immediately evident to the agents that something had gone wrong although neither at first guessed how far they were from the planned landing site. While Gabčík buried the parachutes in the snow, Kubiš made a quick reconnaissance of the area. He found a deserted hut where the two men concealed their equipment under a pile of old sacks. Then, after a quick meal of bully beef and chocolate, they set out over the frozen fields to find a better hiding place before daylight. Near the village they discovered an old stone quarry and went to ground in its abandoned tunnels. Behind them the memory of aircraft engines in the night, the trampled snow of the landing ground and the poorly concealed parachutes told their own story to anyone who was interested. The Gestapo had only to follow up these clues by tracing two sets of tracks across the fields to end the careers of the ANTHROPOID assassins.

By a stroke of luck there were no German troops or police in the vicinity and nobody connected Hockey's bomber with agents and ordered a search. Instead Gabčík and Kubiš were found by a local gamekeeper who had been wakened by the low-flying Halifax and suspected that something unusual was afoot. After a brief search the next morning he found the buried parachutes and the equipment in the hut along with a discarded bully-beef tin with an English label. Following the footprints in the snow, he soon discovered two young men in the quarry. The strangers claimed to be surveyors, assessing the possibility of reopening the abandoned workings, but the gamekeeper noticed that one of them kept a hand in a pocket which obviously concealed a revolver. When challenged about the hidden equipment, the men admitted that they were parachutists from England and asked for help. Informed that they were twenty miles from Prague, the agents became alarmed and upset. This was hardly surprising since it meant that they were hopelessly cut off from their emergency contact addresses in Plzeň. With Gabčík injured, the outlook could not have been bleaker. ANTHROPOID was saved only by a fortunate accident. The miller from a neighbouring village was also roused by the noise of the Halifax and guessed that it was dropping agents. He set out to find the parachutists and soon stumbled on them in the quarry, the most obvious hiding place for miles around. The miller was a member of SOKOL, a sports organisation dedicated to the cause of Czech nationalism since the early days of the republic. Although banned by Heydrich in October 1941, the association continued to exist and the miller offered to put the agents in touch with an underground SOKOL group in Prague. This breached one of the main rules drawn up in London banning any contact with the local resistance until the operation was over, but the parachutists had no real choice. They would be safer in a crowded city than in the countryside where their presence was already the subject of local gossip. Gabčík needed somewhere secure to hide while his foot healed and Prague was in any case where they would find their target, Reinhard Heydrich. With the assistance of SOKOL members the ANTHROPOID team arrived in the capital by train early in the new year. Their equipment, left hidden in the quarry, soon followed and was dispersed to a series of hiding places around the city.

The network which took charge of them was run by Ladislav Vaněk, cover name JINDRA, a former chemistry teacher and SOKOL official from Brno who had been on the run from the Gestapo for the past eighteen months. According to his post-war account, he first learned about the two parachutists in early January although it is likely that he did not in fact meet them until much later, perhaps not until the end of February. The survivors of Heydrich's police dragnet were cautious men and Vaněk's initial reaction was to suspect that the agents were a German plant despatched to infiltrate and compromise his organisation. He ordered the strangers brought to a flat in the Smíchov district of Prague where he could question them personally. Since Gabčík found it difficult to walk, only Kubiš attended the meeting. Although he would reveal neither his name nor the nature of his mission, he managed to persuade Vaněk that he was not a Gestapo spy. The two agents were placed in the care of Jan Zelenka, cover name HAJASKY, a former teacher who had worked for Czech intelligence in the Sudetenland before Munich. Zelenka's speciality was providing safe houses

and documents for 'submarines', people who had to submerge themselves in a new identity because they were living outside the law. With
his help Gabčík and Kubiš procured ration cards and new papers to
replace the ones issued in London which contained errors in the
stamps and ink detectable to even the stupidest German policeman. A
sympathetic doctor was found to treat Gabčík's foot and to provide
medical certificates stating that the two men were unfit for work, one
because of a duodenal ulcer, the other because of an inflamed gall
bladder. These were vital documents. With the Germans mobilising all
available labour, awkward questions were liable to be asked of young
men found wandering in the streets during working hours.

Zelenka hid the agents in a series of safe houses in Prague, moving
them frequently for security reasons. Some of the families with whom
the men stayed knew that they were parachutists and some did not, but
all guessed that they were more than the usual 'submarines' on the run
from the Germans. They were remembered by those who hid them as
cheerful, outgoing but secretive men, who always slept with pistols
under their pillows and never stayed in a building without first
checking for emergency escape routes. At the centre of the network
was the flat of the Moravec family in the suburb of Zizkov, the home of
a middle-aged railwayman, his wife and twenty-one-year-old son, Ata,
who was often used as a courier by the JINDRA group. Through her
work for the tuberculosis league and the red cross, Mrs Moravec had a
series of invaluable contacts throughout Prague and an excellent cover
for underground work. Gabčík and Kubiš soon grew close to 'Aunt
Marie' and her family. Ata was impressed by the parachutists' guns and
by their tales of army life in England where his brother was serving with
the Czech forces. His attitude towards the agents was a mixture of awe
and hero-worship. Despite their easy manner and their willingness to
talk about politics and the war, however, Gabčík and Kubiš kept their
distance in one important respect – they never let slip the nature of
their mission. If pressed on the subject they would laugh and say
'We're counting the ducks on the Vltava,' the river which flows through
the centre of Prague.

It was there, in the network of safe houses provided by the JINDRA
organisation, that Valčik finally tracked them down towards the end of
February 1942, a meeting arranged through Mrs Moravec. Gabčík and
Kubiš were glad to see a familiar face from the Czech Brigade and the
three exchanged news of their experiences since the drop. On 1 March
Bartoš was able to inform London that the two agents were safe and
well although Gabčík had still not recovered from a foot injury which

had immobilised him for eight weeks. The discovery of ANTHROPOID was followed by another cheering development, the renewal of contact with the Abwehr spy Paul Thümmel, the key figure in the Czech intelligence effort since 1937. This was the main priority assigned to SILVER A in December 1941, although security dictated that Bartoš and his men should never know the real identity or even the sex of the mysterious agent considered so important by London. They were to operate through a cut-out, Captain Morávek or OTA, the last of the THREE KINGS and Thümmel's sole contact with the underground. Tracking down Morávek was difficult for he had been on the run since losing his last transmitter and was high on the Gestapo wanted list. In December he barely escaped arrest when the Germans raided a safe house in the old quarter of Prague. He shot his way clear, wounding three security policemen in the process, an incident which Heydrich considered serious enough to mention in a speech to Nazi officials on 4 February. When Valčik arrived in Prague to make enquiries, he met a stone wall. The SS terror and the widespread use of informers had made everyone wary of strangers and he could make no progress. Not until the BBC broadcast a coded message over the Czech service, confirming that he was a parachutist and not a Nazi spy, was anyone prepared to reveal the whereabouts of Morávek. On 14 March Bartoš was finally able to report: 'We have made personal contact with OTA. His reports follow.'

This news was greeted with considerable relief by Beneš, who responded by lavishing extravagant praise on Bartoš. He had always relied on A–54 to boost Czech credibility with the allies and could now look forward to a fresh flood of information on the eve of what everyone predicted would be a series of decisive battles on the eastern front. It was a development likely to improve his bargaining position with Moscow, which had always seemed more than eager for intelligence from this Czech source. A series of urgent questions for A–54 was immediately despatched requesting information about German plans in Russia and the Mediterranean theatre: 'Preparations for spring offensive: Where and what is the probable direction of principal effort? What can be deduced from it? For which countries are new Einsatztruppen being prepared? Relations with Turkey and Sweden. Preparations for new fields of battle: North Africa, Spain, Norway.' This shopping list revealed the preoccupations of Soviet intelligence and SIS, both of which had become disillusioned with the performance of the Czechs since October 1941. They were destined never to receive the answers. The Gestapo was already closing in on A–54, threatening the flow of information which had served the Czechs well since 1937. In a second message from Morávek on 14 March Bartoš warned London that Thümmel was in danger and might have to flee to Switzerland or Turkey. He wanted the underground to fake a kidnapping to save his family from reprisals. This bombshell was completely unexpected and could be traced back to the security sweep which accompanied Heydrich's appointment as acting Reichsprotektor.

When Morávek's last transmitter had been seized by the Gestapo five months previously, on the night of 4/5 October 1941, the Nazis had also netted the intelligence he had been relaying to London. This material confirmed that a traitor was in touch with the Czech resistance and narrowed down the search to three senior figures in the German administration – the state Secretary, Karl Hermann Frank, the head of the Prague Gestapo, Otto Geschke, and the man who ran the Abwehr network, Paul Thümmel. Since Frank and Geschke were above suspicion this left only Thümmel, who was arrested on 13 October. From the beginning Heydrich took a strong personal interest in the case. Thümmel was both a senior Abwehr officer and an old Nazi, a highly decorated party veteran from the days of political struggle. His guilt could be used to the benefit of the SS not only in its historic quarrel with the army but also in the new competition with the party over political supremacy in the occupied east. It would help discredit these rivals and prove to Hitler that the SS was the only reliable pillar of the new order in Europe. But proving a case of treason against such a well-connected figure was not easy. The Gestapo had to proceed with caution and could not employ the methods routinely used against less prominent prisoners. Under questioning Thümmel simply denied everything and nobody dared beat an admission out of him. As his interrogator later recalled: 'He was clever at arousing suspicion against other people. After several days he obtained permission to inform his superiors of these accusations. The result was a cascade of protests from Bormann for the Party, Himmler for the SS and Admiral Canaris for the Abwehr.' On 25 November the Gestapo bowed before the storm and released him with an apology.

Despite this defeat, Heydrich was convinced of Thümmel's guilt and he was kept under police surveillance. According to one account the Gestapo went back to its files and uncovered circumstantial evidence linking the suspect with a series of espionage cases involving an anonymous German officer which stretched from secret contacts with the allies in Holland in 1939 to a leakage of Nazi plans to the Yugoslavs in 1941. A check of Thümmel's movements put him in the right place at the right time on each occasion. According to another, convincing evidence against him was turned up in old Czech intelligence files which Morávec had failed to destroy in March 1939. Whatever the truth of the matter, the security police now felt in a position to act. On 22 February Thümmel was invited to a routine intelligence conference in Prague. There he was rearrested and spirited off to the provincial Gestapo office at Kladno, where he could be interrogated in secret without any interference from Canaris or the Nazi party bosses. This time he admitted that he had been dealing with the Czech resistance but claimed that it was all part of an Abwehr deception operation designed to penetrate the underground. This explanation could not be wholly discounted, for in the murky underworld of wartime intelligence such operations were common. The Gestapo itself routinely tried to infiltrate and exploit resistance groups by the use of agents provocateurs who often posed as parachutists. Thümmel was therefore given the benefit of the doubt and offered a chance to prove his loyalty. At the end of the month he was released on condition that he led the police to Morávek. Thümmel proved reluctant to bait the trap. He tried to drag the situation out while he looked for a means of escape with the assistance of his underground contacts. On at least one occasion he was able to evade Gestapo surveillance and asked Morávek to arrange a fake kidnapping which might save his family from a concentration camp. This was a hopeless appeal, for there was no way of smuggling him out of the Protectorate. In any case, Morávek was given no time to act. On 20 March, the patience of the security police expired and the suspect was arrested for good. The following day Morávek was ambushed on his way to a rendezvous with Thümmel in a Prague park. After a gun battle in which he fired over fifty shots at the Gestapo, he broke through the police cordon and attempted to escape on a passing tram. But his luck finally ran out and, hit in both legs, he fell from the platform into the gutter. As the Gestapo closed in, he shot himself through the head to avoid capture. It was the end of the THREE KINGS and the flow of information to London from A–54. Two months later, on 23 May, Heydrich sent a full report on the affair to Bormann, naming Thümmel as an important agent of Czech intelligence and asking for his expulsion from the party. The case was never brought to trial, perhaps to avoid a public scandal. Instead Thümmel was held in the fortress of Terezin under a false name and murdered by his SS jailers on 27 April 1945, twelve days before the end of the war.

The arrest of A–54 was another coup for Heydrich and put him in a position to launch new political intrigues against both the Abwehr and the party. By contrast it was a severe blow to Beneš, who had always used Thümmel to improve his bargaining position with the allies. In this respect the affair helped seal Heydrich's death warrant. Now the prospects of the exiles seemed to depend solely on the planned campaign of subversion and sabotage, in which the assassination played a leading role. The events of early March also had an impact on both SILVER A and ANTHROPOID. When Morávek was shot, pictures of Bartoš, Valčik and Potuček were found in his briefcase stamped with the name of a photographer in Pardubice. He was carrying them because the men of SILVER A had finally run into trouble with the Germans. At the beginning of March they attempted to legalise themselves by registering with the police, using stolen identity cards provided by their local contacts. A random Gestapo check on new arrivals singled out Valčik for routine investigation and soon discovered that his background was completely fictitious. He escaped arrest only because he was out of town when the Gestapo turned up at the restaurant where he worked. A search began for the suspicious stranger and there was a general check of papers in Pardubice and the surrounding area. Bartoš ordered Valčik to take refuge in Prague and asked Morávek to provide SILVER A with new papers, supplying him with the pictures which he was carrying when he was killed. Valčik was immediately recognised as the vanishing waiter from Pardubice and his former employer was arrested. The other two were unknown to the Gestapo but it was suspected that all three were parachutists. Their descriptions were circulated to every police post in the Protectorate and in Pardubice an intensive hunt began for the men and the clandestine transmitter which was rumoured to be operating in the area. Since it was too dangerous for Valčik to return to the town, he remained in Prague and changed his appearance, dying his hair and growing a small moustache. He took refuge with the JINDRA organisation, staying in the Moravecs' flat at Zizkov and various other safe houses around the city. There he was thrown together with Gabčík and Kubiš, who recruited him for ANTHROPOID early in April. This was another departure from the security precautions imposed by London but an extra man was useful and time was pressing. If the Gestapo uncovered SILVER A and the network in Pardubice, the trail would quickly lead to JINDRA in Prague and compromise the whole assassination plan.

The hole in Heydrich's car blasted by Kubiš's bomb, which had been specially designed for the purpose by SOE explosives experts.

The scene of the crime. Gestapo agents reconstruct the assassination and search for clues.

Heydrich's body is removed from the Bulkova hospital by an SS guard of honour with flaming torches. Heydrich's successor Daluege feared a Czech uprising and insisted that the body should not be moved until after dark.

Heydrich's body lying in state at the Hradčany castle underneath the SS flag, guarded by officers of the security police. The pine branches, typical of Nazi paganism, were meant to evoke the 'Nordic past'.

Heydrich's coffin passes through the centre of Prague, through streets lined with Nazi security police, en route for his funeral in Berlin.

'Uncle Heinrich' with Heydrich's children as the coffin leaves the Hradčany castle for Berlin. Heavily veiled, Lina Heydrich stands in the background like a good Nazi wife.

The siege of the Karel Boromejsky Church—the Prague Fire Brigade pumps water into the crypt in an attempt to force the assassins to surrender.

The SS surrounds the Church—the figures in the dark hats are Gestapo.

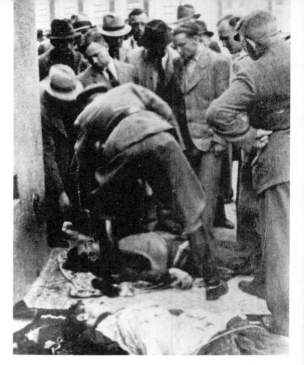

The traitor Karel Čurda identifies the bodies of his former comrades for the Gestapo.

Gestapo and Waffen SS with the bodies of the parachutists, all of whom committed suicide rather than be taken alive.

A hole dug by the trapped parachutists in a desperate attempt to escape from the crypt.

The crypt after the battle. On the left are piles of bones displaced from the coffins during the fighting.

Sergeant Karel Čurda, 'OUT DISTANCE', who betrayed his comrades and became a Gestapo informer. He was hanged for treason after the war.

The severed heads of Gabčík and Kubiš, which were later displayed to their relatives by the Germans.

Heydrich's successor Kurt Daluege delivers a memorial speech on the anniversary of the assassination beneath the death mask of the Nazi 'martyr of Prague'.

The monument erected to the memory of Heydrich at the fatal corner in Prague, with its perpetual SS guard of honour. It was torn to pieces by the Czechs in 1945.

8

Preparations

When the agents began to plan the operation their first requirement was firm information about Heydrich, who moved around a great deal and was often away from Prague on other business. Without reliable intelligence about his daily routine and travel schedule it was difficult to fix a time and place for the assassination. The parachutists were able to learn something by watching the road between Heydrich's residence at Panenské Břežany and Prague, rising early and returning to their safe houses cold and muddy after hours of hiding in hedges and ditches, but the picture built up by these methods was far from complete. It had to be rounded out by inside information, which was to play a vital role in the assassination. Despite the SS guard which surrounded the Hradčany castle, security within the walls was slack. The Nazis employed Czech domestic staff but paid little attention to their activities. The servants were treated as part of the furniture and were in an ideal position to supply information. With the assistance of Zelenka, Gabčík and Kubiš were introduced to František Šefařík, a joiner on the maintenance staff. A married man with a small child, Šefařík was at first alarmed by the enquiries of the mysterious young strangers: 'I told these boys I didn't like it – the whole thing stank of the graveyard – but they calmed me down.' Šefařík took the parachutists to the cobbled square in front of the castle by the Mathias Gate where he pointed out Heydrich's car and the SS guard posts. For safety's sake he avoided further direct contact with them, operating through a cut-out, two girls installed by Zelenka in a flat near the Hradčany. Every evening he would pass a note through the window containing details of Heydrich's movements and whether or not he had been accompanied by an escort. Unknown to Šefařík, the parachutists had a second spy, Josef Novotny, a watchmaker responsible for the maintenance of the castle clocks. His work took him into every room of the building and, since he repaired watches for the German garrison, he was able to pick up a great deal of useful gossip. According to some accounts, they also developed contacts at Panenské Břežany. The Heydrichs regarded the Czech staff there not as a security risk but as a status symbol. As Lina Heydrich remarked: 'Every servant had a servant of his own. It was all . . . very Austrian.' By these methods the parachutists worked out Heydrich's daily timetable and began to look for a suitable ambush spot.

It was soon clear that he could not be killed either at the castle or on his estate. Both were too heavily guarded by the SS. The parachutists had been trained and equipped by SOE for an attack on Heydrich's official car and their attention rapidly focused on his frequent journeys between Panenské Břežany, Prague and the airport where his special JU–52 was stationed. On these occasions Hitler's viceroy was at his most vulnerable because, unlike his predecessor Neurath, he usually travelled without an escort. The problem was to find a suitable spot for an ambush along his normal route to and from the city. Several possibilities were considered, including a steep corner in the old town near the castle, but all were rejected. An attack in the centre of Prague was too risky and might be interrupted by the police and SS, who were always in the vicinity. This left the country road between Prague and Panenské Břežany, which Heydrich travelled twice a day when he was in the Protectorate. After an extensive reconnaissance the parachutists decided on this option, selecting a small wood south of the village of Břežany as the site of the ambush. The sound of firing might reach the SS guards at the estate but it would be all over before they could intervene. The main drawback was that the road was straight, encouraging Heydrich's chauffeur to drive at high speeds. If Gabčík's sten and Kubiš' bombs were to work effectively some means had to be found of stopping the car. With the assistance of a fitter at a Prague factory, the brother-in-law of the family which was sheltering them at the time, the agents procured a steel cable. They planned to string this across the road, forcing the Mercedes to stop or crash. Heydrich and his driver would then be finished off with guns and grenades.

The difficulty about this plan was escaping after the killing. As Vaněk later recalled: 'The country round Panenské Břežany offered not the least possibility of hiding or getting away. For those who carried it out, an attempt in this place would certainly have meant suicide.' Alerted by the noise of the attack, the SS guards at the estate would soon be on the telephone to Prague. The Germans would establish road blocks and comb the entire area with police and troops. Although ANTHROPOID was considered a suicide mission by Czech intelligence in London, the young men involved had no intention of dying if it could be avoided. Both had found girlfriends since reaching the city. Kubiš was involved with Anna Malinova, an acquaintance of Mrs Moravec, while Gabčík intended to marry, after the war, Libena Fafek, the nineteen-year-old daughter of one of the families who sheltered the parachutists. At least one of the girls was pregnant. In these circumstances it is hardly surprising that the agents wished to survive. The trouble was that on bicycles, the only available form of transport, their chances of escape were slim. The assassins tried to improve the odds by procuring a getaway car which Valčik was to drive whilst the two others did the killing, but cars of any kind were hard to come by in wartime Prague. The parachutists continued to refine their plan, always coming up against this final obstacle. Without a car they could not escape and even if one were found they still ran a high risk of being killed or captured: 'The whole thing might easily end very badly.'

At this stage the parachutists were diverted by fresh orders from London. On 28 March two new groups were dropped over the Protectorate. The first, ZINC, was a three-man communications team designed to back up SILVER A and establish an intelligence network in Moravia. The second, OUT DISTANCE, carried a Rebecca beacon to guide RAF bombers to the Skoda works. Bartoš was informed in advance and arrangements were made to contact the new arrivals through coded advertisements in the personal columns of the newspapers. From the beginning things went badly wrong for both teams. The Protectorate was blanketed by cloud and the pilot lost his way, dropping the agents miles from their targets. ZINC had the misfortune to land in Slovakia, the satellite state dominated by the Nazis, and split up to cross the border. The commander, Lieutenant Pechal, was arrested at the frontier and shot his way clear, losing his papers and a briefcase full of money in the fight. A hunted man, he went to ground in the forests near his parents' home. Sergeant Mikš managed to find Bartoš in Pardubice and was sent on to the JINDRA organisation. The youngest member of the group, twenty-two-year-old Corporal Gerik, found his contact addresses useless and fled to Prague, where he surrendered to the Czech police. He was immediately handed over to the Gestapo. Under questioning, Gerik claimed that as a Slovak he felt no loyalty to the exile movement and had volunteered for special duties only as a means of returning home. To confirm this statement, he showed the Germans where ZINC had hidden its radio equipment. OUT DISTANCE had similar bad luck. It was planned as a four-man group, but for some unexplained reason one member dropped out at the last moment. The commander, Lieutenant Opálka, injured his leg when he landed while Corporal Kolařík panicked and lost his papers. Only the third member of the group, Sergeant Čurda, survived the drop unscathed. The men buried the vital Rebecca set and split up. Opálka and Čurda made their way separately to Pardubice and were sent on by Bartoš to the network of safe houses in Prague. Kolařík went into hiding in the town of Zlin but was tracked down by the Gestapo on 1 April and committed suicide to avoid arrest. As for the Rebecca set, it was unearthed by a farmer who handed it over to the authorities. OUT DISTANCE, like ZINC, seemed destined to end in failure.

When Beneš heard of these developments, his immediate instinct was to salvage something from the wreckage. ZINC could be written off, but OUT DISTANCE was another matter. The British had agreed to raid the Skoda plant in co-operation with a parachute group only after months of nagging and the Russians had probably already been informed about the plan. It could not be called off without political embarrassment to the exiles. When London first learned about the problems of OUT DISTANCE on 14 April, the scale of the disaster was still unclear. The mission seemed to be threatened, not by loss of equipment but by a shortage of personnel. It was not simply a matter of erecting a Rebecca beacon to guide the RAF to the vicinity of the Skoda factory, something which could be done by one man. The OUT DISTANCE team was also to light fires on either side of the works as target markers for the bombers. But only Opálka had contacted Bartoš and he was injured. With a CANONBURY raid planned for the end of April, it was decided to call in ANTHROPOID to save the situation. This decision jeopardised the assassins and put their whole operation at risk. It was a classic example of Beneš trying to achieve too much with too little. Despite the warnings of Bartoš he seems to have had no real grasp of the dangers which faced his agents in the Protectorate or chose to ignore the difficulties when it suited his political purposes. In obedience to their new orders, Gabčík, Kubiš and Valčík travelled to Plzeň with Opálka to prepare for the raid. There they were joined by Čurda, who turned up on 23 April. By this stage a new complication had arisen – the Rebecca set could not be found since it was already in the hands of the Gestapo. Rather than cancel the raid, it was decided to proceed without the radio beacon in the hope that the bombers would find the target markers without its assistance. The parachutists were ordered to prepare the fires and await the signal for action over the Czech service of the BBC: 'Have patience, the day of revenge is approaching.'

Skoda was attacked on 26 April by Stirlings of Number 3 Group, detached from a larger raid on the Daimler-Benz and Bosch engine works in Stuttgart. Despite clear visibility and the setting of fires by the parachutists, only one aircraft found the factory and its bombs fell five miles away. A second RAF raid, launched without assistance from the ground on 3 May, also failed to score any hits. A token force of three aircraft was involved and none came within miles of the works. The only result of the CANONBURY raids was the reinforcement of the flak defences around Plzeň. As for the workers, who were supposed to use the bombing as an opportunity for sabotage, they were warned by Heydrich that the destruction of the factory would be followed by their immediate deportation to the Reich. The agents returned to Prague bitterly disappointed at the failure of CANONBURY and angry with Czech intelligence for risking their lives on such a futile enterprise. For Bartoš in particular the episode seems to have marked a turning point. Already doubtful about Beneš' grasp of the realities in the Protectorate, he now became completely disillusioned with his superiors in London. His problems, however, were not yet over.

At the end of April a new wave of parachute groups landed in the Protectorate as Beneš tried to drop as many agents as possible before flights were curtailed by the short summer nights. The majority were sabotage missions, directed against the kinds of targets requested by the Russians as early as August 1941 – the railway network, arms factories, oil-tank farms and the electricity-supply system. There is little doubt that Beneš hoped to impress Moscow with this effort, but the results were disastrous. Of the five missions dropped after ZINC and OUT DISTANCE, not one was successful. The raid on the Skoda works and the surrender of Gerik had forewarned the Nazis. As Heydrich reported to Bormann on 3 May, it was suspected that British air raids were designed to cover the dropping of agents and the security forces were placed on the alert. The Czech agents were soon more concerned with staying alive than with carrying out their missions. On 27 April three groups were dropped over the Krivoklat forest near Prague, two three-man sabotage teams, BIOSCOPE and BIVOUAC, and a single agent, STEEL, with a new transmitter for UVOD, the central council of the home resistance. STEEL also carried spare crystals for Bartoš' radio, which was wearing out. The men landed safely, buried their equipment and dispersed apparently undetected. The following morning, however, a ploughman harrowing his fields unearthed STEEL's transmitter and immediately reported his find to the authorities. The area was searched by Czech police under Nazi control, who soon discovered a second container packed with sabotage equipment and several parachutes. An ambush was set up at the site and the Germans waited to see who would walk into the trap.

The BIOSCOPE team reached Prague safely and made contact with Opálka. Its commander, Sergeant Kouba, wanted to begin operations immediately and asked for help to retrieve his sabotage material. On 30 April he returned to Krivoklat, accompanied by Mikš of OUT DISTANCE, Valčik of SILVER A and the young Ata Moravec. They split up to approach the landing site. Valčik and Moravec walked straight into the police cordon and escaped arrest only because they were warned off by a sympathetic Czech gendarme. Their companions were not so lucky and tried to fight their way out. Mikš was shot dead after killing one policeman and wounding another. Kouba was chased and captured. On 3 May he committed suicide in his cell to avoid questioning by the Gestapo. As for the BIVOUAC team, all three were arrested in Brno within five days of landing. The commander, Sergeant Pospišil, shot a Czech policeman and escaped but was wounded in the leg and rapidly recaptured. His companions gave the Gestapo a fairly complete account of their SOE training and betrayed their contact addresses in the Protectorate, leading to the arrest and execution of ten Czech civilians. Subsequent groups had no better fortune. On 29 April TIN and INTRANSITIVE were dropped near Trebon in southern Bohemia. TIN, the two-man assassination team aimed against the collaborator Emanuel Moravec, was doomed from the start. Sergeant Švarc hurt his legs on landing and suffered internal injuries. Unable to find either his equipment or his companion, Sergeant Cupal, he eventually contacted Bartoš through a newspaper code and was sent to a safe house in Prague. Cupal, also injured in the legs, sought refuge in Moravia, accompanied by a member of the INTRANSITIVE group, a three-man sabotage mission which broke up after losing its equipment canister during the drop. All were later either killed or captured. The Germans were staggered by the amount of material they seized in this period, which included 'arms, ammunition, a large quantity of explosives, 5 transmitter/receivers, 1 homing beacon [the Rebecca set], 72 special charges for sabotage purposes, 6 charges for assassinations, 40 incendiary devices and over 1000 detonators and fuses of various kinds'. This sad catalogue marked the failure of Beneš' plans for an active resistance spearheaded by parachutists. His efforts had only stirred up the Nazis and endangered the lives of the agents already there, something long foreseen by Bartoš. On 21 May the commander of SILVER A reviewed the dismal record of the parachute groups and asked for the cancellation of further drops. His message was bitterly critical of his superiors in London: 'In practice, you are sending us people for whom we have no use. On the contrary, they are a burden on the organisational network which is undesirable in today's critical times. The Czech and German security authorities have so much information and knowledge about us that to repeat these operations would be a waste of people and equipment.'

It was against this background that the whole purpose of ANTHROPOID was challenged, a confused episode which was never properly explained by the main protagonists. The main outlines, however, can be reconstructed. By the end of April it was becoming impossible for Gabčík and Kubiš to conceal the nature of their mission from the JINDRA group. Their obsession with Heydrich and his movements pointed to the conclusion that they had been sent to kill Hitler's representative. Vaněk later claimed to have guessed their purpose as early as January 1942 but his evidence on this point is unreliable. He appears to have taken little interest in the parachutists until April when he was probably tipped off by Zelenka about their activities. While Zelenka approved of the assassination plan, Vaněk was appalled. A survivor of the earlier SS terror, he did not want to touch off a new round of repression which might eliminate the home resistance and leave the communists as the dominant force in post-war politics. In an attempt to forestall the killing, he held a meeting with Bartoš, Opálka, Gabčík and perhaps also Kubiš, at some stage in late April, probably immediately after the failure of the CANONBURY operation. Vaněk seems to have hoped that, as the senior officer amongst the parachutists, Bartoš had the authority to cancel the operation or could persuade his superiors in London to call it off. According to his later account, Bartoš shared his alarm about ANTHROPOID. This reaction is not hard to understand. In the aftermath of the CANONBURY affair, Bartoš considered London's plans reckless and based on a wilful blindness to local conditions. He was already a sick man and collapsed shortly afterwards with rheumatoid arthritis, something which probably affected his judgement. His instinct was to avoid stirring up the Nazis, endangering the fragile resistance movement and jeopardising the intelligence and communications network established by SILVER A. The reaction of the assassins was very different. In their case, frustration with the CANONBURY fiasco took the form of a demand for action. As Vanék recalled: 'The young men asserted that their mission was perfectly clear: they were to organize and carry out the killing. They were soldiers, so they could not find fault with the killing, or discuss its point or lack of point, its timeliness or its untimeliness. At the most, they might think it over; but they could do nothing against an order that they had been given.' When Bartoš tried to carry the discussion further, Gabčík flared up and shouted: 'The killing is necessary and for my part I shall obey the orders I have been given.' He then left the flat, banging the door behind him. Thereafter he made no secret of his dislike for those who, like Opálka, supported Vanék, while he displayed a sense of gratitude to Zelenka, who was prepared to carry the matter through.

Since Bartoš was unable to dissuade the assassins, Vanék decided to appeal directly to London. In early May, he contacted Arnošt Heidrich, a former Czech diplomat and a member of UVOD. Heidrich did not know Vanék personally and refused to deal with him until a coded message had been broadcast by the Czech service of the BBC confirming that he was not a Nazi spy. Heidrich had apparently already heard about ANTHROPOID from his own sources and shared Vanék's reservations. He agreed to draft a message to London protesting against the operation in the name of the home resistance:

> This assassination would not be of the least value to the Allies and for our nation it would have unforeseeable consequences. It would threaten not only hostages and political prisoners, but also thousands of other lives. The nation would be the subject of unheard-of reprisals. At the same time it would wipe out the last remainders of any organization. It would then be impossible for the resistance to be useful to the Allies. Therefore we beg you to give the order through SILVER A for the assassination not to take place. Danger in delay, give the order at once.

This was an understandable plea by men who had barely survived the previous SS terror and wished to keep the remnants of their organisation intact. At the same time UVOD realised that Beneš in London might have a better understanding of the national interest than the hunted remnants of the home resistance in Prague. The message ended by recognising this fact: 'If for reasons of foreign policy the assassination is nevertheless essential, the nation is prepared to offer even the highest sacrifices.' Since UVOD had no radio of its own following the loss of the transmitter dropped with STEEL, the despatch was passed to Vanék for transmission by SILVER A.

The message which was finally broadcast to Beneš on 12 May differed significantly from this original. The crucial final sentence had been altered to read: 'If for reasons of foreign policy the assassination is nevertheless essential, another target should be chosen.' The despatch suggested the quisling, Emanuel Moravec. The result was to give the impression that the entire home resistance movement was united in unequivocal condemnation of the assassination plan. Vanék later claimed that the alterations were made by Bartoš, although his choice of words implies that he colluded in the change: as he recalled, by 'another target' '*we* thought of Emanuel Moravec, minister in the Protectorate government' (author's italics). Moravec was apparently selected in preference to Heydrich before Bartoš learned about Beneš' second assassination team, TIN. He was a natural target for the home resistance. As early as 6 February Bartoš had reported that Moravec was despised as a traitor who 'on the day of reckoning will be dealt with by the first Czech who meets him'. The altered message was an attempt to satisfy Beneš' desire for action and keep the assassins occupied without provoking massive German reprisals which would endanger the JINDRA organisation and SILVER A. While awaiting a reply from London, Vanék persuaded Gabčík and Kubiš to postpone the assassination. According to his post-war account, Opálka actually cycled out to the woods around Panenské Břežany to persuade them to wait. In fact Vanék had little need to worry. When the message to London was sent, Heydrich was out of the Protectorate on a tour of France and the Low Countries. He did not return until the following week when the issue was already settled.

The message from SILVER A must have surprised and embarrassed Beneš since it apparently represented the wishes of the entire underground and revealed that ANTHROPOID was no longer a secret. There are various accounts of how he handled the issue. According to one version, Vanék's request was discussed at a meeting with two exile politicians and two senior officers of Czech intelligence around 13 May. The politicians wanted to respect the wishes of the home resistance and cancel the operation, while the intelligence representatives argued that the allies expected something spectacular. It was too late to retreat. Beneš' reaction is not recorded. This account is partially supported by one of Beneš' secretaries, Prokop Drtina, who remembered long after the war that the President had consulted him about the assassination in the presence of Colonel Moravec: 'I, as a former member of the Czech resistance organisation . . . expressed an opinion that the attitude of the home resistance had to be respected and that no action should be taken without the agreement of the home organisations. The President talked in a similar sense to Colonel F. Moravec who left the meeting with the direct order of the President, the highest commander of the army, to immediately instruct the parachutists to abandon their mission.' Moravec's recollection was different: 'I took the message to President Beneš and the Chief of the British Intelligence Service [Stewart Menzies]. President Beneš ordered me not to answer. The Chief of SIS did not say anything but I have learned since the war that the British . . . insisted on the execution of the order.' This is the only mention of SIS rather than SOE in connexion with the affair, although SIS was of course Moravec's original British sponsor. Menzies certainly had possible reasons for supporting ANTHROPOID. Heydrich carried many secrets in his head which would die with him and his assassination might disrupt the Nazi security service. On the other hand, spectacular killings were not normally favoured by SIS, since they endangered intelligence networks by stirring up the Nazis, and there is no convincing evidence of Menzies' involvement. As for SOE, it knew nothing about the controversy for it was never informed. The Czechs, highly sensitive about national sovereignty, were not in the habit of discussing questions of internal politics with either secret organisation. Moravec's account looks like an attempt to spread the blame. ANTHROPOID had become the subject of bitter controversy in the exile community and many believed that Moravec had organised the operation behind Beneš' back, which was why he finally decided to speak out. In his version the President, with the encouragement of the British, tacitly endorsed the killing by refusing to revoke ANTHROPOID's orders.

After the war, Vaněk maintained that Beneš had gone beyond calculated inaction and issued an order confirming the assassination: 'During the last days of our waiting I had a talk with Zelenka–Hajasky, who told me an interesting thing: Kubiš and Gabčík had disclosed that about 20 May they had received a radioed message in a code known only to them. Bartoš, who sent it to them by the Pardubice liaison agent, was unable to decipher it. And it appeared that this message contained a confirmation of the order – that it said the attack on Heydrich was to be carried out.' His story was supported by the evidence of other survivors. A former courier with the SILVER A network remembered Bartoš receiving a signal for Gabčík and Kubiš which he could not decode: 'I went to Prague to deliver it. . . . Later Bartoš thought that it was the order to carry out the killing.' According to another witness, Gabčík was heard to remark: 'There is nothing else we can do *because the order has arrived*' (author's italics). Although the Gestapo found no trace of the mysterious signal when it captured Bartoš' message files, former radio officers of Czech intelligence argue that it was perfectly possible for headquarters to communicate with ANTHROPOID in a code unknown to Bartoš. Although it was originally intended that Gabčík and Kubiš should operate entirely on their own, they would have carried one-time pads as a matter of course, giving them a secure cipher system should they require one.

Whatever the truth of the matter, one thing is clear – if Beneš did not specifically confirm the assassination order, he certainly never cancelled it. If Drtina's recollection is accurate, Beneš was simply playacting in order to distance himself from what was now clearly a controversial operation. ANTHROPOID would go ahead but the official record would absolve the President of responsibility if it became an issue in post-war politics. In the murky world of intelligence such tactics were not uncommon. When Vaněk's request arrived in London, it was already obvious that Beneš' sabotage and subversion campaign had failed before it had properly begun. His parachute teams were killed, captured or dispersed. Only SILVER A and ANTHROPOID remained intact. Skoda was churning out arms for the Wehrmacht while embarrassing acts of collaboration between the Protectorate regime and the Nazis continued to multiply. On Hitler's birthday Hácha presented the Führer with a fully equipped hospital train for the eastern front as a symbol of solidarity in the struggle against Bolshevism. The Russians, angered by these gestures, asked the exiles to pass a law against collaboration, arguing that this would produce 'a kind of paralysis' in the Protectorate and damage the enemy. The Soviet Foreign Minister, Molotov, was to visit London later in May and Beneš intended to discuss the expulsion of the Sudeten Germans and the future of central Europe during his stay. In these circumstances, it is hardly surprising that he failed to respond to Vaněk's request.

Besides his immediate desire to impress the Russians, Beneš was still haunted by the spectre of a compromise peace. In the spring of 1942 the British received several approaches from German opposition groups. These peace feelers were regarded by Eden as an attempt to split the allies and were frozen off by the Foreign Office, but rumours about them circulated in several neutral capitals. Beneš, ever sensitive to such a possibility, seems to have picked up the stories. As long as Churchill remained in power he knew that Britain would continue to fight, but he suspected that powerful appeasement forces lurked in the shadows awaiting their opportunity. In the Conservative party there were voices which criticised the government for selling Europe to Bolshevism by pursuing an Anglo-Soviet alliance. The Soviet Ambassador,

Maisky, with whom Beneš was on good terms, may have reinforced his fears. On 15 May, the President sent a message to the home resistance emphasising his concern about a compromise peace, which perhaps represented his real answer to Vanék's appeal. According to Beneš, the Nazis would expend their last strength in the impending summer offensive in Russia. If they managed to advance into the Caucasus, a peace offer could be expected which might shake the allies. With Hácha and Moravec collaborating with the Germans and the Slovak premier, Tiso, also a Nazi tool, Czechoslovakia could easily be sacrificed as part of a peace without victory: 'In this situation, a proof of strength in our own country – rebellion, open action, acts of sabotage and demonstrations – may become desirable or necessary. On the international plane action of this kind would contribute to the preservation of the nation itself, *even if it had to be paid for with a great many sacrifices*' (author's italics). The Czechs in other words must demonstrate their hostility to Nazi rule whatever the cost.

It remained to be seen whether ANTHROPOID would be any more successful than the other parachute groups now that the Germans were on the alert. In the spring of 1942, the Nazi leadership was becoming increasingly preoccupied by the threat to the security of the new order in Europe from resistance movements encouraged and supplied by Britain and the Soviet Union. Goebbels returned to this theme again and again in his diaries, noting incidents of sabotage and subversion in France, Holland, Norway and the occupied east, where Soviet partisan units had formed a second front in the German rear areas. As the Propaganda Minister emphasised, terror and assassination were part of this campaign. On 24 February, a bomb attack was launched on Heydrich's old enemy, von Papen, now the German Ambassador in Turkey. The outrage was traced to the Soviet Consulate in Ankara. As Goebbels complained two days later: 'An attempt was made ... to assassinate von Papen and his wife. The man who threw the bomb was torn to pieces by it whereas Papen and his wife remained unhurt. The origin of this attempt is perfectly clear. It was without doubt prepared by the [British] Secret Service in collaboration with the GPU [the Soviet secret police].' In March the head of one of Heydrich's SS murder squads, Franz Stahlecker of Einsatzgruppe A, was ambushed and killed by Soviet partisans. The same month, the Gestapo in Warsaw picked up a traveller who was behaving suspiciously at the main railway station. He claimed to be a German musician on his way to Prague but a search of his luggage revealed a rifle with telescopic sights and a silencer. Under interrogation the suspect admitted that he had been sent from Moscow to kill Heydrich.

By the time this discovery was made, the security police in the Protectorate were already becoming concerned about the safety of Hitler's representative. Although the Gestapo had no direct evidence of a threat to Heydrich's life before this, Germans were being attacked throughout occupied Europe and equipment captured from Czech parachute groups pointed to a possible terrorist campaign, masterminded by the exiles in London. According to Heinz von Pannwitz, the officer in charge of the anti-sabotage section of the Prague Gestapo: 'It became clear from the material which fell into our hands that apart from intelligence and sabotage missions, the agents were equipped and instructed to carry out terrorist attacks and assassinations. Among other items were explosives designed to attach magnetically to cars and some made of black bakelite in a form suitable for telephone stands. Lifting the handset would detonate about 200 grammes of plastic explosive capable of killing a man. . . . Because the number of drops of material increased markedly in April and May 1942 we suspected more and more the possibility of an assassination and stepped up our defences accordingly.' On 1 May, Himmler came to Prague and inspected the explosives captured from BIOSCOPE and BIVOUAC. As a result of this visit, the guard around Heydrich was strengthened and security was tightened at all public appearances. He was asked to stop travelling without an escort and orders were issued for the installation of armour in the bodywork and seatbacks of his official car as a precaution against bomb attacks: 'Heydrich approved all the general measures but categorically refused a personal escort on the grounds that it would damage German prestige in the Protectorate. A certain arrogant pride and his sporting outlook probably prompted his attitude. He really believed that no Czech would harm him.' According to Heydrich's wife, he could not believe that the Czechs would risk national suicide by killing the Reichsprotektor. While his subordinates remained unhappy about his unescorted car journeys, they could do little but report the matter to Berlin.

Heydrich's fatal conceit was encouraged by his belief that the country was firmly under the control of the SS. The threat of the parachutists had been neutralised and an impressive quantity of equipment captured. As for the population, it could be kept in a state of proper subordination by the old policy of carrot and stick. In May 1942 he mounted a propaganda campaign which utilised the Czech police-men killed or wounded in fights with the parachutists to show that collaboration paid. The families of the dead received a large cash gratuity and inflated pensions. As for the wounded, they were presented by the Reichsprotektor with new pistols and German decorations while savings accounts were opened for their children. Informing was encouraged by generous and well-publicised rewards of up to 10,000 crowns. In a despatch to Bormann, Heydrich boasted that these measures had exercised a positive psychological effect on the Czech gendarmerie and on the population where the incidents occurred. On the other hand, opposition continued to be dealt with severely. Those caught helping the parachutists were executed and Heydrich considered a new round of police terror to remind the Czechs of the consequences of disobedience. The contrast between Bohemia–Moravia and the rest of occupied Europe was noted by his superiors. Goebbels' diaries, which constantly lamented a string of assassinations, sabotage and anti-German outrages from France and Holland to the Ukraine, had only flattering things to say about the model policy pursued by Heydrich. Hitler too remained impressed. In a rambling after-dinner discussion on 20 May, the Führer remarked:

> The right, and indeed for the German Reich the obvious, policy is firstly to purge the country of all dangerous elements, and then to treat the Czechs with friendly consideration. If we pursue a policy of this sort, all the Czechs will follow the lead of President Hácha. In any case . . . the fear of being compelled to evacuate their homes as the result of the transfer of population we are undertaking, will persuade them that it will be in their best interests to emerge as zealous co-operators of the Reich. It is this fear which besets them that explains why the Czechs at the moment – and particularly at the war factories – are working to our complete satisfaction, doing their utmost under the slogan: 'Everything for our Führer, Adolf Hitler!'

While the Führer was exaggerating his achievements, Heydrich could hardly have wished for a more ringing endorsement.

The acting Reichsprotektor had always regarded his task as merely temporary, the springboard to yet greater power. As early as January 1942, it was reported by the neutral press that with the reorganisation of the Protectorate government to reflect Nazi supremacy, Heydrich believed that his task in Prague was at an end. In this respect the deteriorating security situation throughout Europe offered him a golden opportunity to deploy his grisly talents elsewhere and he began to press for a personal meeting with Hitler to discuss the problem in the light of his experiences in Bohemia–Moravia. He was already exploiting the rising tide of European resistance as a weapon against his old rivals in the military establishment. His attention focused on occupied

France, where his security police did not enjoy the kind of murderous freedom they were allowed in Russia. France was governed by the army, and the SS was kept in its place. The result was a covert struggle for power with the military authorities. By the beginning of 1942 the balance had tipped towards Heydrich. The army was on the defensive after its failure before Moscow and the sackings which followed, a situation which he was quick to exploit. Moreover senior Nazis believed that it was mishandling the situation in France. As Goebbels complained on 28 February: 'The epidemic of assassination is spreading alarmingly in French cities. Our Wehrmacht commands are not energetic enough in trying to stop it.' In a conversation with Schellenberg that spring, Heydrich 'touched briefly on the question of France and Belgium. His aim was to increase his own authority by appointing supreme SS and police leaders there, since there was no longer likely to be any opposition from the Wehrmacht. . . .' As the army's star continued to wane, his perseverance was rewarded. At the beginning of May he travelled to Paris to install a new police commander, SS Gruppenführer Karl Oberg, and the military administration lost its competence in security matters. While Heydrich seized the opportunity to sample the delights of night life in the French capital, he also found time for business. At a meeting with the head of the Vichy police, he made it clear that the gendarmerie in the unoccupied zone, like the French police elsewhere, would in future take its orders from the SS. Its command was to be purged and suspect officers replaced by Nazi sympathisers. This move was necessary not only to combat the resistance but as the preliminary to the 'Final Solution' in France, the arrest and deportation of all Jews to the killing centres in the east. In a long discussion with the Military Governor, General Heinrich von Stülpnagel, Heydrich emphasised the new powers of his police commander. As he reported to Bormann on 7 May, the situation offered an opportunity to introduce reforms based on his own experiences in Prague which would be 'full of meaning' for the future of the occupation.

The struggle with the army in France was paralleled by the intensification of the old feud with the Abwehr. In the autumn of 1941 Heydrich demanded extensive concessions from military intelligence, attempting to revise the 'ten commandments' of 1935 in his own favour. He no longer pretended to defer to Canaris or to conceal his ultimate ambition to absorb military intelligence into his own empire. When Canaris stalled, the veneer of friendship which had masked their growing rivalry since 1934 was discarded and for a time Heydrich refused to see his former naval superior. Despite Canaris' delaying tactics, his position was soon eroded by incidents which reflected badly on his organisation. He lost favour with Hitler following the successful British commando raid on a secret radar installation at Bruneval, near Le Havre, on 27 February 1942. Hitler was furious at this enemy coup and demanded to know what progress the British had already made in the field of radar. In a conversation with Himmler he 'complained bitterly about Canaris, who had so far given him no real information on this subject', and implied that the SS could do better. Within days of these events, Paul Thümmel was arrested, adding to the problems which faced the Abwehr. Always a political predator, Heydrich probably timed the move to coincide with Canaris' unpopularity at Führer headquarters. Unable to fight back, the Abwehr chief eventually capitulated. On 18 May he arrived in Prague for an intelligence conference, accompanied by his senior staff. There, in the splendour of the Hradčany castle, he signed a peace treaty conceding Heydrich's demands. Canaris was under no illusion that this was the end of the matter. As he admitted to Schellenberg: 'Though a solution had been found for the moment, he could not rid himself . . . of the feeling that Heydrich would attack again. The agreement offered no more than a breathing space.'

In pursuing his old vendetta against the military establishment, Heydrich did not neglect the new struggle with the party for supremacy in the Nazi empire taking shape behind the Russian front. There the SS had to share power with a series of regional commissioners such as Erich Koch in the Ukraine, who enjoyed the tacit support of Martin Bormann. This system of divide and rule, which could be traced back to Hitler's decisions before BARBAROSSA, produced an 'authoritarian anarchy' as each side jostled for position. According to his wife, Heydrich was concerned about the calibre of the party officials despatched to subdue the Slavs. The 'golden pheasants' of the east were certainly corrupt and inefficient but Heydrich's objections owed more to considerations of power than to morality. The rise of the partisan threat offered the ideal opportunity to improve the position of SS police commanders by preaching the virtues of an integrated approach to the problem of resistance and Heydrich hoped to persuade Hitler to apply the lessons of the Protectorate. No doubt he regarded the Thümmel case as a means of neutralising Bormann. Thümmel, like the regional commissioners in the east, was an old Nazi and Bormann had tried to protect him, something likely to embarrass the Führer's shifty secretary. In what was perhaps the model for a wider campaign, Himmler and Heydrich were already trying to remove Hans Frank, the head of the so-called Government-General of Poland. By the spring of 1942 they had constructed an alternative administration based on the security police, and Heydrich believed that he had accumulated sufficient evidence of Frank's staggering corruption to secure his dismissal. Control of the Government-General, added to the position it had already attained in the Protectorate, would guarantee the SS unprecedented power in east and central Europe and a firm base from which to pursue its intrigues in occupied Russia.

In a message from Paris to Karl Hermann Frank on 7 May, Heydrich speculated that Hitler might soon place him in charge of the occupation there 'to act at the same time as the supervisor of the Vichy government'. This appointment would have given the SS control of a major European power for the first time and would have created a western bastion to match the one it was attempting to carve out in the east. Heydrich's own ambitions, however, were not limited to France. Before his trip to Paris he had been considering the problem of resistance throughout Europe and he returned to this theme in the following weeks. According to Heydrich, he was drafting a series of recommendations for Hitler on the entire question of German administration in the occupied territories based on his own experiences in the Protectorate. It is possible that he hoped to persuade Hitler to make him Reichskommissar for all the occupied regions, with power to co-ordinate or override competing jurisdictions. Added to his responsibilities for the deportation of the European Jews, such an appointment would have made Heydrich a major figure in the shaping of the Nazi new order. Others were clearly suspicious that he contemplated some such move, for his meeting with Hitler was repeatedly postponed. Heydrich blamed the jealousy of Himmler and Bormann, claiming that they resented 'the favours showered on him' and were trying to undermine his position with the Führer by a stream of sly hints and slanders. Of the two he considered Bormann the more dangerous: 'Bormann would react by stimulating intrigues; Himmler was more likely to be just mean and bloody-minded.' Heydrich's triumphs after all were victories for the SS, however much Himmler might suspect the ultimate ambitions of his former protégé.

Although Heydrich was concerned about the situation and considered sending Schellenberg to Führer headquarters to protect his interests, he remained 'convinced of his own powers' and confident that he was destined for higher office. His success in Prague was an important step towards the objective of becoming 'the foremost man in

the German Reich'. He symbolised his rising status by an act of
homage to his father, the suspected Jew who was never quite accepted
by polite society in the old Germany. On the evening of 26 May, he
inaugurated the Prague Music Festival with a concert of Bruno's
chamber works, played by a quartet of former pupils of the Halle
conservatory. Heydrich himself wrote the programme notes. According to his wife, the occasion represented the fulfilment of an old dream.
Spurned by the musical establishment of Prussia, his father's talent
was finally recognised by his son, a leading member of the new Nazi
aristocracy. As he strode into the German concert hall that night,
resplendent in his SS uniform and surrounded by obsequious aides,
Heydrich had every reason for satisfaction. He was flying to Berlin the
next day to meet Hitler, who was leaving his field headquarters to
address a parade of officer cadets in the capital on 29 May. It was
rumoured that Heydrich would not be returning to Prague. It is unclear
what new position he hoped to secure from the Führer. Heydrich
intended to visit France and Belgium in the following weeks, a journey
concerned with the implementation of the 'Final Solution' in the west.
Whether he sought to head the occupation there is less certain and it is
probable that he had wider ambitions. When he filled his briefcase for
the encounter with Hitler, Heydrich had been working on his recommendations for a co-ordinated approach to the creation of the Nazi
new order for at least a month. There can be little doubt that he saw
himself as the man to implement the necessary reforms. His meeting
with the Führer, however, was destined never to take place.

While Heydrich was packing his files, Gabčík and Kubiš were
making their own preparations. They had learned about his travel plans
from the clockmaker Josef Novotny, who also passed on the rumour
that Heydrich might not be returning to the Protectorate. The news
increased the pressure on the parachutists to act – to achieve something after the humiliating failures of recent weeks. Hitler's viceroy
could not be allowed to leave Prague in triumph. He must be killed on
27 May, the one day on which, thanks to Novotny, his movements
were known. The problem was finding a site for the ambush. Since
Himmler's visit, Heydrich was well guarded. The military activity at
Panenské Břežany was detected by the ANTHROPOID team and the plan
to carry out the assassination near the estate was abandoned. The risks
were now too great and the chances of escape non-existent. An
alternative site was hastily selected in the Prague suburb of Holešovice,
where there was a crossroads with a sharp bend on a hill leading down
to the Traja bridge. Heydrich's Mercedes had to slow down there on its

way into the city, offering an ideal target. At this point he would be at his most vulnerable, cut off from the SS garrisons at the estate and the Hradčany castle. There were no police stations or barracks in the vicinity and the assassins could escape quickly on bicycles and reach safe houses before the Nazis had time to react. They already knew when Heydrich normally left home and could work out his approximate time of arrival at the bend. The tram-stops near the corner would allow them to wait without arousing suspicion, lost amongst the morning commuters. The plan was probably drawn up by Gabčík, who allocated himself the leading role. Valčik was to stand beyond the bend and signal with a mirror when the car came into sight at the top of the hill. Gabčík was to carry out the actual killing with his sten gun. Kubiš was to hold his bombs in reserve and snatch Heydrich's briefcase after the assassination. It was a crude and desperate scheme but it had the virtue of simplicity. Everything depended on Heydrich sticking to his schedule.

The plan, however, was not adopted without a further argument about the wisdom of the killing. Despite the failure of Vaněk's appeal to London, the opponents of the assassination continued to press for the cancellation of ANTHROPOID. On 26 May, apparently on the initiative of Lieutenant Opálka of OUT DISTANCE, a meeting was held at the flat of a Prague schoolteacher, Josef Orgoun, who was sheltering the assassins. Opálka reiterated the arguments against the operation and appealed to Gabčík and Kubiš to reconsider their position. With Bartoš immobilised by rheumatoid arthritis in Pardubice, he was the senior officer amongst the parachutists but his rank counted for nothing. Gabčík would brook no delay and dismissed Opálka's arguments. Despite Vaněk's request to London, his orders had not been changed and as a soldier he must carry them out. He would not miss the best and perhaps only opportunity of hitting his target. Gabčík was supported by Zelenka and the discussion ended on a sour note. The assassination would take place as planned on 27 May. There is little doubt that Opálka spoke both for Bartoš and for many in the JINDRA organisation when he made his last-minute intervention. It says much for Gabčík's training and strength of will that he never once wavered, despite the moral pressure exerted on him over a period of weeks. This probably owed something to the fact that he had met Beneš in December 1941 and knew that the operation was approved at the highest level. As a mere NCO, it was not his place to question orders from the President of the republic and friend of the great Tomáš Masaryk. After the argument with Opálka, the agents were tense and jumpy. Gabčík disappeared for a while into the streets of Prague, probably to pick up his equipment, leaving Kubiš alone in the flat. That evening, while Heydrich was relaxing at the German concert hall, they made their final preparations. Gabčík checked his sten and Kubiš assembled his bombs, fusing them to explode on impact. The following morning, almost five months after their arrival, they would carry out their mission.

9

Assassination

The morning of 27 May dawned bright and clear, the beginning of a perfect spring day. Gabčík and Kubiš left the Orgouns' flat earlier than usual, giving their hosts no hint of what was to come. Both men carried battered briefcases. Inside, concealed under layers of grass, were the sten gun, broken down into three pieces, and two fused bombs. The grass was intended to camouflage the weapons from a casual police check. Since the food shortages of 1941, many Czechs had started to breed rabbits and it was not unusual for citizens to collect food for their animals in the local parks. They wore caps to conceal the colour of their hair and, despite the fine weather, Gabčík carried a light-coloured raincoat borrowed from a neighbour. The coat was necessary to hide his hands while he was assembling and holding the sten gun. Josef Orgoun later recalled that the men seemed calm and cheerful. As he reached the door, Gabčík turned and remarked: 'Don't worry if we are not back as usual: we have a great many friends and maybe we shall stay with them.' The assassins caught a tram to the suburb of Žižkov, where they collected their bicycles and strapped the briefcases to the handlebars. Gabčík's machine, an old-fashioned woman's model borrowed from Mrs Moravec, was soon to be at the centre of a Gestapo investigation. Just before nine o'clock, they reached Holešovice, dismounted and parked the bicycles against two lamp standards. Valčik was already at the rendezvous and there was a brief discussion between the three men. Valčik went off up the hill, posting himself on the right-hand side of the road, his mirror ready in his pocket. Gabčík knelt down, opened his briefcase and put the sten together under cover of his coat. He did not have to see what he was doing. Assembling guns blindfold was a standard part of weapons training, a drill he had taught many times to the soldiers of the Czech Brigade. With the coat draped casually over his arm, he crossed the street and stood beneath a small grassy knoll near a tram-stop, waiting for Valčik's signal. Kubiš remained on the left-hand side of the road, some yards from the corner, concealed by a lamp post and the shade of several large overhanging trees. The ambush prepared, the assassins waited for their target to appear.

At Panenské Břežany, Heydrich finished breakfast just before nine and his driver, Oberscharführer Klein, brought the official car, an open Mercedes tourer, to the castle door. The normally punctual Heydrich, however, delayed his departure this fine spring morning, strolling with his wife in the castle gardens and playing with his two sons, Klaus and Heider, and his small daughter, Silke. They made a perfect Nazi family group. Heydrich in his SS uniform, his sons in Hitler Youth shirts, his daughter in riding dress and his wife, fair hair plaited severely on top of her head, heavily pregnant with their fourth child. It was almost ten o'clock before his car left the estate, passing the saluting sentries at the gates and turning into the road to Prague. Heydrich sat in the front beside the chauffeur. As usual there was no escort. In the event of an attack, Heydrich and Klein would have to defend themselves with their own weapons, 7.65 mm automatic pistols. Despite the orders issued at the beginning of May for the insertion of armour plate in the bodywork and seatbacks of the Mercedes, nothing had been done, perhaps because Heydrich was soon expected to leave the Protectorate for good. It was an oversight which was to prove fatal.

As the minutes ticked by and Heydrich failed to arrive at the corner in Holešovice, the rush-hour crowds began to clear. Gabčík and Kubiš were left loitering in an empty street, a possible object of suspicion for any passing policeman. Trams came and went, grinding up and down the hill, but there was no sign of the Mercedes with its SS flag. As ten o'clock passed the tension became almost unbearable. Both men knew that this might be their last chance of killing Heydrich. If he had changed his route or altered his plans, ANTHROPOID would end in failure. Kubiš crossed the road for a quick consultation with his companion but was waved back into cover. The waiting continued. Suddenly, at 10.32, Valčik's mirror warned the assassins that their target had come into sight at the top of the hill. Gabčík released the safety catch on his sten and ran to the opposite pavement, positioning himself at the sharpest angle of the bend. Kubiš opened his briefcase and pulled out a bomb. Simultaneously a tram began to climb the slope from the Traja bridge. Although it was likely to be caught in the gunfire, it was too late to abandon the operation. The assassination team had already discussed the possibility of civilian casualties and had agreed that the risk would have to be taken.

As Heydrich's car slowed down and rounded the corner, Gabčík dropped the raincoat, raised his gun and, at point-blank range, pulled the trigger. Nothing happened. The sten failed to fire, either because it had been badly assembled or more likely because there was grass jammed in the mechanism. Gabčík was left standing helplessly at the kerb as the Mercedes swept past. Heydrich then made a fatal error. Instead of ordering Klein to accelerate out of the ambush, he stood up and drew his pistol, yelling at the driver to stop. Neither he nor Klein had spotted Kubiš and believed that they were dealing with a lone assassin. As the car braked in front of him, Kubiš stepped out of the shadows and tossed a bomb at the two figures in the front seats. He misjudged his throw. Instead of landing inside the Mercedes, it exploded against the rear wheel, throwing shrapnel back into Kubiš' face and shattering the windows of the tram which had stopped on the opposite side of the road. There were screams as the passengers were hit by shards of flying glass and metal. The car lurched violently and came to rest in the gutter, pouring smoke. Two SS jackets which had been folded on the back seat were whirled upwards by the blast and draped themselves over the trolley wire.

As the noise of the explosion died away, Heydrich and Klein leaped from the wrecked car with drawn pistols, prepared to fight it out with their attackers. While Klein ran towards Kubiš, who had staggered against the railings half-blinded by blood, Heydrich turned uphill to where Gabčík stood paralysed, holding the sten. As Klein came towards him, Kubiš recovered and, grabbing his bicycle, forced his way through the crowd of shocked passengers spilling from the tram, scattering them by firing in the air with his Colt pistol. Klein tried to bring him down with his automatic but, dazed by the explosion, he pressed the magazine release catch and the gun jammed. Kubiš pedalled furiously downhill, outpacing his pursuer. Within minutes of the bomb explosion, he had reached a safe house in the suburbs of Žižkov. There his bloodstained bicycle was hidden and he was given the uniform of a railway worker. Then, mingling with the lunch-time crowds, he made his way to another safe house where his shrapnel wounds were treated by a doctor. He escaped, believing that the assassination had failed. His last sight of Heydrich was of the German jumping from the shattered car to pursue his companion.

Gabčík found escape less easy. As Heydrich came towards him through the dust from the explosion, lurching and weaving like a drunken man, Gabčík dropped his sten and tried to reach his bicycle. He was forced to abandon this attempt, however, and took cover behind a telegraph pole, exchanging shots with Heydrich who ducked behind the stalled tram. The situation grew more dangerous with every passing second. The longer Heydrich kept Gabčík pinned down, the greater the chance that the agent would be killed or captured when the police arrived at the scene. Suddenly Heydrich doubled over and staggered to the side of the road, obviously wounded and in pain. Unknown to Kubiš, the bomb had severely injured the German, breaking a rib and driving fragments of horsehair and wire from the upholstery of the car upwards into his spleen. As Heydrich collapsed against the railings, holding himself up with one hand, Gabčík seized his opportunity and began to run uphill to his right. But he was not yet out of danger. As he sprinted away from the scene of the ambush, Klein returned from his unsuccessful pursuit of Kubiš to help his wounded superior. Heydrich, his face white with pain, gestured with his free hand and gasped: 'Get that bastard.' As Klein ran after the fleeing assassin, Heydrich staggered along the pavement and fell against the bonnet of the wrecked car. His painful progress was watched by the crowd of tram passengers. Nobody stepped forward to help the crippled figure in the torn SS uniform.

At the top of the hill, Gabčík turned down a side street and hid in a butcher's shop. He could not have made a worse choice. The owner, a man named Brauer, was a Nazi sympathiser and had a brother who worked for the Gestapo. Ignoring Gabčík's request for help, he ran out into the roadway, attracting Klein's attention by shouting and pointing. His automatic still jammed and useless, the SS man rushed into the shop, perhaps believing that his opponent was escaping by a rear entrance. In fact Gabčík had discovered there was only one way out and doubled back, colliding with his pursuer in the doorway. In the confusion, he shot Klein through the legs and the SS man fell forward, dropping his gun. Gabčík leaped over the sprawling figure, firing as he went, and reached the safety of the street. In a desperate attempt to prevent his escape, Klein ordered the butcher to take his gun and pursue his fleeing assailant. Hardly surprisingly, the shopkeeper showed no enthusiasm for this task, taking a few hesitant steps down the road before abandoning the enterprise. Gabčík disappeared into the side streets. Shortly afterwards he arrived at a safe house where he rinsed his hair with camomile to change its colour. He was limping as a result of a fall during his escape from Klein and was bitterly disappointed about the failure of his sten gun.

At the scene of the attack, the crowd began to recover from the shock of the explosion. A young blonde woman recognised Heydrich and took charge, shouting for a car to take him to the hospital. One of the tram passengers, an off-duty Czech policeman, halted a passing baker's van. The driver was reluctant to become involved in the affair and an argument ensued while Heydrich remained slumped against his car, an ominous dark stain spreading across his uniform. A second vehicle was stopped and commandeered, a small truck carrying a load of floor polish. With the help of the policeman, Heydrich was squeezed into the tiny cab and the truck set off down the hill, jolting heavily on the tram lines. The vibration was too much for Heydrich and he asked the driver to stop. He was transferred into the back where he sprawled on his stomach amongst the crates of wax and floor polish, one hand across his face, the other pressed against his wound. In this way the most powerful man in Czechoslovakia arrived at the Bulkova hospital. It was just after eleven o'clock.

Heydrich was immediately taken to the emergency room where his wounds were cleaned by a young Czech doctor, Vladimir Snajdr. He was conscious and had regained his icy self-control. As Snajdr later recalled: 'I took forceps and a few swabs and tried to see whether the wound was deep. . . . he did not flinch although it must have hurt him.' The German Director of the hospital, one Doctor Dick, was summoned to the scene and made a more detailed examination. The prognosis seemed good. The shrapnel had missed the spine and kidneys and appeared to have inflicted only flesh wounds. He insisted, however, on an X-ray. This revealed a more serious situation. Heydrich had a broken rib, a ruptured diaphragm and splinters from either the bomb or the car in his spleen. They were injuries which could have been avoided by the installation of armour plate in the seatbacks of the Mercedes. Dick recommended an immediate operation. Heydrich did not want to entrust his life to a provincial German doctor and demanded a surgeon from Berlin. After some argument, a compromise was reached. Heydrich agreed to surgery but only if the top Nazi consultant in Prague, Professor Hollbaum of the German Clinic, was called in. Shortly after midday, he was wheeled into the operating theatre.

The Gestapo was informed about the attack by the Czech police around 10.45. The Czech liaison officer, Inspector Zenaty, gave no details and merely passed on a rumour that a high-ranking German had been injured in an assassination attempt. According to Heinz Pannwitz, who took charge of the case: 'Similar announcements of attacks on German troops were not uncommon and were often false alarms. The Gestapo therefore was not inclined to take the message seriously and waited for more information.' It was some time before Pannwitz, accompanied by two colleagues, decided to drive to the police station which had reported the attack. There they were informed that an injured general, perhaps the Reichsprotektor himself, had been taken to the Bulkova clinic. At the hospital, nobody appeared to know anything about a wounded German and Pannwitz was forced to make a personal search of the surgical department. There he found Heydrich sitting shirtless on an operating table with two nurses applying ice-packs to his forehead. Pannwitz was appalled by the sight of Heydrich alone and unprotected. Leaving his two colleagues in charge, he telephoned headquarters from Dick's office, demanding the immediate despatch of an SS squad to surround the hospital. He had difficulty persuading his colleagues that it was not all a joke, but eventually they grasped the gravity of the situation. Karl Hermann Frank was informed and rushed to the hospital, followed shortly afterwards by Hácha and the Protectorate government. SS troops cleared all patients from the surgical department and whitewashed the windows as a precaution against snipers. Machine-guns were mounted on the roof and guards posted at the hospital entrances. Signallers installed a direct telephone link with Führer headquarters. At the scene of the ambush, Pannwitz took charge, cordoning off the area, rounding up witnesses and making a preliminary survey of the evidence. This comprised a woman's bicycle, two briefcases, one of which contained a fused bomb, a man's cap, a light-coloured mackintosh, a sten gun and some empty cartridge cases. Pannwitz was convinced straightaway that the assassins were parachutists. The unused bomb contained British plastic explosive, British fuses and British detonators: 'Because the sub-machine-gun was also British, there was no doubt as to where the assassination had been organised.'

Shortly after midday, Hitler was informed about the attack at his headquarters in East Prussia. At 12.30 he telephoned the hospital and spoke to Frank, placing him in charge until Heydrich recovered. According to Frank's notes, Hitler asked if Heydrich had been travelling without an escort and 'sharply condemned' the practice. Frank was forbidden to take similar risks and was informed that he was being sent an armoured limousine from Berlin to protect him against bomb attacks. A reward of one million marks was to be offered for the arrest of the assassins. Anyone caught helping them was to be shot along with his entire family. As a reprisal, 10,000 Czechs were to be arrested. All prisoners already in custody for political offences were to be executed immediately. Frank baulked at the arrests, although for reasons of expediency rather than morality. A resort to reprisals on this scale would repudiate Heydrich's approach and play into the hands of the exiles. Production would be disrupted and the Czechs, feeling that they had nothing to lose, would be pushed towards revolution. He did not dare to argue directly with Hitler but asked if he could fly to Führer headquarters the following day for further discussions, a request which was granted. At 3 p.m. Frank discussed the situation with the heads of his security police. They shared his lack of enthusiasm for reprisals on such a scale. Pannwitz argued that the evidence found at the scene of the crime pointed towards parachutists rather than the Czech resistance. Hitler's order would simply play into the hands of the exile government and its great power allies. According to Pannwitz, Frank left the meeting to telephone Hitler and present him with the evidence of British involvement.

Hitler, however, remained in a bloodthirsty mood. That afternoon, at an interview with Himmler, he raged against the Czechs. If they did not like Heydrich, he would send them someone worse, a man who would not be afraid to wade through blood. Clearly believing that Frank did not have the stomach for the task, he suggested Erich von dem Bach-Zelewski, an SS anti-partisan leader on the eastern front. When Himmler argued that this officer could not be spared because of the military situation, General Kurt Daluege, the commander of ORPO, the uniformed police, was appointed interim Reichsprotektor instead. There seems to have been little logic behind this decision beyond the fact that Daluege was a senior SS officer and was already on the spot in Prague, where he had arrived that morning apparently for medical treatment. He was a former rival of Heydrich's in the early struggle for power and notorious within the SS for his stupidity. Heydrich always referred to him contemptuously by his nickname, 'Dummi-Dummi', or 'the idiot'. Once again Frank's ambition had been thwarted. He had been left in undisputed control of the Protectorate for only a few hours.

After his conversation with Hitler, Himmler returned to his special train in a nearby siding. He had been profoundly moved by the attack on Heydrich, his perfect SS man, and had burst into tears when he first heard the news. Now he backed the Führer's demands for vengeance. At 9.05 p.m. he sent Frank a teleprinter message, backing up Hitler's reprisal order: 'Among the ... ten thousand hostages arrest ... all Czech intelligentsia in opposition. Out of the main body of this intelligentsia, shoot this very night one hundred of the most important.' At the same time Professor Gebhart, Himmler's personal physician and the Surgeon-General of the SS, was rushed to Heydrich's bedside with instructions to report regularly on the condition of 'our good Reinhard'. In Berlin, Goebbels shared Himmler's horror. On 27 May, he noted in his diary: 'Alarming news. . . . There has been a bomb attack on Heydrich in a Prague suburb.' The 'most brutal methods' would be required to deal with the situation. Goebbels believed that the loss of Heydrich at this juncture would be 'irreparable' and vented his anger on the nearest convenient victims, the Jews. As he remarked on 29 May: 'I shall . . . arrest . . . 500 Berlin Jews, and I will warn the leaders of the Jewish community that, for every Jewish plot and every Jewish attempt at rebellion, 100 to 150 Jews who are in our hands will be shot.' In the first few days after the attack, several hundred Jews were murdered at Sachsenhausen concentration camp, an act which met with Goebbels' entire approval: 'The more of this filth that is eliminated, the better for the security of the Reich.'

The savagery of the Nazi leaders was fuelled by fear. The wave of assassinations in occupied Europe had reached their own ranks for the first time, threatening the inner circle of power. As Goebbels remarked on 31 May: 'The Führer's assessment of the political situation is practically identical to mine. He foresees the possibility of a rise in assassination attempts if we do not proceed with energetic and ruthless measures. . . .' According to the Gestapo, the attack was part of a campaign fomented by British and Soviet intelligence in league with international Jewry. The ultimate target was Hitler himself, the 'guarantor of German victory'. If the Nazi leaders were shaken by the attack, their subordinates in Prague were thrown into complete disarray. Nothing was done to prevent the escape of the assassins until late afternoon, when Frank issued an ordinance proclaiming a state of emergency and a curfew. Road and rail traffic out of the city was halted and a reward of 10,000,000 Czech crowns (one million marks) was offered for the arrest of the criminals. Anyone who helped or hid them was to be executed along with his entire family. Later that evening, martial law was proclaimed throughout the Protectorate. These actions concealed a large measure of continuing confusion. Kopow and Wehner, two senior detectives despatched from Berlin, found 'chaos of catastrophic proportions' in Prague. Gestapo headquarters was 'like an anthill. Unimaginable numbers of SS men and SS officers swarmed around each other . . . mingling with senior officers of the police and armed services. . . . Those of the highest rank . . . were crowding round the maps on a large table. They threw whole regiments and contingents of a hundred here and there, discussed court martial orders, new prohibition orders, executions.' The sudden appointment of Daluege did nothing to improve the situation. While Frank accepted Pannwitz's argument that the ambush was the work of parachutists, Daluege feared it was the signal for a general uprising against Nazi rule. His first action was to call in police reinforcements from neighbouring provinces of the Reich, which began to arrive in the Protectorate early on 28 May. In public announcements he emphasised that as a senior SS officer he knew how to deal with revolution and would stop at nothing to maintain the security of the state. On one thing, however, both Frank and Daluege agreed. Whoever had attacked Heydrich, the Czechs must be shown that the master race remained firmly in control. The result was to subordinate police procedures to a show of force, an approach which continued to hamper the proper investigation of the attack in the following weeks.

The curfew took effect at 9 p.m. on 27 May. As the Czechs huddled behind closed doors, a massive search operation began, using German and Czech police assisted by Waffen SS troops and three battalions of regular soldiers. Approximately 21,000 men were involved in checking over 36,000 houses. The Germans were vengeful and trigger-happy. According to one escaped British officer who saw them in action, the SS in particular completely lost their heads and acted like madmen. His account was supported by Kopow and Wehner, who recalled that the Germans were in full battle order and acted as if they expected to come under fire at any second. It was risky to venture out into the street and there was much random shooting at open or lighted windows. The two detectives required a military escort to reach their hotel in safety. As Kopow sourly remarked: 'They are completely mad. They won't be able to find their way out of all the chaos they're creating today, let alone find the assassins.' The sweep netted 541 people who lacked proper papers or could not account for themselves, 430 of whom were later released. The only real prize was Jan Zika, a member of the central committee of the Czech communist party. Of the assassins, the searchers found no sign.

On 28 May, Frank flew to Führer headquarters where he argued in favour of selective terror rather than mass reprisals against the Czechs. According to Frank, the evidence indicated that Heydrich's attackers were parachutists. The arrest of 10,000 hostages would merely disrupt production and play into the hands of Beneš by turning 50,000 to 100,000 of their friends and relatives into active enemies of Germany.

As an alternative he recommended the mobilisation of the Protectorate regime in a propaganda campaign against the exiles and their backers in London and Moscow. Hácha and his ministers were already so terrified they would do anything to placate the Reich. If the criminals were not caught or further disturbances occurred, sharper measures could be taken including the abolition of autonomy and mass executions. While Hitler agreed with these proposals, events were to show that he had not abandoned his desire for a bloody revenge. Frank's recommendations, which reflected an approach previously perfected by Heydrich, were quickly implemented. Hácha and his ministers were easily enlisted in a campaign which called upon the population to condemn the attack and surrender the assassins. Petitions, demonstrations and shop-floor meetings were organised throughout Bohemia–Moravia. On 30 May, Hácha offered 10,000,000 crowns for the capture of Heydrich's attackers, thus doubling the reward, and described Beneš as the number-one enemy of the nation for the misery he threatened to bring upon the Czech people. The following day, the Propaganda Minister, Emanuel Moravec, made a broadcast warning his listeners that the Germans expected deeds and not words. The Czechs must prove their loyalty or face the consequences. The nation must not be destroyed for the sake of Beneš' mercenary gang and its British paymasters. These warnings were reinforced by whispered rumours, deliberately planted by the Gestapo, of the dreadful fate awaiting the Czechs if the criminals were not found.

Propaganda and psychological warfare were backed by a show of force and well-publicised executions. Throughout the Protectorate blocks of flats, suburbs and villages were randomly cordoned off and searched. Everyone over fifteen was ordered to register with the police by 30 May. Those who failed to do so were shot along with anyone found guilty of harbouring them. The evidence discovered at the scene of the crime was displayed in the window of the Bata shoe store in central Prague and photographs were sent to every household in Bohemia–Moravia together with a description of the wanted men. The population was warned that anyone who recognised the criminals or their possessions and failed to report to the police would be executed along with their entire family. Since one of the assassins had been wounded by the bomb explosion, all 7000 doctors in the protectorate had to swear in writing that they had not treated an injured man fitting the description of the suspects. A wave of executions reinforced Nazi threats. The victims included those convicted of martial-law offences or who had merely expressed approval of the attack. The first family groups fell to Nazi firing squads on 31 May. By 4 June, 157 people had died. According to a US intelligence report: 'Victims were chosen from every class of the community; and the Germans do not seem to have had any clearer intention than the satisfaction of their rage. . . . Nevertheless this slaughter was not entirely indiscriminate and occasion was taken to decimate those classes where resistance was felt to be most deeply rooted.' This approach, pursued throughout the summer, followed Heydrich's earlier example and swallowed up the most prominent figure arrested during the terror of October 1941, General Eliáš, who was finally executed on 19 June. The massive manhunt extended into the Reich itself, where the police reserves were called out, along with party organisations like the Hitler Youth and the German Labour Front. Road and rail travellers faced stringent identity checks and the lodgings of foreign workers were repeatedly searched, as were barns and haystacks in the German countryside. A week after the ambush, however, all this activity had failed to produce a single worthwhile lead on the whereabouts of Heydrich's assailants. In Berlin, rumours began to circulate that Heydrich's attackers had not been Czechs at all, and that the ambush had been the product of a murderous Nazi feud.

Gabčík and Kubiš at first sought refuge in the network of safe houses maintained by the JINDRA group throughout Prague. In the discussions which preceded the ambush, little attention had been paid to what might happen afterwards and there was no escape plan. The massive German police search on the night of the ambush took everyone by surprise. It is unclear how the two assassins avoided arrest but two other parachutists had narrow escapes. Opálka had to hide in a wall cupboard which was hastily concealed behind a sofa. Čurda spent an agonising few minutes hanging from a bathroom window over an air shaft. With random searches continuing over the next few days, there were clearly no longer any safe houses in Prague. The presence of the parachutists endangered the JINDRA organisation and the families who concealed them. On the other hand, an attempt to leave the city was equally dangerous, with strict controls on all road and rail transport. It was Zelenka who found the answer. Through his contacts, he arranged to hide all the parachutists in the catacombs of the Karel Boromejsky church, a Greek Orthodox foundation near the centre of Prague. The church had a long association with Czech nationalists, catering specifically for the families of Czech legionaries who had married in Russia during the First World War. The lay preacher, Vladimir Petrek, agreed to shelter the parachutists and won the approval of his bishop, Gorazd.

The church officials were sworn to secrecy before the altar and Zelenka began to smuggle the agents into the crypt in ones and twos. The last to arrive was Gabčík, probably on 1 June. Only Čurda could not be found. In the wake of the great police operation of 27 May, he fled to his home in southern Bohemia, somehow evading the German road blocks, where he hid in his mother's barn. His seven comrades settled into their new refuge, hoping to leave Prague when the heat died down. Along with the ANTHROPOID team were Valčik of SILVER A, Opálka of OUT DISTANCE, Švarc of TIN and the two surviving members of BIOSCOPE, Bublik and Hrubý. The catacombs were a dank and depressing place, made worse for the assassins by their belief that they had failed. Heydrich was not dead and the Czech people were paying a dreadful price for nothing. Gabčík in particular was in a frenzy of frustration, blaming himself for the jammed sten gun.

The exiles first learned of the attack on Heydrich through Prague radio on the afternoon of 27 May. Colonel Moravec recalled that the news was greeted with relief: 'so that was it. Gabčík and Kubiš had done it. Apparently they had fulfilled their mission according to plan and were neither killed nor captured on the spot.' Beneš thanked Colonel Moravec personally for his part in planning the operation, shaking him repeatedly by the hand. As a result of the stringent Nazi security measures, the exiles lost all contact with the parachutists in Prague but the radio link with SILVER A in Pardubice remained. On 3 June Beneš sent Bartoš a congratulatory message, endorsing the assassination attempt: 'From the President. I am delighted that you are maintaining contact and I thank you sincerely. I can see that you and your friends are absolutely determined. It is proof to me that the whole nation is solidly together. I can assure you that it will bring success. The events over there have a great effect here and attract recognition for the resistance of the Czech people.' From the beginning Beneš exploited the dramatic impact of the affair to improve the Czech position in the allied camp. In direct contradiction of the Protectorate regime in Prague, he made no mention of parachutists, describing the incident as the work of the home resistance. On 29 May the Czech government issued a statement which hailed the attack on 'the monster Heydrich' as simultaneously an act of revenge, a rejection of Nazi rule and a symbol to all the oppressed peoples of Europe. The shots of retribution fired by Czech patriots were a sign of solidarity with the allies and faith in ultimate victory which would echo around the world: 'New Czech victims are already falling in the German execution yards. But this new fury of the Nazis will again be broken by the unyielding resistance of the Czech people and will only strengthen its will and perseverance.' The exiles urged the population to hide the 'unknown heroes' and threatened 'just punishment' on anyone who betrayed them. From Moscow, the Czech communist leader, Klement Gottwald, took a similar line in a broadcast on 6 June: 'Our first word goes to those as yet unknown heroes who felled that bloody torturer, Reinhard Heydrich, thereby freeing mankind of one of the worst of Hitler's monsters and glorifying the name of Czechoslovakia throughout the whole world.'

While the propaganda battle raged on and the greatest manhunt in the history of the Third Reich was unleashed against his attackers, Heydrich hovered between life and death in the Bulkova hospital under strict SS guard. No Czech was allowed near him and a clutch of senior consultants clustered around his bed. Himmler phoned almost hourly for reports on his progress. Gebhart, who was in charge of the case, was at first optimistic and believed that Dick and Hollbaum had done a good job. Within days of the operation, however, Heydrich's condition deteriorated. He developed peritonitis, rapidly followed by septicaemia. His temperature soared and he was in great pain, requiring ever larger doses of morphine and repeated blood transfusions. Gebhart refused to operate to remove the infected spleen, relying instead on an early version of sulphanomide to control the poisoning. This was neither as strong nor as effective as penicillin, a drug which the Nazis did not possess, and Heydrich's condition remained acute. On 2 June, a worried Himmler flew to Prague to speak with his protégé for the last time. During their conversation, which centred on the theme of fate and death, Heydrich quoted some lines from his father's fourth opera, *Amen*: 'The world is just a barrel-organ which the Lord God turns Himself. We all have to dance to the tune which is already on the drum.' In one sense this piece of sentimental doggerel, which reflected all his father's faults as a composer, was a fitting epitaph for a life which ultimately lacked either morality or meaning. In death, Heydrich was unable to invoke any great cause or idea. The man who had held power over millions was forced to descend at the last to the level of the trivial and the second-rate. He was as devoid of a coherent intellectual or moral centre as the movement which had shaped him. In another sense, the words reflected a staggering evasion of personal responsibility. For Heydrich, who had murdered thousands in the pursuit of total power, to appeal to fate or predestination was hypocrisy on the grand scale.

Soon after his final meeting with Himmler he began to slip into a coma. At 4.30 a.m. on 4 June, while Daluege and Frank hovered anxiously outside the door, Heydrich breathed his last. According to his doctors: 'Death occurred as a consequence of lesions in the vital parenchymatous organs caused by bacteria and possibly by poisons carried into them by the bomb splinters and deposited chiefly in the pleura, the diaphragm and the tissues in the neighbourhood of the spleen, there agglomerating and multiplying.' The hospital death register was briefer. Beside the name Reinhard Tristan Heydrich an anonymous clerk noted as the cause of death: 'Wound infection'. Hitler reacted angrily to the news, although his anger was directed in the first place against Heydrich himself. As he complained on 4 June: 'Since it is the opportunity which makes not only the thief but also the assassin, such heroic gestures as driving in an open, unarmoured vehicle or walking about the streets unguarded are just damned stupidity, which serves the country not one whit. That a man as irreplaceable as Heydrich should expose himself to unnecessary danger, I can only condemn as stupid and idiotic. Men of importance like Heydrich should know that they are being eternally stalked like game, and that there are any number of people just waiting for the chance to kill them.' Himmler was similarly critical. As he informed a group of high-ranking SS officers on 9 June: 'If, as was the case with Obergruppenführer Heydrich, you are in the habit of leaving your homes every day, at a particular time and taking a particular route, then you are a sitting target for the lunatic who is lying in wait for you. . . . We cannot leave everything to the Good Lord and make him our personal security guard.' According to Himmler, stupidity was always punished. In future all senior SS officers were to travel with an escort. Hitler gave a similar order covering the entire Nazi leadership.

In public, however, Heydrich was presented as the greatest martyr since Horst Wessel, a model Nazi who had fallen fighting for the fatherland. On the evening of 5 June, his body was brought from the hospital to the Hradčany castle where it lay in state for two days surrounded by blazing funeral urns and guarded by senior officers of the police, SS and Wehrmacht. Above the coffin hung a gigantic SS flag, its silver runes sparkling in the torchlight. It was the kind of barbaric display at which the Nazis excelled. On 7 June, in the presence of Himmler and the Protectorate government, Daluege delivered a funeral address composed in equal measure of hypocrisy and sickly sentimentality, hailing Heydrich as a friend of the Czechs, a noble Aryan whose name would be carved forever in the SS hall of fame. As one British official remarked, Daluege's speech was 'a typical example of Nazi bad taste . . . which has a comical and even a bizarre character in the mouth of one of the most notorious scoundrels on the face of the earth'. What his Nazi listeners thought is not recorded, although the mutual contempt and hatred between Daluege and his dear fallen comrade were well known throughout the SS. The speech over, Heydrich's coffin was loaded on to a gun carriage and conveyed solemnly through the hushed streets to the station. For the Czechs, the whole affair was a grim parody of the funeral of Tomáš Masaryk, the father of the republic, eight years before. Throughout the Protectorate, the population awaited the inevitable Nazi reprisals. According to an SD report of 4 June: 'The basis of the Czech mood was an unpleasant anxiety about pending events which were the subject of numerous rumours. These chiefly dealt with a future wave of executions based on decimation, the execution of Czechs in detention and finally the dissolution of the Protectorate.' In a display of loyalty designed to avert such an outcome, Hácha and his ministers accompanied the coffin to Berlin and were present at the state funeral on 9 June along with the leading dignitaries of the Third Reich.

The funeral address was delivered by Himmler, who arrived at the ceremony accompanied by Heydrich's two small sons. The widow, who was expecting her fourth child at any time, remained at Panenské Břežany. Himmler's speech was a carefully edited version of Heydrich's life which slid over the circumstances of his dismissal from the navy and presented him as a convinced disciple of national socialist ideas. In contrast to his private criticism of Heydrich's recklessness, Himmler chose to emphasise his conduct in Prague as evidence of manliness and bravery. Precautions were foreign to a figure who was one of the best sportsmen in the SS, a daring rider, fencer, swimmer and pentathlete. It was typical of his spirit that, although severely wounded, he had pursued and fired at the paid hirelings of the British who had thrown the bomb at his car. Heydrich's name would live in the SS forever as an example of duty to Führer and fatherland. Himmler was clearly upset by the death of his protégé and, like Goebbels, considered him irreplaceable, a view shared by Hitler, despite his earlier remarks about Heydrich's stupidity. The Führer himself was too overcome to say more than a few words at the ceremony but he recognised Heydrich's contribution to the Nazi cause by awarding him 'the greatest honour which I can bestow', the highest class of the German order. It was the second and last such decoration to be bestowed during the entire war.

After the ceremony, the Protectorate government was summoned to a meeting with Hitler. In an attempt to placate the Führer, Hácha began by condemning the British role in the assassination, but succeeded only in provoking an outburst of rage. Hitler worked himself up into a passion against the Czechs, speaking louder and louder, his harsh voice echoing round the audience chamber. He would not tolerate any more trouble in the Protectorate. If the Czechs did not reform and hand over the assassins, he would think nothing of deporting the entire population: 'Let it be absolutely clear to you that I shall resort to extreme measures. Every compromise solution will be ruled out.' When Hácha pleaded for the opportunity to explain the situation to the people of Bohemia–Moravia, Hitler magnanimously agreed. The Czechs were 'intelligent and industrious workers'. He would give them a chance to prove their loyalty to the Reich. At the end of the reception, the Czech ministers went for a walk in the gardens of the Reich Chancellery, accompanied by the state Secretary, Otto Meissner. They plied him with anxious questions about Hitler's outburst and he assured them that the Führer was not bluffing. His 'references to the possible evacuation of the Czechs were, if he knew Hitler, the Führer's last words on the subject'. In fact the whole scene was carefully calculated to exert the maximum psychological pressure on Hácha. Hitler probably was bluffing, as his remarks on the importance of Czech war industry reveal, but his listeners, living daily with the reality of Nazi brutality, had little alternative but to take him seriously.

Rhetoric, however, was not enough for Hitler. Something had to be done to show Hácha that he meant what he said. Besides, a blood sacrifice was required to avenge the death of Heydrich. The Jews were the first to be thrown on the funeral pyre. On 9 June a special train left Prague marked 'AaH' (*Attentat auf Heydrich* or Assassination of Heydrich) carrying 1000 Czech Jews to their deaths in the SS extermination factories. It was followed by two more transports from the ghetto at Terezin. Of 3000 victims only one survived, a man who managed to jump from the train which carried his companions to their deaths. In Poland, the SS dedicated its ghastly work of mass murder to the memory of the lost hero, under the title Einsatz Reinhard (Operation Reinhard). Treblinka, Belzec and Soribor became the final destination of a Jewish population deported eastwards from the ghettos of the Government-General by SS Obergruppenführer Odilo Globocnik and his SS 'resettlement staff'. For the Nazis, however, the murder of Jews was almost routine. Something more was required, a dramatic symbol which would show not only the Czechs but also all of Europe the consequences of defying German rule. On the evening of 9

June a suitable example was chosen – the small village of Lidice, near Kladno in Bohemia. Although neither the first nor the biggest, it was to become one of the most notorious Nazi atrocities of the entire war.

At his trial in 1945, Frank was condemned for the crime of Lidice. Although he was the man who gave the order for the reprisal, the original idea of wiping out the village came not from Frank but from the head of the SD in Bohemia–Moravia, Karl Böhme, a brutal and unscrupulous thug even by the standards of the Nazi security police. Lidice had already come to the attention of the Gestapo before the assassination. Corporal Pavelka of Operation PERCENTAGE, captured in October 1941, was carrying the addresses of two families there, the Horaks and the Stribnys, who had sons serving with the Czech forces in Britain. Moreover it was in an area where parachutists were known to have landed. The ill-fated BIVOUAC group had stayed in the nearby town of Slany before being captured on 2 May 1942. It was probably for this reason that the village was cordoned off and searched by the Gestapo on 28 May, immediately after the attack on Heydrich. Its fate was sealed, however, by a tragic accident. On 27 May a married man named Vaclav Riha sent a letter to his lover, Anna Maruscakova, calling off their affair. It was addressed to her place of work and written in carefully ambiguous language for the sake of discretion. The letter fell into the hands of Maruscakova's employer, Jaroslav Pala, a Nazi sympathiser. He suspected that it was a coded message referring to the assassination and called in the Czech police. The Czechs considered the matter trivial, a simple love letter, but to protect themselves they informed the Germans. Under pressure to produce a lead on the assassination, the Gestapo arrested Maruscakova and her lover. When questioned, the woman claimed that she had been asked by Riha to deliver a message to the Horaks that their son was safe and well in England. Riha confirmed this, adding that the message came from the son himself, Lieutenant Josef Horak, whom he had met some days before the assassination on his way to work in Kladno. It is unclear why these statements were made since at the time Horak was serving with a Czech squadron in the RAF and was nowhere near the Protectorate. A possible clue lies in a statement by Vanék, long after the war, that Riha's mysterious contact was not Horak but Valčik, who was looking for a place to hide the parachutists after the killing. Valčik had passed on the news of Horak during the conversation. It is thus possible that Riha hoped to protect the agents by sending the Gestapo off on a wild-goose chase, pursuing a man who was in fact in England. Like many of Vanék's claims, however, this one must be treated with caution. It is the only evidence linking Lidice directly with the assassins and is unverifiable since all the principals are dead. Whatever the real truth, Riha's statement proved disastrous. The Gestapo in Kladno concluded that parachutists were hiding in Lidice. The village was searched for a second time on 4 June when the Horak and Stribny families were arrested. No trace of parachutists was found but the Germans remained convinced that there was a connexion between the assassins and Lidice. As talk of reprisal grew in the aftermath of Heydrich's death, the village was a natural target. According to some accounts, members of the Gestapo in Kladno were predicting the destruction of Lidice as early as 6 June. It was Böhme, however, who took the final step, phoning Himmler in Berlin on the day of the funeral to present the evidence against the village and recommend retaliation. He did not bother to report to his immediate superior, Frank, perhaps because of his known opposition to mass reprisals. Hitler's decision was taken that evening after the reception for Hácha and his ministers, probably as a result of a conversation with Himmler, although Bormann and Daluege may also have been involved. If Frank had any objections, he kept them to himself. His opposition to mass reprisals on 27 May had damaged his political career and he was not about to make the same mistake twice. At 7.45 p.m. he telephoned Böhme in Prague to pass on the Führer's instructions. Lidice was to be destroyed. The men were to be shot on the spot and the women sent to a concentration camp. Children worthy of Germanisation were to be handed over to SS families. The village was to be burned to the ground and its remains levelled so that no trace remained.

The operation began shortly after 9.30 p.m. on the evening of 9 June. The village was cordoned off and searched. The women and children were taken away and males over fifteen herded together. A squad of security police under SS Hauptsturmführer Max Rostock then began the ghastly work of execution, despatching its victims in groups of ten. The bodies were buried in a mass grave by a work detail of Czech Jews from the concentration camp at Terezin. The houses were set on fire and the ruins bulldozed by the German Labour Service, which spent several months ensuring that no trace of Lidice remained. The final stages of the operation were witnessed by Frank, who flew back from Berlin on 10 June and arrived at the scene when the killing was over. According to Frank, corn would grow where Lidice once stood as a permanent reminder of the fate awaiting those who defied Nazi rule. The Gestapo reported that 199 men were murdered in the operation and 195 women arrested. Of 95 children, 8 were ultimately considered worthy of Germanisation. The majority simply vanished and only sixteen could be traced after the war. In the Protectorate press, this act of mass murder was presented as justifiable retaliation for the assassination. The Gestapo had irrefutable evidence that the villagers had 'sheltered Czech parachute agents, who took a leading part in preparing the assault on Heydrich, and tried to prevent the apprehension of the culprits by the police'. According to Daluege, arms, ammunition and an illegal transmitter were uncovered in Lidice. In fact three searches by the security police on 28 May, 4 June and 10 June had produced only 2 hunting rifles, a rusty revolver and a bag of shotgun cartridges.

The destruction of Lidice added weight to the educational campaign launched by the Protectorate regime on its return from Berlin. In this appeal to the Czech people, Emanuel Moravec, the Propaganda Minister, played a leading role, predicting death and destruction if the assassins were not found. In a speech at Brno on 12 June, he emphasised that there were only two alternatives. The Czechs could either work for the Reich and disregard Beneš or 'follow Beneš and perish in the end . . . and . . . be wiped out as the Czech village of Lidice was wiped out'. His warnings were reinforced daily by the controlled press, which called for the denunciation of not only 'every saboteur . . . but also every neutral . . . before the hand of Reich justice punishes the whole nation'. In the face of these dire predictions there was panic throughout the Protectorate. Every evening crowds formed around the news stands, as the inhabitants of Prague queued to read the latest list of death sentences by the martial-law courts. According to one German bureaucrat, it was rumoured that the nation would be literally decimated if the assassins were not found. The numbers on Czech identity cards would be used to select the victims: 'Those ending in zero would automatically be condemned to death.' The atmosphere of nervous tension reached a level where even Czech officials were incapable of serious work. This deliberate resort to terror, however, failed to bring the Germans any real lead on the assassins. Fourteen days after the attack, the Gestapo had received only 309 statements about the affair, all of them worthless. The investigation seemed to have reached a dead end.

In the dark crypt of the Karel Boromejsky church, relief at the death of Heydrich was tempered by despair at the level of Nazi reprisals. The fate of Lidice horrified the assassins, as did Moravec's threat that worse was in store for the Czech nation unless the guilty men were found. In order to stop the murder of innocent people, they decided to sacrifice themselves. They approached the lay preacher, Vladimir Petrek, and proposed committing suicide in a public park with placards around their necks stating that they had killed Heydrich. They also discussed a more desperate plan with the other parachutists. They would arrange an interview with Moravec himself, confess that they were the assassins, and shoot him in his office. They would then commit suicide by swallowing their cyanide pills. Gabčík and Kubiš were dissuaded by their comrades, led by Opálka, who pointed out that, even if they succeeded, their sacrifice was unlikely to avert Nazi reprisals. It was their duty as soldiers to stay alive and continue fighting for as long as possible. Although dramatic gestures were staved off for the time being, it was clear that the seven parachutists could not remain in the church indefinitely. The atmosphere of terror in Prague and the grim surroundings of the crypt were taking an inevitable toll of their morale. Moreover Bishop Gorazd, alarmed by the savagery of German reprisals, demanded the removal of the assassins, arguing that their presence endangered the interests of the Orthodox Church. The resistance began to look for new hiding places outside Prague. This was difficult, for few were prepared to run the risks involved. A prominent Catholic prelate, asked to find refuge for the men in a monastery, refused to have anything to do with the affair. According to Vanék, a plan was finally worked out to smuggle Bublik, Hrubý, Švarc and Valčik to the mountains where they were to organise partisans. Gabčík and Kubiš were to escape to England by plane. He was to accompany them, leaving Opálka in charge of the underground network. On this point, as on many others, his evidence is unreliable. If such a solution was indeed seriously considered it was the product of wishful thinking. At that time the RAF possessed no aircraft capable of flying to the Protectorate and landing on a grass strip. The plan bore all the marks of improvisation by desperate men in an impossible situation.

While the debate in the crypt was continuing, the Gestapo was increasingly embarrassed by its failure to catch the assassins. In this situation it began to look for a convenient scapegoat and found one in Wilhelm Dennler, a German official at Bertsch's Ministry of Labour. Shortly after Heydrich's funeral, Dennler received a threatening telephone call from the head of the Prague Gestapo: 'On 27 May, the evening . . . of the attack, although a rail blockade was ordered for Prague, you allowed a train with Czech workers to leave in the direction of Berlin. We have meanwhile established that the 3 assassins used this train to escape. They kept themselves hidden under the seats during the journey and, during a short stop in Dresden, they left the train. Do you understand what these discoveries could mean for you?' Dennler was speechless. He knew that the Gestapo was trying to frame him to cover up its own failures and could feel a noose tightening around his neck. He had indeed released a train on the day of the attack carrying key workers for the aircraft plants at Magdeburg after the Air Ministry in Berlin had emphasised their importance to the war effort. Fortunately for him, he had kept a file on the affair and could produce witnesses to testify that the train had left only by agreement with the security police. If the assassins had escaped by this means, the Gestapo must share the blame. Nevertheless, he spent an unpleasant few hours before the matter was resolved.

It was Pannwitz who eventually suggested a way of breaking open the case. A career policeman who opposed mass reprisals, he was convinced that the atmosphere of terror deliberately created after 27 May was working against German interests. Nobody would come forward to claim the reward because they feared that they would be accused of previously withholding information and executed along with their entire family: 'Our special squads . . . confirmed again and again the opinion of the criminologists that fear and anxiety kept back even those who might normally have been prepared to give some information no matter from what motive.' Terror had its place, but people must also be offered a way of saving themselves. An amnesty should be offered to anyone prepared to denounce the assassins or provide information leading to their arrest. The proposition was put to Frank, who issued a proclamation on 13 June promising that anyone who by 18 June denounced the assassins or provided the police with information leading to their arrest would not be harmed. Time was running out for his policy of selective terror. Two days later, Himmler forwarded an order from Hitler for the execution of 30,000 politically active Czechs, a return to the policy of mass reprisal favoured by the Nazi leadership immediately after the assassination attempt.

According to Pannwitz, Frank's new initiative was an enormous success: 'More than 2000 statements by Czechs arrived within three days.' Amongst them was an anonymous letter mailed to the Czech police at Benesov: 'Cease searching for the assassins of Heydrich; cease arresting and executing innocent people. I can't stand it any more. The perpetrators of the assassination are a certain Gabčík from Slovakia, and Jan Kubiš, whose brother is an inn-keeper from Moravia.' The writer knew what he was talking about for he was a parachutist – Sergeant Čurda of OUT DISTANCE. After his act of betrayal, many claimed that Čurda was a weak link from the beginning, a heavy drinker and declared admirer of Hitler who should never have been selected for parachute training. This was probably being wise after the event. Whatever his moral failings, Čurda had done his duty as a soldier during the raid on the Skoda works, but had reached the limit of his courage in the terror which followed the attack on Heydrich. He was disillusioned with his leaders and believed that Beneš was out of touch with the situation at home. The execution of entire families in reprisal for the assassination, culminating in the crime of Lidice, preyed on his nerves and he broke under the strain. Cut off from his comrades in the Karel Boromejsky church, he began to think of saving himself and his family. The anonymous letter to the police post at Benesov was the first step towards betrayal. When it produced no immediate result, Čurda made a fatal decision. On 16 June he caught a train to Prague and walked into Gestapo headquarters at the Peček Palace, a building few Czechs entered voluntarily. There he announced that he had information about one of the briefcases abandoned by the assassins. Perhaps he still believed that his betrayal need go no further.

10

Ending

The nervous figure who appeared at the Peček Palace was immediately brought before the head of the German investigation commission, Heinz Pannwitz. He stuttered so much that it was at first difficult to make sense of what he was saying, but the Gestapo recognised the importance of their unexpected witness when Čurda was able to pick out Gabčík's briefcase from twenty similar cases, identifying it by a tear in the side. According to the report of his interrogation: 'His testimony ... was immediately recognised as being an extremely important clue and Čurda was felt to be credible. ... He had seen the briefcase ... before the assassination ... at the flat belonging to the Svatos family in the possession of ... [a] parachute agent, where he had discovered that the briefcase contained an English sub-machine-gun of a type he knew well. Since the descriptions provided by witnesses matched this parachute agent, attention was turned towards one Josef Gabčík (cover name ZDENEK), formerly residing . . . near Zilina, whose present whereabouts Čurda did not know. ... Čurda also voiced the suspicion that the second assassin might be Gabčík's best friend, Jan Kubiš (cover name OTA NAVRATIL).' These were names previously unknown to the Germans. In the light of the detailed knowledge he displayed, Pannwitz suspected that Čurda was also a parachutist. He was searched and the cyanide capsule issued to every SOE agent was discovered. This led to further intensive questioning. According to Čurda's later account: 'They showed me photographs of a few parachutists and asked whether I knew them. I recognised them all: the photographs were of Lieutenant Pechal, and of Kolařík, Mikš and Gerik. But I said I did not know them. They beat me, saying they had already captured Gerik and they knew more about it than I thought. Then I admitted I knew the men. ... I also admitted that I was a parachutist, dropped on 27 March 1942 in the neighbourhood of Telc in Moravia. . . .' Čurda claimed that he was disillusioned with the exile government and had surrendered to save his family from prosecution.

Čurda was unable to lead the Gestapo directly to the parachutists because he did not know where they were hiding, but he betrayed several of the safe houses provided by the JINDRA group, most importantly the flat in Žižkov occupied by the Moravec family which lay at the centre of the network. Pannwitz had the buildings surrounded and watched. On the morning of 17 June, at 5 a.m., they were raided by the police in a carefully co-ordinated operation. The Moravecs and their neighbours were awakened by the thunder of gun butts on the doors and harsh German voices shouting 'Where are the parachutists?' The Moravecs were lined up in the corridor in their night clothes while the Gestapo searched their flat. The police were extremely nervous, waving their pistols excitedly and jumping at every shadow. In the confusion, Mrs Moravec asked if she could go to the toilet, a request which was surprisingly granted. There she locked herself in and swallowed a cyanide capsule. The door was broken down and a doctor summoned but by the time he arrived she was dead. Still in their pyjamas, her husband and son were dragged downstairs to the waiting black cars. Later that day, Zalenka's apartment was raided. Before the Germans could seize him, he had swallowed poison and placed himself beyond their reach. The clues provided by Čurda seemed to be leading to dead ends. The assassins were no longer in the safe houses and the most important witnesses had killed themselves to avoid questioning.

The Gestapo went to work on those who were left, concentrating on young Ata Moravec. He was taken to the cellars of the Peček Palace where he was tortured throughout the day. When his resistance was at its lowest, he was stupefied with alcohol and presented with his mother's head floating in a fish tank. Broken by pain and shock, he gave his torturers their first real clue to the whereabouts of the assassins, revealing that his mother had told him to go to the catacombs of the Karel Boromejsky church if he was ever in trouble. By this time it was nearly midnight. Pannwitz hastily summoned every city official he could find to give him information about the church and its surroundings but he was unable to find a plan of the crypt or to establish if there were any possible escape routes into the city sewers. It was decided to establish a double cordon around the entire area using over 700 Waffen SS troops from the Prague garrison. To prevent escapes, every manhole and sewerage outlet was to be guarded and soldiers posted on the roofs of the buildings around the Karel Boromejsky, which would then be searched by Gestapo agents escorted by an SS platoon with automatic weapons. Pannwitz emphasised the importance of taking the assassins alive. As a career policeman he wanted to close the case by bringing someone to trial.

At 04.10 hours on 18 June, lorries containing Waffen SS in full battle order converged on the church from several different directions and established road blocks in the empty streets. Five minutes later a Gestapo detail under Pannwitz approached the building and rang the bell. They were admitted by a sleepy janitor who led them into the main part of the church and switched on the lights. The Germans scattered to search the nave, the jackboots of the SS men echoing loudly on the stone floor, but they could find no trace of parachutists. They turned their attention to the metal grille which gave access to the choir loft. It was locked and the janitor claimed that he could not find the key. Pannwitz had the door forced with a gun butt. As the grille swung open there was a rattling sound and a grenade came bouncing round the corner of the stairs. Simultaneously there was a burst of fire from above. The explosion injured one of the Germans and blew out most of the lights. The SS men on the neighbouring roofs, hearing the shooting, began to fire indiscriminately into the church, shattering the tall windows and sending bullets ricocheting amongst the pillars. The altar hangings caught fire, suffusing the dust and smoke from the explosions with a dull orange glow. In the noise and confusion, Pannwitz and his escort were in danger of being hit by their own side and he hastily withdrew his men. The SS commander reimposed discipline amongst the troops and the random firing ceased.

A force of Waffen SS was sent in with orders to storm the choir loft and capture the parachutists alive. This task was far from easy. The only access was by a narrow twisting staircase which put the attackers at a disadvantage. Only after the SS used grenades were they able to fight their way upwards and even then the battle continued for two hours amongst the dim recesses beneath the roof. When the firing stopped, the troops discovered the bodies of two parachutists who had taken poison and a third who was severely wounded and unconscious. According to Pannwitz, this was Kubiš: 'He had tried to use poison on himself but apparently lost consciousness before he could do so. Although he was immediately transferred to the hospital none of the doctors' attempts to keep him alive succeeded. He died within twenty minutes.' The other two agents were identified as Bublik of BIOSCOPE and Opálka of OUT DISTANCE. They had apparently found the confines of the crypt intolerable and were sleeping in the loft when the Gestapo entered the church. The Germans suspected that a fourth parachutist was still at large. None of the corpses fitted the description of Gabčík and there were four coats amongst the débris. The preacher, Vladimir Petrek, was questioned and admitted that there were four more men in the catacombs. In an attempt to save his own life, he showed the Germans the concealed entrance under a flagstone beside the west door. A second larger entrance near the altar had recently been bricked up. The only other access was by an air shaft which emerged through a grille on one of the outer walls.

With three corpses already on his hands, Pannwitz did not want to lose the last remaining witnesses by storming the cellar. Instead he tried to persuade the agents to give themselves up. Loudspeaker announcements were soon reverberating through the morning air, promising that the parachutists would be treated as prisoners of war if they surrendered peacefully. Petrek was sent up to the grille to talk to them but they answered defiantly, shouting that they were Czechs and would never surrender. Karel Čurda and Ata Moravec were brought to the church, handcuffed to Gestapo men. Moravec refused to help the Germans but Čurda approached the vent and called: 'Surrender, boys, it will be all right.' He was greeted with a volley of shots which sent everyone ducking for cover. In an attempt to force the parachutists out, Pannwitz summoned the Prague fire brigade and ordered them to flood the crypt. A fireman climbed up a ladder and knocked out the iron grille over the vent. The hoses were connected and began to pump 660 gallons of water a minute into the catacombs. Trapped inside, the parachutists placed a short ladder against the wall and ducking under the powerful jets of water roaring through the opening, cut the hoses or pushed them out. When the Czech firemen tried to replace them they were repulsed by gunfire and Molotov cocktails. According to the German report of the action: 'The Waffen SS was then ordered to throw tear-gas grenades down the shaft. . . . However, the criminals quite often managed to throw them back out. Hoses were again put into the shaft; a few hand grenades were used to stop the criminals pushing the hoses out again.' Pannwitz hoped that the flooding and the gas would eventually persuade the parachutists to surrender. He reckoned without their grim determination and the interference of his political master, Karl Hermann Frank, who arrived on the scene shortly after dawn.

As the morning dragged on with the situation unresolved, Frank grew impatient. The Karel Boromejsky was near the centre of Prague and most of the population could hear the firing. The continued resistance in the crypt was setting a bad example to the Czech people, one he wished to discourage by a crude display of Nazi power. This primitive sentiment was soon to override Pannwitz's desire to capture the men alive. Frank's impatience was shared by the Waffen SS commander, who believed that the restrictions imposed by the Gestapo were hampering his soldiers and making them a laughing stock. The issue was finally decided when it was discovered that the water level in the catacombs was only rising very slowly. It was feared that 'the water might be escaping somewhere and, even worse, that the criminals would be able to use this to find an escape route through some kind of drainage canal or underground passageway'. The Waffen SS commander recommended storming the crypt. The siege was a matter best resolved by soldiers and mere policemen should stand aside. Pannwitz protested strongly, pointing out 'the absurdity of the order and . . . the importance of taking the agents alive. They could have been killed six hours earlier if that had been desirable. . . .' After a heated argument, he was overruled by Frank. An SS combat detachment entered the catacombs through the entrance by the west door and tried to end the siege with automatic weapons and grenades. The soldiers had to struggle forward through waist-deep water, wearing masks to protect them against the drifting tear gas. Unable to find the parachutists in the darkness, they were ambushed from concealed niches in the walls and fell back, carrying two wounded.

The military commander, embarrassed by this failure, ordered the main entrance near the altar to be blown open with explosives. He hoped to catch the defenders between two fires by a simultaneous assault through both openings. As the SS prepared to renew the attack, four shots echoed underground, followed by a long silence. A soldier was sent down the hole to investigate and emerged a few moments later shouting: '*Fertig!*' ('Finished!'). According to the German report on the action: 'Four dead criminals were found in the crypt. Apart from serious injuries, they had wounds in the temple showing that they had killed themselves with their own revolvers.' The parachutists had resisted the SS for over six hours and committed suicide with their last bullets rather than surrender. The bodies were carried from the wrecked church and thrown on the pavement where Gabčík was identified as the second assassin by Čurda. Amongst the eleven pistols found in the débris were the two Colt revolvers used in the ambush at Holešovice. While Frank was still savouring this triumph, an urgent message arrived from the Reichsführer SS: 'Any means should be employed to reassure the assassins in order to capture them alive.'

Without the parachutists, Himmler lacked the living evidence required to counter allied propaganda and show the world that the killing was 'made in England'.

Three days after the battle at the Karel Boromejsky, Bartoš of SILVER A was tracked down in Pardubice and fatally wounded after a gun battle with the Gestapo. His radio operator, Potuček, met the same end on 2 July when he was killed by Czech police. The village of Ležáky, which had concealed SILVER A's transmitter, suffered an even grimmer fate than Lidice. On 24 June all the adult inhabitants were murdered. Of the children, only two little girls were considered worthy of Germanisation and handed over to Nazi families. The remainder disappeared. The JINDRA group was rolled up and its leader arrested. When Pannwitz interrogated him, Vaněk offered to co-operate with the Gestapo, suggesting that he restore the radio link with London. By this means the Germans would be warned in advance about new parachute groups and could arrest them when they landed. Agents captured by the deception plan could be interned until the end of the war and the exiles fed false information about their activities. As a guarantee of good faith, he offered to nominate hostages from his own resistance group. According to Pannwitz, Vaněk:

> gave the impression of being a middle-class man, afraid that after the war, which he considered lost by the Germans, Czechoslovakia would turn to communism. Apart from that, he did not feel that the allies should put the Czech nation at risk for their war aims, after having deserted her in 1938 and 1939. . . . Besides the strength of the German army was so great that the Germans would not hesitate to use any means . . . to keep the Protectorate in their hands. . . . unrest or revolt . . . would be suicide for the Czech people.

Unknown to Vaněk, his captors were already trying to initiate a deception operation, using Potuček's radio and material from Bartoš' message files captured in Pardubice, which gave details of the codes and cover names used by the parachute agents. The Czech transmitters at Woldingham responded to SILVER A's call sign, but the Gestapo lacked a captured parachutist who knew the proper radio procedures and Operation HERMILIN was abandoned in September 1942. It was attempted again the following year, with a radio operator captured from a subsequent group. As for Vaněk, he told his captors everything he knew. He identified captured resistance colleagues for the Germans and urged them to follow his example and confess. He was the only major figure in his underground group to survive the war.

Nazi reprisals continued throughout the summer. Between 28 May and 1 September 1942, 3188 Czechs were arrested and 1357 condemned to death by the emergency courts. A high proportion were ex-officers or members of the intelligentsia, groups defined by the Nazis as irreconcilable representatives of the 'national idea', an independent Czechoslovak state. This total did not include the victims of Lidice and Ležáky or the 3000 Jews deported to the east. Nor did it include the 252 relatives and helpers of the parachutists condemned in Prague on 29 September. During their interrogation they were beaten and confronted with the heads of the seven agents, impaled on spikes. Their conduct in the face of such brutal treatment impressed even their jailers. As the chief of the Prague Gestapo reported on 25 June: 'Most of the people who helped the assassins took a pronounced Czech, chauvinist, anti-German stance, especially the women. . . . They were often heard to say: "We are proud to die for our country."' Sentence was carried out on 24 October at Mauthausen concentration camp. The men were shot and the women and children sent to the gas chambers. Amongst the victims were twelve relatives of Kubiš and thirteen of Valčik. Gabčík's family escaped reprisal because he was a Slovak and the Nazis found it convenient to maintain the fiction that their satellite state of Slovakia was independent.

Bishop Gorazd and the officials of the Karel Boromejsky were condemned to death on 3 September. The role of the clergy enraged Hitler, who intended to settle accounts with organised religion at the end of the war. As he complained on 3 July, the Churches could not be trusted: 'One need only recall the close co-operation between the Church and the murderers of Heydrich. Catholic priests [*sic*] not only allowed them to hide . . . but even allowed them to entrench themselves in the sanctuary of the altar.' After the trial, the Orthodox Church throughout the Protectorate was dissolved and its property confiscated. As a deterrent against further assassinations, Frank rounded up 4000 people with relatives amongst the exiles and held them as hostages at camps in Moravia. Those interned included members of the Beneš family. The Germans considered putting Beneš himself on trial and condemning him to death *in absentia*, but this plan was abandoned. A final reckoning with the exile president was deferred until after the war. Čurda received 5 million crowns for the betrayal of his comrades, paid in monthly instalments by a German bank in Prague. His mother and sister were released from custody and avoided the grim fate awaiting the families of the other parachutists. Čurda changed his name and adopted German citizenship, marrying the sister of an SS officer and pursuing a new career as a Gestapo spy. He toured the Protectorate posing as a parachutist, a role he knew well, denouncing those who assisted him, and helped the Germans track down the radio group ANTIMONY, dropped in October 1942. He also identified the bodies of parachutists killed in action, allowing the Gestapo to arrest and murder their families. Convinced that the Nazis would win the war, he hoped eventually to settle in the east as one of the warrior peasants of Hitler's imperial dreams.

For the remainder of the occupation, the Nazis tried to keep the memory of Heydrich alive as a heroic figure who had died for the cause of the greater German Reich. He was held up to the Czechs as a symbol of what was to be gained by collaboration and as a warning of the consequences of resistance. A Reinhard Heydrich Foundation was created in Prague to study national, economic and cultural conditions 'in the territories for which he fought and fell' and throughout the Protectorate streets and squares were renamed in his honour. On the anniversary of his death in June 1943 a carefully scripted propaganda exercise took place in the Czech capital. That morning a bust of Heydrich was unveiled at the fatal corner in Holešovice with a permanent SS guard of honour. In future passers-by would have to doff their caps as a mark of respect for the dead hero. In the afternoon, his widow, accompanied by Karl Hermann Frank, received delegations of workers and peasants, the social groups he had supposedly tried to help. A special stamp was issued with a picture of Heydrich's death-mask flanked by SS runes and the inscription '*Deutsches Reich*'. Throughout the Protectorate the press carried laudatory articles on his life and work, while in Berlin wreaths were laid on his grave.

In April 1943, Hitler gave the estate at Panenské Břežany to Heydrich's wife and children in perpetuity as a symbol of the permanent union of Bohemia–Moravia with the Reich. Himmler took responsibility for the family of his ideal SS man, a task he did not find easy. The widow wrangled over the terms of the gift and became involved in a sordid argument with the SS over payment for the concentration-camp labour employed to improve the house and grounds. The Reichsführer SS regarded the estate as a focus of future German settlement, the centre of a corridor of Aryan peasants designed to break up the Slav population into smaller and more manageable units. As one of his subordinates in Prague emphasised in April 1943, such a solution would be welcomed by the Heydrich family, who missed the experience of living in a proper German community. As late as 1944, 1300 ethnic Germans were settled on land to the north of Prague, but these schemes were brought to an abrupt end a few months later by the arrival of the Red Army. Panenské Břežany, the permanent gift of the Führer, was left tenantless, as the Heydrich family packed all the valuables it could carry and fled into Bavaria, accompanied by swarms of German refugees.

The Czechs paid a heavy price in blood for the death of the tyrant, with over 5000 victims of Nazi reprisals. In the light of this casualty list, the majority innocent civilians, the inevitable question must be asked – despite the heroism of the parachutists and their helpers, was anything achieved by the assassination? ANTHROPOID certainly fulfilled one of its main aims by focusing world attention on the Czech cause. The death of Heydrich came at a time when the allies were retreating on nearly every front. On 27 May, Rommel launched an offensive in North Africa which by the end of June had taken the fortress of Tobruk and carried the Germans to the gates of Egypt. In the North Atlantic, U-boats scored success after success, sending 834,000 tons of shipping to the bottom in June 1942. On the eastern front, the Germans defeated the Red Army at Kharkov on 17 May and also drove forward in the Crimea, capturing Sebastopol on 3 July. As the Permanent Under-Secretary of State at the Foreign Office, Alexander Cadogan, ruefully remarked on 15 June: 'Libya bad, sinkings awful . . . Malta convoys badly mauled. No good news anywhere.' Amongst the neutrals, allied diplomacy had been dealt 'a fearful blow'. Only in the distant Pacific, where the US Navy halted the Japanese at the Battle of Midway, was there anything positive to record.

It was therefore hardly surprising that the assassination was hailed as a significant victory by Britain, Russia and the United States, a symbol that the people of occupied Europe rejected Nazi rule and that the tide of battle must eventually turn. As *Izvestia* proclaimed on 29 May, the report of an attack on 'the Hitlerite executioner, Heydrich, shows how serious is the situation in Czechoslovakia. . . . The shots at Heydrich are a further sign that the Slavonic nations will never be slaves of German imperialism.' The European Service of the BBC took a similar line, employing the killing to boost morale amongst the peoples of occupied Europe. It was given a priority second only to reports on the fighting. As a General News Directive emphasised on 29 May:

> The Russians stand firm against the worst Hitler can do, the British stand firm and the Czechs stand firm. All three are suffering heavy losses but so are the Germans and all the Allies have to do is to hold fast and return blow for blow. . . . The blitzkrieg is dead and the terror instrument is broken in Hitler's hand. War is now war on the battle fronts and on the Underground

Front. The days when it was only the Germans who could strike hard are over. . . . The Germans must be frightened by what is happening. The Czechs and all the other enslaved peoples must be made proud in the knowledge that they have cast out fear and thus have turned the terror against the Nazis.

As Beneš had intended, allied comment generally attributed the attack to the home resistance and hailed it as a symbol of Czech opposition to Nazi rule. Parachutists were never mentioned.

The widespread public sympathy for Czechoslovakia created by the killing was reinforced by the crime of Lidice, which was condemned as an act of barbarism throughout the civilised world. In a speech typical of allied comment, the US Secretary of the Navy, Frank Knox, proclaimed: 'If future generations ask us what we were fighting for in this war we shall tell them the story of Lidice.' According to Jan Masaryk, Nazi reprisals played straight into the hands of the exiles: 'I was in the US at the time of Lidice and making no progress in our propaganda, having exhausted all the possibilities of the situation. Then came Lidice, and I had a new lease of life. Czechoslovakia was put on the map again and we had an easy time.' In Britain, Beneš was able to use the favourable atmosphere to political advantage, securing the concessions for which he had fought tenaciously since 1939. The Foreign Office was careful to avoid a direct endorsement of the assassination, which it regarded as an internal Czech affair. As Frank Roberts of the Central Department remarked on 11 June: 'However much we may welcome Heydrich's fate it is not, I imagine, the policy of HM Government to go out of their way to glorify political assassinations.' At the same time, the Czechs had to be given some recognition. The Dominion Prime Ministers were informed on 8 July that 'In view of the trials through which the Czechoslovak people have been passing since the death of Heydrich we think it desirable for psychological reasons to give Beneš such satisfaction as is possible.' While Britain still had reservations about the juridical continuity of the Czech state and would not commit itself on borders, the government was prepared to repudiate Munich unequivocally and to make it clear that the legal status of the Czech government was in no way inferior to that of the other exile regimes by raising the British legation to the rank of an embassy. The settlement was announced in the Commons on 5 August when Anthony Eden stated that, since the Munich agreement had been unilaterally destroyed by Hitler, Britain was 'free from any engagements in this respect'. When a final settlement of the Czechoslovak frontier was decided, London 'would not be influenced by any changes effected in and since 1938'. He went on to pay tribute to the 'tenacious and courageous stand' which the Czechoslovak people were making against their 'ruthless German oppressors'. Acts like the destruction of Lidice had 'stirred the conscience of the civilized world' and would not be forgotten when the time came 'to settle accounts with their perpetrators'.

The British not only repudiated Munich but also washed their hands of the Sudeten Germans, opening the way to a radical solution of the minorities question in the post-war period. During the negotiations in July which led to the final settlement, the British Ambassador informed Beneš and Masaryk that after the war London 'did not intend to oppose the principle of transfer of the minority population from Czechoslovakia in an endeavour to make Czechoslovakia as homogeneous a country as possible from the standpoint of nationality'. The republic would never again have to live with a German revolver aimed permanently at its heart. In talks with the Russians, the exiles received similar reassurances. On 4 June, the Soviet Ambassador to the Czech exile government, Bogomolov, confirmed that Russia wanted the restoration 'of a strong, independent Czechoslovakia. This means . . . complete restoration of Czechoslovakia in the pre-Munich boundaries.' He raised no objection to the expulsion of the Sudeten Germans. Molotov, who was visiting London, took a similar line in a long conversation with Beneš on 7 June, confirming that for the Soviet Union Munich did not exist. The Soviet Foreign Minister promised to support the expulsion of up to one and a half million Sudetens after the war. According to one of Beneš' closest associates, Prokop Drtina, this was the most important outcome of ANTHROPOID: 'The response to the assassination and Lidice in Allied opinion was so enormous that it equalled for us a victorious battle. . . . without Gabčík, Valčik, Kubiš and other fighters determined unto death, we would never have achieved the purification of the Czech lands from the German settlements.' Beneš himself was justifiably jubilant. In a message to the Czech people, broadcast by the BBC on 8 August, he proclaimed that the shame of Munich had been finally expunged: 'I know today as an absolute certainty, that we shall win this war and that the gains registered in the negotiations we have just concluded with the Soviet Union and Great Britain will be realised. I therefore regard this diplomatic task which I had set to our whole liberation movement and to myself, as having been substantially fulfilled.'

Beneš believed that the assassination and its aftermath not only had saved the nation from the old Munich but also guaranteed it against a new betrayal. After Lidice he remarked to Jaromir Smutný:

> It is terrible what the Nazis do but from the political point of view these events brought one surety to us: the situation now cannot develop in which Czechoslovakia would not be recognised as an independent state. All the time I feared a negotiated peace. Negotiated peace is still the only hope for Germany, but now I feel secure. . . . I was afraid that they would leave us in one way or another integrated with Germany. . . . The executions . . . consolidated our state of affairs. This is the great political consequence of these events.

Beneš, obsessed with his experiences in 1938, greatly exaggerated the impact of the assassination and Nazi reprisals in this area. With the benefit of hindsight, it is clear that there was little chance of a compromise peace with Hitler after three years of bitter warfare and innumerable broken promises. If such an outcome had ever emerged, it is extremely unlikely that the position of Czechoslovakia, whatever its sacrifices for the allied cause, would have been proof against great power self-interest. Beneš himself seems to have had second thoughts on this score, informing Lockhart in March 1943 that he feared a separate peace between Russia and the Axis and a new Nazi–Soviet pact. Partly for this reason, he emerged as a fervent advocate of an early second front.

Colonel Moravec claimed that the effects of the assassination went beyond these diplomatic gains. The death of Heydrich damaged the German war effort and thus more than justified the casualties involved. This is harder to substantiate. While Hitler compared the loss of Heydrich to a lost battle, the killing had no impact on military operations and, as for the 'Final Solution', the deportation trains continued to roll across Europe towards the killing centres in the east. Heydrich's eventual successor at the Reichsicherheitshauptamt, Ernst Kaltenbrunner, may have lacked the combination of intelligence and ferocious energy which characterised his predecessor, but the security police remained a powerful instrument of terror throughout the occupied areas. In the Protectorate itself, the Nazis probably lost production as a result of events in June and July, but this was a temporary hiccup. The Czech arms industry continued to serve Hitler well for the remainder of the war as Heydrich's creature, Karl Hermann Frank, pursued his dead master's established tactics of carrot and stick. If Heydrich's assassination had any effect, it was in the less tangible area of psychological warfare. The Germans no longer felt safe even in their formerly model Protectorate where they had taken their position for granted. Frank's threats of dreadful reprisals in the event of another assassination and the heavily armed escort which always accompanied his specially armoured car proved this. Nor was Heydrich's family, the symbol of the eternal union between the Czech lands and the Reich, immune from fear. In January 1944 Heydrich's widow received a threatening letter which sparked off a correspondence with Himmler on the best means of guarding the Panenské Břežany estate. The Reichsführer SS took the matter extremely seriously, ordering the Gestapo to deal with it at the highest level, a duty owed by the security police 'to the memory of our dead comrade and friend Heydrich'. Later that year Frau Heydrich petitioned for her son to be excused Hitler Youth membership for the remainder of the war, rather than expose him to the risks of travelling through Prague unprotected. As she informed Himmler, it was a scandal that young German boys should be allowed to brave the dangers of the streets on their own. The myth of the special relationship established between Heydrich and the common people of the Protectorate was clearly wearing thin.

In a broader perspective, when allied propaganda attributed reprisals like Lidice to fear, it was not far from the truth. The assassination was a symbol that even the most powerful men in the Third Reich were not invulnerable and it was a portent of the fate awaiting the Nazis if they lost the war. In this respect, ANTHROPOID and its consequences lent a strong impulse to the movement to try the Axis leaders for their crimes. On 17 June, the exile regime sent a note to all the allied governments, proclaiming its determination to secure retribution for Lidice and the other Nazi reprisals. Hitler, Himmler, Daluege and Frank were held responsible for these crimes against humanity and justice, as well as the subordinates who carried out the killings and all Germans who aided them 'though only indirectly or approved of their conduct'. After the war special courts would be established to deal with the culprits. While the Foreign Office, which had been dragging its feet on the war crimes question, had reservations about the sweeping nature of this statement, it realised that it was impossible to avoid some commitment. On 1 July 1942, Eden sent a message to the Czech Institute in London to mark the opening of an exhibition of war pictures which read: 'His Majesty's Government will not forget the crimes committed by the Nazi hordes, and least of all will they forget Lidice and Ležáky. The view of His Majesty's Government was stated once and for all by the Prime Minister last October when he said: "Retribution for these crimes must henceforth take its place among the major purposes of the war."' On 21 August, President

Roosevelt went further and issued a statement warning the Nazis that one day they would be 'compelled to stand in courts of law . . . and answer for their acts'. At the end of this road lay the International Military Tribunal at Nuremberg and the gallows.

As even Moravec admitted, the assassination had other, less beneficial effects. Far from rallying the Czech people around the home resistance, as Beneš expected, it shattered the remnants of an organisation already weakened by the SS terror of October 1941. Apart from Lidice and Ležáky, the Nazis avoided mass reprisals likely to drive the population to the point of desperation. Frank was cunning enough to offer the majority the prospect of survival while eliminating the most dangerous anti-Nazi elements, a development which the exiles were powerless to prevent. According to Daluege: 'The development of the current political line – i.e. the hard grip . . . the public mood artificially created by us, and the nervous tension of the Czechs, the things which led to an escalation of fear circulating as rumours of an impending decimation of the whole nation – has proved correct.' This judgement was shared by the allies. In November 1942 a report on the political situation in Prague emphasised that the population was cowed and reluctant to take risks. While the Czechs were convinced that the allies must eventually win, they expected a long war and were 'afraid of what the Germans may do to them in the meantime'. The British also noted the success of Frank's approach. According to a Foreign Office report of November 1942, compiled after consultation with SOE and the Political Warfare Executive: 'We all feel that the German repression has been to some extent successful, in so far as resistance has been discouraged, contacts with London interrupted and the Czech war machine made to function not unsatisfactorily for the German war machine. There are unfortunately indications that a certain proportion of the population . . . is collaborationist, although not by choice. SOE put this proportion as high as 65% and General Sikorski [the Polish leader] as high as 80%.' SOE concluded that 'the spirit of open resistance' in the Protectorate had been broken. In the following years the underground had to be rebuilt out of the wreckage of the old networks.

The scale of German reprisals in 1942 and the consequences for the resistance made the exiles more careful in future about the sacrifices they demanded of the home population. When the Russians pressed for the destruction of the Skoda arms works, regardless of the human cost, in the spring of 1943, their demand was rejected. The British received a similar response on 28 February when they requested extensive sabotage of the railroad network to impede German troop movements on the eve of the spring offensives in the east. According to Beneš: 'With a second front one might do something; without it not much chance. If Churchill and Roosevelt demanded, he would make the appeal. But responsibility would be ours. The Russians – and the Czechs were pro-Russian – had been asking for direct action, but had not succeeded.' As for assassination, while Beneš was still prepared to contemplate action against prominent collaborators like Emanuel Moravec, he forbade attacks on Daluege and Frank because 'the death of a German national would mean great reprisals.' The President remained embarrassed by the lack of widespread resistance activity at home until late in the war. According to Moravec: 'He was particularly jealous of France, failing to appreciate her far more advantageous position, her relatively easy communications with England, from which the Maquis were being supplied with arms and other necessities.' Until 1944, the Protectorate was simply too far from the fronts for the underground to be supported by either the western powers or the Soviet Union, which was given the main strategic responsibility for east and central Europe. As the British Ambassador, Philip Nichols, reported in July 1943, it was unrealistic to expect large-scale acts of resistance from the Czechs such as those in France and the Low Countries until the fighting came closer, particularly in view of strict Nazi security measures. Over 50,000 Czechs had been tortured and murdered since 1939, a much larger total than 'Czech Government circles in London had ever thought probable'. The majority consisted of 'the most active and resolute patriots, the bitterest enemies of Germany. This fact . . . has obviously reduced the strength of the most . . . aggressive elements to a large extent.' Active resistance in the Protectorate did not really resume until the end of 1944, when the Russians were in a position to offer direct support. By then the shape of allied military strategy had rendered Beneš dependent on the Soviet Union and unable to deal with the Czech communists from a position of strength as he had earlier wished. When he established his first government on liberated soil at Košice in April 1945, it was by courtesy of the Red Army and the communists held most of the key ministries. Thereafter he had to spend much of his time and energy trying to prevent them from gaining a monopoly of power.

As the exiles had pledged in 1942, the Nazis paid for their crimes when Czechoslovakia was liberated. When the Protectorate collapsed in 1945 there was an outburst of Czech rage against everything German. In the bitter fighting which marked the final days of Nazi rule, members of the SS and party formations were ruthlessly hunted down. Some were burned alive or hanged from the lamp posts in the streets of Prague. In the following months the Sudetens, the Trojan horse within the Czechoslovak state at Munich, were the main sufferers. Those who did not flee were expelled over the border into Germany. By the end of 1946 1,859,541 had been deported. Konrad Henlein, Gauleiter of the Sudetenland and Hitler's tool in 1938, committed suicide to avoid the gallows which undoubtedly awaited him. As for Karl Hermann Frank, he hoped to save himself by a deal with the western allies, but was handed over by the Americans to face justice in Prague. At his trial in March 1946 the prosecution paid particular attention to his role in 'the holocaust that followed the assassination of Heydrich and to the crime of Lidice'. He tried to avoid responsibility by blaming Hitler but his wartime boasts about his own role in the affair came back to haunt him. As one witness remarked: 'You didn't have to make yourself small in those days.' Frank was condemned to death and hanged at Pankrac prison, where the Gestapo had murdered many of his Czech victims, on 22 May 1946. His end was witnessed by an invited audience of 5500, which included the surviving mothers of Lidice. He was followed to the gallows by Kurt Daluege on 20 October. The Czech ministers of the Protectorate regime were arrested and tried for collaboration. Hácha, however, did not survive to face the courts. On 1 June 1945 he died in his cell, 'an old and gravely ill . . . man, to whom no one showed any pity'. An attempt to extradite Heydrich's widow from the British zone of Germany failed and she was condemned to life imprisonment *in absentia* in October 1947. Frau Heydrich lived out her life as a hotel keeper on the island of Fehmarn, where there was always a welcome for SS acquaintances from the old days of power. In 1953 she was awarded a pension as the widow of a general killed on active service. The traitor, Karel Čurda, was not so lucky. He was arrested by the resistance on 5 May 1945 near Plzeň, trying to flee towards the Americans with German papers and a large quantity of banknotes. Brought before a revolutionary tribunal, he was insolently defiant. When the judge asked him how he had been able to betray his fellow parachutists he replied: 'I think you would do the same for one million marks.' Čurda went to the scaffold 'completely unrepentant, joking obscenely with his executioner'.

Despite the undoubted benefits which the assassination brought the exile cause, there was little recognition of the parachutists and their bravery after the war. No memorials were erected to commemorate the dramatic deed at the Holešovice corner or the heroic defence of the

Karel Boromejsky church against overwhelming odds. Beneš was
determined to avoid any connexion with ANTHROPOID and never
discussed the subject. The origins of this attitude stretched back to
1942. When the Germans captured Bartoš' message file, they found
Vaněk's request for the cancellation of the operation and Beneš'
message of congratulation after the event, items which proved that the
assassination was 'made in England'. Goebbels scented a propaganda
coup and the material was published by Frank on the anniversary of
Heydrich's assassination in an attempt to divide the home population
from the exiles. Beneš was accused of risking the existence of the
nation from the comfort and safety of his bolt-hole in Britain. According to Frank, he had planned the killing 'to revive an interest in his
clique of émigrés among British official circles'. The exiles replied by
denying any role in the affair, arguing that the attack was carried out by
the underground without any assistance from London. The Foreign
Office was informed that the Nazi claim was a mixture of half-truths
and lies: 'The radiogram quoted by Frank, in which the secret
organisation allegedly asked not to make any attempt on Heydrich's
life, is a complete fabrication. No order for Heydrich's murder was
ever issued from London. In fact the whole Nazi theory about a fight
for freedom being conducted and ordered from London is false, as all
acts of resistance in the homeland are directed and decided by its own
headquarters there.' The supposed message of congratulation dated 3
June 1942 did exist but referred to the 'maintenance of the secret link
with London' and general resistance activity, not to the attack on
Heydrich. The whole affair had been fabricated by the Germans to
'foment opposition to the London Government among the weak-willed
and the defeatists'. If any Foreign Office official noticed the difference
between this statement and Beneš' earlier claims to control anything
and everything which occurred at home, they refrained from comment.

The situation did not change after the war. Amongst the former
exiles, 'There was not a single person who would stand up and say with
pride, I am the one who ordered the assassination or, at least, organised
it.' Beneš was embarrassed by the number of victims swallowed up in
Nazi reprisals and realised that the issue could still be a divisive one in
domestic politics. He remained vulnerable to the charge that he had
plunged his people into a Nazi bloodbath and left them to face the
consequences. In the interests of national unity and post-war
reconstruction, it was inadvisable to stir up controversy between those
who had spent the war abroad and those who had stayed at home. Such
divisions would only be exploited by the communists. In discussions

with former resistance leaders he categorically denied any role in the killing. Unofficial efforts to discover the truth ran into a conspiracy of silence. When the communists seized power in 1948 as the cold war began, they had no interest in paying tribute to the assassins because they had not been responsible for the death of Heydrich. Anyone who had worked for the London Czechs or SOE was in danger of arrest as an agent of imperialism. Gottwald's praise for the unknown heroes in June 1942 was expunged from history. As for Colonel Moravec, who knew the real story, he kept his knowledge secret out of loyalty to Beneš until 1964 when he finally spoke out in a public lecture to refute the charge that he had set up the operation behind the President's back to please the British. An advocate of resistance at Munich, he was unrepentant about ANTHROPOID despite the scale of Nazi reprisals. According to Moravec, his country was at war and had to fight for its liberation: 'If . . . Czechoslovakia, instead of yielding to the Munich decision, had fought Germany, as I am convinced it should have done, it would have suffered much greater losses than it did after Heydrich's death, but it would also have earned a worthier place in history. . . . Given the circumstances in which we were placed at the time, it was a good try. . . . it is a good page in the history of Czechoslovakia in the Second World War. The Czech people should be proud of it. I am.' It was a view shared by the surviving comrades of the parachutists, the former soldiers of the Czech Brigade, who erected a monument to their memory in a Leamington park far from the country for which they had fought and died. On the plaque, these words appear: 'IN TRIBUTE to all Czechoslovak Soldiers, Airmen and Patriots who fell in World War II. From Royal Leamington Spa in 1941, volunteers from free Czechoslovak forces stationed in the town were parachuted into their homeland to rid it of the tyrant Protector SS General Heydrich. Two of them – Jan Kubiš and Josef Gabčík – accomplished their mission in May 1942. They and their companions laid down their lives FOR FREEDOM.'

Appendix 1

Acronyms and Codenames

A–54	The Abwehr officer, Paul Thümmel, who spied for the Czechs.
Abwehr	German Military Intelligence.
ANTHROPOID	Codename for the plan to kill Heydrich.
BARBAROSSA	The Nazi plan to invade the Soviet Union.
C	Traditional codename for the head of British Intelligence.
Deuxième Bureau	French Intelligence.
Einsatzgruppen	SS murder squads organised by Heydrich which operated behind the German lines in Poland and Russia.
GPU	The Soviet Secret Police, later renamed the NKVD.
GRU	Soviet Military Intelligence.
HAJASKY	Codename for the resistance worker, Jan Zelenka.
JINDRA	The resistance group in Prague which hid the parachutists. The codename was also used by the group's leader, Ladislav Vanék.
Kameradschaftsbund	A secret society involved in the Sudeten German movement.
Maffia	The Czech home army.
MI5	The British counter-espionage organisation.
MI(R)	Covert warfare branch of British military intelligence.
NKVD	The Soviet secret police.
ON	Obrana Národa, the nation's defence, a resistance organisation founded by former Czech officers as the basis of a secret army.
ORPO	The Nazi uniformed police.
OTA	Codename for Captain Václav Morávek.
RSHA	Reichsicherheitshauptampt or Reich Main Security Office, headed by Heydrich.

SA	Sturmabteilung or Stormtroops.
SD	Sicherheitsdienst, the SS intelligence service created by Heydrich.
SEA LION	The German plan for the invasion of Britain.
Section D	Covert warfare branch of the British Secret Intelligence Service.
SIPO	The Nazi security police, headed by Heydrich. It included both the Gestapo and the criminal police.
SIS	The British Secret Intelligence Service or MI6.
SOE	The British Special Operations Executive, founded in 1940 to encourage European resistance.
SOKOL	The Czech gymnastic association, an organisation closely associated with nationalism.
Sonderbehandlung	'Special Treatment', the SS term for murder.
SS	Schutz Staffel or 'Protection Squad'. The SS expanded into a vast organisation of which Heydrich's security apparatus was only a part.
THREE KINGS	Czech resistance group which collected intelligence for the exiles.
ULTRA	Signals intelligence derived from cracking the secret of the enigma coding machine used by the Germans.
UNCLE	Czech codename for Soviet military intelligence.
UVOD	The central council of the Czech home resistance which represented all groups except the communists.

Appendix 2

Czech Parachute Groups 1941/42

BENJAMIN   Otmar Riedl with codes and crystals for home army. Dropped over Austria due to navigational error on 16/17 April 1941 and arrested after dumping his equipment. Undetected as a parachutist and charged only with illegal crossing of a border.

PERCENTAGE   Corporal František Pavelka with a transmitter and ciphers for the home army. He was dropped near Caslav on 4 October 1941 and arrested on 25 October in Prague.

ANTHROPOID   Sergeants Josef Gabčík and Jan Kubiš who were sent to kill Heydrich. They were dropped on 28/29 December 1941. Intended dropping zone Borek aerodrome near Plzeň. Actual dropping zone was village of Nehvizdy outside Prague. Both men were killed at the battle of the Karel Boromejsky Church on 18 June 1942.

SILVER A   Lieutenant Alfred Bartoš (promoted captain while in the field), Sergeant Josef Valčik, and Corporal Jiří Potuček with the mission of contacting A–54, establishing intelligence networks and co-ordinating the arrival of subsequent groups. They were dropped on 28/29 December, between Kolin and Podebrady. Valčik was killed at the Karel Boromejsky. Bartoš was arrested in Pardubice on 21 June 1942 and died the following day from his wounds. Potuček was shot dead by Czech police on 2 August 1942 while on the run.

SILVER B   Sergeant Vladimir Skacha and Sergeant Jan Zemek, dropped on 28/29 December 1941, with the mission of delivering a transmitter to the underground and arranging supply drops. They went to ground after losing their equipment.

ZINC   Lieutenant Oldrich Pechal, Sergeant Arnost Mikš and Corporal Vilem Gerik, a radio group with the mission of backing up SILVER A, establishing an intelligence network in Moravia and delivering money to the resistance. Dropped in error near Gbely in Slovakia on 27/28 March 1942. Pechal shot two German customs officers while crossing into the protectorate and was later arrested. Mikš joined the JINDRA group in Prague and was shot dead by Czech police while picking up equipment in the Krivoklat forest near Kladno on the night of 30 April/1 May 1942. Gerik surrendered to the Czech police in Prague on 4 April and was handed over to the Gestapo. He became a collaborator and according to the Gestapo 'contributed substantially to the discovery of other parachute groups by getting into their safe houses'.

OUT DISTANCE   Lieutenant Adolf Opálka, Sergeant Karel Čurda and Corporal Ivan Kolařík, dropped near Telc in Moravia on 27/28 March 1942 with the mission of planting a Rebecca beacon to guide RAF bombers to the Skoda works in Plzeň. This was originally a four-man group but one member dropped out and was not replaced. Kolařík was arrested by the Gestapo in Brno and committed suicide on 1 April 1942. Opálka was killed at the Karel Boromejsky on 18 June 1942. Čurda surrendered to the Gestapo on 16 June 1942 and became an informer. It was his information that blew the JINDRA network and led to the deaths of the parachutists in the church.

BIVOUAC   Sergeant František Pospišil, Sergeant Jindřich Čoupek and Corporal Libor Zapletal dropped on the Pozary estate, north-west of Krivoklat on 27/28 April 1942 with the mission of sabotaging the railway bridge and signals at Přerov and the power station at Brno. Zapletal and Čoupek were arrested by the Gestapo on 2 May 1942. Pospišil was captured a few days later.

BIOSCOPE   Sergeant Bohuslav Kouba, Sergeant Josef Bublik and Sergeant Jan Hrubý dropped on the Pozary estate, north-west of Krivoklat on 27/28 April 1942 with the mission of sabotaging the railway bridge at Hradnice and the transformer station at Vsetín. Kouba was detained by Czech police on 3 May 1942 in Kutna Hora and committed suicide in his cell. The two others were killed at the Karel Boromejsky on 18 June 1942.

STEEL A   Lance-Corporal Oldřich Dvořák dropped on the Pozary estate, north-west of Krivoklat on 27/28 April with a transmitter for the home army and spare crystals for SILVER A. The transmitter was buried but betrayed to the Germans by a farmer. Dvořák was shot on 30 June 1942 as he tried to flee to his family in Slovakia.

INTRANSITIVE   Lieutenant Václav Kindl, Sergeant Bohuslav Grabovský and Corporal Vojtěch Lukaštík dropped on 29/30 April near Trebon in southern Bohemia with the mission of sabotaging the oil refinery at Kolin. The group lost its equipment in the drop and went into hiding. Kindl and Grabovský were captured in March 1943. Kindl became an informer and was shot in error during a Gestapo operation he was assisting on 20 May 1944. Grabovský was executed at Terezin in October 1944. Lukaštík was shot dead on 8 January 1943.

TIN   Sergeant Ludvik Cupal and Sergeant Jaroslav Švarc dropped on 29/30 April near Trebon in southern Bohemia with the mission of killing the Minister of Education and Propaganda in the protectorate government, Emanuel Moravec. The men lost contact with each other in the drop and could not find their equipment. Both were injured in the legs and Cupal also sustained a serious internal injury. Švarc went into hiding with the JINDRA group in Prague and was killed at the Karel Boromejsky on 18 June 1942. Cupal joined Lukaštík of INTRANSITIVE at Velehrad in Moravia. On 18 September both men attempted to sabotage the railway line between Polešovice and Nedakonice, sparking off a Gestapo search. Cupal shot himself when surrounded at Velehrad on 15 January 1943.

CHROME   A supply drop on 25 May 1942. No record of location.

SHALE   A supply drop on 29 June 1942. No record of location.

ANTIMONY   Lieutenant František Závorka, Sergeant Stanislav Srazil and Lance-Corporal Lubomír Jasínek, a radio group dropped on 23/24 October 1942 to re-establish contact with the home army and to ascertain the fate of SILVER A. It was tracked down with the help of Karel Čurda (ex-OUT DISTANCE) in January 1943. Srazil collaborated and his companions committed suicide.

Primary Sources and Select Bibliography

1 Primary Sources

(a) BBC Written Archives Centre, Caversham Park, Reading

Daily Digest of World Broadcasts (From Germany and German-Occupied Countries)
European News Service, Broadcasts and Guidelines

(b) Modern Military Records, National Archives, Washington DC

Microfilm T–77, Roll 1050, Sammlung von übersetzen Funkdepeschen des Geheimsenders Sparta–1
Microfilm T–84, Roll 437, Der Reichsprotektor in Böhmen und Mähren
Microfilm T–175, Roll 9, Befehlshaber der Ordnungspolizei
Microfilm T–175, Roll 82, Personlicher Stab Reichsführer-SS
Microfilm T–175, Roll 90, Gedenkrede zur Trauerfeier für den durch Morderhand gefallenen SS Obergruppenführer und General der Polizei Reinhard Heydrich
RG–238, Interrogation of Walter Friedrich Schellenberg
RG–266, OSS Records

(c) Foreign and Commonwealth Office, London

SOE Papers

(d) Public Record Office, London

Air 20/307
AIR 27
CAB 79
FO 371

(e) YIVO Institute, New York

Abschlussbericht Attentat auf SS Obergruppenführer Heydrich

2 Select Bibliography

Amort, Čestmír, *Heydrichiáda*, Prague 1965.
Amort, Čestmír, and Jedlička, I. M., *The Canaris File*, London 1970.
Andrew, Christopher, *Secret Service*, London 1986.
Aronson, Shlomo, *Reinhard Heydrich und die Frühgeschichte von Gestapo und SD*, Munich 1971.
Beneš, Eduard, *Memoirs of Dr Eduard Beneš*, London 1954.

214   *Primary Sources and Select Bibliography*

Berton, Stanislav F., 'Das Attentat auf Reinhard Heydrich von 27 Mai 1942 Ein Bericht des Kriminalrats Heinz Pannwitz', *Vierteljahreshefte für Zeitgeschichte*, Vol. 33, 1985, pp. 673–706.

Berton, Stanislav F., 'Who Ordered the Assassination of R. Heydrich and Why?', unpublished.

Berton, Stanislav F., 'Secrets Of Lidice', unpublished.

Brandes, Detlef, *Die Tschechen unter deutschem Protektorat*, Munich 1969.

Brissaud, André, *Canaris*, London 1973.

Brissaud, André, *The Nazi Secret Service*, London 1975.

Burgess, Alan, *Seven Men at Daybreak*, London 1960.

Calic, Edouard, *Reinhard Heydrich Schlüsselfigur des Dritten Reiches*, Düsseldorf 1982.

Cameron, Norman, and Stevens R. H. (trans.), *Hitler's Table Talk 1941–1944*, London 1953.

Cave Brown, Anthony, *'C': The Secret Life of Sir Stewart Menzies*, New York 1987.

Chmela, Leopold, *The Economic Aspects of the German Occupation of Czechoslovakia*, Prague 1948.

Czechoslovak Information Service, *Czechoslovak Sources and Documents No. 2*, New York 1943.

Dawidowicz, Lucy, *The War Against the Jews*, London 1983.

Dennler, Wilhelm, *Die bohemische Passion*, Freiburg 1953.

Deschner, Gunther, *Heydrich: The Pursuit of Total Power*, London 1981.

Dodds-Parker, Douglas, *Setting Europe Ablaze*, London 1984.

Doležal, Jiří, and Křen, Jan (eds), *Czechoslovakia's Fight 1938–1945: Documents on the Resistance Movement of the Czechoslovak People*, Prague 1964.

Dollman, Eugen, *The Interpreter*, London 1967.

Erdely, E. V., *Prague Braves the Hangman*, London 1942.

Fest, Joachim C., *The Face of the Third Reich*, New York 1970.

Fleming, Gerald, *Hitler and the Final Solution*, Oxford 1986.

Foot, M. R. D., *Resistance*, London 1978.

Foot, M. R. D., *SOE: The Special Operations Executive 1940–1946*, London 1984.

Fuchik, Julius, *Notes from the Gallows*, New York 1948.

Gajan, Koloman, and Kvaček, Robert, *Germany and Czechoslovakia 1918–1945*, Prague 1965.

Georg, Enno, *Die Wirtschaftlichen Unternehmungen der SS*, Stuttgart 1963.

Gilbert, Martin, *The Holocaust: The Jewish Tragedy*, London 1987.

Graber, G. S., *The Life and Times of Reinhard Heydrich*, London 1980.

Grant Duff, Sheila, *A German Protectorate: The Czechs Under Nazi Rule*, London 1942.

Groscurth, Helmut, *Tagebücher eines Abwehroffiziers 1938–1940*, Stuttgart 1970.

Haag, John, 'Knights of the Spirit: The Kameradschaftsbund', *Journal of Contemporary History*, Vol. VIII, No. 3, 1973, pp. 133–53.

Hamšík, D., and Pražák, J., *Eine Bombe für Heydrich*, East Berlin 1964.

Heinemann, John L., *Hitler's First Foreign Minister Constantin von Neurath: Diplomat and Statesman*, Stamford 1979.

Heydrich, Lina, *Leben mit einem Kriegsverbrecher*, Pfaffenhofen 1976.

Hirschfeld, Gerhard, *The Policies of Genocide Jews and Soviet Prisoners of War in Nazi Germany*, London 1986.

Hoettl, Wilhelm, *The Secret Front: The Story of Nazi Political Espionage*, New York 1954.

Hoffman, Peter, *Hitler's Personal Security*, London 1979.

Höhne, Heinz, *Canaris*, London 1979.

Höhne, Heinz, *The Order of the Death's Head*, London 1969.

Huss, Pierre J., *Heil! and Farewell*, London 1943.

Huták, J. B., *With Blood and Iron: The Lidice Story*, London 1957.

Ivanov, Miroslav, *Target: Heydrich*, New York 1974.

Jelínek, Zdenek, *Operace Silver A*, Kolin 1984.

Kersten, Felix, *The Kersten Memoirs*, London 1956.

Koutek, Jaroslav, *Tichá Fronta*, Prague 1985.

Král, Václav (ed.), *Lesson from History*, Prague 1962.

Krausnick, Helmut, and Brozat, Martin, *Anatomy of the SS State*, London 1968.

Lochner, Louis P. (ed.), *The Goebbels Diaries*, London 1948.

Lockhart, R. H. Bruce, *Comes the Reckoning*, London 1947.

Luža, Radomír, *The Transfer of the Sudeten Germans*, New York and London, 1964.

Mackenzie, Compton, *Dr Beneš*, London 1946.

Mamatey, Victor S., and Luža, Radomír (eds), *A History of the Czechoslovak Republic 1918–1948*, Princeton 1973.

Mastny, Vojtech, *The Czechs Under Nazi Rule*, New York 1971.

Moravec, František, *Master of Spies*, London 1981.

Otáhalová, Libuše, and Červinková, Milada (eds), *Dokumenty z historie československé politiky 1939–1943*, Prague 1966.

Pimlott, Ben, *Hugh Dalton*, London 1986.

Pimlott, Ben (ed.), *The Second World War Diary of Hugh Dalton 1940–1945*, London 1986.

Reitlinger, Gerald, *The Final Solution*, London 1971.

Reitlinger, Gerald, *The SS: Alibi of a Nation*, London 1981.

Schellenberg, Walter, *The Schellenberg Memoirs*, London 1956.

Smelser, Ronald M., *The Sudeten Problem 1933–1938: Volkstummpolitik and the Formulation of Nazi Foreign Policy*, London 1975.

Speer, Albert, *The Slave State*, London 1981.

Stafford, David, *Britain and European Resistance 1940–1945*, London 1983.

Stevenson, William, *A Man Called Intrepid*, London 1976.

Ströbinger, Rudolf, *Das Attentat von Prag*, Landshut 1977.

Táborský, Edward, *President Edvard Beneš Between East and West 1938–1948*, Stanford 1981.

Taylor, Fred (ed.), *The Goebbels Diaries 1939–1941*, London 1982.

Vaněk, Ladislav, 'Atentát na Heydricha', *Dějiny a Současnost*, vol. IV, No. 5, 1963, pp. 10–12.

von Schmöller, Gustav, 'Heydrich im Protektorat Böhmen und Mähren', *Vierteljahreshefte für Zeitgeschichte*, vol. 27, 1979, pp. 626–45.

West, Nigel, *MI6*, London 1985.

Wiener, Jan, *The Assassination of Heydrich*, New York 1969.

Wighton, Charles, *Heydrich: Hitler's Most Evil Henchman*, London 1962.

Young, Kenneth (ed.), *The Diaries of Sir Robert Bruce Lockhart 1939–1965*, London 1980.

Notes

Introduction

The claim that Heydrich was killed to protect a prominent German traitor appears in Lauran Paine, *The Abwehr: German Military Intelligence in World War Two*, London 1984, D. Hamšik and J. Pražák, *Eine Bombe für Heydrich*, East Berlin 1964, and C. Amort and I. M. Jedlička, *The Canaris File*, London 1970.

The theory that he was assassinated to avert the extermination of the Jews appears in William Stephenson, *A Man Called Intrepid: The Secret War 1939–1945*, London 1976. The book is so inaccurate as to hardly warrant serious consideration.

The story about the Duke of Windsor can be found in Peter Allen, *The Crown and the Swastika: Hitler, Hess and the Duke of Windsor*, London 1983.

The memoirs of František Moravec were first published in English as *Master of Spies*, London 1970. The result of Miroslav Ivanov's research, *Target: Heydrich*, was published in English translation in New York, 1974.

Chapter 1: Funeral In Berlin

The details of Heydrich's funeral on pp. 3–4 are drawn from Gunther Deschner, *Heydrich: The Pursuit of Total Power*, London 1981, and Charles Wighton, *Heydrich: Hitler's Most Evil Henchman*, London 1962.

The quotations on p. 3 are from Deschner, pp. 267–8, and Wighton, p. 277.

The quotation on p. 4 is from Helmut Krausnick and Martin Brozat, *Anatomy of the SS State*, London 1968, p. 340.

The descriptions of Heydrich's character on pp. 4–5 are from Walter Schellenberg, *The Schellenberg Memoirs*, London 1956, pp. 30–1, Eugen Dollman, *The Interpreter*, London 1967, pp. 91–6, Wilhelm Hoettl, *The Secret Front: The Story of Nazi Political Espionage*, New York 1954, pp. 32–41, and Pierre J. Huss, *Heil! and Farewell*, London 1943, pp. 117–20.

The details about Heydrich's family background and early life on pp. 5–9 are drawn from Deschner, Edouard Calic, *Reinhard Heydrich Schlüsselfigur des Dritten Reiches*, Düsseldorf 1982, Shlomo Aronson, *Reinhard Heydrich und die Frühgeschichte von Gestapo und SD*, and G. S. Graber, *The Life and Times of Reinhard Heydrich*, London 1980. Calic emphasises the nationalist and anti-Semitic attitudes of Bruno Heydrich.

The social background comes from V. Berghahn, *Modern Germany*, Cambridge 1985, Lucy Dawidowicz, *The War Against the Jews*, London 1983, F. L. Carsten, *The Rise of Fascism*, London 1967, and S. J. Woolf (ed.), *European Fascism*, New York 1969.

The quotations on p. 6 are from Berghahn, p. 12, and John M. Steiner, *Power*

Politics and Social Change in National Socialist Germany, The Hague 1975, p. 264.
The quotation on p. 8 is from Graber, pp. 23–4.
The quotation on p. 9 is from Graber, p. 14.
The details of Heydrich's naval career on pp. 9–15 are based on Deschner, Aronson, Calic, Graber, and Lina Heydrich, *Leben mit einem Kriegsverbrecher*, Pfaffenhofen 1976. Calic emphasises his authoritarian sympathies and interest in the Nazis at this time.
The naval background is based on Holger H. Herwig, *The German Naval Officer Corps*, Oxford 1973, and Keith W. Bird, *Weimar, the German Naval Officer Corps and the Rise of National Socialism*, Amsterdam 1977.
The quotation on p. 10 is from Deschner, p. 24.
The long quotation on p. 10 is from Bird, p. 268.
The quotation on p. 13 is from Calic, p. 36.
The long quotation on p. 14 is from Graber, pp. 26–7.
The quotations on p. 15 are from Lina Heydrich, pp. 8–20, and Deschner, pp. 35–7.
Details on Heydrich's decision to join the SS on pp. 16–18 are from Calic, Deschner and Lina Heydrich.
The background on the SS is drawn from Heinz Höhne, *The Order of the Death's Head*, New York 1969.
Details about his early SS career and his relationship with Himmler on pp. 18–20 are drawn from Deschner, Aronson, Lina Heydrich and Graber.
The quotation on p. 18 is from Wighton, p. 35.
The first quotation on p. 19 is from Felix Kersten, *The Kersten Memoirs*, London 1956, pp. 98–9.
The second quotation on p. 19 is from Graber, p. 59.
The quotations on pp. 20–1 are from Kersten, pp. 219–20, and Deschner, p. 54.
The quotation on p. 21 is from Höhne, p. 154.
The quotation on p. 22 is from Joachim C. Fest, *The Face of the Third Reich*, New York 1970, p. 157.

Chapter 2: Hitler's Secret Policeman

The description of the struggle to control the police, pp. 23–6 is based on Deschner, Aronson, Krausnick, Höhne, and André Brissaud, *The Nazi Secret Service*, London 1975.
The quotation on p. 23 is from Krausnick, p. 143.
The description of the Röhm purge on pp. 26–7 is based on Deschner, Graber, Höhne, Brissaud, and Robert J. O'Neill, *The German Army and the Nazi Party*, London 1968.
The quotations on pp. 26–7 are from J. W. Wheeler-Bennet, *The Nemesis of Power*, London 1967, p. 310, Stephen H. Roberts, *The House That Hitler Built*, London 1938, pp. 106–7, and Höhne, *The Order of the Death's Head*, p. 114.
The consolidation of police power on pp. 27–9 is based on Deschner, Aronson, Krausnick, Höhne, Brissaud and Graber.

The quotation on p. 29 is from Höhne, p. 231.

The description of the security police and the 'Jewish question' on pp. 29–30 is based on Höhne, Deschner, Dawidowicz, Gerald Reitlinger, *The Final Solution*, London 1971, and Karl A. Schleunes, *The Twisted Road to Auschwitz*, London 1972.

The description of the attack on Catholicism on pp. 30–1 is based on Deschner, Hoettl, Guenter Lewy, *The Catholic Church and Nazi Germany*, New York 1965, and Franz von Papen, *Memoirs*, London 1952.

The quotation on p. 31 is from Hoettl, p. 39.

The description of the intrigues against the army and the Abwehr on pp. 31–7 is based on Deschner, O'Neill, Höhne, Schellenberg, André Brissaud, *Canaris*, London 1973, Heinz Höhne, *Canaris*, London 1979, and J. W. Wheeler-Bennett, *The Nemesis of Power: The German Army in Politics 1918–1945*, London 1967. Details of the Formis affair from Höhne, *The Order of the Death's Head*, and Brissaud, *The Nazi Secret Service*.

Details of the Tukachevsky affair from Schellenberg, Brissaud, Höhne and Hoettl. Schellenberg was not always a reliable informant and it is possible that Hitler took no direct hand in the Tukachevsky affair.

The quotation on p. 34 is from Brissaud, *Canaris*, p. 56.

The quotation on p. 35 is from Höhne, *Canaris*, p. 252.

The details on Operation TANNENBERG on pp. 37–8 are from Calic and Höhne, *The Order of the Death's Head*.

The quotation on p. 37 is from Höhne, pp. 294–5.

The details on the Einsatzgruppen in Poland and the tension with the army on pp. 38–9 are from Höhne, *The Order of the Death's Head*, Höhne, *Canaris*, Brissaud, *Canaris*, Deschner, Calic, O'Neill and Harold C. Deutsch, *The Conspiracy Against Hitler in the Twilight War*, Minneapolis 1970.

The quotations on p. 38 are from Brissaud, *Canaris*, p. 153, and Höhne, *Canaris*, p. 363.

The background on the Einsatzgruppen in Russia, the Wannsee Conference and the 'Final Solution' on pp. 39–42 is based on Deschner, Calic, Dawidowicz, Höhne, *The Order of the Death's Head*, Reitlinger, *The Final Solution*, Gerald Hirschfeld (ed.), *The Policies of Genocide: Jews and Soviet Prisoners of War in Nazi Germany* (London 1981), Martin Gilbert, *The Holocaust: The Jewish Tragedy*, London 1987, Gerald Fleming, *Hitler and the Final Solution*, Oxford 1986, and Gerald Reitlinger, *The SS: Alibi of a Nation*, London 1981.

The quotations on p. 40 are from Reitlinger, *The SS: Alibi of a Nation*, p. 177, Graber, p. 184, and Calic, p. 438.

The first quotation on p. 41 is from Gilbert, p. 283.

The second quotation on p. 41 is from Schellenberg, p. 207.

The quotations on p. 42 are from Gilbert, p. 285, Fleming, pp. 59–60, and Krausnick, p. 340.

The details of Heydrich's personal life on pp. 42–4 are drawn from Deschner, Graber, Wighton, Schellenberg and 'Der Spiel ist aus', *Der Spiegel*, 9 February 1950.

The first two quotations on p. 43 are from Brissaud, *Canaris*, p. 157, and Fest, p. 172.

The last quotation on p. 43 is from 'Der Spiel ist aus'.

The quotations on p. 44 are from 'Der Spiel ist aus', Dollman, pp. 94–5 and Fest, p 154.

Chapter 3: The Czech Connexion

The treatment of the Sudeten crisis on pp. 45–8 is based on Schellenberg, Hoettl, Brissaud, *The Nazi Secret Service*, Brissaud, *Canaris*, Höhne, *The Order of the Death's Head*, Höhne, *Canaris*, Ronald M. Smelser, *The Sudeten Problem 1933–1938*, London 1975, Radomir Luža, *The Transfer of the Sudeten Germans*, New York and London 1964, Helmut Groscurth, *Tagebücher eines Abwehroffiziers 1938–1940*, Stuttgart 1970, and John Haag, 'Knights of the Spirit: The Kameradschaftsbund', *Journal of Contemporary History*, Vol. VIII, No. 3, 1973, pp. 133–53.

The quotation on p. 45 is from William L. Shirer, *The Rise and Fall of the Third Reich*, London 1967, p. 447.

The quotations on pp. 46–7 are from John L. Heinemann, *Hitler's First Foreign Minister Constantin von Neurath: Diplomat and Statesman*, Stamford 1979, p. 313, and Brissaud, *The Nazi Secret Service*, p. 239.

The quotation on p. 47 is from Brissaud, *The Nazi Secret Service*, p. 241.

The details of Beneš' career on pp. 48–50 are based on Eduard Beneš, *My War Memoirs*, London 1928, Eduard Beneš, *Memoirs of Dr Eduard Beneš*, London 1954, Godfrey Lias, *Beneš of Czechoslovakia*, London 1940, Compton Mackenzie, *Dr Beneš*, London 1946, Victor S. Mamatey and Radomír Luža (eds), *A History of the Czechoslovak Republic 1918–1948*, Princeton 1973, and Edward Táborský, *President Edvard Beneš Between East and West 1938–1948*, Stanford 1981, and Gordon A. Craig and Felix Gilbert (eds), *The Diplomats 1919–1939*, 2 vols, vol. 1, New York 1967.

The quotations on p. 48–9 are from Beneš, *War Memoirs*, pp. 74–5, and Robert Bruce Lockhart, *Comes the Reckoning*, London 1947, p. 64, Mackenzie, pp. 122, 262, and Taborsky, p. 13.

The details of intelligence co-operation on pp. 50–55 are based on František Moravec, *Master of Spies*, London 1981, Rudolf Ströbinger, *Das Attentat von Prag*, Landshut 1977, C. Amort and I. M. Jedlička, *The Canaris File*, Hamšik and Pražák, Christopher Andrew, *Secret Service*, London 1986, and Nigel West, *MI6*, London 1985.

The quotation on p. 50 is from Moravec, p. xix.

The quotations on pp. 50–1 are from Moravec, pp. 20–1 and p. 35.

The quotation on p. 52 is from Moravec, p. 49.

The quotation on p. 53 is from Moravec, p. 93.

The quotation on p. 54 is from Andrew, p. 533.

The background to the aftermath of Munich on pp. 55–6 is from Mamatey and Luža, Beneš, Moravec, Hubert Ripka, *Munich Before and After*, London 1939, and Leonard Mosley, *On Borrowed Time*, London 1971.

The quotation on p. 56 is from Beneš, p. 197.

The discussion of Moravec's plans on pp. 56–8 is drawn from Moravec, pp. 124–35.

The quotation on p. 57 is from Andrew, p. 580.

The background on Hitler's plans on pp. 58–9 is based on Brissaud, *Canaris*, Höhne, *Canaris*, Groscurth, Luža and Moseley.
The quotations on p. 58 are from Krausnick, p. 177, and Brissaud, *Canaris*, p. 121.
Details about the fate of the Kameradschaftsbund can be found in Haag.
The quotations on p. 59 are from Brissaud, *Canaris*, pp. 124–5.
The background to Moravec's flight on pp. 60–61 is drawn from Moravec and Amort and Jedlička.
The quotations on p. 60 are from Moravec, pp. 137–42.
The quotation on p. 61 is from Moravec, p. 143.
The background to the Nazi occupation of Prague on pp. 61–3 is from Mamatey and Luža, Luža, Moseley, Detlef Brandes, *Die Tschechen unter deutschem Protektorat*, 2 vols, vol. 1, Munich 1969, Vojtech Mastny, *The Czechs Under Nazi Rule*, New York 1971, and Heinemann.
The quotation on p. 61 is from Mackenzie, p. 245.
The quotation on p. 62 is from Heinemann, p. 188.

Chapter 4: Exiles

The description of the political position of the exile government on pp. 67–70 is based on Beneš, Moravec, Mamatey and Luža, Mackenzie, Táborský and Sir Robert Bruce Lockhart, *Comes the Reckoning*, London 1947. The Foreign Office view of Beneš is summed up in C6283/2/12 FO 371 and C7646/2/12 FO 371/24289.
The quotations on p. 67 are from Moravec, p. 145, and Mackenzie, p. 249.
The quotations on p. 69 are from Mastny, p. 143, Lockhart, p. 60, Moravec, p. 148, and Libuše Otáhalová and Milada Cervinková (eds), *Dokumenty z historie československé politiky 1939–1943*, Prague 1966, Document No. 84.
The first quotation on p. 70 is from Kenneth Young (ed.), *The Diaries of Sir Robert Bruce Lockhart 1939–1965*, London 1980, p. 83.
The description of the relationship with British intelligence on pp. 70–72 is based on Moravec, Beneš, Otáhalová and Červinková, M. R. D. Foot, *Resistance*, London 1978, M. R. D. Foot, *SOE: The Special Operations Executive 1940–1946*, 1984, and C1739/2/12 FO 371/24287.
The second quotation on p. 70 is from Moravec, p. 218.
The quotations on p. 71 are from Otáhalová and Červinková, Document No. 135.
The first quotation on p. 72 is from C4850/2/12 FO 371/24288.
The subsequent quotations on p. 72 are from C1739/2/12 FO 371/24287, Otáhalová and Červinková, Document No. 178, and C7642/2/12 FO 371/24289.
The description of the founding of SOE on pp. 72–3 is based on Andrew, Foot, Ben Pimlott, *Hugh Dalton*, London 1986, Hugh Dalton, *The Fateful Years*, London 1957, and David Stafford, *Britain and European Resistance 1940–1945*, London 1983.
The impact of the strategic position on the Foreign Office view of Beneš can be found in C7642/2/12 FO 371/24289.
The quotation on p. 73 is from Lockhart, p. 94.
The description of Czech diplomacy and intelligence activities on pp. 73–7 is based on Moravec, Amort and Jedlička, Beneš, Lockhart and Táborský. Details on SOE are

drawn from Foot, Stafford and Andrew.

The first quotation on p. 75 is from Amort and Jedlička, p. 95.

The second quotation on p. 75 is from C10775/6/18 FO 371/24392.

The description of Czech relations with Soviet intelligence on pp. 77–8 is based on Brandes and Moravec.

The quotation on p. 77 is from Stanislav F. Berton, 'Who Ordered the Assassination of R. Heydrich and Why', unpublished manuscript, p. 30.

The first quotation on p. 78 is from Otáhalová and Červinková, Document No. 178.

The description of Beneš' dealings with the British on pp. 78–9 is based on Beneš and Lockhart.

The quotations on pp. 78–9 are from C1627/1627/12 FO 371/26395, Andrew, p. 627, Lockhart, p. 115, and Beneš, p. 158.

The description of the underground and Beneš' contacts with Eliáš and Hácha on pp. 79–80 is based on Luža, Mastny, Brandes and C10775/6/18 FO 371/24393.

The long quotation on p. 80 is from Mastny, p. 163.

The details of the power struggle between Frank and Neurath on pp. 80–4 are based on Mastny, Luža, Brandes, Mamatey and Luža, Heinemann and Fred Taylor (ed.), *The Goebbels Diaries 1939–41*, London 1982.

The first quotation on p. 81 is from Heinemann, p. 200.

The second quotation on p. 81 is from J. B. Huták, *With Blood and with Iron: The Lidice Story*, London 1957, p. 41.

The quotations on p. 82 are from Heinemann, p. 204, Mastny, p. 147, and *Goebbels Diaries 1939–1941*, p. 167.

The first quotation on p. 83 is from *The Goebbels Diaries 1939–1941*, p. 356.

The second quotation on p. 83 is from Václav Král (ed.), *Lesson from History*, Prague 1962, Document No. 14.

The quotation on p. 84 is from Král, Document No. 12.

The quotation on p. 85 is from Stafford, p. 32.

Chapter 5: Time for Action

The description of the Czech army on pp. 86–8 is based on Beneš, Moravec, Lockhart and C7921/1419/62 FO 371/24366, C8530/1419/62 FO 371/24366, C8316/1419/62 FO 371/24366, CAB85/19 AFO (40) 1, CAB85/19 (40) 25.

The first quotation on p. 87 is from CAB85/19 (40) 46.

The quotations on pp. 87–8 are from C1132/6/12 FO 371/26376 and C12431/12431/12 FO 371/30855.

The quotation on pp. 88–9 is from Miroslav Ivanov, *Target Heydrich*, New York 1974, p. 40.

The description of Czech and SOE plans on p. 89 is based on Beneš, Mastny, Moravec, Ivanov, Stafford and Zdenek Jelínek, *Operace Silver A*, Kolin 1984.

The description of events in the Protectorate on pp. 89–90 is based on Brandes, Heinemann, Amort and Jedlička and Mastny.

The quotation on p. 90 is from Amort and Jedlička, p. 111.

Beneš' attitude to BARBAROSSA on pp. 90–1 is based on Táborský, Otáhalová and Červinková, Beneš and Mamatey and Luža.

The first quotation on p. 91 is from Táborský, pp. 139–40.

The second quotation on p. 91 is from Otáhalová and Červinková, Document No. 193.

The description of Czech–Soviet and Czech–British relations on pp. 91–7 is from Beneš, Moravec, Lockhart, Mastny, Otáhalová and Červinková, Táborský, Amoret and Jedlička, Brandes, Ivan Maisky, *Memoirs of a Soviet Ambassador: The War 1939–43*, London 1967, C7680/7140/12 FO 371/26410, C7765/7140/12 FO 371/26410, C7883/7140/12 FO 371/26410, C8376/57/12 FO 371/26381, C9515/57/12 FO 371/26381 and Microfilm T–77, Roll 1050, Sammlung von übersetzen Funkdepeschen des Geheimsenders Sparta-1.

The quotation on pp. 91–2 is from Táborský, p. 145.

The quotation on p. 93 is from Moravec, p. 215.

The quotation on pp. 94–5 is from Jiří Doležal and Jan Křen (eds), *Czechoslovakia's Fight 1938–1945: Documents on the Resistance Movement of the Czechoslovak People*, Prague 1964, Document No. 14.

The quotation on p. 96 is from Microfilm T–77, Roll 1050.

The quotation on p. 97 is from Microfilm T–77, Roll 1050.

The description of the parachute groups from Britain and the USSR on pp. 98–102 is based on Brandes, Ströbinger, Ivanov, Hamšik and Pražák, Huták, Jelínek, Foot, Moravec and Microfilm T–77, Roll 1050.

The quotation on p. 100 is from Burgess, p. 29.

The quotation on p. 101 is from Ivanov, pp. 137–8.

The description of the press boycott on pp. 102–3 is based on Mastny, Brandes, C10976/57/12 FO 371/26381 and Microfilm T–77, Roll 1050.

The quotation on p. 103 is from Huták, p. 44.

Chapter 6: The Butcher of Prague

The description of Heydrich's appointment on pp. 107–11 is based on Brandes, Mastny, Deschner, Lina Heydrich, Schellenberg, Heinemann, Wilhelm Dennler, *Die bohemische Passion*, Freiburg 1953, and Gustav von Schmöller, 'Heydrich im Protektorat Böhmen und Mähren', *Vierteljahreshefte für Zeitgeschichte*, vol. 27, 1979, pp. 626–45. Mastny, von Schmöller and Dennler do not believe that the security situation was as dangerous as Heydrich claimed.

The quotation on p. 107 is from Deschner, p. 191.

The quotation on p. 109 is from Král, Document No. 19.

The quotation on p. 111 is from 'Der Spiel ist aus', pp. 21–2.

The first quotation on p. 112 is from E. V. Erdeley, *Prague Braves the Hangman*, London 1942, p. 51.

The subsequent quotations on p. 112 are from Král, Document No. 19.

The description of Heydrich's measures on pp. 112–16 is based on Brandes, Deschner, Dennler, Mastny, Otáhalová and Červinková, Král and Microfilm T–84, Roll 437, 'Der Reichsprotektor in Böhmen und Mähren'.

The first quotation on p. 113 is from Dennler, p. 58.
The second quotation on p. 113 is from Král, Document No. 20.
The quotations on pp. 114–15 are from Král, Document No. 20, and Otáhalová and Červinková, Document No. 453.
The quotations on p. 115 are from Mastny, pp. 197–8.
The quotations on p. 116 are from Král, Document No. 20, and Ivanov, p. 97.
The description of Heydrich's personal life on pp. 116–17 is based on Deschner, Lina Heydrich and Huták.
The quotation on pp. 116–17 is from 'Der Spiel ist aus', p. 27.
The description of the assassination plan on pp. 117–25 is based on Moravec, Ivanov, Berton, 'Who Ordered the Assassination of R. Heydrich and Why?', and SOE papers. The latest exponent of the theory that the plan was put forward by SIS is Anthony Cave Brown, *'C': The Secret Life of Sir Stewart Menzies*, New York 1987. His chronology undermines his entire case.
The quotations on pp. 117–18 are from SOE papers and *Czechoslovak Sources and Documents No. 2: The Struggle for Freedom*, New York 1943, Document No. 85.
The first quotation on p. 119 is from Moravec, p. 192.
The subsequent quotations on p. 119 are from Moravec, pp. 193 and 205.
The long quotation on p. 121 is from Ivanov, pp. 43–4.
The first quotation on p. 122 is from SOE papers.
The second quotation on p. 122 is from Dalton, p. 368.
The first quotation on p. 123 is from SOE papers.
The second quotation on p. 123 is from Ben Pimlott (ed.), *The Second World War Diary of Hugh Dalton 1940–1945*, London 1986, p. 329.
The quotation on p. 124 is from SOE papers.
The quotations on p. 125 are from Táborský's diary and Moravec, p. 199.
The description of SILVER A on pp. 125–6 is based on Jelínek.
The description of the aircraft problem on pp. 126–7 is based on Stafford, Foot, Huták, Ivanov, C1368/10893/12 FO 371/26148, C1394/10893/12 FO 371/26148 and C286/51/2 FO 371/30823.
The quotations on pp. 127–8 are from a letter by R. Hockey to the author, and Moravec, p. 199.
The quotations on p. 128 from Moravec, p. 199, and AIR 27/956.
The last quotation on p. 128 is from Hamšík and Pražák, p. 148.

Chapter 7: Return

The description of political economic and cultural reorganisation in the Protectorate on pp. 130–5 is based on Deschner, Mastny, Brandes, Dennler, Mamatey and Luža, Otáhalová and Červinková, Albert Speer, *The Slave State*, London 1981, Enno Georg, *Die Wirtschaftlichen Unternehmungen der SS*, Stuttgart 1963, Leopold Chmela, *The Economic Aspects of the German Occupation of Czechoslovakia*, Prague 1948, OSS Report 22900, 'Under German Domination – Czechoslovakia May–August 1942', and Microfilm T-84, Roll 387.
The quotation on p. 130 is from Shirer, p. 1036.

The quotations on p. 131 are from Mastny, pp. 199 and 200.
The quotation on p. 132 is from *The Times*, 21 January 1942.
The quotations on pp. 133–4 are from Král, Document No. 22.
The quotations on p. 134 are from Král, Document No. 22 and No. 24.
The first two quotations on p. 135 are from Deschner, pp. 221 and 218.
The last two quotations on p. 135 are from Král, Document No. 22.
The first two quotations on p. 136 are from Deschner, p. 234, and C14048/57/2 FO 371/26301.
The quotations on pp. 136–7 are from *Hitler's Table Talk 1941–1944*, London 1973, pp. 237–8, and Louis P. Lochner (ed.), *The Goebbels Diary*, London 1948, p. 51.
The quotation on p. 137 is from *Goebbels Diary*, p. 3.
The description of Beneš' policies on pp. 137–9 is based on Beneš, Táborský, Mastny and Brandes.
The quotations on p. 138 are from BBC European News Service, News Summary 31 May 1942, and *Czechoslovak Sources and Documents No. 2*, Document No. 57.
The quotations on pp. 138–9 are from SOE Papers.
The description of the CANONBURY operation is based on SOE Papers, C5286/5286/12 FO 371/26380, C5694/52/2 FO 371/26380, C2915/589/12 FO 371/30837, C3527/3527/12 FO 371/30844, C3852/3557/12 FO 371/30844, Letter Air Historical Branch, Ministry of Defence, and Ivanov.
The description of the activities of SILVER A on pp. 139–42 is from Jelínek and Ivanov.
The quotations on p. 140 are from C1651/3091/12 FO 371/30837.
The first two quotations on p. 141 are from Ivanov, pp. 92 and 109.
The quotations on pp. 141–2 are from Moravec, p. 200, and Jelínek, p. 30.
The background on the early experiences of ANTHROPOID is based on Ivanov, Hamšik and Pražák, Ströbinger, Huták and Alan Burgess, *Seven Men at Daybreak*, London 1960.
The quotation on p. 144 is from Ivanov, p. 25.
The background on the arrest of A–54 on pp. 145–8 is from Jelínek, Ivanov, Amort and Jedlička, Deschner, Brissaud, *Canaris*, Jaroslav Koutek, *Tichá Fronta*, Prague 1985, and Microfilm T–84, Roll 437.
The first quotation on p. 145 is from Amort and Jedlička, p. 133.
The second quotation on p. 145 is from Amort and Jedlička, p. 133.
The quotation on p. 146 is from Brissaud, *Canaris*, p. 256.

Chapter 8: Preparations

The description of the planning on pp. 149–51 is from Ivanov, Hamšik and Pražák, Huták and Burgess.
The quotation on p. 149 is from Ivanov, p. 104.
The first quotation on p. 150 is from Deschner, p. 217.
The second quotation on p. 150 is from Ivanov, p. 98.
The quotation on p. 151 is from Ivanov, p. 98.

The description of the new parachute groups on pp. 151–5 is based on Jelínek, Ivanov, Burgess, SOE papers, C. Amort, *Heydrichiáda*, Prague 1965, Document No. 50, and Stanislav F. Berton, 'Das Attentat auf Reinhard Heydrich von 27 Mai 1942 Ein Bericht des Kriminalrats Heinz Pannwitz', *Vierteljahreshefte für Zeitgeschichte*, Vol. 33, pp. 668–706, and Microfilm T–84, Roll 437. Berton's article presents the memoir of Pannwitz, the Gestapo man who investigated the assassination.

The description of the CANONBURY raid is based on Ivanov, Jelínek, Microfilm T–84, Roll 437, and 'Abschlussbericht Attentat auf SS Obergruppenführer Heydrich'.

The quotation on p. 153 is from Ivanov, p. 128.

The quotation on p. 154 is from Amort, *Heydrichiáda*, Document No. 50.

The quotation on p. 155 is from Jelínek, pp. 46–7.

The description of the debate over the assassination and the appeal to London is based on Ivanov, Jelínek, Ströbinger, Hamšik and Pražák, and S. Berton, 'The Despatch at the Request of Jindra Pertaining to the Assassination of Reinhard Heydrich', unpublished.

The first two quotations on p. 156 are from Ivanov, p. 143.

The long quotation on p. 156 is from Berton, 'The Despatch at the Request of Jindra', p. 40.

The first three quotations on p. 157 are from Berton, 'The Despatch at the Request of Jindra', pp. 35–6, and Ivanov, pp. 143–4.

The quotations on pp. 157–8 are from Berton, 'Who Ordered the Assassination of R. Heydrich and Why?', p. 16, and Pannwitz, p. 702.

The second quotation on p. 158 is from Ivanov, p. 146.

The quotations on pp. 158–9 are from Ivanov, p. 197, and letter from S. Berton. See also Ströbinger, p. 138.

The description of Beneš' preoccupations on pp. 159–60 is based on Brandes, Mamatey and Luža, Táborský, C3135/29/18 FO 371/30898 and C51225/539/12 FO 371/30837.

The quotation on p. 159 is from C5404/5404/12 FO 371/30848.

The quotation on p. 160 is from Brandes, p. 253.

The description of the security situation on pp. 160–1 is based on Deschner, *Goebbels Diary*, Amort, *Heydrichiáda* and Pannwitz.

The quotation on p. 160 is from *Goebbels Diary*, p. 63.

The first quotation on p. 161 is from Pannwitz, p. 678.

The second quotation on p. 161 is from Pannwitz, p. 679.

The description of Heydrich's activities at this time on pp. 161–6 is based on Brandes, Deschner, Mastny, Wighton, Lina Heydrich, Schellenberg, Brissaud, *Canaris*, Amort, *Heydrichiáda*, and Microfilm T–84, Roll 437. For details of the struggle with the party over the occupied east, see Höhne, *The Order of the Death's Head*, and Alexander Dallin, *German Rule in Russia*, New York 1957.

The quotation on p. 162 is from *Hitler's Table Talk*, pp. 464–5.

The first quotation on p. 163 is from *Goebbels Diary*, p. 65.

The subsequent quotations on p. 163 are from Schellenberg, p. 331, and Microfilm T–84, Roll 437.

The quotations on p. 164 are from Schellenberg, pp. 399 and 405.

The quotations on p. 165 are from Mastny, p. 203, and Schellenberg, p. 331.

The quotation on pp. 165–6 is from Hoettl, p. 30.
The description of the preparations of the parachutists on pp. 166–7 is based on Ivanov and Ströbinger.

Chapter 9: Assassination

The description of the attack on pp. 169–74 is based on Ivanov, Pannwitz, Huták, Burgess, Deschner and Wighton.
The quotation on p. 169 is from Ivanov, p. 140.
The quotation on p. 173 is from Ivanov, p. 176.
The quotation on pp. 173–4 is from Pannwitz, p. 681.
The first quotation on p. 174 is from Pannwitz, pp. 682–3.
The description of the Nazi reaction to the attack on pp. 174–83 is based on Brandes, Deschner, Ivanov, Huták, Dennler, Ströbinger, Pannwitz and BBC Monitoring Service, Daily Digest of World Broadcasts (Broadcasts from Germany and German Occupied Countries). The rumour that Heydrich was killed by his own side appears in Arvid Fredborg, *Behind the Steel Wall*, London 1944. In 1942, Fredborg was a Swedish journalist in Berlin.
The last quotation on p. 174 is from Jan Wiener, *The Assassination of Heydrich*, New York 1969.
The quotation on pp. 175–6 is from Wiener, p. 100.
The quotations on p. 176 are from Deschner, pp. 248–9 and 276, and Fleming, p. 115.
The quotations on pp. 176–7 are from Peter Hoffmann, *Hitler's Personal Security*, London 1979, pp. 119–22, and 'Der Spiel ist aus', pp. 26–7.
The quotation on p. 177 is from 'Der Spiel ist aus', p. 28.
The quotation on p. 179 is from OSS Report 22900.
The quotation on p. 180 is from Moravec, p. 200.
The quotations on pp. 180–1 are from Amort, *Heydrichiáda*, Document No. 37, and BBC European News Service, 29 May 1942.
The quotations on p. 181 are from Jelínek, pp. 183–7, and 'Der Spiel ist aus', p. 28.
The quotations on p. 182 are from Ivanov, pp. 178 and 275.
Robert Harris and Jeremy Paxman claim in *A Higher Form of Killing*, London 1982, pp 88–94, that Heydrich died because Kubiš' grenade had been filled with a special lethal toxin developed by the British biological warfare establishment at Porton Down. Their general account of the assassination is riddled with inaccuracies and they present no documentary evidence to support their claim. A moment's thought indicates the absurdity of Kubiš risking a night drop from an aircraft carrying lethal biological toxins and then transporting them round the Protectorate for the next five months. Moreover, Kubiš was hit by splinters from his own bomb, but he did not die as a result. As M. R. D. Foot has remarked, 'The gutters of Prague contained enough germs to infect Heydrich without resorting to the theory of a biological warfare attack.'
The quotations on pp. 182–3 are from *Hitler's Table Talk*, p. 512, Deschner, p. 263, and C6484/539/12 FO 371/30837.

The quotation on p. 183 is from Heinz Boberach (ed.), *Meldungen aus dem Reich: Die geheimen Lageberichte des Sicherheitsdienstes der SS 1932–1945*, Berlin 1984, Document No. 289.

The quotations on pp. 183–4 are from Microfilm T–175, Roll 90, and Deschner, p. 268.

The description of the crime of Lidice and the reprisals against the Jews on pp. 184–7 are based on Pannwitz, Deschner, S. Berton, 'The Secrets of Lidice', unpublished, Gilbert, Fleming and Reitlinger, *The Final Solution*.

The quotations on p. 184 are from Deschner, pp. 270–1.

The description of the propaganda campaign by the Protectorate government on p. 187 is based on Brandes, Dennler, Deschner and Pannwitz.

The quotations on p. 187 are from OSS Report 22900 and Dennler, pp. 78–80.

The description of the assassins in hiding is based on Ivanov, Wiener, Burgess, Ströbinger and Hamšik and Pražák.

The description of the changing Gestapo policy on pp. 188–9 is based on Pannwitz.

The quotation on pp. 188–9 is from Dennler, pp. 80–2.

The first quotations on p. 189 are from Pannwitz, pp. 686–7.

The last quotation on p. 189 is from Huták, p. 128.

Chapter 10: Ending

The description of the discovery of the parachutists and the fight at the church on pp. 191–6 is based on Ivanov, Pannwitz, Amort, Dennler, Huták, Wiener, Burgess, Ströbinger and Hamšik and Pražák.

The quotation on p. 191 is from Amort, Document No. 49.

The quotation on p. 192 is from Ivanov, pp. 246–7.

The quotation on p. 193 is from Pannwitz, p. 695.

The quotation on p. 194 is from Amort, Document No. 42.

The first two quotations on p. 195 are from Amort, Document No. 42, and Pannwitz, p. 697.

The quotations on pp. 195–6 are from Amort, Document No. 42, and Pannwitz, p. 697.

The description of the destruction of Ležáky and the fate of the parachutists' helpers on pp. 196–8 is based on Brandes, Jelínek, Pannwitz, Ivanov, Hamšik and Pražák and Berton, 'Who Ordered the Assassination of R. Heydrich and Why?'

The quotation on p. 196 is from Pannwitz, pp. 703–4.

The first quotation on p. 197 is from Amort, Document No. 49.

The second quotation on p. 197 is from *Hitler's Table Talk*, p. 554.

The description of the Heydrich myth and the fate of his family on pp. 198–9 is based on Deschner, Lina Heydrich, Reitlinger, *The SS: Alibi of a Nation*, and Hamšik and Pražák.

The description of Beneš' diplomatic dealings on pp. 199–202 is based on Beneš, Luža, Mamatey and Luža, Táborský and Berton, 'Who Ordered the Assassination of R. Heydrich and Why?'

The quotations on p. 199 are from David Dilks (ed.), *The Diaries of Sir Alexander Cadogan 1938–1945*, London 1971, pp. 458–9, European News Service Broadcast, 29 May 1942.

The long quotation on pp. 199–200 is from BBC European News General Directive, 29 May 1942.

The quotations on p. 200 are from C6627/5404/12 FO 371/30848 and *The Diaries of Sir Robert Bruce Lockhart*, p. 605.

The quotations on pp. 200–1 are from C5922/5404/12 FO 371/30848, C6788/326/12 FO 371/30835 and *Czechoslovak Sources and Documents*, Document No. 65.

The quotations on p. 201 are from Beneš, p. 206, and Berton, 'Who Ordered the Assassination of R. Heydrich and Why?', pp. 20 and 7.

The last quotation on p. 201 is from Beneš, pp. 209–10.

The description of the situation in the protectorate after Heydrich is based on Brandes, Mamatey and Luža and Lina Heydrich.

The first quotation on p. 203 is from Luža, p. 236.

The quotations on pp. 203–4 are from *Czechoslovak Sources and Documents*, Document No. 88, Cordell Hull, *The Memoirs of Cordell Hull*, vol. 2, New York 1948, p. 1184, and Mamatey and Luža, p. 315.

The quotations on p. 204 are from C11965/539/12 FO 371/30838 and C10581/326/12 FO 371/30835, and Stafford, p. 108.

The quotations on p. 205 are from *The Diaries of Sir Robert Bruce Lockhart*, p. 229, Otáhalová and Červinková, Document No. 259, Moravec, p. 206, and CC8610/372/69 FO 371/34337.

The description of the end of Nazi rule on pp. 205–6 is based on Luža, Brandes, Mamatey and Luža, Jürgen Thorwald, *Flight into Winter*, London 1953, and George Bilainkin, *Second Diary of a Diplomatic Correspondent*, London 1946.

The first two quotations on p. 206 are from CU5559/2828/73 FO 371/57642 and *The Times*, 6 April 1946.

The last two quotations on p. 206 are from Mamatey and Luža, p. 321, and Moravec, pp. 204–5.

The description of the Nazi propaganda campaign against Beneš on pp. 206–7 is based on *Goebbels' Diary* and C7606/372/12 FO 371/34337.

The first three quotations on p. 207 are from C7606/372/12 FO 371/34337.

The last quotation on p. 207 is from Berton, 'Who Ordered the Assassination of R. Heydrich and Why?', p. 7.

The quotation on p. 208 is from Moravec, p. 207.

Index

In the following index, 'Reinhard Heydrich' is abbreviated to 'H.'; 'Czechoslovakia' to 'Cz.'; and 'Operation ANTHROPOID' to 'ANTH.'

BURY ME WITH MY PEARLS

Humor with a Spiritual Twist

JANE JENKINS HERLONG

Lighthouse Publishing
of the Carolinas

www.lighthousepublishingofthecarolinas.com

Praise for
Bury Me with My Pearls

Jane (Jenkins) Herlong is one of the happiest, funniest, most awe-inspiring people I have ever known. Even in the most stress-filled occasions she has a way of turning it all into a nice, funny, happy joke ... called "life." I met Jane at the Miss America 1980 pageant, and we were instantly friends. Friends forever, I like to say, because we will spend eternity together at the feet of our Lord, worshiping, laughing, loving and singing His praises! This book, like Jane, is filled with those little stories that help you move along through this journey we call life. She has a heart of gold, words of pure silver, and a life filled with victories that only Jesus can give. She is the real deal ... I love her! I like her! And you will too! Thank you, Jane, for your efforts to bring humor to all situations that life has to offer. Thank you for being a shining example of who Jesus is on this earth!

Cheryl (Prewitt) Salem
Miss America 1980 (Wow, that was a long time ago!)

Just as a mother passes down her pearls to her daughter, Jane Herlong shares pearls of wisdom and life lessons in *Bury Me with My Pearls: Humor with a Spiritual Twist*. By combining the folksy wisdom of a Southern belle with spiritual truths from Scripture, Jane weaves whimsical tales of growing up in the South with stories of the love and challenges of adulthood. With wit and charm, Jane guides you to discover the mothers-of-pearl in your life, the people you look to, lean on, and learn from. She helps you string your strand of people and experiences that bless you with truth, love, safety, and respect. This delightful book will tug your heart and inspire your faith.

LeAnn Thieman CSP, CPAE
Author, *Chicken Soup for the Christian Woman's Soul,*
Chicken Soup for the Soul: Answered Prayers,
Chicken Soup for the Soul: A Book of Miracles

Get a glass of iced sweet tea (unless you are from the North) and get ready to laugh from the first page to the last! But, subtly, subtly, you will get the impact of how truly amazing "good people" influence "truly amazing good people"! You may even decide to be buried with your pearls on! Jane, congratulations! This is a precious book, to "take your heart home" to influence mine!

Naomi Rhode
Professional Speaker, Author, Speaker Hall of Fame

Bury Me with My Pearls is a must read for anyone who wants to be encouraged, inspired, and who wants to laugh a lot! Jane's down-home way of sharing her powerful message will lift you up and inspire you to face any of life's challenges. I have watched Jane face incredible family challenges, but through it all she displayed incredible faith, amazing grace, and a powerful sense of humor. I am thrilled that the inspirational and hilarious stories she has shared with me for years will now be part of your life. I know her Momma, Miss Eleanor, and Tootsie are smiling from heaven, with their pearls on.

Dale Smith Thomas
International Empowerment Speaker,
Television Personality, and Author of *Good Morning Gorgeous*

Jane Jenkins Herlong is not only one of the funniest speakers in America but also one of the smartest people you will ever meet. She is able to share her wisdom in ways that anyone can grasp and to do so using a unique combination of humor and strategic "pearl" thinking. This book will inspire you, empower you, and entertain you!

Willie Jolley
Best Selling Author of
A Setback Is A Setup For A Comeback
and *An Attitude of Excellence*!
CSP, CPAE (Member, Speaker Hall of Fame)
Named "One of the Outstanding 5 Speakers in the World"
by Toastmasters International
Host of *The Willie Jolley Show* on CBS-TV, PBS,
Sirius/XM & WHUR-FM

While it's a toss-up whether I laughed or cried more while reading *Bury Me with My Pearls*, one thing is certain, when I finished it I was a better person than when I first picked it up. I have been a fan of Jane Jenkins Herlong's humor from the first moment I first heard her speak; however, I had no idea that she had such a magnificent gift for balancing humor, hope, and spirituality through storytelling. If you're looking for a book that will help you find your spiritual center, while comforting you with humor and warming you with inspiration, look no further.

Bree Boyce
Media Personality, Professional Singer,
Miss South Carolina 2011

BURY ME WITH MY PEARLS: HUMOR WITH A SPIRITUAL TWIST BY JANE
JENKINS HERLONG
Published by Lighthouse Publishing of the Carolinas
2333 Barton Oaks Dr., Raleigh, NC, 27614

ISBN 978-1-938499-33-3

Brought to you by the creative team at
LighthousePublishingoftheCarolinas.com: Denise Loock,
Eddie Jones, Rowena Kuo, and Brian Cross.

Library of Congress Cataloging-in-Publication Data
Herlong, Jane Jenkins.
Bury Me With My Pearls: Humor with a Spiritual Twist /
Jane Jenkins Herlong 1st ed.

Printed in the United States of America

TABLE OF CONTENTS

DEDICATION

This book is dedicated to the greatest pearl in my life,
the queen of all gems, my mother,
Eleanor Welch McElveen Jenkins.
She was priceless.

A capable, intelligent and virtuous woman—who is he who can find her? She is far more precious than jewels and her value is far above rubies or pearls. Proverbs 31:10 (AMP)

Again, the kingdom of heaven is like unto a merchant man, seeking goodly pearls: Who, when he had found one pearl of great price, went and sold all that he had, and bought it. Matthew 13:45-46 (KJV)

MY MOTHERS OF PEARL

Grandmother McElveen had two suitcases packed: one for a possible hospital stay and the other for her funeral. "Eleanor, bury me with my pearls," she said one day to my mother.

"Oh, Mother!" exclaimed my mother. Then Grandmother McElveen glanced at Tootsie, my second momma, who worked for my family for almost fifty years. "Eleanor doesn't want to listen, Tootsie. Please make sure I'm buried with my pearls."

My mother told me that story during one of her many stays at Roper Hospital in Charleston, South Carolina. *Please make sure I'm buried with my pearls.* The sentence looped through my mind all night. *What a great title for a book.*

"Jane, I want you to remember how I want to be buried." I didn't want to discuss the topic. But my mother continued, "For my music, I want my favorite song, 'Please Release Me,' by Engelbert Humperdinck." Momma always made me laugh; it was one of her pearls.

The beginning of the formation of pearls —and in the South we do love those gems—is the nacre, the inner shell of an oyster (which also forms the outer layer of a pearl). Nacre is the mother-of-pearl. Its iridescent beauty is considered a treasure. It is crucial to the formation of the pearl.

Mother-of-pearl is strong and resilient. Just like Momma and Tootsie.

Friends called them all kinds of names: Maude and Florida, smoke and fire, Bert and Ernie, or Lucy and Ethel. Momma and Tootsie were an amazing team. I've seen them beat wayward lizards to death with brooms, leap onto the kitchen table when they spotted a mouse, and put out fires with aprons. I've seen Tootsie drop to her knees laughing after my mother said something funny, and I've seen them embrace in tears.

Momma, Tootsie, and I were a superglue trio until I started first grade. I thought my heart was going to explode when I sat in that cage-like wooden school desk. All I could think of was how much fun I was missing. No more watching *I Love Lucy* with Tootsie at 10:00 a.m. No more running around the house as Momma and Tootsie tried to brush my honey-colored ringlets that Momma called knots. No more flour fights with Tootsie when she made her delicious biscuits. And no more clothesline tents; the family's bed linens would just be white sheets hanging lifeless on a wire.

Once Tootsie gave me a good tongue-lashing after I had fallen off a ladder and torn a ligament in my foot. "Girl, I done told you not to git yo'self up on no ladder! Dat is man's work," exclaimed Tootsie in her Gullah brogue.

Then Momma grabbed the phone, "How many times have I told you that your uterus will fall out onto the floor if you climb a ladder?"

No kidding. If Tootsie and Momma were shopping in Wal-Mart and saw a woman on a ladder, they would always whisper, "She gonna be sorry. Her uterus is going to fall out onto the floor."

Can't you just hear the Wal-Mart folks on the loudspeaker? "We need some help. We have a uterus on aisle four . . ."

After both my mother and Tootsie passed away, I was speaking in Virginia Beach, Virginia. My driver was an older gentleman with a unique accent. "Tom, you aren't from around here, are you?" I asked.

"Oh, no ma'am. I'm from Beaumont, Texas."

"Do you go home much?"

"Oh, yeah. I go see my mama."

This guy was no spring chick, so I quizzed him again. "Is your mama in pretty good health?"

"She's okay but we most lost her about three months ago."

"Really, what happened?"

"Well," said Tom with a stammer, "her uterus just fell out."

I knew in the pit of my soul that Momma and Tootsie were still sending me that uterus speech. They were also reminding me of our many moments of laughter. That's what this book is all about: laughter, living well, and putting the Lord in the center of your strand of pearls.

Momma and Tootsie are the women, my mothers-of-pearl, who shaped me into the woman I am today. They made me laugh. Many times they made me snort in a non-Southern Belle fashion. They also held me when I cried. They encouraged me. They're the backbone of my character, a constant reminder of the importance of surrounding yourself with the right people. They also popped me on the bottom when I did wrong. They taught me to live well, to love others, and to do the right thing regardless of how you felt. Their lessons stuck with me just like a Charleston-Rice-Spoon-size helping of Tootsie's steaming hot grits.

Mother-of-pearl is a metaphor for something rare, fine, admirable, and valuable. We should all aspire to share the legacy of our deeds as we develop our talents. Just like a mother passes down her pearls to her daughter, so should we proudly and courageously leave the next generation valuable lessons.

Sometimes our mothers shared "words of wisdom" we thought were hilarious, but eventually we realized those "rhinestones" were priceless gems. For example, right before my wedding Momma said to me, "You know, somewhere in the Bible it says to keep your husband happy. I don't know the exact verse, but it's something like 'for every headache you have, there's a woman out there somewhere with an aspirin in her purse'" (Book of Eleanor, chapter one, verse one).

Who are the people you look to, lean on, and learn from? Find the mother-of-pearl in your life and pray for that protective shell. Seek out someone who provides safety and beauty at the same time. Seek someone who will tell you the truth in love, a person you trust and respect. Find that person or persons who have journeyed through life well and have accumulated a beautiful, eclectic strand of valuable pearls. Then model that person.

Aspire to inspire before you expire.

But the fruit of the Spirit is love, joy, peace, forbearance, kindness, goodness, faithfulness, gentleness and self-control. Against such things there is no law.

Galatians 5:22-23 (NIV)

CHAPTER 1

The Power of the Irritant

Becoming a Pearl Inspector

My friend Linda has some of the most beautiful pearls I've ever seen. Every time she wears them, I grab the long strand and act like I'm fixin' to give the pearls the ultimate test for genuine authenticity—rubbing them across my teeth. If the sensation is grainy, then they're the real jewels. I guess you can say I am a pearl inspector.

I've been taught all of my life not to judge others. My parents would follow that advice with "you are who you associate with." Those statements confused me. Certainly, it's wrong to play God and condemn a soul to spend eternity in the "smoking section." But when we discuss the fruit of the Spirit, we should all be fruit inspectors and pearl inspectors with godly discernment. Each of our pearls should represent the same qualities as the fruit of the Spirit. We'll never know if we have love, joy, peace, forbearance, kindness, goodness, gentleness, and self-control unless we're put to the test.

I can honestly say that I avoid relationships when I see bad fruit in someone's life. If I want to be a loving person, I hang around with loving people. The fruit of the Spirit is also contagious. With the help of the Holy Spirit, our life's work should be crafting a strand of pearls that represents all the fruit of the Spirit.

I always experienced "Holy Spirit butterflies" when pondering the pearl of love … sounds so sweet and pretty, doesn't it? Well, hold on to your strand because the Lord may place you among unlovable folks. (And remember, you're not qualified to look at anyone else's pearls unless you inspect *your* strand first.)

In Matthew 5:44 Jesus said, *But I say unto you, Love your enemies, bless them that curse you, do good to them that hate you, and pray for them which despitefully use you, and persecute you* (KJV). Ah, come on? Love these folks? Yes. But we don't have to like them. Many times I've said, "I love them with the love of Christ, but I don't like them." God in His wisdom knew that loving the unlovely is possible only through the power of the Holy Spirit.

Thank God for *agape* love, the purest form of love—the love Jesus Christ has for His Father and for His followers. We can't operate in *agape* love without divine intervention. The good news is that I, in my humanness, can't make this happen. I just have to be obedient. I can say with conviction that praying for our enemies benefits us. We rob ourselves of peace and blessings by not praying for those who come against us. 1 Corinthians 13:13 reminds us that the greatest of gifts is love—especially loving our enemies. So, give the Enemy a black eye and pray.

The Spirit's pearl list continues with joy, peace, kindness, goodness, faithfulness, gentleness and self-control. What about forbearance? According to the Hebrew and Greek definitions, *forbearance* simply means to hold back and be still. Refrain from action. Let God do His work with His perfect timing. That's been a difficult lesson for me to learn because I am a fixer.

God knows every inch of us, so He allows circumstances to teach us who we are. As life unfolds, only we can decide how to handle its challenges. Trials will do two things: reveal our lack of spiritual maturity and give us an opportunity to increase our spiritual maturity. If we're wise, we'll recognize our weaknesses and grow stronger.

In the language of pearl formation, these times of growth are called irritants. The growth cycle of a pearl starts with a grain of

sand, the first irritant that begins the formation of a jewel. Oh, yes. I met my first irritant when I was in the first grade.

I Don't Like You, Debra Sue

I remember the day well. The high school girls were coming to my first grade class to select the cutest girls to compete for the coveted title of Little Miss Merry Christmas.

I was a tomboy. I had chosen to wear corduroy pants, a flannel shirt, and penny loafers. I had brushed my hair and shined the coins in my shoes. I was looking fine.

The only glitches were my oversized lips and the loss of my two front teeth. But that didn't stop me from marching myself to the front of the classroom and smiling my heart out.

Snickers and lots of whispering rippled across the room when I took my place. Making matters worse was the "irritant" standing right beside me.

Her name was Debra Sue, and she was the class diva. Her momma had put her in a "stick-out" (crinoline) dress and poodle socks. She was wearing her Easter shoes. Bright red lipstick coated her lips. (I'm sure she had used the tester tube left by Miss Ann, the local Avon lady.)

Debra Sue's hair was a mass of ringlets and bows, glued in place by Extra-hold Aqua Net. As we say in the South, "Her hair was jacked up to Jesus." A Category Five hurricane couldn't have ruffled her "do." To make matters worse, she had *all* of her teeth.

Of course, she was picked to be in the pageant.

Something strange happened to me that day. I became more determined than ever to be "better." I was motivated. Debra Sue was my first grain of sand.

My brother was helping with the pageant, and he told me they needed a fishbowl because the contestants were going to select questions out of it. I flushed my fish and cleaned up my fishbowl for the pageant.

The night of the pageant was magical. I sat on a broken chair on the front row of the old high school auditorium. I was mesmerized by the wannabe beauty queens as they glided across the stage, wearing Mike Benet empire waist gowns with matching shoes. My heart pounded as *my* fishbowl was brought to center stage. The big-hair girls each put their long, white-gloved hand into my fishbowl and retrieved a small slip of white paper.

That night irritated me enough to redirect my young mind. It was the beginning of something big, something special. A seed pearl began to form in my soul. I heard God say, "Jane, you will be doing this one day."

Little did I know that seventeen years later, I would walk across the stage competing for one of the most prestigious titles of all, Miss America. Sometimes life isn't fair, but those occasions can allow God to give us a holy nudge. Irritants can take our lives to the next level and actually plant dreams. And it all started with a girl who was my first irritant.

Columnist Ann Landers wrote, "If asked to give what I consider the single most useful bit of advice for all humanity, it would be this: Expect trouble as an inevitable part of life and when it comes, hold your head high, look it squarely in the eye and say, 'I will be bigger than you. You cannot defeat me'."[1]

The Bible says: *Consider it pure joy, my brothers, whenever you face trials of many kinds, because you know that the testing of your faith develops perseverance. Perseverance must finish its work so that you may be mature and complete, not lacking anything* (James 1:2-4 NIV).

Here's my paraphrase of that passage: You do not know who you are until you have to be what you think you are.

Thank you, Debra Sue. But I still don't like you.

---

1   Wake-Up and Smell the Coffee. Ann Landers. New York: Random House Value Publishing, 1998.

God-Love-Her Pearls

The phrase used to be "Bless your heart." For more serious cases the expression has been upgraded to "God love her."

Irritants can be a great gift. Many outstanding feats have been accomplished when adversity presented itself: my academic career is a stellar example.

Academically, I struggled. In elementary school I was placed in the "C" section—not to be confused with a surgical procedure to give birth. There was an "A" section for the Einsteins, a "B" section for the normal children, and the "C" section for those who needed medication and supplication.

One day in the sixth grade, I was carrying a stack of paper to the office for my teacher and she said, "Jane, don't look at those papers. It's your IQ." I thought, *Lady, you are stupid.* Then I looked at my IQ and realized that I was the stupid one.

When it was time to take the PSAT in high school, I made the lowest score in the class. I was told that scores increase considerably when you take the SAT. Well, that didn't happen. I even took classes to make a higher score on the math section, and I actually made a lower score. I took the SAT for a second time. My score was low again. Then I tried the ACT and my score was still pitiful. Is there a test called DUMB?

In the meantime, I began teaching dyslexic children on weekdays after school and every Saturday. The head of the program fired me and told me she thought I was dyslexic.

I sat on some rocks at Folly Beach, "boo-hooing" and having a pity-party. Then I realized that no one could tell me who I was and that no one knew what was inside me except my Heavenly Father. With faith and prayer, I determined to prove the experts wrong.

I decided to go to college.

I met with my high school advisor. She reviewed my transcript and college entrance exam scores. Then she asked if I had any "pull." All I could think of was that Daddy had a brand new John Deere tractor.

None of the colleges and universities that grabbed my interest were interested in me. However, one day I received a letter from the admissions office at Columbia College in response to my application. They weren't accepting me either, but they wanted me to come to an interview. That was good enough!

I drove to Columbia, South Carolina, determined to become a Columbia College girl. Over and over again I said to the admissions counselor, "Just give me a chance. I will make you proud." I wore that man down.

When I returned to Johns Island, I ran into the tomato field and yelled, "Daddy, I got in!"

My parents couldn't afford my college tuition. That was another hurdle. But God blessed me with a grant and gave Daddy some cucumber rebate money.

That August I entered Columbia College as a freshman on academic probation, but four years later I walked across the stage with a diploma in hand. My peers awarded me the college's highest honors. I even made the Dean's List.

God did a work in my life many years ago with Debra Sue, the class diva, and my academic challenges. But He didn't stop there. God is a God of possibilities and life lessons. I can testify that irritants and adversity can become your best friends.

I've learned that the Lord uses many opportunities to teach us lessons, even a checkout line at Wal-Mart.

I Gave Up Wal-Mart for Lent

Living in Johnston, South Carolina, makes going to Wal-Mart a treat. I've admitted many times that I love Wal-Mart so much I gave it up for Lent. When you give something up for Lent you have to replace it, so during the Holy Season I shop at a smaller store named Fred's. This store is the love child of Wal-Mart and Family Dollar.

One day as I waited in the Wal-Mart checkout line, I noticed the people in front of me were aggravated. The checkout guy was

the reason. He had everything pierced you could possibly have pierced. He had a safety pin above his eyebrow, a metal spike through his cheek, and enough rings above the other eyebrow to hold a small shower curtain.

I wanted to ask him to unhook the safety pin over his eye just to see if his eyebrow would fall off. The guy had so much metal on his face a series of questions ran through my mind: *If you ran real fast would you whistle? Is your name Pierce? Did you fall into a tackle box?* I enjoyed thinking of funny questions as I watched the people in front of me—they obviously had no sense of humor.

I placed the space bar on the belt between my merchandise and the person checking out in front of me. When my turn came, "Pierce" started to scan the space bar. I just stood there thinking, *You've got to be kidding. Is your brain pierced?*

The magic continued, "Where'd you git this frommm?" he said.

I could hardly understand him. He had a huge silver-colored ball lodged in the middle of his tongue. I thought, *Did he lick that tackle box when he fell into it?* But I said, "Uh, I don't believe I want that space bar."

Some people would have lost their temper, and hey, why not? After all Wal-Mart is an acceptable place to pitch a hissy fit. Instead, I chose humor.

What if I had unleashed my anger? How would that have affected the rest of my day? Laughing is a much better option.

And I also reminded myself of the way I looked when I was that age.

Golden Arch Pearl

When my children were small, I did what most families in America do: take the children to McDonalds. There I discovered the pearl of patience, which was a much-needed addition to my strand.

One day we were all in a bad mood. The children were getting on my nerves. They wanted this toy and that toy, so I decided to use the drive-through. No playground today.

When I pulled up to order, the microphone girl said, "Welcome to McDonalds. Would you like to try our fish sandwich and orange mint milkshake?"

Just thinking about that combination of food made my stomach turn. "No thank you," I said politely. "I'll have a dozen chicken nuggets."

"What?"

"I want a dozen chicken nuggets," I repeated.

"Uh, it don't come like that, ma'am. It only comes in four, six, and twelve."

With the children being tired and unhappy, I could have lost it. Once again, I tried to find the humor and learn patience from being irritated. I chose to entertain myself by asking, "Can I have two orders of six nuggets?"

"Oh, yes ma'am. Now we can do that."

Pearls in the Ladies Room

I had a layover at Hartsfield International Airport, so I decided to make use of my time and visit the ladies' room. In the privacy of a bathroom stall I heard, "Duh-nah, duh-nah, dunta, dunta, dunta, dunta." It was the song that struck fear in my heart and kept me from swimming in our small creek for *years*—the theme song from *Jaws*. "Dunta, dunta, dunta, dunta . . ."

Yes, I looked in that potty just to make sure.

I mean, if you've ever heard that song near a body of water—regardless of how small—you just make sure.

Then I heard, "Hello?"

Yes sirree, the woman in the next stall was talking on her cell phone. Sadly, that's quite common these days. Every cell phone should have an app called When and Where Not To Talk on Your Cell Phone. Free Download.

Well, my curious was up (Johns Island phrase) and I had a long layover, so I listened. Have mercy. That woman was on a job interview. The kicker was when she said, "Yes, I'm great with paperwork."

The humorist in me took over. I handed her a wad of toilet paper.

A voice whispered, "Very funny. I'm on a job interview."

To which I replied, "No job is finished until the paperwork is done."

Another pearl was formed that day on my ever-growing strand.

We all have a choice: let a situation control us or take control of it. Many times we're tempted to let a dumb situation have the upper hand.

In *The Eight Concepts of Bowen Theory*, Dr. Roberta Gilbert discusses high functioning thinking as opposed to low functioning reacting. A good example of this is to watch CSPAN and then change the channel to Jerry Springer's show. Jerry Springer may be more entertaining, but the best way to manage our emotions is to be a thinking person.

The small things in life may stump us. We allow our emotions to take over, and we give in to our feelings. Managing our emotions is important; they reveal what's inside of us. Life situations reveal who we really are and what we need to change.

Yes, pearls can be produced in the most unlikely places—Wal-Mart, McDonalds, and even an airport bathroom stall.

Our Heavenly Father loves to teach us lessons about ourselves in unusual places.

Joe's Funeral Hole

My friend Joe was enrolled in mortuary school and desperately wanted a full-time job at the funeral home where he was being trained. One of the town's most respected patriarchs had passed away, and the funeral was going to be one of the largest the town had ever seen. Joe wanted to impress the owner

of Carter Funeral Home, so he made sure that every detail was covered . . . no pun intended.

Joe was nervous about the big day. He believed his entire future hinged on that funeral, and he desperately wanted things to go well. Before the graveside service was held, Joe asked the owner, Mr. Carter, about his chances of being hired by the prestigious funeral home.

"Well," said Mr. Carter, "we do need a new staff member and we will consider you, but we must see extreme professionalism. Make sure that no matter what happens you know how to make it look excellent."

The solemn service concluded with the Baptist church soprano singing the classic hymn, "It Is Well with My Soul." The nervous funeral director wannabe stepped too near the edge of the grave that was covered in Astroturf and tumbled to the bottom of the red Georgia clay hole. Covered in mud, Joe realized he had ruined the largest funeral in the history of the county and buried any chance of employment with the Carter Funeral Home. Embarrassed and literally "red-*clay*-faced," Joe was hoisted out of the grave by his colleagues.

The soloist sang, "It is well, it is well, with my soul." Suddenly, Joe had a thought. The song inspired him. Mr. Carter's words— "make it excellent"—resonated in his brain. He walked over to the grieving widow, knelt down on one knee with red clay dripping on his shiny, black patent leather shoes and calmly said, "I took it upon myself to personally inspect the grave, and I want you to know all is well with that hole."

Joe got the job. He turned an irritant into an opportunity.

Someone once told me a story about a young man who approached the corpse at a wake and asked the deceased if he could marry the departed man's daughter. No one could figure out what the young man was thinking.

To me, it was obvious. At one time or another, the deceased must have said to this young man, "Over my dead body will you marry my daughter . . ."

Another opportunity born from an irritant.

Deep South Funeralizing

Nothing is more delightful than meeting folks from other areas of the country (particularly the South) who are just down-home-not-trying-to-impress-you types. Down in South Georgia at a city's chamber of commerce banquet, I had the chance to meet a whole family like that. They were the definition of "laid-back"—flesh and blood examples of the proverb that "a relaxed attitude lengthens a man's life."

The family had won the coveted award for "Small Business of the Year." The triplet brothers, named Henry, Harry, and Herman, owned a funeral home.

As they accepted their award, they gave the praise for their success to "Momma." Those fellas were no "spring chicks." As they spoke, "Momma" stood right next to them, just beaming. I thought I was going to cry it was so sweet. Here's a universal truth about us Southerners: no matter how old we are, we continue to refer to our parents as Momma and Daddy.

After the banquet ended, I just had to get more acquainted with the triplets and "Momma."

All I said was "I bet y'all have fun together." Well, that launched them into the latest tale. Their South Georgia drawl alone could have entertained me for hours.

"Hey, Herman," said Harry, "Tell 'er 'bout Miss Lizzie's funeral last week."

"Well, it was sump'in. We never had nothin' like at before," Herman lamented. "Henry was standing by the preacher at the graveside with the whole family settin' underneath our biggest tent. I was standing over to the right of the family and noticed an ol' stray dawg. That dawg jist walked up to me and starts to be friendly. You know, it was embarrassing. I didn't know what to do so I just said in a strong voice, 'Sit!' The family thought I was talking to them, and they all sat down real fast like. Well, Harry

most lost it 'cause we was all in our funeralizing mode. And the preacher just kept readin' like nothin' was wrong: 'Yea, though I walk through the valley of the shadow of death, I shall fear no evil.' Lawd, have mercy I know I was fearin' some evil al'right. Fearin' makin' a scene with this dawg. Well, I shook him off and darned if that dawg didn't start up again. Miss Lizzie's son took one look at all the commotion and started cryin'. He nudged his brothers and sisters and they cried too. I just knew we was in a heap of trouble.

"Well," Herman continued, "I shook the dawg off again and decided to set down, thinkin' maybe that dawg would quit. The only place to set down was on the front row. Well, doggone, as soon as I set down that dawg jumped up and sat in my lap. We was eyeball to eyeball. There was not much to do then but pat the ol' stray. I figured we was good friends by then anyhow."

"After the service, one of the family members walked up to where we was standin'. He had a funny look in his face. We was worried," said Henry.

"'How did you know?' the son asked Herman. 'That dog coming up here in the tent was just a precious memory . . . it was a blessing. Thank you for your customer service'."

"Come to find out, Miss Lizzie took in stray dawgs," said Herman. "It was the perfect way to send her on home."

I love when folks can turn an unexpected event into an entertaining story. Their stressing turned into a blessing.

A stranger came and I took him in. Matthew 25:35
(NLT, slightly tweaked by author)

The Possum Drop

In the South, we entertain ourselves in some unique ways— even when folks from other places who, as we say in the South, "jist don't git it" try to stop something fun and harmless.

In one sleepy North Carolina town of 240 citizens, the owner of the local Citgo station started a tradition of lowering a live possum in a plexiglass cage—his way of simulating the dropping of the ball in New York City's Times Square, Southern style. However, someone from PETA (People for the Ethical Treatment of Animals) called the organizer and threatened to sue the town since the event, in their words, was "perverse, reckless, and terrifying for the possum." The event was so popular that the organizers "thunk up" a solution: Substitute the live possum with another possum, not one that was "playing possum" but one that actually had departed to the great trashcan in the sky. The Brasstown Drop would go on.

Personally, I never saw the problem with using a live possum because the townsfolk were so good to it. It was fattened up on cat food, slowly lowered in the cage, and released back into the wild to go about its business. Sounds like a pretty good deal to me. In fact, if that possum could talk I bet it would be angry with PETA. After all, it had been spared from the indignity of homelessness, living trashcan to trashcan and using its playing-dead skills to survive; instead it was cared for in a comfortable environment complete with cat food cuisine. To top it all off, it enjoyed a ride from the Citgo sign to the ground in a plexiglass box, then rose to celebrity status on video. Just a matter of perspective.

A representative of *The New York Times* phoned the Possum Drop organizer, but he was too busy to talk: he was duplicating videos of the Possum Drop. People actually bought the video.

To be sure, the people of Brasstown are going to be surprised when folks from all over the country come for a visit so they can participate in the town's unique way of ringing in the new year, especially since they figured out how to work around that irritant, the PETA.

Oversized Texas Pearls

I spent two wonderful days in Georgetown, Texas, speaking to the Texas Baptist Weekday Education Association. The one thousand attendees were nurturing women with hearts as big as the Lone Star State who deeply love children. The conference theme was "Imagine That," based on the fabulous Christian song by Mercy Me, "I Can Only Imagine."

My transporter, Celina, was delightful. She was kind enough to drive me to see where I was speaking. Yes, everything is bigger in Texas, proven again when I saw the Georgetown Texas Baptist Church looming in the distance. After I toured the education building, I knew the sanctuary would be spectacular. I wasn't disappointed. My little hometown church, Harmony United Methodist, could have fit in the church lobby. As always, the fun part is connecting with women from all over Texas. Some wore cowgirl hats, some had big hair, and others were more understated. We bonded when I told them that W. Bush (42) had made me an Honorary Texan. I have the proclamation hanging in my office. I knew the former President had given me a title almost as prestigious as Miss South Carolina. When I went home, I knew what I had to do. I bought a Suburban and got my concealed weapons license. I enjoyed every second of sharing my presentation. Afterwards, many were dear enough to make comments and share some of their struggles. One woman looked very beaten down and stressed out. She thanked me many times over and then gave me a glimpse into her life.

I heard some of my favorite colleagues speak the next day. Suzie Humphreys, on the fringe of her seventies, is as sharp as a Texas boot spur. Along with her hilarious humor, Suzie throws in a zinger or two just at the right time. A bottom-line, hip-shooting Texan, Suzie tells it like it is. I love Suzie's take on depression. She said if you are going to be depressed, get into it. "Call in sick, put on that old terrycloth robe with grape stains on it, complete with non-waterproof mascara on your eyelashes. Then cry. I mean really cry. Then think of more sad stuff and let

that mascara run down your face. Top it off with looking in the mirror. In about two hours, you will decide that you are sick of all of this. Here is what to do next: get cleaned up, dressed up, and eat some Mexican food."[2]

Suzie acknowledged that depression can be serious, but after her presentation an audience member scolded her for making light of it. Suzie listened to that hurting woman whose husband had abandoned her many years ago. Suzie was brave enough to comment, "You're angry at this man. Depression is simply anger turned inward. Do yourself a favor and forgive him."

After "carrying on" with Suzie—sharing speaker tricks and new ideas—I was greeted with a hug from the same stressed woman I had met the previous day. For a moment, I didn't recognize her. She was different. Her walk was straighter, her face brighter, and her personality charged. I told her the difference in her look was an amazing transformation. "I needed this," was her response. "I needed to hear what you all had to say. I'm tired of being stressed-out and irritated."

Messages filled with honesty, encouragement, and pure godly love can change a person's heart. Imagine that.

> *We can rejoice, too, when we run into problems and trials, for we know that they help us develop endurance.*
> *And endurance develops strength of character, and character strengthens our confident hope of salvation.*
> Romans 5:3-4 (NLT)

Miss Ludy's Skin-Deep Beauty

Ludy Godbold was the treasure of Columbia College, my alma mater. Just stroll through the campus and check out the gym—the Godbold Center, named after Miss Ludy. She brought home six medals from the 1922 Federation Sportive Feminine

---

2   Humphreys, Suzie. First Baptist Church of Plano Women's Event. Georgetown, TX. 15 July 2011.

International Games—the alternative to the male-only Olympic Games. She was a physical education professor at Columbia College and loved by all. I was fortunate enough to be a student in the waning years of the Godbold era.

My first semester in college I decided to take a tennis class for beginners. The information we received about this class was most unusual . . . bring a racket, a can of tennis balls, and write your last name on a piece of notebook paper and pin it to the back of your shirt. Little did I know that the challenge of Miss Ludy's tennis class would slam me into the net.

The first day of class I followed the instructions: I sat by the tennis courts waiting for the teacher, my last name written in uppercase letters pinned to the back of my shirt. I was amazed when I saw an elderly woman approach me carrying a tennis racket. Yes, it was Miss Ludy Godbold, and I was fixin' to get more than a tennis lesson. "Jenkins!" Miss Ludy yelled when it was my turn. "Get over here and hit."

Miss Ludy put up with no foolishness, but her rare humorous moments were legendary. She once said that her sister was the ugliest woman who ever walked the earth. When her sister died, Miss Ludy said, "Now I am the ugliest woman alive."

The first few weeks I did what she said and stood where she told me to stand. The word on the Columbia College "street" was that she gave everybody a C. I decided to try for a B. An upperclassman told me that Miss Ludy only gave B's to students who were brave enough to ask her to hit with them.

I love a good challenge so I asked Miss Ludy to hit with me. Sure, I was afraid, but I asked anyway. Really, how bad could it be? The woman was *old*. I could take her on . . . or so I thought.

As the other students watched, I stepped onto the court to go head-to-head with the legend. I positioned myself exactly where she had taught me to stand. My palms were moist with fear. I felt as though I were standing on the grass courts of Wimbledon—Game Point, Set Point, Match Point, and Championship Point. That very elderly woman gave the tennis

ball a few bounces, threw it straight up, and down that racket came. The ball became a registered weapon of the federal government. It rocketed past me, one za-billionth of an inch from my head. No human being could have returned her speed-of-light serve. I chose the only graceful move available—I thanked Miss Ludy and left the court. The class was stunned.

At the end of the semester, I opened my report card and smiled ... Miss Ludy had given me a B. I can't imagine what it would have taken to receive an A.

I had asked Miss Ludy what most students wouldn't ask. I was afraid, but I refused to let fear stop me.

Years later, standing in the wings of the legendary Miss America stage in Atlantic City, New Jersey, I heard another treasure, Bert Parks say, "Welcome, Jane Louise Jenkins, Miss South Carolina!" At that moment, I said to myself, "Jane, you can do this. After all, you are brave. You hit with Miss Ludy Godbold."

Thank the Lord for that irritation that helped me take the next step, and the next—all the way to the Miss America Pageant.

Be strong and of good courage; do not be afraid, nor be dismayed, for the LORD your God is with you wherever you go. Joshua 1:9 (NKJV)

Monopoly and Mudslinging

It was the call I desperately wanted. "Jane, we want to hire you to speak and sing all over the country, each night in a different city. You will be paid." The caller mentioned a name several times that I thought was the name of the production company that was hiring me.

Almost two months after that phone call, I was speaking and singing in LA—not Los Angeles but Lower Alabama. Dressed in a cowgirl outfit, black hat, and tan boots, I sang my heart out promoting tractors, implements, and the N-7 Gleaner Combine to farmers and ranchers from the tri-county area. The "production

company" was not the name of a woman as I had assumed; it was an agricultural equipment company named Allis Chalmers.

The job was fun. Traveling, meeting new people, and just being on the road was an adventure. I particularly liked my driver, Joel.

In the South, we refer to folks like Joel as a "wash-foot Southern Baptist." They are strict, conservative, and unshakable. You can imagine my surprise when Joel made a startling confession: "Jane, you need to know something about me. I have a problem with gambling." Let me clarify that Joel's "gambling" was driving through McDonalds and playing Monopoly. Each time he purchased something, he earned stickers. My job was to lick. We won Coca-Colas, French fries, and Happy Meals.

Then came the fateful day when we drove up to the Holiday Inn in Macon, Georgia, and read the marquee: Tonight Only, Female Mud Wrestling. I said, "Joel, we're going."

He was upset. "I can't," Joel replied. "I'm the head deacon at church."

I thought for a moment and said, "Joel, Jesus healed people with mud."

There was a pause. Joel looked at me and said, "Let's go."

We stood in the back of a dark room with bright lights shining on the mud pit that looked like a sea of chocolate pudding. Joel stayed in the shadows, hoping no one from his hometown would see the head deacon from First Baptist Church in a bar watching female mud wrestling. The ring/mud master announced, "Our first contestant weighing in at 250 pounds from Tifton, Georgia ... and her challenger weighing in at 92 pounds all the way from Valdosta, Georgia. Give it up for Amazing Grace."

"Joel," I said, "this has to be divine intervention."

We watched the mud fly. To our amazement, the 92-pounder pinned face down her much "healthier" opponent. Amazing Grace was declared the winner and awarded $200.

Joel couldn't help himself. He approached the mud-covered winner and asked her what gave her that strength. She replied, "I gotta pay for my new mobile home."

The next morning Joel seemed different. "Well," I said. "What did you think of last night?"

"It was inspiring," replied Joel. "Yep," he continued, "I'm teaching Sunday school this Sunday and I got the title: How to Handle Mudslinging with Amazing Grace."

Sometimes the Lord places us in situations with people who stretch our minds and challenge our hearts. I was reared a loose Episcopalian and Joel was a strict Southern Baptist—a combination that created many interesting experiences. By the end of our travels all over the South, our stomachs were filled with lots of McDonalds food; our hearts were packed with memorable adventures and a greater respect for each other's uniqueness.

CHAPTER 2

The Oyster Shell—Our Homes

B arbara Bush once said, "Your success as a family, our success as our society depends not on what happens at the White House, but on what happens inside *your* house"[3] (author emphasis). The former First Lady understands pearls; she wears multiple strands every day.

As our pearls are formed, they must be protected so they can grow into the fullness of their beauty. Crafting your home or oyster shell is the beginning of having a healthy home life. Some of us may have had cracks in our shells, and our homes became polluted. I prayed for a Christian husband and was determined to raise my children in a wholesome environment. My goals were to live a Christian life, celebrate my Southern heritage, and make wise decisions to ensure a peaceful future. I treasure God's promise in Jeremiah 29:11-14:

> *I know what I'm doing. I have it all planned out—plans to take care of you, not abandon you, plans to give you the future you hope for. When you call on me, when you come and pray to me, I'll listen. When you come looking for me, you'll find me. Yes, when you get serious about finding me and want it more than anything else, I'll make sure you won't be disappointed. I'll turn things around for you … You can count on it.* (MSG)

---

3   Bush, Barbara. Wellesley College Commencement. 1 June 1990.

The older I become the more I realize the utmost importance of rearing children in a godly environment with Christian values. I remember the rich lessons of the family experiences with my own husband and children. Hopefully, some of the following stories will make you chuckle, but mostly I hope they'll remind you that home life and parenting are serious matters that should be bathed in prayer.

Gumpa and Lou: The Tide That Bonds

One generation shall commend your works to another, and shall declare your mighty acts. Psalm 145:4 (ESV)

When I was a child, we all referred to going to my grandparents' home as "going up to the yard." Gumpa built the white clapboard home for his wife and six children. The house was always filled with the sounds and smells of comforting welcome. A ten-minute bicycle ride took me to visit my grandparents where I enjoyed all the amenities of living down a dirt road that connected me to family.

Imagine March in the Lowcountry with a sea of yellow daffodils covering the yard. My grandmother, Lou, would sit on the green porch swing and watch her grandchildren de-daffodil her yard. My grandfather, Gumpa, was either fishing in Abbapoola Creek or working in his garden.

Lou was a textbook example of a grandmother. When we were sick, she fixed her famous homemade custard accompanied by cherry Jell-O. It was worth being sick just to have her deliver that amazing boiled custard in a Mason jar sealed with serrated wax paper. We poured the cream-colored custard over the bright red Jell-O. It not only pleased the eyes but also tasted heavenly.

I remember Gumpa driving by our house in his dark green pickup truck, his weathered arm extended out the window as he drove down the long dirt road to the highway. He was always singing, but we never understood the song. I knew he was on a mission to buy groceries or farm supplies.

The years passed. By the time I could drive, Gumpa was confined to casting for shrimp in the creek or working in his "geaarden" growing "vegee-tables" as he would say in his Gullah brogue. He always kept busy even when his body began to fail him.

One spring day when I visited my grandparents, Gumpa was working in his garden. He sat on a plastic chair. He had attached wheels to the bottom of it so he could move it down the rows. I watched him as he maneuvered the chair with his feet, dug a hole, dropped in a seed, and covered the hole with his foot. He spent hours repeating the procedure until his garden was planted. Gumpa was determined to sow those seeds because my grandparents lived off the land. All the food they ate was either caught in the creek or grown on the farm. Maybe that's why they both lived into their nineties.

There's much to be said about keeping active in the twilight years. Gumpa and Lou had a passion for their land and loved sharing both produce from the garden and delicious Lowcountry cooking. Their friends often said, "I had some cucumbers and tomatoes outside of my door this afternoon. I knew the vegetables were from Mr. Frank [Gumpa]."

My grandparents were wealthy people regardless of their financial worth. Many measure success in terms of money. As I travel and meet people, I've learned that following your heart's desire and serving others is the true definition of success.

In a day when many children don't even know their families, I consider it a blessing to have such fond memories of my grandparents and the timeless values they taught me: love of family, the worth of hard work, and the responsibility of serving others. What a gift to be reared in a family that loved the land and shared its bounty. The older I grow, the more I appreciate stories like that. The highest calling is to love what you do and to serve others.

Do all the good you can . . . by all the means you can . . .
in all the ways you can . . . in all the places you can . . . as
long as you can. John Wesley[4]

My Pitiful Tree House

The Lowcountry of South Carolina is famous for its beautiful live oak trees. Spanish moss draped from the branches of hundred-year-old trees gives tourists and nature lovers breathtaking memories. At my childhood home, we had both oak and pecan trees in our yard. Both types of trees taught me valuable lessons.

One old pecan tree outside of our house on Johns Island, South Carolina, had a good climbing branch that was almost parallel with another branch. One day I decided to build a tree house, but I encountered some problems with the limbs of that tree. First of all, pecan trees don't have strong branches. Second, the limbs weren't level enough or consistent enough in height to provide a level floor for my tree house. My next challenge was the lumber. The only lumber I had was the frail sticks Daddy used to stake his tomatoes. Daddy had tons of sticks, but they broke all the time. And, of course, I was growing taller and heavier every day. I did manage to create a kinda-sorta-looking floor. Of course, when the wind blew, my "tree house" became a pile of sticks.

Eventually, I lost faith in the pecan tree and the tree house. I wised up and went on the hunt for a stronger tree. Down the old dirt road not too far from our home, I discovered the most amazing oak tree. Climbing it was a bit of a challenge, but once I hoisted myself to the first branch, it was like a stairway to heaven. The branches were strong and made me feel secure. I didn't have to walk gingerly from one branch to the other. I had confidence in that tree. I spent many fun hours dangling upside-

---

4   *John Wesley's Sermons: An Anthology.* Ed. Albert C. Outler and Richard P. Heitzenrater. Abingdon Press. 1991.

down from that tree, standing on its strong branches, or just using my imagination.

Not too long ago I noticed that the old pecan tree has gone to the big forest in the sky; however, that oak tree still stands as strong and mighty as ever.

When I think back on my childhood tree house experience, I realize how many spiritual lessons I learned. To have a solid structure, you must first have a firm foundation. The Bible is our foundation for developing life skills. Whether we are building a family, a business, or a friendship, the principles of the Bible should be our values. Having faith in the world's beliefs is like the weak branches of that old pecan tree: they will not support us during our trials. As time goes on and our difficulties increase, the weight of life's challenges can give us a heavy heart. The foundation we use for support must be strong enough to handle the winds of change. If our foundational values are weak like those frail sticks, we risk breaking what means the most in life.

But the Word of God, like the old oak tree, gives me the security I need to climb to new heights. Many times it's tough to grab the first branch, but once I have a firm grip on it, the next level is so rewarding. Climbing one branch at a time requires that first leap of faith. The view from the top is glorious. I rise above my circumstances and soar with eagles instead of looking down in fear.

I hope you can take to heart the lessons of the tree house. The weak branches of the old pecan tree taught me to search for the strong branches of the oak. And it all began with acorn-sized faith.

The Long Branches of the Angel Oak

A magnificent oak tree can be seen down a dirt road on the way to St. John's Episcopal Church on Johns Island. When I was young, I considered it a treat to travel the dirt road instead of the normal route down Maybank Highway to get to church because

we passed the Angel Oak. This phenomenal Lowcountry tree is at least 300 years old (some sources have cited its age between 500 and 1500 years old).[5] For years we visited that tree and climbed on its long branches. It reminded me of the octopus from *Twenty Thousand Leagues under the Sea*. Climbing on the Angel Oak was like being in a tree house mansion. For a young girl, it was an unforgettable experience.

Unfortunately, some people literally made their mark on the Angel Oak by carving their names or initials on its bark. I guess they thought their carvings would live on for another one thousand years. But they never considered that making their mark was killing the tree.

Carving the bark of a tree is like engaging in a pointless argument that will cause irreversible damage to people and relationships. The deep wounds caused by hurtful words and actions leave an indelible mark.

My father had a fit when he saw the abuse on the Angel Oak. He taught us never to put a nail in a tree or to carve its bark. As a farmer and true steward of nature, my father impressed upon us the importance of respect, not only for the environment but also for those who stood like that giant tree, whose arms are much like the branches of the Angel Oak—arms that give comfort, shade, and a sense of family, our roots.

For many years, enjoying the Angel Oak was restricted to those who were willing to pay a small fee to visit it. For a long time, I didn't visit it. Maybe I was afraid it wouldn't live up to my memories.

I never made a mark on the Angel Oak; however, that tree did mark me. I remember the lesson Daddy and the tree taught me, to treat the people in my world like I treated that tree—with love and respect. I pray that the other lessons Daddy taught me will stay as strong and large as the Angel Oak.

---

5   www.sciway.net/sc-photos/charleston-county/angel-oak.html. 24 Feb 2013.

Love one another with brotherly affection.
Outdo one another in showing honor.

Romans 12:10 (ESV)

I Won Miss America's . . . Boyfriend

A couple of years ago, I was asked to judge the Miss Mississippi Pageant. I was relieved to have this diversion since it was the one-year anniversary of my mother's death and also the anniversary of my winning the title of Miss South Carolina. Another twist was Miss Mississippi had won Miss America the year I competed in the pageant *and* she had dated my future husband, Thomas Herlong.

Thomas was known throughout South Carolina as a peach farmer and a bachelor who was always looking for the perfect peach. More specifically, Thomas escorted three Miss Americas, dated two of them, and was quite taken with one of them. You guessed it. She was the Miss Mississippi who stomped me at Miss America.

Thomas and I first met at a Jaycee luncheon when he introduced me as the reigning Miss Charleston. I thought he was very cute. I loved the way he introduced me, "Miss Cha'leston." He dropped the "r." How cha'ming.

Our paths crossed again a few months later when I was trying to find judges for the Miss Charleston Pageant. I called Thomas. Determined to come across as being mature and queenly, I casually asked, "So, what have you been doing lately?"

Without missing a beat Thomas replied, "Artificially inseminating my cows."

I couldn't muster a reply to that, queenly or otherwise. Even though I was on top of my game in interviewing and only months away from competing in the Miss South Carolina Pageant, I was answerless. For some strange reason, that increased my attraction to this country boy/gentleman.

We met again when Thomas booked me as Miss South Carolina to sing at the Annual Jaycee Awards Banquet in Myrtle Beach. Thomas knew then that I was the one and only heifer for him. One week later, he proposed.

It wasn't the most romantic setting for a marriage proposal. We were dining at Lizard's Thicket, an iconic family-style restaurant. Between bites of the mashed potatoes and collard greens, Thomas popped the question.

Later I asked him why he felt compelled to propose to me at Lizard's Thicket. He said he got a funny feeling in his stomach and thought it was love. It turned out to be the collard greens.

God gave me another sign that Thomas was truly a country boy—a perfect fit for me. After he popped the question he said, "I guess the wedding will have to be sometime after peach season and right before dove season."

At public speaking engagements, I often quip, "I didn't win Miss America, but I did marry her boyfriend." The best part is that Thomas is the strong Christian man I had prayed for ever since I was a teenager, not to mention what a cutie-pie he is.

The Wal-Mart RV Extravaganza

At one point in my life, a particular family and their adventures provided me with much laughter. In the South we refer to these families as "just good folk." I would be proud to be a member of this family.

For many years, I was the "AgFirst Farm Credit Girl" at the Sunbelt Ag Expo in Moultrie, Georgia. The Farm Credit folks made me a float and toted me, the old beauty queen heifer, around the grounds of the Expo to sing, speak, and host ribbon cuttings.

I was in the care of a wonderful man named Kenneth. He was so proud of his small town that he took me to the hardware store that his daughter and son-in-law had just bought. We stood on the street in front of the hardware store in the middle

of the town's main drag. Across the street, I noticed a restaurant with an unusual name, Keith-A-Que. I asked Kenneth, "What's with the name?"

He said, "Yep, Keith just bought that restaurant from a fella named Bob." Bless his heart. Obviously, Keith did not get it.

Kenneth and his wife have a great family. They took me out to eat at their favorite place. No, not Keith-a-Que. We went to Cracker Barrel. Kenneth had the whole clan seated at a long table in the middle of the restaurant. Toward the end of the meal, Kenneth stood up to get everyone's attention. "All right," he said, "who's going Saturday morning?" Several family members offered comments and suggestions. Kenneth quieted his crowd once again. "Let me make myself clear. We aren't leaving at 6:05 a.m., and we aren't leaving at 6:01 a.m. We are leaving at 6:00 a.m. sharp."

The family discussed food, lawn chairs, and who was responsible for this and that. I realized I was in the middle of a big family meeting. My head was moving back and forth like a windshield wiper trying to take it all in. Whatever they were planning, I could tell from the tone and comments that it was a major family event.

"Here's the deal," Kenneth continued. "We're not going to miss the new Wal-Mart opening in Valdosta like we missed the one last week in Tifton. So the RV is leaving at 6:00 a.m. with or without you."

I have no idea who went or how it went. All I know is that I woke up Saturday morning seven hours away from Valdosta, Georgia, wishing I was in that RV.

Secret World of Men and Do-dahs

I wish God had included a verse in the Bible about the Proverbs 31 woman picking up a part for her husband from a tractor supply store.

"Jane, I need for you to go to . . . just take the first left at . . . the part number is . . . see if they have . . . don't get the part with the serrated edge." This is the kind of conversation that challenges a couple's marriage.

Every woman I know understands that when she's asked to run this kind of errand, it's going to tie up both her day and her mind. My first bit of advice is to remember the directions to that particular business because you'll be returning at least twice before you get the right part.

Typically, pickup trucks are parked around the building like covered wagons circling for security purposes. Walking down the aisles inside, you realize you've entered a secret world of men and their big toys.

Eavesdrop on a few conversations, and you'll discover the men are all discussing do-dahs that fit on thingamajigs. More experienced men advise their younger protégés. They go back and forth into the secret confines of long, narrow aisles lined with little boxes only they recognize, filled with do-dahs only they understand.

I was standing in line behind other dazed women like lambs in line for slaughter. We do not understand nor do we want to understand what is about to happen.

I witnessed the do-dah experts behind the counter humiliate the woman in front of me. When she left to get the whatchamacallit so they could see what she was trying to explain, the cashiers made fun of her. They get their kicks out of women like me who are clueless about do-dahs. I knew I had to defend my own kind.

Out of my unfiltered mouth (I lose more of my filter every day) I said, "Excuse me!" I must have been loud because all eyes within a twenty-five foot radius focused on me. "I think I'll ask my husband to go to Dillards and pick up a pair of Hanes-Her-Way-Pantyhose CD, control top, cotton crotch, reinforced toe, anti-cellulite paneled shapers, with a high extended waistband in Travel Buff or Barely There."

My little one-liner must have done some good. When the woman returned from her car, she was greeted with greatly improved customer service.

Sometimes you have to remind people how to treat each other whether you're dealing with parts or pantyhose.

Hummingbirds, BB Guns, and Jesus

"Your daddy's back," said my mother, "and he's brought a girlfriend."

Don't assume I'm referring to an unfaithful husband. "Your daddy's back" meant that my mother's hummingbirds had returned. We don't believe in reincarnation, but every year after my father passed away, my mother pretended Daddy was a hummingbird and visited her every summer. She even named him "Bully."

That's the lighter side to the annual hummingbird visits. When my mother filled the hummingbird feeder, it also attracted what she calls the "monster birds." They hung on the rope, drank the syrup, and scared her "babies." Momma's partner in crime, Tootsie, knew to slam the sliding glass door and yell, "Git yo' self 'way from yuh!"

The problem became so bad that Momma and Tootsie devised a plan to get rid of the "monsters." Their plan was pure evil. They wanted to murder one of the monster birds and attach it to the cord by the feeder with Scotch tape. That would hopefully intimidate the other birds—sort of a Mafia-style method of problem solving. But Momma and Tootsie both chickened out.

I couldn't help but share their dilemma with my cousins who will remain nameless. These cousins are mild-mannered, church-going, precious people. You would never imagine they have a Darth Vader dark side.

Apparently they had been plagued with European sparrows, which are just plain angry birds. They would fly into the bluebird's house, peck the bluebird babies to death, and then build their

nest on top of the carcasses. To rid themselves of these criminals, my cousins found a refrigerator box, decorated it with branches and leaves, poked holes in the cardboard, climbed under it, and shot their BB gun at those bird cannibals. In between reloads, my cousins studied their Sunday school lesson with a flashlight. Once a nosy neighbor called and said, "It's none of my business, but you have a refrigerator box in your yard and it's moving."

Their confession reminded me of some song lyrics: "His eye is on the sparrow and I know He watches me."[6] What a comfort to know that even when I do unkind things, God still loves me. He doesn't grab His BB gun and shoot at me when I do things to make Him angry. Come to think of it, He doesn't have to. Usually, He just lets me shoot myself.

My Uncle Joe

You would have liked my Uncle Joe. As a child, I was captivated by the six-foot rattlesnake skin he had mounted on a long pine board. Uncle Joe was also the master of "Bourbon Dogs" (small hot dogs cooked in his secret sauce). He sold insurance and was an appraiser. As a hobby, Uncle Joe raised chickens and shipped them to faraway places. He served in the Coast Guard and was a World War II veteran who gave life service to the words of Lee Greenwood's song, "God Bless the USA." He was a storyteller. He loved people and cherished his family. If you met his wife, my Aunt Binny, you would understand the kind of man he was just by looking at her gentle face and hearing her loving voice.

One Christmas I told him that I had named my cat "Uncle Joe" since the cat was fearless. Uncle Joe loved it when I told him the cat slapped one of the horses in the face to get to the pan of horse feed. It made him proud to know that he had a fearless feline namesake, even if it was an old tabby cat with a broken tail.

---

6   Lyrics by Civilla D. Martin. "His Eye Is on the Sparrow." 1905. Public Domain.

The years passed. Uncle Joe developed illnesses that required a multitude of medications. Unfortunately, he had a terrible reaction and wasn't supposed to live through the night. Uncle Joe rallied time and time again. He was tough. All he wanted was to be surrounded by his family. Momma and I told him we loved him. We stroked his head and held his hands.

I didn't want to see him die, but I didn't want to see him live in that condition either. Uncle Joe deserved better.

The room in the funeral home was decorated with family, friends, flowers, and all of his medals. Prominently displayed were photographs of glorious days when he served our country during World War II. Uncle Joe was a credit to the "Greatest Generation."

At the service, the Masons praised Uncle Joe. He was given a 21-gun salute and serenaded by Taps. Each of the presiding ministers spoke of the unshakable foundation of his life: faith, family, and friends. His grandchildren each placed a single red rose on his casket. His one and only granddaughter kissed her hand and lovingly touched his casket. A wealth of love had gathered under that funeral tent. I was proud to sit there.

> *You are not here merely to make a living.*
> *You are here to enable the world to live more amply, with greater vision, and with a finer spirit of hope and achievement. You are here to enrich the world.*
> *You impoverish yourself if you forget this errand.*[7]
>   Woodrow Wilson

---

7   Wilson, Woodrow. *Congressional Government: A Study in American Politics.* Reprint. Transaction Publishers. 2002.

Old Flame at the Class Reunion

After thirty years, the email-invitation finally arrived:

First Baptist High School
Invites you to
30 Years of Classes.
Join us at the
Carolina Yacht Club,
Charleston, South Carolina

Hmm. I was impressed!

Then more emails arrived. Douglas, Jayne, Emily, Terry, Linda, Leize, Kathy, Pat . . . and how about Ricky? A month or so before the reunion, I ran into another classmate. I was so excited because I hadn't seen this person in years. At first, I couldn't remember why I hadn't been fond of this individual, but after thirty seconds of conversation, it all came back. I remembered having to listen to complaints about acne issues in high school; now it was tedious details about their colon. Some people never change; they just switch topics.

That incident reminded me of going out with Joe Ben and Martha. "Okay," Joe Ben says, "before we leave this house, there are a few rules. No talk about cholesterol, medicine, acid-reflux or chiropractors." Good thinking.

Most of the class members were not bringing their spouses. Either they were divorced or the spouse would rather "take a bullet" than go to their partner's class reunion. I "replied to all" saying I wanted to show off Thomas since no one would believe that someone that nice married me. I copied Thomas on the e-mail and he just loved what I said. I was going to show him off, my trophy hubby.

When we arrived, I went to the table and pinned on my name and high school picture. After about two minutes, I realized the best route to recognizing the masses was first staring at the yesteryear photo we were all wearing for identification, then

proceeding to the proverbial squeal and hug.

Classmate Douglas had pinned his picture to his pants because he didn't want a pin-mark in his new shirt. Note: It's a bad idea to force someone to stare in that vicinity trying to figure out who you are.

Other class members arrived. I saw Dr. Carolyn Dodds who was the brain of the class. She looked super and has done well. A big surprise was that Dr. George, another classmate, was a closet brain. George apparently had dumbed himself down for high school popularity purposes. He married another doctor and they are a handsome couple. Basically, all my classmates had followed predictable paths.

Everyone wanted to meet my trophy husband.

The reunion had been planned on the worst football Saturday of the year: Clemson v. Miami. I had to have "words" with Thomas to peel him away from the television at home. As soon as we arrived at the yacht club, Thomas disappeared upstairs to listen to the Clemson game. In fact, he had his own private reunion with First Baptist grads who went to Clemson. To think, at my high school reunion, Thomas had a reunion with his own kind.

Then, from across the room, our eyes met. Yes, it was *him*—the heartthrob of my high school life. As we approached, time shifted into slow motion. I remembered when he used to pick me up in his brand new MGB GT. He still had a million-kilowatt smile—as dashing as ever.

No need for small talk. We embraced. Then he whispered in my ear, "I've always loved you. I knew it could've happened in another time, if only . . ."

"It took me a long time, Clay" (name changed to protect me from his wife), I said, "but I finally found another you. I want you to meet my husband, Thomas."

I ran upstairs where Thomas was listening to the Clemson game to fetch him. "Thomas," I exclaimed, "you have to meet Clay." I launched into my story . . . blah, blah, blah. Thomas looked like he was in a trance. "Thomas," I said, "Clay just told

me he has always loved me and I said . . . Thomas, *say something!*"

Thomas looked at me passionately and said with great excitement, "Clemson and Miami are in overtime!"

I could have had a Jerry Springer moment and made up all kinds of junk. "Clay was my first husband, he's my baby's daddy, we ran off to Vegas . . ." It wouldn't have mattered. Clemson and Miami were in overtime.

Maybe the key to a happy marriage is being able to go to your class reunion, reunite with your old flame, tell your husband all about it, and then hear him say, "I'm okay with that."

After reading this section to Thomas, I asked, "What would be the most exciting way to end it?"

He replied, "Clemson won."

What's on Your Refrigerator?

Some families use refrigerator doors as family messages boards and bragging spots. When my children were young, they arranged letters and numbers on our refrigerator. Now I use the outside of my fridge as an entertainment center. I constantly add unique reminders to help me have a good attitude and to teach my children. One of them came from Mount Vernon.

Here's the story: When Thomas and I went on a trip to Washington, DC, I decided to take the water taxi on the Potomac to visit Mount Vernon, the home of George Washington. It's not often you have the opportunity to tour a historic landmark and read a sign that says, "Please do not photograph the President's teeth."

George Washington was a brilliant, talented man, but one thing he struggled with was his teeth. He had excellent dental hygiene but genetically bad teeth. Contrary to popular belief, Washington's 'sto bought' teeth were made of porcelain, not wood.

At Mount Vernon, you can view a video that shows how they made his teeth and how painful it was for him to wear the apparatus. He's the father of our country, but we could also call

him the father of dentures. I've never seen one portrait of Washington with a big beauty queen smile on his face. Now I know why.

My mother once told me that her dentist friend, Dr. Felix, told her not to marry my daddy because they both had soft teeth. Come to think of it, that was probably the extent of their marriage counseling. And after I experienced root canal number two, I decided that Dr. Felix was correct. Maybe Washington was the product of poor dental genes too.

I'm amazed by what businesses try to sell to tourists and what people buy for souvenirs. In Mount Vernon's gift shop, I spotted a refrigerator magnet of Washington's teeth. Well, I had to have it.

Having an authentic replica (don't you love that expression) of George Washington's teeth on my refrigerator reminds me of the importance of smiling and having a good sense of humor. It also reminds me that stuff just happens that you cannot control. George "whupped" the British, but his teeth "whupped" him. It's a visible lesson—my children even comment on it—that teaches perseverance, courage, and history.

Although toothless, George Washington had a big bark and much bigger bite. He chewed up the British and spit them out. Thanks to George, we can all smile.

Only One Aunt Josie

When I became a Herlong, I bonded with Aunt Josie. She was a public servant, a Southern Belle, a wonderful educator, and a fabulous entertainer. I just loved her. Aunt Josie had a personality as fragrant and lovely as her award-winning roses. Aunt Josie was truly a rare and genuine pearl, the strength of her family and a role model for future generations.

From the moment I met Aunt Josie, her abilities amazed me. The big silver Airstream hitched to the back of Aunt Josie and Uncle Henry's Suburban made an immediate impression. In jest I said, "Aunt Josie, I bet it's hard to drive that rig!"

"Honey," she replied, "I just use the mirrors."

When she saw another Airstream she exclaimed, "Henry, get the book and look up that number." (All Airstreams have a number on the back, identifying the owner.) Aunt Josie never met a stranger.

She was Scarlett O'Hara, Martha Stewart, and Margaret Thatcher rolled into one.

From the grandness of her home on Columbia Road to the quaintness of the Methodist Oaks retirement community, Aunt Josie remained a southern lady of grace and hospitality. At my last visit, I laughed with Aunt Josie as she wound her way through the hairpin turns of her new home. She introduced me to everyone as if we were at one of the many Clemson football games we had attended together. She showed me numerous articles written about her son, Henry. She was so proud of his accomplishments as a federal judge. And Aunt Josie spoke so beautifully of Mary Jo, her daughter. Her Blocker and Herlong roots run deep and wide.

Only a few months later, I was standing in the choir loft singing one of Aunt Josie's favorite songs, "In the Garden." I stared at her gleaming silver casket draped in an assortment of roses and greenery cut from her yard. I thought of her long, wonderful life. The big silver Airstream had become her little silver truck. Her silver casket would be her last ride.

Get the book, Saint Peter. Here comes Aunt Josie.

I Love You More Than My Luggage

The following is a tribute to John Poter Herlong, a cousin by marriage and a dear friend. John died unexpectedly of a massive heart attack . . . way too young.

Many times John told me, "I love you more than my luggage." I will miss his one-liners. Cousin Joe Ben said it best, "That rascal up and left us."

You did leave us, John. My heart hurts. I will miss so many things about you that it's hard to list them all.

I remember twenty-five plus years ago when I journeyed to Uncle Robert and Aunt Flora's house for my appointment at your makeshift beauty shop. I sat on a wooden stool in their utility room so you could illegally cut my hair. Most of the women in Edgefield County sat on that same stool, waiting for you to do your magic. You transformed us so well that we followed you here, there, and yonder. You also were one of the best makeup artists I've ever known. I've seen you transform little girls into Peach Queens, Junior Misses, and several Miss Statesmen. Our local girls did well: One became a model and adorned the cover of a top European magazine. Another one became a finalist in the Miss USA Pageant.

Your talents weren't limited to just hair and makeup. You were a superb decorator. I loved the way you helped prepare my home for the Johnston Women's Club Tour. How many times did we watch you create an elegant ballroom out of a cow pasture? We gasped as we entered a wonderland of lights and romance ... your gift to many Edgefield County brides.

I'll miss your candor. Johnny-Boy, you threw grenades of honest truth. Ouch! You told me things that I didn't want to hear, but you knew I needed to hear them.

I'll miss your wisdom. Countless times I called you with an "issue." In a few seconds, you said just the right words. You were one of the wisest friends I've ever had.

But we all knew the drill. You had to have your times of solitude. We worried about you, but you always bounced back. Eventually, emails appeared or our phones rang. Thank God, you were back.

Only a month or so before you died, you called me while I was sitting with Momma in ICU. I cried when I heard your voice. I'll miss how much you loved and cared. All of us experienced your kindness. Not once did you demand attention or praise. Just like your final wishes ... no praise, no special attention.

We also witnessed your unconditional love for your precious mother. You gave up so much to be with Aunt Flora, but you never complained and loved every second of your time with her.

I loved the deep faith your emails expressed, a side of you many weren't privileged to know. In one of the last emails you sent me, you quoted Philippines 4:13: *I can do all things through Christ who strengthens me* (NKJV).

Promise me that when my time comes, you'll be waiting for me with a round brush, hair spray, some rollers, and shoes that are the same color (post funeral humor). As always, you'll tell me with choice words to sit down and be quiet. You'll want me to be introduced in heavenly style. You always want me to be at my best.

John, you blessed me. Thank you, my cousin, and my friend. I love you more than my luggage.

Conchs and Mermaid Pocketbooks

As a child I roamed Bird Key Beach, a lump of sand sandwiched between Folly Beach and Kiawah Island. I walked along the shoreline for hours, searching for the perfect shell. I collected conchs, sand dollars, and "mermaid pocketbooks"— empty egg casings. I gathered the best treasures and left the damaged ones behind.

Family times and childhood experiences are priceless treasures, perfect for crafting a healthy home. Just as we value unblemished seashells, we all desire a perfect home. As much as I loved my family, I knew there was fracture in our family shell. As children we may believe that we're the only ones who have issues, but as we mature we understand that's not true. What I saw happen in my family was of great value. Painful experiences taught me what not to do. I also know it's healthy to find the good in every situation since it can be an extremely valuable opportunity for learning. The best we can all do is to celebrate the positive whether our family shells are cracked or airtight.

CHAPTER 3

Precious Pearls: Our Children

Since I was an avid tomboy, the gifts I received during my childhood consisted of cowboy accessories, popguns, slingshots, and toy tractors. Finally, to my parents' relief, I asked for a doll. The female/mothering pearl began to form.

When the time came for Thomas and me to start a family, nothing happened. But God had a plan. Through patience and prayer, I realized that children are as delicate and priceless as the formation of the seed pearls. It took years of infertility for me to appreciate valuable lessons and the amazing honor of having the greatest title of all: mother.

Surviving Infertility with a Fertile Sense of Humor

One of the greatest challenges Thomas and I faced as a couple was trying to start a family. I think back on those years as the "best worst times." My heart was broken month after month, but the Lord is a faithful, comforting, and miracle-working God.

"You only have a ten percent chance of having a baby." The words stung like a bumblebee. I had taken rounds of fertility drugs, suffered through endometrial biopsies, a laparoscopy, not to mention the endless number of sonograms and tests. I stared at the fertility specialist in disbelief. I wanted to cry.

I had prayed about our family plans. It seemed like nothing was working. I wanted to scream, "Somebody get me off of this emotional roller coaster!"

I didn't like myself. I felt like part of me had died because of the stress of wanting a family so badly. I had always been a positive person, living life with joy and purpose. I prayed that God would help me be myself again.

With tears streaking my face, I left the fertility specialist's office and drove to my new job. My husband had purchased a stockyard, and he had drafted me to work in the office. A stockyard is a place where cows, goats, sheep and—you name it—are sold. I asked Thomas what I should wear to work. He replied, "Something you may not want to see again since your clothes will smell like the bottom of the animal pens."

I knew by the smell that I was close to the stockyard. As I looked around, I felt like one of the cast members in the television show, *Bonanza*. I was surrounded by cowgirls, cowboys, and cow pies. My cute light blue skirt and matching blouse with hand-painted fish on the collar did not blend.

One cowboy fixed his eyes on me as I entered the office door. The left cheek of his face was stuffed with Redman Chewing Tobacco, and about ten toothpicks hung out of the other side of his face. He stared at me like I was the weirdo.

He said, "Hey, ain't you that Herlong girl whose husband done bought this place?" "Yes," I replied nicely. I didn't feel nice or want to be nice. In fact, I thought he needed to look at himself in a mirror. I just wanted him to leave me alone.

Then he asked the question I hated: "You got any chaps?"

Chaps? What are chaps? I wondered. *Is he talking about Chap Stick?* "Chaps?" I asked. "What do you mean?"

"Young'ns," he replied. "You know, children."

Oh boy. That was the one topic I didn't want to hear about or be asked about.

I felt the tears filling my eyes. "We don't have any children," I sputtered. "We want children, but we've been under the care of

a fertility specialist and he said . . ." I couldn't believe I was giving this perfect stranger an update on my ovaries.

He interrupted me, "You ain't got no chaps?"

"No," I sniffed.

"Well, if you was my heifer . . . I would've done drove you to the meat processing plant."

Oh no. That cowboy did not call me a cow, did he? Not to mention that I would have been considered a bum cow for not being able to have a calf.

"Honey, if I were your heifer," I shot back, "I'd drive myself to the meat processing plant."

At that moment my attitude began to change. I could have continued to feel sorry for myself, but I chose to laugh. A small step in the right direction. Even that annoying cowboy eventually became a good friend.

Thomas and I survived many years of testing: our faith and our patience along with a variety of medical procedures. The Lord graciously honored our prayers. He taught me to let go completely and trust Him with all things. On July 8, 1988, our son Holmes was born; twenty-two months later, we were blessed with Caroline.

Thanks be to God for giving us nudges in our darkest hours. Even at a smelly, old stockyard, God used an unlikely situation and a gruff person to help me on my journey of faith.

> *Children are an heritage of the LORD: and the fruit of the womb is his reward.* Psalm 127:3 (KJV)

A Time to Jitterbug and a Time to Waltz

I admit it. I ignored the letter from OBGYN and Associates informing Dr. Gamewell Watson's patients that he was "transitioning out of clinical medicine." In other words, I had to replace my dear, precious 102-year-old gynecologist.

How could I replace the man who had delivered my newborn babies? The man who had the wisdom to send me to a fertility specialist when pregnancy plans "weren't happening." The man who wouldn't leave town when my children were due, and who let me stay in the hospital for five days after my children were born. Dr. Gamewell Watson, the man who had delivered my husband, Thomas, and even had made an unexpected house call when our son Holmes was a newborn.

Along with all those wonderful qualities, Dr. Watson's homespun wisdom is remarkable. When I finally became pregnant, he told me, "Now Suga', you have to stop doing the Jitterbug and learn how to do the Waltz."

I saw the name on the caller ID—OBGYN and Associates. I hadn't wanted to read the devastating news. Why would I want to hear it? *This is crazy. Something is wrong with me.* I forced myself to answer the phone.

"Mrs. Herlong, this is Shemetra at OBGYN and Associates. I'm calling to help schedule you with another one of our physicians. I'm sure by now you've received the letter about Dr. Watson."

The young lady was kind, professional, and carefully phrased her words. I just listened. "Now, Dr. Watson is still coming to work a couple of days a week and he will have an office," said Shemetra. "Uh, Mrs. Herlong, are you still there?"

"Did you say he *will* have an office?" I asked.

"Oh, yes ma'am."

Then right out of my mouth came this bombshell: "Well, I guess I'll bring my own equipment to his office because I am *not* giving him up."

Well, that girl started to laugh and she didn't let up. "Oh, thank you, Mrs. Herlong for making me laugh," said Shemetra. "You have no idea how hard it's been to call all of Dr. Watson's patients. I've never seen such devotion. Last week I had to tell one of his patients the news, and she became so weak we had to take her outside to get some air. Another woman in the office

had already reluctantly switched doctors. When we called the name of another patient for Dr. Watson, boy, that woman was *not* happy. She wanted to know why this other woman was still his patient and she wasn't!"

Yes sirree, Dr. Watson is our OBGYN rock star.

Dr. Watson decided to enter the field of obstetrics and gynecology in a rather unorthodox manner. When he returned home after his college graduation, his father asked him to follow a pregnant mule around their Trenton farm. All summer Dr. Watson took care of the mother-to-be mule. When that job was completed, Dr. Watson decided to take care of humans instead of animals.

"You know, Mrs. Herlong," Shemetra lamented, "some of these women have been under his care for over sixty years. They just do not want to let him go. I believe they love Dr. Watson more than they love their own husbands. These women think they're cheating on Dr. Watson if they go to another gynecologist. I've never seen anything like it."

I guess you could say we were all acting like that old mule Dr. Watson took care of. We were just plain stubborn.

I reluctantly told Shemetra to schedule my next appointment with a doctor who Dr. Watson actually delivered. If I can't have Curly Watson, I decided, at least I'll have a Curly Watson baby as my gynecologist.

"And please tell Dr. Watson when my appointments are, Shemetra," I added. "I want him to make an appointment to come to the office when I have my appointments."

Now that this amazing man is in a new stage of life some may wonder if Dr. Watson will jitterbug or waltz. That's easy. His body might be doing more of a waltz, but his heart and mind will never stop doing the jitterbug.

I feel very blessed to have had this wonderful man in my life, the first person to touch my much-prayed-for babies. Dr. Watson was an inspiration to all and his memory will live on forever. Rest in Peace, Curly.

Always give without remembering; always receive without forgetting. William Barclay

Is the Enjoli Woman in Therapy?

As a teenager, I was fascinated by a commercial that advertised a particular brand of perfume. It seemed that if a woman wore this product, handling the challenges of womanhood would be as fragrant as the product itself.

I'll never forget the jingle that accompanied the beautiful, svelte blonde as she whirled across the television screen: "I can bring home the bacon, fry it up in a pan, and never, never, never let you forget you're a man."[8] Ooh, baby, what a woman.

That song played in my head for years. That's me, my inner self would chant. I can do it all, have it all, and be it all. Aren't Christian women encouraged to be perfect at everything in the name of Jesus? To witness to others as holy, unblemished, fragrant saints? I couldn't wait for the chance to prove that I, too, was an Enjoli woman.

Reality check. Where is that perfect chick when I need her the most? I'm in the throws of wife and motherhood. I need to ask her so many questions. Is it okay to give my children leftover lasagna for breakfast? Can I ask Thomas to turn his underwear inside out and wear it one more time? Can Sunday be considered a real day of rest, like staying in bed all day?

Remember the jingle? "I can bring home the bacon." No, I do not bring home the bacon. At best, I bring home imitation bacon bits. "Fry it up in a pan." When I announce that it is time to eat, my family doesn't come to the table. They get into the car. "And never let him forget he's a man." No problem here. He won't let me forget.

I'm confused. Commercials on TV are telling me one thing while Aretha Franklin says I need r-e-s-p-e-c-t. Then I'll feel like a natural woman. At least Mary Chapin Carpenter is honest when she sings, "Sometimes you're the windshield and sometimes

---

8   Lyrics and music by Jerry Leiber and Mike Stoller. "I'm a Woman." 1962.

you're the bug."[9]

I Am a SHE: Southern Home Executive

In the midst of the confusion brought about by being a wife, mother, and woman, I'm also having guilt. I have to cleanse my soul and confess that I'm domestically challenged. I wake my children up to get dressed for school, and they get their clothes out of the dryer. When Thomas asked me if I had washed his favorite pair of dress socks, I spotted them on the floor, dirty. He turned his head and in one swipe I grabbed those suckers, sprayed them with Lysol, and threw them into the dryer on "fluff." I admit I even thawed out the steaks in the dishwasher on "rinse and hold." Oh, how I wish I could have the domestic skills of *Leave It to Beaver* mom, June Cleaver, and the patience of *Little House on the Prairie* mom, Carolyn Ingalls.

After many years of careful research, I've finally discovered where the Enjoli woman is. She's in therapy. No woman, or person for that matter, can be perfect and wear all the many hats that the world tells us to wear.

But to whom do I listen in an effort to discover the truth? How do I handle my responsibilities as a Christian wife and mother and do a good job? Between the Internet, self-help information, and my "sistahs" at church, I am bombed with tons of advice.

First, be honest. No, I won't do it all right. Yes, I'll make mistakes. But I believe in the healing power of grace and a good sense of humor. The grace of God is there to help me through the years of molding my children and keeping my marriage healthy. Grace reminds me that I don't need to fear failure. God is forgiving. I must remember that *a merry heart doeth good like a medicine* (Proverbs 17:22 KJV).

Here's my tribute version to the songs that shaped me: the Enjoli jingle, The Bug Song, and R-E-S-P-E-C-T:

9   Lyrics by Mary Chapin Carpenter. "The Bug." 1992.

"I Am a SHE . . . Southern Home Executive"

Words by Jane Jenkins Herlong and Matt Herring
Music by Matt Herring

Nascar, football, have our hearts
Cracker Barrels and Wal-Marts;
I wear Spanx, shorts, and tanks.
Don't judge me, I'm no skank.
I became a beauty queen,
Rode in fancy limousines.
Now I vacuum, cook, and clean;
All I eat is Lean Cuisine.

Chorus

I am a SHE ... Southern Home Executive
I married HE ... A Hottie Everything-to-me
A Southern Belle, Momma taught me well
Raised on grits and hissy fits
Met Jesus at the altar rail
He loves me even when I fail
I am a SHE ... Southern Home Executive

Years of infertility,
Got a child with ADD
I love him but Doctor, please,
Is there any medication for me?
I drag my weary self to bed
Don't touch me, I'm half dead
My "drawers," I declare,
Are my "leave me alone" underwear

Bridge

Southern women may seem hard to please,
But deep down we're sweeter than our tea

Chorus
I am a SHE ... Southern Home Executive
I married HE, A Hottie Everything-to-me
A Southern Belle, Momma taught me well
Raised on grits and hissy fits
Met Jesus at the altar rail
He loves me even when I fail
I am a SHE ... Southern Home Executive, Home Executive.

Here She Comes . . .The Queen of All Queens

Thank God for Esther. Talk about respect. She was clever, beautiful, bold, and brave.

I think she was the first lady of beauty pageants since she mastered the onstage question. "Esther, what do you want more than anything else in the world?" asked King Ahasuerus as Esther stood on the royal stage.

"I want to save my people and have *world peace* throughout the 127 provinces," replied Esther boldly.

Wait a minute—she had already won the title and she was the queen. What was the prize? The prize was not only saving the lives of her people but her own life as well. Esther broke all the rules but always covered herself in prayer. You go, girl! God honored her as Queen Esther, but first she developed the heart of a servant. No doubt she was the titleholder and voted Miss Congeniality of the Jewish people.

Lord, do I need to develop a heart like Esther?

The Proverbs 31 woman used all of her talents. I think one can accurately say she was the windshield *and* the bug. She was diligent as a homemaker, but she also had authority outside of the home. And she took good care of herself. She dressed in colors fit for royalty.

Okay, so she had servants. Yes, I do too and probably so do you. My servants are my dishwasher, vacuum cleaner, dryer, computer, washing machine, and the list goes on.

Actually, Esther and the Proverbs 31 woman were both queens. They knew that their influence began with a pure heart and God-directed steps. Both women began their journey of womanhood not with the right brand of perfume but with the sweetness of prayer. Godly women have a special beauty and confidence. Can I go so far as to say they had the spirit of the Enjoli woman without the perfume bottle?

Are there women today that have such a spirit?

Miss Margaret: the Queen of Prayer

Oh, yes. Miss Margaret was one such woman. Maybe it was the scent of the flowers that day at her funeral. Maybe it was the atmosphere of the church. Whatever the cause, it was a day I'll never forget. A sea of vaguely familiar faces filled the room. Present were young, old, black, white—some folks I recognized and many I didn't. The thread that held us together was Miss Margaret. We all sat in silence—remembering and celebrating the life of one remarkable woman.

I remember walking with Miss Margaret to her prayer garden and listening to her heartfelt prayers. Under the shadow of a huge wooden cross, surrounded by beautiful flowers, Miss Margaret spoke simple but powerful words of faith. Today when I look at my two miracle children, I think of her fervent prayers and her precious witness.

Like the Proverbs 31 woman, Miss Margaret's arms stretched out to the community. Her clothes were strength and dignity. She was known in the county as someone to turn to in times of need. Her life and laughter were contagious. The joy of the Lord was her strength. Miss Margaret was both a woman of grace and a merry heart. I found the spirit of what I was looking for when I saw the Holy Spirit living in Miss Margaret.

Thank You, Lord, for the gift of her friendship.

Girlfriends, this is what we're looking for. We want real-life, modern day Esthers and Proverbs 31 women who have the spirit

of the Enjoli woman. Women who focus on being the best they can be through the power of the Holy Spirit. We'll make mistakes. We'll be deceived by the world. Just lighten up and learn to laugh at yourself.

So all of you Enjoli wannabes listen carefully. You can't do it on your own and that is good news. Learn from women who have found the truth and lived it. The answer to a woman's success certainly doesn't come in a bottle of perfume or any other product. But the spirit of the Enjoli woman can be found in Scripture, and it emanates from the lives of godly women.

How sweet the scent of a woman filled with God's love and grace. Tune out the world, tune into the Word, and lighten up.

> *Dear Lord, please help me to be a woman after Your own heart, a praying wife and mother. May my actions and thoughts reflect You, and may I always be reminded of the privilege of motherhood. May our home be covered in prayer and may all who enter it experience Your grace and peace. Amen.*

Oyster Shells and Oyster Roasts— a Southern Tradition

In the Lowcountry, we love our oyster roasts. Opening the oyster shell is one of the roast's greatest challenges since oyster shells resist invasion. I've seen folks armed with the latest oyster shell weaponry finally give up trying to open the stubborn shell. The oyster shell is in protection mode, guarding the growing delicacy inside.

Oyster shells should be just like our homes, the covering that protects our most precious assets, our children. Our homes should protect our values—what we pray our children will embrace. Many years ago, I bought a plaque and displayed it in our kitchen. It read, "Christ is the Head of this house, the unseen Guest of every meal, the silent Listener to every conversation."

Parenting generates countless challenges. I carefully monitored what my children watched on television. We didn't have any kind of cable or satellite television until the children were teenagers. They didn't like it one bit. I ordered movies from a company in Utah that sold wholesome family entertainment. The company was funded by the Mormon Church, but I didn't care. It was one of the only companies I knew that produced decent entertainment.

The standing joke in our family is, what happened to Bambi's mother? When my children were small, I recorded over the part when Bambi's mother is shot. They asked, "What happened to Bambi's mother?" I answered, "Doing what mothers do—talking with Jesus."

Navigating children as they mature is a difficult task, especially concerning relationships. They may develop relationships that aren't beneficial, the outside toxins that endanger your family's shell. Godly children from godly homes sometimes get involved with the wrong crowd. The results are disastrous. The solution is to get on your knees, parents, and pray for wisdom.

Our family encountered the challenging task of stopping family dysfunction from poisoning the next generation. On the rides back home after we had spent time with family, my children began asking questions and making comments about family behavior. Those long rides gave Thomas and me an opportunity to help our children set boundaries and borders without inflicting our children with the same unhealthy behavior. On many occasions we held hands in the car and prayed before entering a place where we knew there was conflict.

Parenting is a twenty-four/seven job. I used to think that couples without children were odd. Now I appreciate their decision not to have children. The last thing this world needs is a parent who lets the world raise their young'ns. The parents I know who are trying their best to raise godly children say that their children are their hobbies. Amen to that!

Even though parents try to dot every *i* and cross every *t*, they can still encounter tremendous challenges. There are no guarantees. But nothing compares with the peace that comes

when parents lay their heads on their pillows at night knowing they did their very best.

Proverbs 22:6 says, *Train a child in the way he should go, and when he is old, he will not turn from it* (KJV). I've heard that verse quoted many times and the meaning is obvious. That verse also encourages parents to allow their children to follow their natural talents and gifts.

When my children were small, I was an avid reader of Dr. James Dobson's books. They contain such godly common sense. I highly recommend reading his books on strong-willed children and discipline. He says that after parents discipline children, the children should be sent to their rooms. Then after several minutes have passed, parents should go to their children's rooms and talk about the incident. Dobson also teaches that parents make mistakes, and they should pray to be better parents in front of their children.

One night, while my family was praying, I did what Dobson suggested. I asked God for forgiveness and correction when I didn't properly handle a moment of discipline for the children. All of a sudden, our son Holmes decided to be a television evangelist and said in a very loud voice, "Yes, Lord . . . thank You, Jesus . . . correct this woman."

A second grader came home from school and said to her mother, "Mom, guess what? We learned how to make babies today."

The mother, more than a little surprised, tried to keep her cool. "That's interesting," she said. "How do you make babies?"

"It's simple," replied the girl. "You just change *y* to *i* and add *es*."

My friend Morgan Jones was engaged to a young man who was coming to visit her kindergarten class and read to them one afternoon. Morgan told the children that her fiancé was coming after lunch. The children were so thrilled they could not contain their excitement. They asked repeatedly, "When, Miss Jones? When, Miss Jones?" Morgan kept telling the children, "After lunch." As expected, Cal, her fiancé, walked into the classroom

after lunch. The children took one look at Cal and started to complain. "Miss Jones, you lied to us! That ain't Beyoncé!"

Another teacher friend was substituting and overheard a young child in the class exclaim to another classmate, "I'm glad we have a prostitute teacher today."

I loved those precious moments of laughter with my children. I also know that currently only 30 percent of families are considered "traditional."[10] Guiding our children to Christian adulthood is a massive undertaking.

Our home is filled with reminders—I call them monuments—that symbolize for my children the important lessons we have tried to instill in them. Decorate your home with photos, plaques, and other family treasures that create an environment filled with value-packed messages for your children and grandchildren.

If Only the Old Kitchen Table Could Talk

"The more this table ages, the better it looks," said the salesperson when Thomas and I bought our kitchen table. Years later I realized that the statement applied to much more than the aging of the wood.

When I dust the kitchen table, I see the words "Daniel C. Herlong" imprinted in the grain of the wood. One day, Thomas's father, Daddy Big John, taught Holmes and Caroline how to write in cursive. The lesson was obviously repeated several times. That's the reason we have an indelible memory of my father-in-law's signature to cherish.

To the right of the signature is a memory from a Herlong brother. Uncle Frank came to visit. If you've ever had a Frank Herlong visit, you have a story. Uncle Frank talked about his track career at Clemson University, and he used an oval place mat to simulate how he ran. By the time Uncle Frank finished running laps, we had an oval shape permanently marked in the wood.

---

10   "Married Couples Are No Longer a Majority, Census Finds." *New York Times.* 26 May 2011.

If the old kitchen table could talk, it would tell many stories. High chairs have scuffed its edges in many places. It heard Holmes and Caroline's first words. It witnessed the funny expressions on their faces when they tried new foods for the first time. It marveled over the contagious laughter that can only come from a giggling baby. That table shared many of the milestones that all parents cherish.

Our kitchen table is our gathering place. It has been decorated with Pocahontas-themed birthday parties, cowboy round-ups and grown-up monumental birthdays. The Easter Bunny left jellybeans and chocolate bunnies on its sturdy surface. Thomas's pitiful sock bunny has sat on that table every year since 1980.

Our table has seen its share of failed meals and tears; it has heard laughter, serious conversation, and countless drills from those elementary grammar books, *Wordly Wise*. Term papers and graduation thank-you notes have been written there.

My parents sat around that table with Thomas's parents. They laughed and told stories about growing up and the places they had seen. We laughed and learned with them.

I miss the family members who are no longer with us. They sit in new places of honor around the Father's table. My prayer is that our children, their children, and their grandchildren will continue our table tradition.

Our kitchen table is a storybook of a cherished past and a gathering place for tomorrow's memories.

> *The words of wise men are like goads, and masters of these collections are like well-driven nails; they are given by one Shepherd.*
> Ecclesiastes 12:11(NASB)

The Blue Beauty Queen

Many times in our families we decide we can't afford to go places or invest in big toys for family entertainment. However,

within reason and budget, there are some things we can't afford *not* to do. Memories are some of the most valuable gifts we can create for our children. They can be revisited, with no cost, for many years to come.

A few years ago Thomas phoned with a big announcement, "I have a surprise for everybody. I'm driving up now." The children and I raced outside and saw the object that challenged my wedding vows and changed my life forever—a boat. Not just any boat. A blue boat, its glittering paint sparkling in the sunlight. It reminded me of the Mike Benet pageant gown I wore in the Beaufort Water Festival. The children were thrilled. They thought it was beautiful.

Thomas is a man of good taste. Seeing him behind the wheel of that mirage-like, rhinestone blue sequined boat seemed totally out of character. Thomas is more like Ward Cleaver than Larry the Cable Guy, or so I had thought.

Maybe that sparkly boat was his queenly tribute to the fact that he had dated two Miss Americas. "Did you know the boat was this color?" I asked hesitantly.

"Well, I knew the boat was blue, but not *this* kind of blue," Thomas replied, not making sense. What frightened me the most was the massive engine attached to the stern. Yes, I said stern. Here lies yet another problem. I know very little about boats. Honestly, the entire thing resembled a piece of blue, rhinestone-encrusted plywood with a space shuttle engine attached to its rear.

To make boating even more interesting, Thomas honors only two speeds: dead still and g-force fast. We were in trouble.

The boat did well in the lake near our home, but taking it to the ocean brought new challenges. Tide changes create banks— big islands of pluff mud and/or oyster shell beds. We knew where practically every bank was located—we hit all of them. I kept an old pair of shoes in the boat because I became the designated "pusher." You may ask, don't you have a depth finder? Yes, but by the time it beeps you're already "up the crick."

Cousin Bubba, an Abbapoola Creek cuz, recommended a way to figure out where the banks were located. He said, "Follow the ebb tide flow." In other words, imagine how the ebb tide pull creates these mounds of mud. Wise boaters launch their boats at low tide so they can easily find, and avoid, the banks.

Piles of pluff mud are dangerous. Pluff mud is composed of dead shellfish, and it smells to the high heavens. It will suck you down and not let go.

Sadly, there are also people who will do the same thing. God bless the "Blue Beauty Queen" for teaching me that finding and avoiding the dangerous piles of dead shellfish and pluff mud people is the best way to protect yourself.

Wisdom chooses to do well in the present so that you will be satisfied later.

Mrs. Blume—A Jewel of an Educator

Show yourself in all respects to be a model of good works, and in your teaching show integrity, dignity, and sound speech that cannot be condemned, so that an opponent may be put to shame, having nothing evil to say about us.
Titus 2:7-8 (ESV)

I was afraid. I had heard about this particular third-grade teacher. She was tough and tender at the same time. We felt blessed that our children had an educator like Mrs. Blume, a woman who reflected our family values in her classroom. She had taught for many years and called it like she saw it. Her shtick was giving each student a creative nickname, rolling girls' hair with strips of cloth on Halloween, and keeping the room temperature on "hang meat" because germs weren't allowed in her classroom.

Mrs. Blume had been my eldest child's teacher about a month when she called me in for a conference. I knew it was coming. I walked into her perfectly arranged classroom and

asked the question most parents would ask, "Well, what's wrong with my son?"

To which she replied, "He's fine. You're the problem."

I fell in love with Mrs. Blume that day. She explained that third grade was the all-important grade for parents to "let go" and in her words, "Let [your children] fail. They'll learn faster."

Mrs. Blume was well known for both her common sense and sense of humor. When telemarketers called her home, Mrs. Blume always responded, "Honey, I'll buy anything you're selling as long as you buy a Trenton United Methodist Church Cookbook." One young lady made the mistake of trying to sell HBO to Mrs. Blume. "Well," said Mrs. Blume, "you're selling pornography. Do you go to church?"

The young lady replied, "Why, yes. I am Roman Catholic."

"Real-ly," Mrs. Blume drawled. "Then I suggest you go to confession and get another job."

Mrs. Blume was a classic hip-shooting educator who knew how to handle all kinds of people: third graders, controlling parents, and even unwanted telemarketers. She told it like it was with no apologies. I learned to appreciate her long history of preparing children for middle school. She also taught me something that's terribly difficult for parents to learn: allow children to learn from their mistakes.

Alligators, Bugs, and Anchors

One Saturday on Johns Island, we were greeted by a six-foot gator hiding behind a tree in my mother's yard. It would walk a few feet, then crouch down in the yard looking for something to eat. We figured it had left the pond to find some nourishment in the creek. Between the two bodies of water surely there was something for it to eat. I called Animal Control but no one was there. I left a message. *That's just great,* I thought. *By the time Monday morning rolls around, that gator could be on the other side of Johns Island.* But we couldn't do anything about it.

That Saturday night was the eve of Thomas's birthday. We decided to spend the evening eating out with some friends. Just as we were about to leave the house, Thomas announced that he didn't feel too well. Yes, a nasty stomach bug gripped him that night, the following day (his birthday), and several days after that.

You know the old saying about "threes." Sure enough, the next day my daughter Caroline announced, "Momma! Grandmother's bathroom is flooded." In fact, all the bathrooms were flooded, indicating a problem from the ground up. You can't call a plumber on Sunday afternoon to fix that kind of trouble either. We spent the afternoon bailing water and listening to the toilet gurgle in unison with Thomas's stomach.

For Thomas's birthday, I had bought him a much-needed anchor for the stern of the boat. Every time we tried to anchor the boat, it just dragged on the bottom. We just couldn't get that front anchor to hold the boat on its own. Surely, I reasoned, a second anchor would secure the craft. Along with the ten-pound anchor, I also had to buy rope, four feet of chain, and special fasteners. It turned into an investment gift.

On Sunday afternoon, Thomas finally had the strength to sit at the kitchen table to open gifts and read his cards. I had bought a beautiful cake, decorated with Clemson University tiger paws and Happy Birthday written in orange. After a chorus of "Happy Birthday to You," I presented the cake, hoping it would cheer him up.

"Momma," said Holmes, "the cake is moving." We watched as the cake slid off its foundation onto the table. Apparently, the bilingual clerk at Publix wasn't so bilingual after all. I had repeatedly told her that I didn't want an ice cream cake. In seconds, we had a melted cake that was almost impossible to eat. What made the moment even more festive was the background music provided by the gurgling toilets.

Trying to "save the day," I presented Thomas with his brand new ten-pound galvanized anchor. He took one look at it and said, "Do you think we need an anchor that big?" I couldn't help but think: *We have a six-foot gator in the yard, you're sick on your*

*birthday, your birthday cake is sliding across the kitchen table, and my
mother's septic tank is exploding. With so much happening, the answer
is yes. Y-E-S. I need a huge anchor right now. I need something that
will hold me steady so I won't lose my mind. This ten-pound anchor
represents everything we need right now.*

My faith was shaped like a boat anchor that evening.

All of us need a physical reminder of what's important when
the alligators, stomach bugs, and septic tanks in life give us
trouble. Anchor your lifeboat with the faith it takes to fight
things that we have no control over.

Cast all your anxiety on him because he cares for you.
1 Peter 5:7 (NIV)

A Southern Belle in Training

Nothing warms the heart of a Southern mother more than
seeing their young embrace Southernisms, like the moment you
hear them say, "Yes, Ma'am" or "No, Sir." Those moments are as
sweet as hearing them recite The Ten Commandments or asking,
"Momma, was Jesus born in Southern Bethlehem?"

The Sunday after Labor Day, Caroline ran down the stairs on
her way to church. I stared at her feet in disbelief. "Caroline!" I
exclaimed. "Your shoes!" My voice sounded as shrill and dramatic
as if a robber had broken into the house. A moment only those
who understand the nuances of our Southern ways can fully
comprehend.

"Oh, Momma! I forgot. It's after Labor Day!"

She ran upstairs and reappeared wearing a darker, more
appropriate color. To my relief, the child understood the importance
of the unspoken rule: No White Shoes after Labor Day.

"Oh," I bragged, "I've raised a true Southern young lady."
Caroline didn't protest, fuss, or whine. She protected herself
from scandal and preserved our family honor. That's simply what
a Southern mother does—she teaches her chir'in.

The day after Labor Day is secretly celebrated as Find Out Who Is One of Our Kind Day. A true Southern woman only has to glance down to satisfy both her curiosity and heritage. It's a private club with no name, no meetings, and only one activity. The dues, however, are enormous.

Not twenty-four hours later, another Southern "sistah" and I were answering questions regarding the No White Shoes rule. The person asking questions was a transplant . . . a Northerner.

My "sistah" Belle is an Olympic gold medalist in Southern accents and our treasured Southern ways. Her explanation was as smooth as molasses. "Why, Honey," she said to our Northern friend, "it's our-uh Southern ways. You ah here-uh now, and this is how we ah. I was taught by my momma and othah kin the golden rule of No White Shoes after Labor Day when I was fo-wa years old."

Believe it or not, there's a book titled *A Southern Belle Primer or Why Princess Margaret Will Never Be A Kappa Kappa Gamma.* Apparently, Princess Margaret actually wore white shoes out of season when she visited Texas. The author, Maryln Schwartz, reminds her readers that every Southern belle learns the white shoe rule from birth. Roots are everything in the South, and a true belle would never think of breaking the code. She would never wear white shoes after Labor Day or put dark meat in chicken salad. "Never wear white shoes before Easter or after Labor Day. The only exception, of course, is if you're a bride. Bridesmaids' shoes should match the punch."[11]

Frankly, our Northern friend impressed me. She didn't say, "Well, it's a stupid rule. Up North we wear what we want to when we want to." Bless her Yankee heart, she was trying to adapt to our Southern ways.

What's all this fuss about not wearing white shoes after Labor Day? Maybe it started at the Twelve Oaks barbeque when our dear Scarlet was "pea green with envy" when her beloved Ashley was taken up with his cousin, Melanie Wilkes. Maybe it

---

11   Schwartz, Maryln. *A Southern Belle Primer or Why Princess Margaret Will Never Be A Kappa Kappa Gamma.* New York: Doubleday, 1991.

was after Labor Day and Melanie hiked up her skirt, revealing her white petticoat and a pair of virgin white church pumps.

I'll bet Scarlet was so angry she blurted the words that started the whole trend, "That ole tacky Melanie Wilkes is wearing white shoes after Labor Day. I thought her kind knew better."

I looked up the real answer—something about white shoes in the summer being cooler and dark shoes in cooler temperatures being warmer. I like my explanation much better.

This "shoe tale" has a rather cute ending. My Northern friend, in her best attempt at a Southern accent quipped, "Why Suga, I cannot believe you ar-uh actually drivin' that white car after Labor Day."

We all have unique ways of teaching values to our children. Adding humor, with a few cultural nuances, usually helps. Of course, the most important things are not what we wear on our feet but what we teach from our hearts.

A Sense of Holy Offspring Humor

I think the Lord sits on His mighty throne and decides to give parents different types of children for His heavenly entertainment.

One day Holmes came home from school and asked me to sign his Shakespeare test. I glanced down and saw a big red grade of "38." At the same time my phone rang. It was Cousin Connie, his English Literature teacher.

"Jane, Holmes scored a 38 on his Shakespeare test."

"By some stroke of divine intervention is the grading system based on a scale of 40 points?" I asked.

Cousin Connie continued, "I want you to know how he answered his questions on the test. His answers are very catty. Question one: Name Shakespeare's three children. Holmes wrote Huey, Louie, and Dewey. And the next answer isn't any better. Where is Shakespeare buried? Holmes's answer: Somewhere in the dirt."

Which leads me to Facebook. I stand firm on this advice: Do not friend your adult children on Facebook.

Recently, Uncle Stanley (Thomas's brother) called and said, "Ya'll better see what Holmes is puttin' up on Facebook."

"Well, Stanley, I'm not his friend," I replied.

"Well, I might not be either after what I just read. Your son said and I quote, 'When I was very young, I felt like a man trapped in a woman's body'."

I immediately called Holmes and repeated the conversation.

"Oh, Momma," he said, "I just forgot to write the rest of the sentence . . . and then I was born."

Holmes's Cruise

"I will graduate with honors," said our son Holmes proudly.

"Need I remind you that you have an F?" I said.

To which he replied, "Momma, the F stands for Fabulous."

"Okay, Son, but I'll bet you a cruise that you will not graduate with honors."

Thomas shot me a look that years of married life had taught me to interpret—the "have you lost your mind" look.

A week later, we all gathered in the high school gym to witness the graduates receive their scholarships and awards. Holmes turned around and said, "Daddy is coming, right?"

"Yes," I answered. "He'll be here."

When Thomas arrived, Holmes gave him the "thumbs-up" sign. Thomas looked at me and I reminded him, "Holmes has an F. We're safe. There'll be no cruise."

The ceremony began. Eventually, the time arrived for the last and most important announcements—the Honor graduates. Last names beginning with the A's, then B's, and so on. Then the guidance counselor started on the H's . . . Holmes Herlong . . . Thomas and I stared at each other in disbelief. Just as if Holmes had thrown the winning pass at the last second of the Super Bowl, he jumped up and announced to the entire crowd, "I'm

going on a Caribbean cruise!"

After the ceremony and still in shock, Thomas and I practically assaulted the guidance counselor. In unison we demanded, "Re-average his grades!"

My bet with Holmes became reality a few weeks later. We boarded the *Sovereign of the Seas*, the Royal Caribbean ship that housed more people than Johnston, South Carolina.

Two words describe our cruise—big and small. The ship was big but the rooms were small. Big people ate lots of food. Bigger people ate lots and lots of food. We had a large amount of fun with small toys—Jet Skis to be more specific.

One day we rented two Jet Skis and enjoyed a high-speed adventure. Thomas knows two speeds: stop and hold-on-and-pray. When we snow ski, he's either at a dead stop or flying down the slope. Whether he's on the top of the Rockies or in the beautiful blue waters of the Caribbean, Thomas has a need for speed.

After bouncing around on the back of the Jet Ski, I decided it was my turn to drive. Time for Thomas to experience the joy of feeling out of control on the back of that thing.

When the Jet Ski stopped, I jumped into the water. All of a sudden, Thomas yelled the unthinkable, "Shark!"

"Oh, stop it!" I commanded.

"No, really!" Thomas retorted. "It's right under you. It's the biggest one I've ever seen!"

I panicked. "Thomas, help me get back on the Jet Ski!"

Thomas just stood there and pointed. He was so taken with the size of the shark, he didn't do one thing to help me hoist myself onto the Jet Ski. Thankfully, I remembered what the instructor said about mounting it: one knee on the back and then pull up on the seat. It was a miracle I remembered that bit of information with my heart pounding and my fist ready to pound Thomas. I thought, *I'll show him! I'll teach him a lesson and let that shark attack me. Then he'll be sorry!* I even wondered if he had taken out a shark policy on me before we left home. It's amazing what stupid things you can think up.

With all my strength I maneuvered myself back onto that Jet Ski. "I can't believe you just stood there without helping me."

Again Thomas said, "Just look at the size of that creature!"

To my relief, I looked into the crystal clear Caribbean water and saw the biggest starfish I had ever laid eyes on. "That's a starfish!" I said to Thomas.

He looked so aggravated and said, "I said *starfish*, Jane!"

"You said *shark*!" I shot back.

"Oh," said Thomas rather sheepishly, "I meant to say *starfish*. I wondered why you had such a big reaction to something as small as a starfish."

At the time I wanted to scream. But now when I think of that cruise, I just remember having fun with my family. That large event combined with small experiences has become a huge family memory.

Not Quite a Chevy Chase Vacation

We made our pilgrimage from Orlando to Panama City for part two of our summer extravaganza. It was a long, desolate drive to the Emerald Coast, also known as Redneck Riviera.

We didn't know what to expect as we traveled from two lane roads to four lane highways, but we were entertained by the directional battles waged between On-Star, our smart phones, and the Garmin.

As we neared our destination, the scenery began to resemble downtown Myrtle Beach. "I thought you said this place was nice and resort-ish," one of our offspring said.

After a few more miles, the roadside looked more like Las Vegas. Mopeds buzzed around like giant gnats. I couldn't believe my eyes. A replica of the *Titanic* housed a Ripley's museum. Across the street stood a large mansion, upside down—its roof hugging the pavement. Some kind of fun house. Weird.

Then we heard high-pitched screaming. Turning our heads, we saw an apparatus that looked like a gi-normas toothpick with

a swing on it. That thing was so high the screaming people looked like ants.

The high-rise condos were massive. Honestly, I had never seen a building with so many condos. In fact, I had never seen a building that large.

More commentary from the backseat: "Oh great, I bet we're on the ninety-fifth floor overlooking the parking lot. Some resort."

I snapped back, "Y'all hush. This is free."

I was speaking at a convention for the Southern Peanut Growers. The meeting planner had been kind enough to give us three nights in a condo.

We finally found our building. When we checked in, the girl at the front desk handed me a stack of papers. One "freebie" was for three DVDs. A sheet of ten coupons advertised 10 percent off of any meal on Wednesday after 6:00 p.m.—if you ordered more than six shrimp and a slab of fish. Another perk was 15 percent off any raft from a store named Jaws if you could prove that you were a Florida resident born after 1984 during the month of July.

While Thomas parked the car, Holmes and Caroline helped me push the luggage cart to the second floor. They complained to each other about how "touristy" the place was.

I opened the door to our condo and the world changed. Our place was a brand new, deluxe condo with marble counter tops, leather furniture, and beautifully tiled floors. We were immediately drawn to the large sliding glass door. We pulled back the long shades and saw the magic. The beach sand looked like sugar. The water was Caribbean deep turquoise blue. Paradise.

My offspring were speechless.

We enjoyed a few days of relaxation. One night we decided to escape the tourism and eat at a local haunt. The GPS took us right to Hunt's Oyster Bar. The line of hungry patrons almost wrapped around the entire building. The window decor featured crude paintings of drunken sea creatures holding adult beverages.

We discovered that there was a two-hour wait for a table and a one-hour wait for the bar. Donna, the drink chick, kept all of us entertained as we sweltered in the humidity. She was the queen of the oyster bar. In that world, she knew everyone and everything.

Suddenly, a woman in a convertible drove by. Two giant parrots perched on the roll bar. Donna said, "Well, I'm glad she found 'em. One flew off last week, and they found one of them birds settin' on the courthouse stairs."

Holmes can't stand to just sit and wait. He evaluated all the choices around him and fixated on a building across the street. "Momma, don't you and Caroline get those spray fake tans? You should get a touch up. Just walk across the street. We'll wait on you." I tuned him out and continued to fan myself. Once again he tried to convince me to visit the business across the street.

Holmes kept talking about the place across the street. I looked at Thomas who had a smirk on his face. They were both up to something. Then I looked at the sign on the building: Tan Fannies. Both Thomas and Holmes had a good laugh since it was definitely *not* a tanning salon.

Maybe Chevy Chase should visit Panama City and consider making a new movie, *Vacation—Southern Style*.

I realized on that trip how precious and few our family moments were becoming. Soon our children would be absorbed in serious relationships, jobs that might take them far away, and families of their own. What a blessing to enjoy that part of our lives as a family, just having fun.

The Prom Creature Is Slain

All families experience monumental occasions: births, deaths, weddings, and The Prom. The Prom introduces mothers and daughters to the enchanting world of appropriate fashion, patience, and all the amenities that accompany this first official hoopla—revered as a milestone in maturity. I learned an

unexpected lesson when I began to see Caroline's prom through her eyes and respect her view. I also celebrated that evening in a delightfully creative way—minus the perfect dress, shoes, bag, jewelry, etc.

A few years ago, I had a speaking engagement in Texas. The person who introduced me at the luncheon stood up, and to my surprise, said, "I'm looking for a size eight and a half, three-inch-heel acrylic sling back shoe with a T-strap, with or without rhinestones. If any of you ladies can help me, I'd appreciate it." Then she added with a quiver in her voice, "My daughter's prom is this weekend and we cannot find the perfect shoes." Without missing a beat, she continued, "Our speaker today is originally from Johns Island, South Carolina . . ."

At the time I thought, *This is too strange. What's the deal about prom? Must be a Texas thing.*

Then, this past October, I heard these chilling words: "You know, this year is The Prom."

After lengthy discussions about who to ask, what to wear, what kind of hairstyle, where to eat, and what to ride in, I realized that The Prom is not a Texas thing; it is a Prom Thing. It stands on its own two feet and has a mesmerizing, potentially life-threatening personality. The Prom Creature consumes the minds of teenagers and makes parents spend money on stuff they pray their parents will *never* know about.

No kidding, a few years ago, I was told to bolt the door of an alterations shop in Augusta to keep out the "prom people" because there were other prom-goers having their dresses fitted. It was like being in charge of security at the Pentagon.

High school parents have told me the two things they dreaded most were SAT exams and The Prom. Yes, the Prom Creature reared its ugly head and I fell prey. It got me last year, too.

Caroline and I were shopping in Greenville, buying a pageant dress. My mind was preoccupied with Holmes since his prom date had been forced to cancel. Then, through the door of that

beauty queen place, entered a goddess. She and Caroline had the best time getting acquainted. Out of my mouth came the unthinkable, "Are you busy on April___? My son needs a date to The Prom." I couldn't believe I'd said it! But guess what? It worked. Holmes had, as he described it, "The Perfect Trophy Prom Date."

Checking out at Stein-Mart only a few weeks later, I realized The Prom's lingering effect. With the final prom dress in hand, after the third attempt to shop for earrings and the right evening purse, one of the young clerks said, "Oh, is that your daughter's dress?"

"Yes."

"We just had our prom last weekend," the clerk continued. "My dress was yellow. It was from Caché."

"The bright yellow satin dress that was in the window?" I asked.

"Yes!" she answered with a gleam in her eyes.

"We saw that one. It was so pretty!" I exclaimed.

Then from the other checkout lane came these words, "My dress was green, fitted to the top, full at the bottom with beading."

"Oh, yes, we saw that one at Dillard's and took it home on approval," I said. After only a few minutes of talking to the checkout chicks, I realized I had seen practically every prom dress in Georgia and South Carolina.

Everyone rides to The Prom in a limousine. The thought crossed my mind to ask Betty Bland Dowd (Bland Funeral Home) if she would do me a big favor.

After calling twenty limousine companies to the tune of way-too-much-money an hour, I called my good friend, Calvin. "No problem!" he exclaimed. "I'll give my friend Happy a call." Only Calvin would have a friend named Happy. And with a name like that, I prayed he wasn't a pimp. He wasn't.

Happy and I sealed the deal. At 5:30 p.m. on Friday night, a stretch limo rolled down our driveway. I must admit that it gave me a thrill.

Some of you may be thinking, *how stupid*. That's fine. Let me share the rest of the story. What does one do with a limousine that's booked for several hours and will only be used less than half of that time? The answer is, call eight girlfriends and enjoy a fun-filled trip of frivolity.

We followed the prom limo filled with our young and decided to wait at the Waffle House for Happy to return and take his second group out on the town. As soon as that limo turned gingerly into the parking lot, an explosive sound rocked the Waffle House. I thought the doors and windows would burst. The waitresses jumped up and down, screaming, "We won! We won!" Oh, yes. They thought they had won the Publisher's Clearing House Sweepstakes. Although I hated breaking the waitresses' hearts, my friends and I had a fun evening with Happy and the prom limo.

The Prom Creature had to be slain. And I can't wait until next year. I'm already wondering who to ask, what to wear, where to go eat . . . Maybe we'll ask the Waffle House ladies to join us.

Some People Are Scarier Than Snakes

Since we live on a farm, it's not uncommon to have snakeskins under the house. They just hang there like coats in a closet. I sympathize with snakes. They're just hot and sick of another layer. I understand. I imagine that, if they could, those snakes would put on a halter top and thong to keep cool. I know. How I think is scary.

One day I was bringing in groceries, and there it was . . . alive and in person, stretched across the steps all wrinkled up. It looked like it had eaten a long accordion, or maybe a thousand ticks.

I knew what had happened. Thomas had replaced some old wood on the side of the house. One very small opening had now become non-existent. Well, Mr. or Miss Snake didn't get the memo and tried to slither through the hole that wasn't there anymore. The poor thing looked like me after I gave birth . . .

spent, wasted, done, stick me with a fork.

I wanted to talk to it. If possible, I would have conducted an interview with a little microphone: "So, tell me, what have you been up to? Do you bite? How was your winter? See any of your friends down there under the house? Do you have babies? How many mice do you consume in an average year?"

For once, I had pity on a snake. (I've come a long way from screaming when I saw a snake in a *National Geographic*, then turning the page with a pencil eraser.)

However, I still need to work on my children.

As I compiled my interview questions for the snake, Caroline acted like a coroner: she leaned over to take a better look and pronounced the snake dead. Holmes, however, pulled up on his four-wheeler, took one look, and put that vehicle in fifth gear. In the words of the former Gov'ner of Cale-forn-ya, he acted like a "girly-man."

Cuz Joe Ben has a great snake story about my father-in-law, Big John, bringing a dead snake in a bucket to Brother Ben at the tractor dealership, pretending to look for some parts. When Uncle Ben tilted the bucket, the massive snake head hit the countertop with a loud thump. Uncle Ben literally ran around the counter, swearing he would kill Big John. Then Uncle Ben confiscated that bucket so he could pull the same stunt on countless others.

Working in the fields, I used to be deathly afraid of reaching into a tomato plant and picking a snake. I feared that one would bite me, and I would drop dead in a hot-as-Hades Johns Island tomato field.

When I married Thomas, I soon discovered that his father, Daddy Big John, entertained himself by pulling snakes out of peach trees and throwing them at people. I also learned that some snakes are actually helpful—not all of them are satanic.

One last story about snakes. Said the snake to the traveler, "Please give me shelter in your warm pocket? For I'm a lonely snake and freezing!"

The traveler obliged and put the snake in his pocket. A little while later, to the traveler's surprise, the snake bit him when he put his hand in his pocket to warm it. "Why did you bite me?" asked the man.

"Well," replied the snake, "you knew I was a snake."

Another valuable lesson to teach our children is that there are good snakes and there are bad snakes. Just like in life there are the good folk and the others. Some are full of poison and try to bite; others just hang out and protect us from the mice and bugs in life. God grant me, and my young, the wisdom to know the difference.

> *I have given you authority to trample on snakes and scorpions and to overcome all the power of the enemy; nothing will harm you.* Luke 10:19 (NIV)

Sprinklers, Mud Pies, and Shuckin' Corn

"I want my children to enjoy running through a sprinkler, making mud pies, and shucking corn." Many folks have told me that recently. Maybe that could be a tagline for our Chamber of Commerce: Edgefield County, South Carolina ... where children still make mud pies and play in sprinklers.

The ringing of the last school bell of the year was a sweet sound when I was a child. I couldn't wait to get home. It was summer. That meant Daddy would take us to Bird Key in the boat that he and my Uncle Horace built. They named it *The Minx*.

Momma said some people laughed as they cruised past us in their state-of-the-art open boats. They made fun of our homemade, hooded boat—until a thunderstorm came up. When Daddy lowered the wooden sides, *The Minx* was transformed into a floating box. We were protected from the drops of rain that stung like BB gun pellets. The boaters who had laughed at us were soaking wet in their fancy boats.

On summer weekdays, I played outside all the time. I spent many days making mud pies on the back steps and carefully stacking them on the concrete steps of our old clapboard house.

My parents set aside one day in July to shuck corn. Momma, Daddy, Tootsie, Alonzo, and I had an assembly line. Family members were assigned stations—from pulling the corn to making sure all the air was out of the small plastic bags. By the end of the day, we were up to our ears in corn. Resisting the urge to take a bite out of a fresh cob of Silver Queen was almost impossible.

On hot days we cooled off with the sprinkler. Our sprinkler rotated in a clockwise circle. We had fun trying to outrun the stream of water that spewed from all four sides. Trying to avoid the spray, we got soaked.

As life becomes more complicated, many people want a slice of simplicity. There comes a time in life when bigger is not always better. I want to preserve and celebrate the simple, valuable treasures in life and pass them down to future generations.

Enjoy present pleasures in such a way as not to injure future ones.[12] Seneca

Poison to the Pearl

We celebrate family life and do our best, with the help of the Holy Spirit, to instruct our children. But one of the most destructive forces that can threaten a family is enablement. Some of the finest families I know are saturated with enabling behavior. It gradually destroys many lives, including the person being enabled. In *Necessary Endings*, Dr. Henry Cloud says of enabling: "There is a difference between helping someone who is disabled, incapable or otherwise infirm versus helping someone who is resisting growing up and taking care of what every adult (or child, for that matter) has to be responsible for: herself or himself.

---

12   The Quotations Page. http://www.quotationspage.com/quotes/Seneca 11 Feb. 2013

When you find yourself in any way paying for someone else's responsibilities, not only are you stuck with a delayed ending, but you are probably harming that person."[13]

One of the best places to take the pulse of America is at the checkout line. Children throw hissy fits trying to get the toy or candy they want. I watch how parents handle those moments of discipline, which can be a precursor to full-blown enabling. One of the most poignant moments I ever witnessed was a young child sitting on the floor crying. When I asked him what was wrong, his words shocked me: "There's nothing else I want."

My two children wanted "this toy" or "that candy bar" too. Could I have bought it for them? Yes. Should I have bought it for them? No.

When those "I want" tantrums erupted, I used the Mr. Trapeze muscle. Mr. Trapeze is located on the top of the shoulder. I first saw this technique used on *Star Trek*, compliments of Mr. Spock. That sci-fi scene replayed itself in my head, and I can assure you that it works. When the slightest pressure was applied, my children knew I meant business.

The Million Dollar Gas Can

Like a surveillance expert, I watched for any enabling that had the potential of poisoning my children. I agree with Dr. James Dobson when he suggests that one strong punishment on the onset should send the signal and set a boundary with children. Honestly, it depends on the child as to how strong the signal.

Thomas has trouble with standing firm when events need attention. Holmes had his daddy in his back pocket when it came to running out of gas in his very used SUV. About once a month, Holmes phoned and said, "Hey, Momma. Is Daddy there? I ran out of gas ... again." Kind and generous Thomas would refuel Holmes's car every time. On one out-of-gas occasion, Holmes was unaware that his daddy was on a business

---

13   Cloud, Henry. *Necessary Endings*. New York: Harper-Collins Publishers, 2010.

trip. I was thrilled to get The Call. I bought a red plastic gas container and attached a note to the side:

Dear Holmes,

This is a special day for you since you will learn a lesson that will last a lifetime. You may not appreciate this in the present but I can assure you that this is a valuable lesson. This is an empty gas can and there is no money included for you to buy gas. The good news is that you have friends that can drive you to the station to buy gas. Ask them for the money. You will pay them back from money you earn cutting the grass. Congratulations on your new life lesson.

Love, Momma
P.S. Daddy is out of town.

P.S.P.S. Holmes never ran out of gas again.

I am ultra-sensitive to enabling since I've witnessed the consequences. I saw my mother try to stop enabling after my father died. He was a very good man, but Daddy tried to fix things with money. He just didn't have the skills to handle situations, and it really grieved him. Daddy talked with me about all the things he had done out of the goodness of his heart that only made the problems worse. I just wanted to cry for him. He died one year after our conversation, at the ripe old age of seventy-two.

Boundaries must be established when dealing with people whom you dearly love but who have been helped way too much. I've learned that the enabler will never be able to do enough for the person they are enabling. Did you get that? *Never.* And every act of enabling will be accompanied by more stress, anger, pain and hurt. It cripples both parties.

For even when we were with you, we would give you this command:
If anyone is not willing to work, let him not eat.
For we hear that some among you walk in idleness, not busy at work, but busybodies.
Now such persons we command and encourage in the Lord Jesus Christ to do their work quietly and to earn their own living.
As for you, brothers, do not grow weary in doing good.
If anyone does not obey what we say in this letter, take note of that person, and have nothing to do with him, that he may be ashamed.

2 Thessalonians 3:10-15 (ESV)

CHAPTER 4

Stringing Your Strand

S eed pearls, irregular pearls, and dark pearls should all be part of our strand. Each pearl is added, refined, and polished as the Lord allows events and people to cross our paths. It's all about becoming valuable in this world and bringing glory to God.

The seed pearl symbolizes our God-given talents and natural gifts that, through time, will be polished. We can't permit life's hard lessons to ruin our natural gifts. Momma always said to me, "You've always been a sweet person. Don't ever let anyone or anything take that away from you."

The dark pearls are those difficult times that allow God to do His best work. We don't welcome those gifts. We would never choose dark pearls for our strand. We're forced to add them. But as we mature, we learn to appreciate their value.

The irregular pearls represent those events in life that challenge our faith. Something goes wrong and we end up in a tough situation. These irregular pearls also provide a wonderful opportunity to develop a sense of humor.

Sowing Seed Pearls

Years ago when our son Holmes was around five years old, we took him to homecoming at Clemson University. Going to the Clemson football games with my parents was always a treat because Daddy had a motor home.

After the tail-gaiting feast, Thomas, a Clemson graduate, wanted to take the children to see the floats around campus. I stayed with my father, who had just had knee replacement surgery, and helped him clean up the motor home.

My last words to Holmes were, "Hold on to Daddy!" When Thomas is immersed in an experience like Clemson University homecoming, he doesn't pay much attention to details—like our children.

About twenty minutes after Holmes and Thomas left, I heard someone banging on the metal motor home door. I opened it to find Holmes, tears streaming down his face.

"Daddy lost me!" he said through his sobs.

I was so thankful to see the child, but I was also upset that Thomas had let it happen. Then it dawned on me that Holmes had only been to Clemson twice. Miraculously, he had found his way back to my father's motor home. "Holmes, how did you know how to find your way here?" I asked. I'll never forget his answer.

"Momma, you told me I was smart. I ran and said I am smart, I am smart . . ."

I looked up and saw a very frantic Thomas talking with a university security guard.

"There's Daddy!" Holmes exclaimed.

Then Thomas ran to another security guard.

"Don't tell Daddy where we are, Holmes," I said. "Daddies need to learn some lessons too." I allowed the search to continue a little longer before we flagged Thomas down.

We learned many lessons that day. I learned the power of my words, Thomas learned to pay attention to the children, and Holmes gained self-confidence.

I began telling Holmes he was smart early. When he ate a dead bird in the yard, I told him he was too smart to do that. When our as-the-crow-flies neighbors brought him back home after he had left his clothes lying in a pile in our yard, I told him he was too smart to run around with no clothes on. I could have just as easily told him that he was stupid on those occasions. I could have planted a seed in him that destroyed his confidence and sense of identity. But I didn't.

The seed pearls we string on our children's strands are invaluable. Words can make or break our children.

Thirteen years after the homecoming incident, we moved Holmes into his dorm at Clemson University and hugged him goodbye. As tears filled my eyes, the Lord reminded me that Holmes was capable of handling the new challenge.

"Holmes," I said, "remember, you are smart."

Dear Lord, please help me to remember the impact of my words, that something as small as my tongue has tremendous power. Amen.

I Wear My Seed Pearls My Way

Tiffany is the daughter of a good friend of mine from Columbus, Ohio. Becoming a physician's assistant was Tiffany's dream, so she bravely moved to Charleston, South Carolina, to pursue that dream. Without question, Tiffany had the temperament and the personality for the job. She was an ideal candidate. Her determination and passion to be accepted into that highly competitive program impressed me.

Tiffany submitted her application and waited. Many weeks passed. She was surprised that she hadn't received any word from the admissions office. When she finally called the office at the medical university, she received disappointing news. She was not one of the thirty accepted students. In fact, she hadn't even been considered. They had misplaced her application.

Tiffany called me for advice. A professor had suggested that she call the admissions office to vent her frustration over being treated unfairly. Tiffany didn't feel comfortable with that approach since it was counter to her nature. I advised her to call the admissions office and ask for priority consideration the following year.

Tiffany handled herself with character and grace when she contacted the individual in charge. Her attitude served her well. Within a few weeks, the director of admissions called her and admitted her into the PA program. Someone had dropped out and Tiffany was the first person called. The director of the PA program had been impressed with Tiffany's ability to handle disappointment and her effective communication skills—two qualities every physician's assistant needs.

Our Most Powerful Weapon

Roger Rabbit says, "Sometimes a laugh is our only weapon."[14] That's one of the wisest things I've ever heard even if it was spoken by a cartoon character.

To be able to laugh at oneself is a wonderful quality. Laughter truly is the best medicine. As the Bible says, *it doeth good like a medicine* (Proverbs 17:22 KJV).

At one of my recent speaking engagements, a woman shared a story with me that was a hoot. To celebrate a "round birthday" (zero at the end), she bleached her brunette hair and became a blonde. A week after the big change, she had a good laugh with her new "do."

Here's her story: "I was sitting in a restaurant waiting for my husband, Jerry, when I spotted a woman who looked like me. I could tell that this stranger had just bleached her hair too. I tell you, she was so friendly! We waved to one another and then smiled. I just had to meet her! I got up from my table and walked

---

14   *Who Framed Roger Rabbit?* Robert Zemeckis, Producer. Bob Hoskins, Director. Touchstone Pictures. 1988.

right toward this blonde stranger. That's when I realized I'd been looking in a mirror!"

What a healthy person! She was able to tell this story and laugh at herself. Nothing tickles my ears more than hearing someone say, "Jane, I had something happen to me that is so funny." At most conventions where I speak, the masses trail the humorists around the hotel like the Israelites followed Moses en route to the Promised Land.

So the next time you to want to destroy the blues, call a friend who makes you laugh or read something humorous. Blaze your way back to emotional health by using your best weapon: laughter!

New York Life or Death?

Before I formed thee in the belly I knew thee; and before thou camest forth out of the womb I sanctified thee.
Jeremiah 1:5 (KJV)

I love that verse since it addresses so many questions about who we are. Since I'm a humorist, I always look for the humor in life. It's just the way I see things.

In the early 1990s, Thomas decided to enter a new profession—financial services. Because we live in such a small town, Thomas approached the funeral home folks and asked if he could set up his office in the same building with them. No kidding, traveling down (or up) Calhoun street, people see a sign that reads Bland Funeral Home on one side of the building and Herlong Financial/New York Life on the other side.

Just to have some fun, when folks walk into the building, I ask them, "New York Life or *Death?*"

It Is What It Is

Some readers may have heard me tell one of my favorite stories about my Cudin' Titta LaRoach. She had a sense of humor that is legendary on Johns Island.

Here's the story: On the last day she taught school, an irate parent said to her, "I'm so angry with you, I have a good mind to knock your teeth down your throat!" Cudin' Titta kept her cool and said, "I'll save you the trouble." She then took out her false teeth and handed them to the angry woman.

Many relationships or circumstances in life cannot be fixed. The healthiest folks I know use humor or a relaxed attitude to handle those issues.

I was in Charleston taking care of my mother when Cudin' Robbie (Cudin' Titta's husband) passed away. When I went to the funeral home to pay my respects, I saw their son, Stanny (his real name is Stanyarne—so Southern). As always, he wore a grin. Stanny, his brother, and his sister took great care of Cousin Robbie and continue to take care of their mother. The funeral was a celebration of Island people who loved Robbie and appreciated his faithful service to St. John's Episcopal Church.

Stanny is so much like his fun-loving parents. At the funeral he told me a funny story that had happened a few months before his father's death.

His parents, Cousin Robbie and Cousin Titta, were sitting side-by-side when his father announced to Stanny, "I need to tell your mother that I'm working late."

"Well," said Stanny, aware of their dementia, "tell her yourself. She's sitting right next to you."

"That's not Titta!" declared Robbie.

"Daddy," said Stanny, "that is your wife."

Stanny then proceeded to dial the landline number with his cell phone. He handed the cell phone to his father and his mother answered the house phone. Sitting side-by-side, Robbie and Titta talked to each other on different phones.

"I'm still at work and wanted to let you know," said Robbie.

"What are you doing?" asked Cousin Titta.

"All you need to know is that I'm working late," said Robbie. With that, Robbie gave the phone to Stanny and said, "Your mother doesn't need to know where I am or what I'm doing. You can't tell women everything."

After Stanny finished the story he said, "You know I had a choice to either be upset or go with the flow. I mean it is what it is."

Then he burst out laughing and gave me a big hug.

Yes, it is what it is. How we all handle "what is" is what life's all about.

The Breast/Best Pearls

Speaking to a group of ladies, I shared a story about a family member who had a bout with breast cancer. I emphasized how a positive attitude can help as we face difficulties.

After the meeting ended, an older woman approached me who obviously had a story to share. That happens lots of times to speakers. Many times you just tolerate the tale. Then there are those rare times when the story or joke is unbelievably hilarious. This is one of those times. "I got me a friend who had both her breasts removed," said this friendly woman. "The doctor said she was a candidate for one of them special reconstruction operations. Well, she asked me go to the doctor and help listen 'cause her husband is the kind that don't get it. You know it's like—the wheel is turning but the hamster is dead.

"Anyhow, I was setting in the office with my friend and her husband when the doctor said, 'What I'm gonna do is cut yo' abdomen and pull it up to make you new breasts. Y'all understand?'

"Well," the woman continued, "that husband of hers was so confused. The doctor looked right square in his face and said, 'Let me explain it like this. We gonna take yo' wife's stomach and pull it up and make new breasts. Y'all got any questions?'

"'Sho nuff,' her husband said, 'yes sir, I do. If she goes to gettin' hungry, are them things gonna growl'?"

She said that doctor kept his composure until he left the room; then he let out a laugh that echoed throughout the office. "Yes," said my new friend, "we all needed a good laugh."

But the Lord in heaven laughs . . . Psalm 59:8 (RSV)

Dixie Diva in an Ann Taylor World

Sometimes our friends become our families. The precious pearls we call friends accept us for who we are. What a blessing to have girlfriends who carry us through tough times.

Several months after my mother passed away, dear friends took me on a beach trip to help me get through my first birthday without my mother. That act of kindness was a seed pearl I deeply appreciated.

Momma always told me to be myself and seek friends who love me for who I am. That lesson hit home with me on that beach trip. One day we visited a recently opened complex of interesting shops filled with a delightful mixture of clothes, shoes, and furniture.

"Look!" one of my friends said, "There's an Ann Taylor and they're having a 20 % off sale." So off we went, down the street to shop at Ann Taylor.

As we neared Ann Taylor, the sign above another shop caught my eye: Dixie Divas. Just like a crow attracted to shiny objects, I flew into the store.

It was old beauty queen heaven. Rhinestones accented almost every article of clothing in the store. Time stood still as I studied the pocketbooks, shoes, and jeans—all featuring some kind of decorative do-dah splashed across it.

Then it hit me. I am a Dixie Diva with Ann Taylor friends. The best part of my "ah-ha moment" was that it was okay. My "friend-girls" had no trouble with me browsing and weaving through that store.

As always, Momma's lesson was confirmed: be yourself and seek those who celebrate your uniqueness.

Thank you for reminding me of that lesson, Momma. In my heart I know it was your way of telling me Happy Birthday.

The Lord is near to the brokenhearted.

Psalm 34:18 (ESV)

A Pearl of a Tribute

Several years ago, I was asked to speak at a banquet to honor office personnel who worked for a large agricultural organization. The event's organizers had planned a predictable schedule: After a prayer, the folks would proceed to the serving area. During dessert I would speak for about thirty minutes.

The president of the group was an older gentleman; he had served in that role for many years. He wanted me to sing a special song at the end of the evening to honor Miss Mabel, a woman who had worked forty-seven years for the organization and had decided to retire.

You could have spotted Miss Mabel a mile away. When she entered the banquet hall, she wore a lovely rose corsage on her jacket. She walked from table to table. At each one she was greeted like a rock star. Her many acts of kindness through the years had made her the office icon.

"Do you have a special song to sing to Miss Mabel after we give her the gifts?" asked the president.

"Oh, yes I do. It's called 'The Wind Beneath My Wings' and you'll love it."

"I don't believe I've ever heard that song," he replied.

"Oh, I know you have," I said to reassure him. "Just remember to say this sentence: 'Miss Mabel, you are the wind beneath my wings.' It'll be perfect."

"Now, what was that line for me to say?" he asked again.

"You are the wind beneath my wings," I repeated.

"I sure hope I can remember it," he said.

I knew right then that it was definitely not going to be perfect.

The moment arrived. Miss Mabel, complete with handkerchief in hand, made her way to the stage for her tribute: lovely gifts, plaques, flowers, and a montage of memories and hugs. This poster woman for all administrative professionals was honored beautifully.

"Now, Miss Mabel," said the president, "we have one more thing to say to you."

I was holding my breath, hoping he could remember the introduction to my song for Miss Mabel. "Uh, Mabel, uh, you are the . . ." stammered the president.

Oh, boy. This is rich. He can't remember the line!

The misery continued. "Miss Mabel, you are the . . ." Then the unthinkable. "Miss Mabel, you are the wind inside of me."

No words can describe how I struggled to sing to that dear woman. The amazing part was that she loved it and cried harder. I was crying right along with her, but mine were tears of laughter.

A speaker friend, Karen Buxman, once said, "There are times when you laugh so hard tears may run down your leg."

Holy Smack-down at
Harmony United Methodist Church

Harmony United Methodist Church is always "bursting at the pews" when the talented young Harmonites entertain. One year the theme of the show was Noah's ark; it featured some of the cutest costumes I've ever seen. Witnessing the church sanctuary's transformation into a miniature Broadway stage with lots of singing and laughter is an annual delight for all of us in the congregation.

Unfortunately, show time coincides with wasp time—not to be confused with White Anglo-Saxon Protestants. No, I'm referring to the flying creature that injects fear and venom into

unsuspecting pew people. Since I sit in the choir loft, the entertainment created by the wasps is like having a box seat for a Broadway production.

With perfect precision, the pest zoomed past me as if it were landing at Dallas/Fort Worth International Airport. The first landing site was a female visitor's hair. The attraction was the hairspray. No big surprise. Wasps love sweet-smelling sticky goo. Unaware of the wasp, the visitor fluffed her hair gently, prompting the insect to light on another victim. Suddenly, the congregation fixated on the pest. Almost everyone bowed their head—not in prayer, but in protection—as the intruder swooped up and down the aisles, landing on various people.

One Sunday morning a few years ago, Virginia Honeycutt decided to outsmart the flying menace by concealing a can of Hot Shot in her choir folder. The critter didn't have a chance. Virginia shot it right out of the sky. You go, girl.

Another memorable moment occurred during Christmas one year. A wasp hatched during the off-season. As Cudin' Connie Herlong sang, "Jesus, Jesus, Rest Your Head," an older church member jumped up with her church bulletin rolled to kill. Cudin' Connie's angelic voice was overpowered by the sounds of the wasp being pulverized repeatedly by the bulletin, complete with several stomps on the floor. Miraculously, the wasp rose from the dead. Connie, unfazed by the cacophony, didn't miss a beat of the song.

Not too long ago, during the Noah's ark production, veteran wasp-killers sprang into action. You see, not only do we learn how to develop a deeper faith at Harmony, we also learn how to handle the wasp. One person grabbed a pew Bible and hit the wasp with The Word. An additional swat was delivered with the church bulletin. It was all over.

Yep, just like the enemy of our souls, Satan. He swoops in, full of venom, and flies around. Everyone panics. Oh, he can buzz and he can sting. He may target you, but you have the weapon to defeat him. Just use The Word.

And all God's creatures, even the wasps, said, "Amen."

God Love Him, Joe Lee

To be surrounded by people who make you laugh is one of the best gifts you can give yourself. Joe Lee McCarter, my good buddy from Clover, South Carolina, is just plain fun. There are those who make me laugh, and there is Joe Lee who makes me snort. We all need friends that make us snort from time to time.

I'll never forget the big night at the Miss South Carolina Pageant when Joe Lee sat right beside me in the auditorium. I was trying so hard to act queenly since I had just finished my reign as Miss South Carolina and my Miss America judges were seated right in front of me. "Jane, behave," I told myself.

Have mercy! The first contestant in evening gown was the Shrine Queen. That girl's dress, no kidding, was one solid mass of tassels. Joe Lee got up in my face and whispered, "Don't you know them Shriners sacrificed them hats for that dress."

I bit my lip, pinched myself, and asked God to please stop me from snorting. Well, to top it off, the contestant's hair was bright yellow. And yes, Joe Lee does hair. After composing myself, he got right back in my face and said, "Number 62 on the color chart. Honey Chile, that color chart only goes to 37." That did it. We made a scene, yes we did.

Joe Lee says he's the last of the dirty dozen (the last of twelve children). He loves his momma, too. He told me he and his brothers were painting the funeral home in Clover one summer and found a pair of dentures in the shrubbery. Just for a joke they wrapped up those teeth and mailed them to his momma. She had ordered some new teeth through the mail. Joe Lee said, "Me and my brothers are all the time playing tricks on Momma. Jane, it was just a hoot. Honey, she wore them dentures almost a month before she figured out they weren't mail-order teeth. She liked them funeral home teeth so much she mailed back her sto' bought teeth. Momma said that people give up their organs

when they pass, so why not donate dentures?"
It's just cleansing to have friends like Joe Lee.

When you were born, you cried and the world rejoiced.
I hope when you depart this life, the world will cry but
you will rejoice.

Ancient Indian Proverb

One Man's Pearl Is Another Man's Chicken Dinner

Definitely there are pearls that only we can appreciate. Like
Leroy. I met Leroy several years ago. He's an entertaining fellow.
Just throw him a couple of boiled peanuts ("bald" for those of
you with Southern ancestry), and Leroy danced up a storm.
Leroy also had a certain stride—he walked with confidence but
was a hint shy.

Actually, Leroy is a chicken—a rooster to be more exact. My
son swears that he played checkers with Leroy and almost lost.
Hmm. Leroy—the pecker who plays checkers?

As I see it, all visitors to Edgefield County, South Carolina,
should visit Leroy. The bonus feature is listening to the wonderful
stories and folktales of his owner and friend, Ike Carpenter. Ike
is a history buff and loves to blend the believable with some
pretty tall tales.

One of Ike's passions is re-enacting days gone by. He takes
Leroy along, and Leroy the rooster re-enacts too. Ike places him
in what looks like a cage made of hay bales, ties a small rope
around his leg, and puts a stake in the ground. It's all for show
since Leroy is tame. At times, Leroy perches on Ike's shoulder.
Leroy is a pearl to Ike. They just go together.

It's a treat to stop by Ike's "Whatever Stand" and chat. If
Leroy shows up, the visit is even better. It's one of those sit-
around-and-listen places.

Once Ike was re-enacting with his feathered friend and some
folks in the Confederacy thought he was "fair game" and, well,

took an axe to Leroy. This caused quite a stir amongst the locals. Now visiting Ike is sad. But Leroy lives on. Ike has erected a memorial to his friend: a plastic Wal-Mart chicken decorated with pictures of Leroy.

Ike has more tales to share and, as always, we'll be there to laugh and listen.

Better Than Weight Watchers—Chicken Farmers

That time of year when clothes must be cooler had arrived, which meant more flesh may be exposed. I remember when I could throw something on, not ponder whether it looked good, and go about my business. Not so easy anymore. So I decided to diet.

Around that time, I spoke to a group in Birmingham, Alabama. The client asked if I would repeat a workshop several times one morning. Consequently, I was exhausted and very hungry by the time noon arrived. I had been carefully watching every bite of food I ate, but after talking all morning, I couldn't wait to sit down and enjoy lunch.

When I arrived in the ballroom, one seat was available in the front. I sat down by several farm families who were up for the big award to be announced at the luncheon. They were all chicken farmers. On the plate right in front of me was a large chicken breast smothered with everything I shouldn't put in my mouth. Chicken Cacciatore. *This is going to be hard to resist.*

My table partners were quiet and visibly nervous. They had hardly touched the delicious-looking meal. I took a bite of chicken and then decided to start conversation. "So, how is the chicken business?" I inquired.

One by one my tablemates told me their poultry woes. KFC wants smaller chickens; Tyson wants big chickens. Chicken feed was expensive. Typical chicken talk.

Then one woman leaned in and whispered, "Y'all had any mutants?" As she described the chicks, I thought they sounded

like the cutest little fuzzy things. Some sort of secret treasure. "Oh," I said, "how sweet!" In one rapid move they all turned and stared at me.

Then the lady said, "The others peck 'em to death."

"Well," said one man, "you ain't gonna believe this, but I seen one of my chickens runnin' and it was draggin' two other legs behind it. Yep, it had four legs."

I realized I was in the middle of a horror movie, *Nightmares in the Chicken House.* The stories did not stop: a chicken with three wings, a chicken born with no eyes, etc.

One man sat there listening with no expression on his face. I recognized the type. He had the best/worst chicken nugget of all, and he was waiting for his turn. When everyone was silent he said, "I'm still waitin' for one with two heads."

I looked at my Chicken Cacciatore and renamed it Chicken-tell-a-story. I couldn't help but wonder if it was one that had been blind, deaf, with three wings, or four legs.

The bad news is none of my chicken friends won the award. The swine folks walked away with the John Deere Gator. The good news is that I resisted the dish and probably lost a few ounces.

Thank the Lord I sat with the chicken people and didn't have to listen to pig tales.

Cultured and Uncultured Pearls: Both Are Valuable

I-40W to 440W to 65S to 64W—Waynesboro, Tennessee. I had been hired to speak at a teacher in-service in that lovely East Tennessee town, which appeared to be lifted directly out of a Norman Rockwell painting. Through the mountains of Tennessee, the song "Rocky Top" echoed in my rental car as I accelerated up one incline and braked down the other. Country stores, complete with window displays of quilts and jars of cider, dotted Highway 64W.

Driving up to the hotel, I was reminded of The Three Pines Hotel in Waynesville, North Carolina. My parents took their annual pilgrimage to The Three Pines after tomato season to escape the unforgiving Lowcountry heat. It was a far cry from the Ritz Carlton.

As I turned into the parking lot, I noticed a blue princess phone hanging outside of the one story building. A large sign read, "For assistance dial 511." I followed instructions and heard a friendly, "Ho-te-el!"

What made it so funny was the lady was only about two feet from me. We could see each other, but she still insisted on using that blue princess phone. I didn't even get half of my name out before the attendant said, "I know who you are. You spostah speak to them teachers tomorrow. We bin speckten you." With that, she appeared from behind the building and said, "We puttin' you in the nice room. Let me git in there and cut on the wind'r unit so you won't git hot."

I asked if she had an iron. After much to-do, she handed me an apparatus so covered with duct tape you could hardly make out what it was. A small stick was anchored on the top, secured with more tape to keep the thing "on."

"If I was you, I'd wear my rubber shoes when I plug it in. This thing's liable to spit at ya," she warned, then laughed.

What more could you ask for? The room was whistle clean and cool; the hotel was equipped with friendly, accommodating service. I loved it.

The school's Director of Instruction and his attractive wife met me for dinner that night at the town watering hole. Sunday evening worshipers had filed into the restaurant one by one. It seemed I was introduced to the entire town. They were all so friendly and informative—offering many comments about each other's health and happenings. After the meal, which concluded with "worms and dirt," we drove around Waynesboro. I loved it too. The tour even included my host and hostess's neighborhood. "This is where we live and down this street is where our daughter

lives. Next to her live our daughter's best friend and family …"

The following day I thoroughly enjoyed meeting the teachers and giving my presentations. I knew they would be kind and appreciative. They were.

My visit to Waynsboro concluded with All-You-Can-Eat Catfish Night—another local favorite. It featured table talk about football, colleges, and UT—who went to UT and who at the table shamefully attended another university. One of the gentleman said, "I went to Austin Peay [pronounced pea] University."

"Hey, Gailand, tell Jane about y'alls cheer."

"At games," Gailand said, "we yell, 'Let's go Peay'."

Just as I regained my composure, Gailand continued, "One time we had a basketball star with the last name of Fly. So we all got flyswatters, waved them in the air and cheered—okay, y'all forgive me—'The Fly is open. Let's go Peay.'"

You can't make that stuff up.

Top Reasons Older Women Should NOT Be Beauty Queens

10. They do not make tennis shoes with stiletto heels.
9. If you wave in a parade, your arm fat may hit you in the face.
8. Can't wear spanx in swimsuit competition.
7. Your platform is called "PLAW"– Panty Liners for All Women.
6. Your hair is too thin to keep the crown on your head.
5. No underwire bra is strong enough to keep the "girls" up.
4. Extra-curricular activities are having mammograms and colonoscopies.
3. Angry menopausal women will attack the judges.
2. Can't look surprised when you win because you've had too many Botox injections.
1. If you win the title, you may literally "wet your pants."

CHAPTER 5

God Loves Damaged Pearls

I've been involved in pageant competition since I was in high school. I judge and emcee these days rather than parade across a stage. I don't consider myself a pageant person, but I am a woman who challenged herself to become the best she could be through pageant competition. Because I've sat on both sides of the judges' table, I've watched young women be transformed from the inside out. I view pageant competition as one of the best self-improvement venues available to young women. It has been of tremendous benefit to me.

There She Is . . .

When I competed in the Miss America pageant, I met Miss Mississippi, Cheryl Prewitt. Her bio stated that she had been in a terrible automobile accident when she was eleven years old. Cheryl was thrown through the windshield. She ended up with one hundred stitches in her face, and her leg was crushed so badly that the bone was destroyed. The passenger in the other car was killed.

Cheryl put her faith in God, believing He could perform a miracle. The doctors were amazed when her leg was ex-rayed; they noticed a "cocoon of calcium," the semblance a bone, being formed. It seemed impossible, but our God is a miracle working God. Cheryl's prayer was answered, but God wasn't finished yet.

As Cheryl entered adolescence her body grew, but her bad leg stayed the same length. She developed a limp and tried to hide her problem with the help of hemming tricks and an unusual gait. Cheryl knew that if God could heal the bone in her leg, He could also heal the length of her leg.

One evening Cheryl attended a faith revival in Jackson, Mississippi. When the evangelist asked those who needed prayer to come forward, Cheryl was front and center. Under the cover of that worn tent in a remote southern town, Cheryl Prewitt watched in wonder as her leg grew until it became the same length as her other leg.

As we stood next to one another at the Miss America pageant on one of most prestigious, iconic stages in American culture, Cheryl Prewitt told me that she knew the Lord had purposed for her to become Miss America.

Years later, she was crowned Miss America.

Joyce Meyer says, "It is not as important how we start (our past), but how we finish."[15] Cheryl had a rough start, but what a glorious finish!

Bless Their Hearts...

Sometimes when I'm sitting at the judges' table and a contestant enters the room, I immediately recognize that she isn't a summa cum laude graduate of an Ivy League institution. I know to ask non-challenging questions.

On one occasion, I asked a young lady if she had any special talents. She thought for a moment and replied, "Yes, I can write with my right hand and my left hand. I am amphibious."

At another pageant I asked a contestant to tell us about her friends. "Well, I like to hang out with people who've been in bad accidents. I got one friend who can't use his arms or legs. They call them people paraphernalias."

---

15   Meyer, Joyce. *Battlefield of the Mind*. New York:Warner Books, Inc.1995

Mikimoto, Meet Rasheeda . . .

When I judged the Miss North Carolina pageant, one contestant quickly became my favorite. Her name was Rasheeda. She caught my eye the first night of competition when she walked across the stage in her leopard print swimsuit. The next night was talent and she wowed us with a beautiful aria. She looked regal in her purple, rhinestone-studded evening gown.

I was excited when it was my turn to ask her the all-important onstage question since it was my first chance to communicate with her. I asked her to share any advice she had received for the competition. Rasheeda's answer was humorous and heartfelt. She talked about losing weight and mentioned that at one time her thighs rubbed together. Then she asked her mother, who had lost forty pounds, to stand up. I knew then that Rasheeda would more than likely be in our top five. On Saturday night, Rasheeda was thrilled to be named third runner-up to Miss North Carolina.

I observed and admired several qualities in Rasheeda. First, she had journeyed a long way from her roots. She made a decision to reach for the sky and matured into a beautiful woman both inside and out.

Secondly, in our private interview, one of the judges mentioned that Rasheeda and another contestant in her group had worn the same gown for talent. That's one of pageant competitors' biggest fears. Rasheeda's response was amazing: "Well," she quipped, "looks like the other contestant and I both have great taste!" She didn't know how unkindly the other contestant had responded to the same question.

Another Rasheeda moment occurred when she was asked in the judges' interview how she felt as the only African-American in the pageant. She simply replied, "I hadn't noticed."

A priceless pearl had been formed in that beautiful young woman's life. She was determined to have a great finish no matter what challenges she faced. Along the way she developed a jewel of an attitude.

A Moo-ving Lesson

When I was a contestant in the Miss South Carolina pageant, one of my judges told me a story that I'll never forget.

A young woman wanted to win the coveted title of Miss Normal from the great state of Illinois. At the organizational meeting, the young lady asked, "What should I do for talent?"

The director of the program replied, "You do what you do best!"

The young lady thought for a moment and then wrote down on her talent sheet, "I'll be performing a classical music rendition." The pageant director assumed she would sing or play an instrument.

On Friday night at the dress rehearsal, she pulled into the parking lot in a four-wheel-drive pickup truck pulling a cattle trailer. In that trailer was a Holstein cow that hadn't been milked all day. The pageant director asked, "What's this?"

"This is my talent," said the wannabe beauty queen.

"What do you mean?"

"You said to do what I do best, and I am the 4-H cow milking champion for the state of Illinois."

The pageant director reminded the contestant that the Miss America pageant didn't allow live animals on stage. But that girl was no dummy. She had read and re-read the rulebook, and it didn't say anything about live animals on stage. (You can bet that the rulebook now is several inches thicker because of that one issue.)

The young woman scattered hay on the stage and positioned the cow. She had a three-legged stool and a galvanized bucket with dents in it. With great confidence, she grabbed her "instruments" as confidently as any great musician. Then she gave the soundman a nod. Dah, dah-dah, dah-da . . . squirt, squirt, squirt, squirt . . . She milked that cow to a Viennese waltz.

In between squirts, the director asked, "Wait a minute . . . what if that cow has a need?"

"Oh, I know this cow. I raised her. Don't worry, unless she is terribly startled, she'll be fine." But she had placed a large galvanized bucket behind the curtain, just in case.

Well, there was nothing they could do to stop her. On Saturday night, she was the last to perform her talent. The curtains opened and she walked on stage in molded, 4-H green, sequined hog washers. She sat down on her three-legged stool and played that cow. Dah, dah-dah, dah-da ... squirt, squirt, squirt, squirt ...

The crowd was frozen. The local photographer thought the scene was a perfect photo-op for the front page of the paper. He walked to the front of the stage with his super flash Nikon camera and fired away.

The cow stopped chewing and bellowed a moo that rocked the auditorium. Then its tail started to wiggle. I've lived on a farm and I know that a twitching cow tail is the international signal for something-is-gonna-happen-fast. The contestant jumped up to get the big bucket and the director ran to help. They both tripped over the main power source and the entire auditorium went dark. All you could hear in the darkness were the sounds of a much-relieved animal.

The power outage created a stampede. The audience evacuated the building and the stage crew fumigated, water-gated, and mop-pa-gated. The pageant directors prayed that no one would litigate.

The young lady walked over to the director who wanted to kill her and asked, "Can I try it again?"

The moral to the story is to always keep trying to do your best. Be responsible and clean up your mess. If someone moves your bucket, don't blame that person. Take the initiative. Never give up.

Galatians 6:5 says, *Each one should carry their own load.* (NIV)

The Bucket List

One of the most dramatic events I ever witnessed in pageant competition occurred in North Carolina. I had been asked to judge the Miss North Carolina USA program. As I was marking

my ballot for the swimsuit portion of the Teen Competition, the Miss North Carolina contestants began their onstage swimsuit phase.

Swimsuit competition is what separates the Miss USA and Miss America pageants. Body sculpting and attention to muscle tone are a huge part of the USA competition.

As one of the contestants walked onto the stage, a deafening hush swept across the crowd, followed by several audible gasps. I looked up in disbelief and saw a physically deformed young woman. She literally walked across the stage on all fours. No one knew exactly what to do. One by one, the audience members began to clap until the auditorium was filled with thunderous applause.

Obviously, there was a story behind her presence in the pageant.

After she walked across the stage, she left town. We later discovered that the experience had been an item on her "bucket list." With the short time she had left to live, that young woman wanted to check off another item: competing in a beauty pageant. And the pageant officials had made it possible.

That courageous woman reminded me that we're all valuable and that we should take advantage of each precious moment of every day. She was determined to have a great finish.

Can You Love You?

Constance Bess recently shared a presentation with members of the Johnston Women's Club. Her topic? "How to Live a Romantic Life." As a speaker myself, I couldn't imagine how to speak on that broad topic until I heard the theme of the presentation: be good to yourself.

Bess's very simple suggestions were based on a powerful Scripture: *"Love the Lord your God with all your heart and with all your soul and with all your mind and with all your strength." The second is this: "Love your neighbor as yourself." There is no*

commandment greater than these (Matthew 12:30-31 NIV). The fact is that many women do not love themselves. In my opinion, you cannot love others unless you first understand the love of Christ and love yourself. Constance encouraged women to wear a special piece of jewelry to bed each night, something that made them feel special:

> *Put on an attractive robe in the morning and match your lingerie. Enjoy your coffee in a lovely cup and saucer. Lift the cup to your mouth in a graceful and elegant manner. Play classical music and close your eyes. Another suggestion is to budget for flowers. You can purchase inexpensive flowers from the grocery store or cut some greenery from your yard. Make yourself feel special and valued. Regardless of your past or the damage that has been done, know that our Heavenly Father is loving and forgiving.[16]*

Just for awesome added information: Constance wears her pearls to bed.

---

16   Constance Bess. "How to Live a Romantic Life." Johnston Women's Club. Johnston, South Carolina. 12 Feb. 2013.

CHAPTER 6

Dark Pearls

Don't ask God to get rid of your problems, and don't merely tolerate them. Welcome them as gifts and you will find God's way through them. View your problems as the next steps to growth for you.[17]

Dr. Henry Cloud

We all dread those times when a dark pearl is added to our strand of beautiful creamy white pearls. We don't want to put that particular pearl on our priceless strand, but ironically it can become the most valuable one of all. Its value depends on how we use and display it. It can be a treasure or a tragedy. Our dark pearl may be produced by a variety of irritants: the death of a loved one, illness, betrayal, divorce, unfair treatment, abuse, or financial ruin. Only one out of every ten thousand pearls becomes a dark pearl, so its price is steep. Will we find value in this rare treasure or will we allow it to devalue our life? It all depends on how we handle that dark period in our lives.

On the DVD outtakes of the movie, *Bruce Almighty*, Jim Carrey is given the power of God, who is played by the legendary actor, Morgan Freeman. The scene opens with a young boy being

17   Cloud, Henry and John Townsend. *What to Do When You Don't Know What to Do: Discouragement and Depression.* Nashville: Thomas Nelson. 2009

punched in the face by an older, larger boy. The younger, smaller child asks God to make him bigger. The next scene shows that his prayer has been answered: the young child has become very large and inflicts the same pain on other small boys.

Freeman's character scolds Bruce for answering the young boy's prayer. "I was planning on using this young man's childhood hurts and gifting him as a writer," says Freeman's character. His next line is powerful: "Many times God uses dark colors to paint beautiful pictures."[18]

Will you allow God to turn your dark colors into beautiful pictures? Will you celebrate the value of the dark pearl? Will you make your pain someone else's gain?

Please Remove This Pearl from My Strand

Lord, please let this cup pass from me. For many years, this was my one line prayer. I can say with conviction that this dark time in my life was a feeling that had been inside me since childhood. I knew in the pit of my soul that God had given me a job that required all of the fruit of the Spirit plus a few leaves, vines, and roots. When the events finally unfolded many years later, I experienced the worst hurt of my life.

It's almost impossible to imagine that someone you've loved and trusted for years may say and do things totally out of character. While discussing family financial business, a sibling made the comment to me, "Well, you had a bigger wedding, a college degree, and other events."

My heart broke. I realized the real issue wasn't those events, but something much deeper and more serious. That one sentence uncovered deep roots, from which many sad events sprouted—dark years of deep hurt and emotional pain. I was trapped in an impossible family problem in a role I didn't want, which led to events every family fears.

---

18 *Bruce Almighty.* Tom Shadyac, Dir. Jim Carrey, Morgan Freeman, and Jennifer Aniston. Universal. 2003.

The most devastating part was watching my mother's grief. As Momma's health declined, she needed her children to rally, to come together, for her best interest. I prayed for wisdom. I read and studied Christian literature. I wanted the emotional pain to stop. I begged the Lord to use His mighty power to fix the problem. Balancing the love message while taking a stand on moral absolutes required tremendous effort. I believe many Christians struggle, as I did, with striking that balance.

Talk Is Cheap Unless You Go to a Therapist

We can talk day and night about what wrong has been done to us. Many people experience the unspeakable pain of the tragic death of a loved one. Mine was a living death that seemed to have no end. When we deal with difficult people, situations, or horrible events beyond our control, all arrows eventually point to how we handle those times. Ask the Lord to reveal your shortcomings or mistakes. Seek His guidance on handling life's challenges in a healthy way. Be honest and look inward. Numerous resources are available to help us during those dark times. There are amazing self-help books and counselors, but make sure to ask trusted folks for names of therapists.

John 10:10 says that the thief comes only *to steal and kill and destroy* (NIV). Did you catch the part about the thief? Thieves are sneaky and will rob you blind if you let them.

Someone sent to me a lovely prayer on a crumpled piece of paper that addressed my hurt:

- Begin this way: "Father, I have been hurt. Please heal my wounded heart. Heal me of these feelings of rejection, alienation, sorrow and loss."
- Then confess to the Lord: "I confess that I want to retaliate against this person. I am angry, frustrated and in pain. I know these are not emotions that are going to be helpful to me or that will resolve the situation. I ask You

to forgive me of these negative feelings. I desire to forgive this person, Lord. Please help me to forgive."

- Then declare before the Lord with faith: "I free this person right now from the wrong he or she has done against me. I let him or her go and turn him or her over to you. You deal with this person, Lord. I turn over all responsibility to you for this person. Free me from any memories that may try to haunt me or discourage me in the wake of this hurtful experience. Help me to walk in freedom and strength in relationship to this person and to all others who know of this incident. I trust You to do this, Holy Spirit. And I ask this in Jesus' name. Amen."

Many issues can only be resolved by the Lord. Momma used to say, "That is a huckleberry above my persimmon." In her own humorous way, she was admitting that a certain situation was way beyond her ability. Only our Heavenly Father has the power and the wisdom to handle those kinds of problems.

Don't Pop My Pearls; Don't Shred My Coat

For many years I asked, "Why is God allowing this to happen to my family?" The answers seemed to jump off the page when I read the story of Joseph. Genesis 37 gives us powerful lessons on patience, perseverance, and God's perfect timing.

Joseph was an unashamed dreamer who wore his coat. That impresses me. He didn't hide his coat or his dreams. But Joseph found himself in an unexpected pit of trouble. Unfortunately, his big mistake was thinking everyone else should have been excited for him. Bless his clueless heart. Through his ordeal, Joseph developed talents that he never thought possible. I can certainly identify with Joseph.

Thank You, Dr. Broome

Many people are afraid of developing their gifts and talents. That's sad. I never thought I would write a book since I received an F in my college composition class. Years later, I was invited to speak at Convocation. As fate would have it, on the third row sat the professor who had given me the big, fat F. I had the pleasure of holding up my newly published book and presenting it to him. I gave him a big hug and thanked him for challenging me and making me a better writer. That F was the best thing he could have ever done for me.

Unfortunately, many may never discover who they are because their fear of rejection is so strong. Are you stuck in a cycle of not being all God created you to be? Develop the gifts with which God has so richly blessed you.

Will you compromise being your absolute best so someone else can feel better about himself/herself? Some may try to pop your strand since they envy your pearls or, in Joseph's case, tear your coat. Others may resent your accomplishments since they're bearing the personal consequences of making unhealthy choices. We can choose our choices, but we cannot choose our consequences.

In pageant competition, the one phase I loathed was swimsuit competition. I didn't have a swimsuit figure. The thought of wearing a bathing suit in front of a ka-zillion people was not a fun thought. One of my graduate school professors suggested I wear my swimsuit under my clothes so it would feel more natural. Desperate to feel more confident, I followed his advice.

The night of the swimsuit competition at the Miss South Carolina Pageant, I walked down that runway and did my very best. Another more competitive contestant, trying to "psyche me out," said, "Oh, Jane, did I tell you how great your hair looked *last* night?" That comment just sailed right over my head. Years later, I figured out that she was trying to shake my confidence. Her tactics didn't resonate with me since I don't think or act like that. She was trying to pop my pearls.

My response to pearl poppers is, "Do yourself a favor and develop your own pearls. Don't pop my pearls; don't tear my coat." Above all, pray for them. And pray for yourself—ask God to give you the wisdom to handle them.

How pathetic Joseph's story would be if he had cowered under the pressure of his brothers. What if the Genesis account read like this: "So Joseph, being fearful of what his brothers thought, refused to wear his beautiful coat and kept it in the back of his closet. Joseph stayed in the land, tending sheep. He never left the region because his brothers told him what to do and when to do it." Thank God Joseph chose to wear his coat, develop his talents, and become the man God intended him to be. Joseph got out of the pit.

Some families, and people in general, operate under the rule of "stay in the pit; don't climb out." They act like crabs in a bucket. If one tries to get out of the bucket, the other crabs pull down the crab that's trying to escape. The unhappiness and frustration that family members bury for years can erupt like a smoldering volcano when parents, due to age or illness, are no longer able to be the head of the household. Sadly, one person may bear the burden of unresolved, buried issues and by default become a target. I know. I wore that bull's eye.

If You String It, They Will Come

Many times the dark pearl allows us room to grow, change, and step out of our comfort zones. The Lord may be using the hard times to prepare us for the next level. I never imagined that I would speak across the country or be given so many other wonderful opportunities. I never thought that I would write articles and books or that my singing and my humor would be broadcast on satellite radio. The Lord has been preparing me for the desires of my heart through the dark pearl. God meant it for good; I praise Him for helping me find the value of the dark pearl.

The oft-repeated sentence in the movie *Field of Dreams* is "if you build it, they will come."[19] A similar statement could be made about our pearl strands: "if you add one, more will come." In other words, if we choose to make great choices and add more experiences, our strand will become longer and stronger. Many doors of opportunity will open as we continue to open our hearts and minds.

One of the best words in the English language is *next*. Don't look back unless you are planning to go there.

"Miss Ruth was a lady and a lady always knows when to leave." That's another great movie line, taken from *Fried Green Tomatoes*.[20] The wise sage, Sipcy, played by Cicely Tyson, spoke those words when one of the main characters passed away.

Anyone who wears pearls should wisely practice the art of timing. Know what to do and when to do it. Know how to appear calm even when you're screaming on the inside. Both my mother and my sister died within a five-month period. It was a very emotional time for many in my family. I became a target for many whose emotions were out-of-control. Seeing such ungodly behavior was very painful. All the divisive emotions should have been left at the door of the church, funeral home, or family gathering. Respecting the occasion should be the goal, not making the event all about one person's feelings. Anyone who chooses unruly behavior and inappropriate words should be pitied. Unprincipled behavior speaks volumes about the character of the person spewing the venom.

A Half a Valium and a Whole of Jesus

No, I'm not kidding. I have Christian friends, people I deeply respect, who have taken medication to get through some tough times. Wise counselors who offer good advice are another option.

---

19   *Field of Dreams*. Brian Frankish, Executive Producer. Phil Alden Robinson, Director. Universal Studios. 1989.
20   *Fried Green Tomatoes*. Anne Marie Gillen, Executive Producer, *et al.* Jon Avnet, Producer and Director. Universal. 1991.

Many resources are available that can help us deal with emotional pain. I'm thankful I sought the help of a wonderful Christian counselor.

Some Christians are so focused on the "love message" they fail to see that they can become someone's punching bag. Some will try to devalue your gifts. In those situations, boundaries and borders need to be recognized and practiced. Sadly, some people will use us as doormats. Christians may allow themselves to be treated like that "in the name of Jesus." I don't intend to be sacrilegious, but I don't recall Jesus being another person's doormat.

In *Fool-Proofing Your Life*, Jan Silvious writes:

> *God knew there would be those to whom you could not entrust yourself, so He offered an alternative way to behaving with these particular people. Nowhere did He exempt us from the call to forgiveness or love, but He did issue warning upon warning that, if heeded, would liberate the captive from the hostage-taker . . . the victim from the victimizer . . . the wise from the foolish.[21] Silvious warns that the other cheek may get you into a deeper mess. She encourages the reader to use wisdom she calls "relational intelligence."[22]*

In Joseph's case, he matured and learned all about relationships involving difficult people. Things went from bad to worse, but Joseph maintained his godly attitude when he was rejected, sold into slavery, falsely accused, and thrown into jail. When he was brought before Pharaoh and his circumstances improved, he still remained godly. What a guy!

When Joseph's brothers discovered his identity, he responded with kindness and compassion. God had exalted him to a position of leadership in Egypt, but Joseph's leadership qualities were already in place. His coat may have been torn to shreds, but

21   Silvious, Jan. *Fool-proofing Your Life*. New York: Random House, 2009.
22   Ibid.

his natural talents and gifts were protected, nurtured, and used for a great good.

In *Talent Is Never Enough*, John Maxwell writes, "When it comes to dealing with others, there are really only three routes we can take:

- *The low road: where we treat others worse than they treat us*
- *The middle road: where we treat others the same as they treat us*
- *The high road: where we treat others better than they treat us*[23]

Thank the Lord for high roads and for Joseph's example. Taking the high road is a difficult path. It requires great courage. But in time, when we've matured, we'll realize the value of choosing this route.

Joseph understood the value of the difficult path: "Ye thought evil, but God meant it unto good—In order to make Joseph a greater blessing to his family than otherwise he could have been" (John Wesley's paraphrase of Genesis 50:20).

Joseph exchanged his torn coat for a royal robe fit for a king. That robe may have even been decorated with a pearl or two!

When God Allows Your Pearls to Pop

Sometimes when our strand of pearls pops and rolls, we become confused. Some of us feverishly chase these valuables as they roll out of control. Some wonder how God could allow such a thing to happen; some try to figure out how to fix it.

Wise believers understand that God is doing *His* work in *His* way in *His* time. These pearl-popping times challenge our character. Remember, all of our pearl strands should be an eclectic blend of both beautiful and jagged jewels, created by the

---

23   Maxwell, John. *Talent Is Never Enough*. Nashville: Thomas Nelson, 2007.

Lord's will for our spiritual growth. What if the strand must be broken so He can add a tremendous blessing?

The strand of pearls we were stringing may be a noose around our necks. The only way the Lord can set us free is to allow the pearls to pop and roll. If you're frustrated, trying to restring your strand with the same "pearls," then pray and ask the Lord to reveal His plan for a new strand.

One of my dearest friends unexpectedly lost her husband in a tragic plane crash. Charles's death rocked our small community. It was a personal loss for Thomas and me because Mary and Charles were so dear to us. I watched Mary grieve Charles's death. She became a single mother with young children.

At first Mary fought moving into the new life the Lord had prepared for her. I remember the day when sorrow and pain overwhelmed her. She thought she had thrown her wedding rings away by accident. In despair she cried out to God, thinking she had lost her last sacred connection to Charles. The Lord spoke to Mary's heart that day about trusting Him for her future. She realized that she needed to let go of the past in order for the Lord to move her into His future.

A few years later, I watched Mary walk into her wedding reception, arm in arm with her new husband, Harry. God restored Mary's life, but it may not have ever happened if Mary had refused to trust the Lord. As Mary and Harry danced their first dance, we all praised God for bringing them together.

What about the wedding rings she cherished? Mary found them a few days after she thought they were lost forever. Today her daughters are wearing those precious stones in their wedding rings.

Wintley Phipps, amazing singer and Christian speaker, once introduced his incredible rendition of "Amazing Grace" by saying, "It is in the quiet crucible of our personal private sufferings that our noblest dreams are born and God's greatest gifts are given, and often given in compensation for what we've been through." [24]

---

24 Phipps, Wintley. National Speakers Association Convention. Orlando, FL. 11 July 2010.

Lessons from Mr. Kitty

A few years ago, I hired a marketing coach for my speaking business. He told me to create some phrases and print them on postcards. One of the expressions I came up with is, "Mend your fences *before* you have a stampede."

On that same theme, one day I noticed that one of my favorite hanging baskets was totally flat on the top. Obviously, some creature had been parking itself on the top of my basket. I was determined to catch the plant-squisher in the act.

It didn't take me long to identify the culprit. Mr. Kitty (our cat, of course) was perched in the basket. Only his glassy eyes and pointed ears were visible. The scene reminded me of watching lions stalk their prey in *Mutual of Omaha's Wild Kingdom* when I was a child.

We hoisted the hanging baskets higher on the chain. But super kitty managed to out-smart us. Jumping a few inches higher was no problem. He was determined to enjoy his perch in the hanging basket. Napping in it was important to him.

One evening we heard the low-pitched growls, screams, and all the trimmings of a full-fledged catfight in the making. Our sweet little kitty was using the hanging basket in a covert operation to possibly ambush the other cat. He devised his plan and executed it flawlessly. Mr. Kitty "tended his fences before he had the stampede." He was determined to let the other cat know that he had crossed the line and invaded his turf.

Many things change in life, and many people we care about change too. Momma always said in her colorful way, "If you live long enough, you see every #@*! thing."

Set boundaries for yourself and for your family. Some of us may have the difficult task of setting boundaries with our adult family members. Ouch! Thank the Lord for borders and boundaries.

Dr. Henry Cloud writes:

> *Boundaries, in a broad sense, are lines or things that mark a limit, bound or border. In a psychological sense,*

*boundaries are the realization of our own person apart
from others. This sense of separateness forms the basis of
personal identity. It says what we are and what we are
not, what we will choose and what we will not choose,
what we will endure and what we will not, what we feel
and what we will not feel, what we like and what we do
not like, and what we want and what we do not want.
Boundaries, in short, define us.*[25]

Think of a counter in a department store. This is your side
and this is my side; do not cross the boundary. It's as simple as
that.

Mend your fences now—before it's too late. Avoid the
stampedes. Come over to our house, sit awhile on the porch, and
watch Mr. Kitty jump into the flattened hanging basket. Maybe
that will motivate you.

The Darkest Pearls

Don't allow others to contaminate your pearl strand with the
darkest and most dangerous pearls: jealousy, greed, and hatred.
I've seen these horrible qualities take root in people I love. What
heartbreak! Responding in a godly manner to those who target
you is what Christianity is all about.

Unfortunately, sometimes people are just plain mean. For a
long time I thought that the love of Christ in my life as I related
to these people would heal the relationships. Not necessarily so.
In *Changes That Heal,* Dr. Cloud encourages us to stay away from
hurtful people.[26]

Psalm 129:4 assures us that God *has cut [us] free from the cords
of the wicked* (NIV). Dr. Cloud also courageously observes in
Necessary Endings that there are three kinds of people:

---

25   Cloud, Henry. *Changes That Heal: How to Understand Your Past to Ensure a Healthier
       Future.* Revised Edition. Grand Rapids: Zondervan. 1992.
26   Ibid.

1. With wise people, talk to them, give them resources, and you will get a return.
2. With foolish people, stop talking to them about problems; they are not listening. And stop supplying resources; they squander them. Instead, give them limits and consequences.
3. With evil people, to quote a Warren Zevon song, the strategy is "lawyers, guns and money." The reason? You have to go into protection mode, not helping mode, when dealing with evil people. Lawyers, guns and money usually get their attention. This introduction is not only for effect. The truth is that I am not kidding.[27]

Dr. Cloud's wise words finally freed me from a difficult family problem that I had attempted to repair for many years. I thank God for helping me understand that some things cannot be fixed.

Some Baggage Can't Be Fixed

I stood around the baggage carousel in Portland, Oregon, with many other travelers hoping to spot my temporary closet on wheels. Finally, I saw my wheeled suitcase with fluorescent luggage tags making its way down the belt. I grabbed the suitcase and headed to the rental car terminal. Glancing behind me, I stared in disbelief. My practically new roller-board had a large gaping hole on one side, a crushed zipper, and missing front pockets. To make matters worse, one leg of my pantyhose was tucked inside my suitcase and the other leg was dragging behind it. A perfect split.

Prudent female travelers utilize the multi-tasking convenience technique of leaving their undies in the pantyhose. Yes, my drawers were sunny-side up tucked into the hose. I quickly reeled in the unsightly undergarments as I silently thanked my mother

---

27   Cloud, Henry. *Necessary Endings*. New York: Harper Collins Publishers, 2010.

for teaching me the clean underwear rule ... both on and off the body. You just never know ...

Making a U-turn, I headed toward the luggage lady standing only a few feet away. She took one look at my terminally damaged suitcase and said, "Are you sure we did that?"

It was just one of those moments when my mouth got ahead of my brain: "Well, I can assure you this didn't happen during the twelve-foot trip from the belt to here."

The luggage lady inspected the large hole in the side of the bag complimented by an exposed wire while she attempted to open the main compartment with a crushed zipper. She lifted what remained of the outside pockets and asked, "Do you think it can be repaired?"

I've framed the picture of my damaged suitcase since its message is clear: some things cannot be repaired. However, my luggage has been *replaced* with another bag of equal value.

Many times when life hands us difficult circumstances, the best thing to do is replace what is damaged. Pour your energy into something more hopeful. According to Dr. Henry Cloud, it's healthy to lose hope in hopeless situations. Search for a new hope in another direction. We need to learn the difference between wishing and hoping. Wishing is based on false hope since it may be unrealistic wanting. When we are faced with these types of realities, it's wise to consider a necessary ending.[28]

As much as I loved my family, I realized that many of my family members didn't feel the same way about me. I needed a healthy end. Just like that damaged suitcase, I tried to repair something that had no hope. Talk about dragging around excess baggage! No thanks.

Hope deferred makes the heart sick, but a longing fulfilled is a tree of life. Proverbs 13:12 (NIV)

---

28   Cloud, Henry. *Necessary Endings.* New York: Harper Collins Publishers, 2010.

Soaring above Buzzard Meat

Grace also means that there are things we should *not* do.

Driving to Aiken, South Carolina, I had to look twice to see if my eyes were deceiving me. There lay a dead buzzard on the roadside. Not that a dead buzzard is such an unusual sight in South Carolina. What struck me as odd was this: no other buzzards were crowded around the carcass, enjoying a feast. On my return trip I noticed the same dead buzzard, all alone.

Buzzards feed on things that are filthy and corrupt. They don't even attempt to catch prey. They simply look for lifeless animals.

What a contrast to an eagle.

Traveling to a speaking engagement in Leavenworth, Washington, I was fascinated by the beautiful streams nestled between the Cascades. My driver kept saying, "Look! There goes another eagle. Watch as it gracefully swoops down and catches fish." It was an incredible sight.

Eagles are magnificent. They gather tree limbs and build their nests high on rocks. An eagle's nest can be as large as eight to ten feet wide and up to twenty feet deep. They can weigh as much as two tons. A mother eagle actually pulls feathers from her breast to cushion the nest for her babies.

To prepare for flight, the mother eagle picks up the eaglets on her wings and takes them for a ride. Once she is high enough in the sky, she drops them. Just before they hit, she catches them and sweeps them high into the sky again, repeating the process until her young learn to fly. What a ride!

Life introduces us to both eagles and buzzards. The buzzards in life are attracted to problems; they make a sport out of ripping folks apart with their mouths, creating rumors, and attacking reputations. Just like the buzzard carcass I saw on the roadside, no one really has use for them, not even their own kind. On the other hand, eagles are known for their boldness, strength, and dedication. Eagles are to be admired and imitated; the buzzards in life need to be avoided. God help us all not to end up like that lonely, dead buzzard.

To attract eagle-like people, we need to live like eagles. Maybe the first eagle-like step toward better living is feasting on a change in attitude, which will surely lead to a change in altitude.

Isaiah 40:31 says, *But they that wait upon the Lord shall renew their strength; they shall mount up with wings as eagles; they shall run, and not be weary; and they shall walk, and not faint* (KJV). I pray that when those dark times come, and they will, we'll remember this scripture and learn to soar above our circumstances with grace, beauty, and dignity.

The Priceless Pearl of Grace

Allow God to speak to your heart when you're hurting and know that He has every tear in a bottle (Psalm 56:8). When I couldn't pray any more, the Lord sent my Christian friends to literally hold me, pray for me, and share wonderful books and media to lift me up. He sent me His grace through their love and support.

Praise God that the pearl of grace comes free of charge with every dark pearl we're given. As we add each experience to our strand of pearls, the pearl of grace should remain the centerpiece of our strand since it is the very essence of our Christian life. *For by grace you have been saved through faith. And this is not your own doing; it is the gift of God; not a result of works, so that no one may boast* (Ephesians 2:8-9 ESV).

Grace is the cornerstone of Christianity. In *Growing Deep in the Christian Life*, Charles Swindoll defines grace as "that which God does for mankind through His Son, which mankind cannot earn, does not deserve, and will never merit."[29] Grace is powerful because it signifies that we're no longer under the Law and that Christ dwells within us. We've inherited the hope of glory, and we've been baptized and circumcised in Christ unto new life. Grace also means that the Spirit of God lives within us and enables us to live the Christian life.

---

29   Swindoll, Charles. *Growing Deep in the Christian Life.* Portland, OR: Multnomah Press, 1986.

Grace, grace—so beautiful and precious since the blessings that follow are joy and peace. That's why we should protect our strand and knot our pearls.

My Newest, Most Valuable Dark Pearl

How can you possibly call a horrible time in your life "the most valuable pearl"? The answer is simple: I searched for and I found the value.

I have been asked what I learned through those many heartbreaking years of loss, rejection, financial issues, and personal attacks on my character. I learned the value of adding the pearl of peace to my strand. I sought the Lord's direction and I was obedient. I asked my sister to forgive me if I had done anything to hurt her. It was a confusing time, though. I had already had that conversation with her many times, but the Lord continued to lay it on my heart. Eventually, He showed me the reason: my sister died almost one year to the day after that conversation.

I prayed for those who turned against me, and I didn't retaliate with mean actions or words. At times I was bold but never mean or spiteful. When I see the family members who hurt me deeply, the Holy Spirit helps me see them through the eyes of our Father. I refuse to carry any hateful feelings since I know that is like drinking poison. If I harbor deadly emotions, the first one destroyed will be me. I keep my distance and guard my heart, but mostly I continue to ask the Lord to guide me, to direct my path, and to restore my life in His time and in His way. Relationships have begun to heal. As communication has been reestablished, I have no regrets and no reason to apologize since I'm confident the Holy Spirit directed my path in the past and continues to guide me with principled words and deeds. I just continue to do the next right thing.

I felt The Comforter's hand on my shoulder as I held my mother when she took her last breath. Just days before Momma

died, she said, "Life wouldn't have been worth living if it hadn't been for you." We traveled such a heart wrenching journey together, and we supported each other through laughter and tears. I promised her I would be by her side until the end. I kept my word.

My life began with Momma being the nacre or protective coating in my life. As her life ended, I had the honor of serving as her protector, helping her celebrate and culture the beautiful pearls on her strand.

Thanks be to my Heavenly Father that He is faithful to His Word. All is well . . . His peace fills my soul and sparkles on my strand.

CHAPTER 7

Priceless Pearls of Laughter

A merry heart doeth good like a medicine . . . but a crushed spirit dried the bones. Proverbs 15:13

My absolute favorite pearl, a jewel of great value, is the pearl of laughter. My mother was very comical. We laughed together all the time. On many occasions, Momma maintained a merry heart when there was nothing on the outside to make her merry. For example, her declining health could have been a spirit-crushing experience. But the Lord sent Anna, a dear Johns Island friend, to live with Momma. The many heartfelt prayers and knee-slapping conversations they shared filled their hearts with much joy during those last difficult weeks.

I'll never forget a couple that attended one of my speaking engagements. They laughed more than anyone else in the audience. They thoroughly enjoyed themselves. After the speech, they both gave me a big bear hug and said, "We haven't laughed in months. We've been holding our sweet grandbaby until she drew her last breath."

I was speechless. You never know what folks are dealing with, and you can never underestimate the healing power of humor.

I hope you'll laugh, possibly snort, at some of these stories. Yes, they're true stories with just a hair of embellishment. For now, just take a spoonful of "merry" and laugh!

Eleanor's Valuable Fur Vest

It was time to tackle the closet in the front hall. Accumulated over a lifetime, my mother's coats hung in the closet, lonely and neglected. If they could have spoken, they would have admitted they were sad and confused.

One item stood out—Momma's reversible vest. The perfect length and weight. Momma's dream vest.

I remember the morning she called me to share the news. "I got a surprise today, a reversible fur and leather vest. It came from Goodwill and cost $25. It's just what I've always wanted."

Momma and I loved a good deal. I was excited for her. "How does it look?" I asked.

"It's dark leather with a collar and it zips up the front," she boasted.

"Tell me about the fur. What kind is it?"

"Well, huh, I don't know. It looks kind-a mangy. It has some fur missing and, well, it's just different," she said.

"What kind of fur is it?" I repeated.

"Let me look," Momma said. There was a gasp. Her next sentence will live in my memory forever. "It's possum!" she shouted. Followed by another line I'll never forget: "Wait, it's from New Zealand. Aren't they better than our possums?"

Several thoughts ran through my mind: *Does she actually believe that New Zealand possums are superior to other possums? That New Zealand possums don't play dead or live in trashcans or eat trash? That they don't become squished "buzzard bait" when they try to cross the road?*

Momma always wore that vest with the fur side in and the leather side out. She insisted that she was proud of her possum, but she still never wore the fur on the outside.

Several weeks later, I invited her to attend one of my speaking engagements in Myrtle Beach. The possum vest made the trip with us. For the first time, Momma wore the possum on the outside.

On the way, we stopped at one of our favorite restaurants for dinner. As always, many people were waiting in line for a table. I parked across the road and told Momma to wait in the car until I found out if we could get a table. Inside, the hostess told me that a table for two was available. So I went outside and motioned for my mother to come in.

There stood Momma on the other side of the road, wearing her possum fur for the first time. It was a moment. Suddenly, she removed it, switched it to the leather side, and began her walk across the highway to the restaurant side of the road.

As soon as she reached me, Momma switched the vest back to the possum side. She said with a chuckle, "Well, since I was crossing the highway, I didn't want to get hit." We had a great laugh together.

KIAMIAPOW

Once I asked Momma to travel with me to Jacksonville, North Carolina, for a speaking engagement. If you've ever been to that part of the state, you know Jacksonville has a military base.

On the interstate, we passed an exit that would have taken us to the base. The green exit sign read, KIA MIA POW. As soon as I read the sign, I knew the initials meant Killed in Action, Missing in Action, and Prisoner of War. Momma looked at me and said, "That's a crazy name." Very slowly, she sounded out the words, "KEE-UH, ME-UH, POW." Then she asked, "Is that some kind of Indian village?"

My Mother's Many Boyfriends

My mother loved all her doctors and had nicknames for each of them. She called her number one doctor, her internist, Dr. Boyfriend. Momma's cardiologist was Dr. Sweetheart and her lung doctor was Dr. Cootie. Obviously, she wasn't too fond of

him. She tried on several occasions to make him laugh, but he just didn't have a very good sense of humor.

Once she took a break from Dr. Cootie for a while. When she finally returned to see him, he asked her, "Mrs. Jenkins, where have you been?"

Momma said, "I gave you up for Lent and Lent lasted for two years."

For the first time, he responded with a smile. From then on he became known as Dr. Cutie.

Wear Your Humor Eyes

Years ago, I was sitting in my car one day and witnessed something that has stuck with me. A woman was walking down the street around a construction site. One of the men in the high-rise building whistled at her. She put on the brakes and yelled, "Who whistled at me?" There was a long pause, then a sheepish reply, "I did."

The woman glanced up and said in a loud voice, "Thank you so much!"

How pitiful, I thought.

Now jet ahead with me.

My mother was having cataract surgery. We were sitting in a room with a group of folks, waiting for my mother to be called into the surgical area. Momma was her usual fun self, answering all the questions she overheard the nurses asking all the other patients.

Unexpectedly, a gentleman rounded the corner where we were sitting. "May I make a comment?" he inquired.

"Yes," I said, sort of bewildered.

The gentleman continued, "You're a pretty lady."

I had just celebrated a birthday the week before, so I blushed. "Thank you so much!" Momma and I sat there glowing. Then Momma said, "She won a pageant."

I blushed again but secretly loved it. We giggled like two silly schoolgirls.

"Mr. Adams?" said one of the nurses, breaking the magic of the moment. "Your cataract surgery is next."

I've always heard it said that beauty is in the eye of the beholder. I wonder if "cataract eyes" count.

Laughter in the Waiting Room

Momma and I took countless trips together to her many doctor appointments. We had many opportunities to find the humor in those experiences—even when we were filling out numerous medical forms. Sometimes our only entertainment was reading the list of every disease known to mankind and circling the ones that applied.

As we sat in a waiting room one day, an elderly couple shuffled into the office and over to the receptionist's window. She said in a loud voice, "Y'all need to fill out the back of this sheet and circle all the problems you have."

The husband replied in a louder voice, "Why don't you save us the trouble and circle the whole sheet?"

"You know I can't do that, Mr. Crosby," chuckled the receptionist. Obviously, these folks were no strangers to the office staff, and their friendly banter revealed their affection for each other.

"Did you bring your glasses?" asked the wife.

"No, just read the list," said the husband.

"But you can't hear," replied the wife in a loud voice.

"Well, you're deaf yourself," answered the husband.

I was looking at the same list of ailments and thought, *this is gonna be good.*

The wife began reading. "You got gas?"

"Right now?"

"No."

"Have you had gas?"

"Yes," he said. "I get it when we eat Mexican."

"I'll circle this next one 'cause I know you got arthritis."

"That ain't right. You're the one with arthritis," he said correcting her.

"Oh, yeah. You're right."

"How about pain?"

"You can be a pain," he said in a joking voice.

"I definitely know the answer to what's next," she said, "irritability." They both laughed.

I knew what was coming. The next ailment was "menstrual cramps," but the typing was faded. The wife stammered and stuttered and finally asked, "You got mental cramps?"

"Cramps?" he asked. "Yeah, when we eat Mexican."

Momma and I could hardly control ourselves. We were about to pop with laughter. The good news is that couple loved to laugh too.

Sometimes You Gotta Act Queenly

Beauty Queendome is still alive in the South. Just the other day a friend from church attended the Catfish Feastival in Ware Shoals. No, that's not a typo. The event isn't a festival; it's a feastival because so many catfish are consumed. Years ago, I emceed the Miss Catfish pageant. No, the girls didn't have to have long whiskers to win.

Events like the Catfish Feastival remind me of the many parades I participated in as queen of the festivals I was fortunate enough to win. In Beaufort, South Carolina, I was Queen of the Carolina Sea Islands. The pageant committee thought it would be unique for the contestants to be interviewed on a yacht. I think I won that pageant because the heel of my shoe got stuck between two of the planks on the long dock. One of the judges had to rescue my high heel, and my shoe catastrophe was a great icebreaker.

As Queen of the Carolina Sea Islands, I was scheduled to ride in the Railroad Days Festival parade in Branchville, South

Carolina. I wore a white jersey dress with rhinestones on the bodice that matched my float.

I loved the Water Festival float and couldn't wait to ride on it for first time as the Queen of the Carolina Sea Islands. It was covered with blue and white plastic discs. A blue, sparkly skirt covered the bottom and hid the float's wheels. When the driver increased his speed, the skirt rippled in the wind. It was what all beauty queens live for.

Momma and Miss Ada Rast transported me to the festival in our big yellow Buick with the white hard top. We arrived in plenty of time, but my float never showed up. To compensate for the absence of the float, the Branchville people made two signs on white poster paper with magic markers. They were the tackiest things I had ever seen, but those pathetic signs were nothing compared to what happened next.

"Jane doesn't care about riding on a float. I'll drive her in the parade," said Momma. "Jane," she directed, "get on the hood of the car and act queenly."

I thought I would die of embarrassment. Ride on the hood of the big yellow Buick with posters taped to the sides?

As I climbed onto that hood, it never occurred to me that my mother had never driven in a parade. Neither had I ever ridden on the hood of a moving car. After the second block, my bottom was cooking like a rump roast in an oven set at 300 degrees. That car hood was hot! Then my mother slammed on the brakes to speak to someone she knew and I slid off the hood.

I climbed back on the hood and said, "Momma, you are way behind the car in front!"

She gave it the gas. My body was plastered across the windshield. All I could think of was Momma's instructions, "Jane, act queenly."

That sort of thing happens to all of us. We just don't want to act queenly. We want to have a hissy fit or throw-down—something as inappropriate as slapping a Wal-Mart Greeter . . .

"We raised you to act right, so do it," Momma told me many times. I've said it to my children. It's wise advice—whether you're riding in a parade on the hood of a big yellow Buick or just walking down the aisle at the grocery store.

> *Hear counsel, and receive instruction, that thou mayest be wise in thy latter end.* Proverbs 19:20 (KJV)

An Ode to Eleanor's Electrolux

All my life I've heard that cleanliness is next to godliness, but I've seen lots of clean folks act pretty dirty. The closest thing to a scriptural mandate I can find is Hebrews 10:22: *Let us draw near to God with a sincere heart in full assurance of faith, having our hearts sprinkled to cleanse us from a guilty conscience and having our bodies washed with pure water* (NIV).

My mother always preached that "physical cleanliness is a prerequisite to godliness." Momma just had her own translation of certain verses in the Bible, and the Electrolux vacuum was instrumental in the cleanliness process. It was pampered and loved—one of my mother's favorite items in her home. The sacred Electrolux was housed in the "Holy of Holies," my mother's closet.

Let me reminisce about my first encounter with this machine. I recall the fateful day it was purchased. The Electrolux wasn't obtained because of its power or because of the pristine aftereffects of using it. No, humiliation brought it into our home.

You know what happened. The Electrolux Man makes his way into your home and challenges the power of the machine, boasting that he can vacuum stuff out of a mattress. Unfortunately, my mattress was chosen to be vacuumed, followed by a revelation of the grotesque "molting" from my flesh. After my family subjected me to an emotional frenzy of ridicule and many inappropriate personal hygiene comments, the checkbook became their next victim. I heard muffled whisperings of my

loved ones: "don't know what would've become of Jane if the Electrolux man hadn't vacuumed her mattress."

Yes, the Electrolux has become another symbol of Americana. I can actually guess how old someone is just by asking if they own an Electrolux. Seriously, going into the Electrolux store (if you can find one) is like going into a library. The salespeople are at least 150 years old. My new theory is that Electrolux employees start out working at a Hallmark shop, then spend at least sixty years in a library before they finally land in an Electrolux store.

For many years, Thomas, the children, and I spent the last days of summer in Charleston. It was fun—the beach, the boat, the seafood. Then the day of reckoning arrived. I would have to spend my last day in Charleston getting my mother's house back in order.

My mother's voice whispered in my ear, "You know how I like this house to look." Yes, I knew. Momma's definition of clean was "sterile." I mean hospital-operating-room clean. Major surgery could be performed on her kitchen table. Momma even put newspaper underneath the coo-coo clock. Her hair hadn't moved since 1962—the year Aqua Net was invented. Momma was particular. And so much fun to tease (no hair pun intended).

For me, cleaning anything is the opposite of fun. The only benefit is seeing the grime, grit, or dirt disappear.

But it was time to drag out the old, scarred Electrolux.

Momma's Electrolux has a brain. It sensed I wasn't happy. Out of pure spite, it decided to lock its wheels. So I had to tote that mass of steel around the house. (I vividly remember my grandmother's Electrolux looked like a little sled that had to be dragged.) And, of course, Momma's Electrolux has 250 attachments. The rug "beater" about did me in. What a great name for the thing. It will beat the user to death when or if it decides to work.

Every time I use that vacuum, it throws up. The top just pops open, and it pretends to be full. How is this possible? There's no dirt in it. I think it's programmed to rebel so the salespeople have a job. Basically, I had war with the Electrolux. It won.

I know these machines are fabulous and have the power of the space shuttle. And I know there are ka-zillions of Electrolux fans out there. In fact, one fan told me that she would rather have her Electrolux than her children. Now I understand: owning an Electrolux is like belonging to a cult.

I have a central vacuum system. Just one hose. I've been liberated. I guess it's a choice: "burning the bra" or wearing the harness of being married to a family tradition.

I needed a few days to recover from my bout with Momma's Electrolux. Now I look at my central vacuum system (Wal-Vac) with more love in my heart than ever.

Sometimes a bad experience teaches us to appreciate what we have. The moral of the story? There's good in all dirty situations if we choose to look hard enough.

You will make known to me the path of life; in Your presence is fullness of joy; in Your right hand there are pleasures forever. Psalm 16:11(NASB)

Momma's Pink Hair Pick

One day when I was rummaging around the bottom of my purse, I felt an unexpected twinge of pain from some metal prongs. My mother's infamous pink hair pick. I always figured that thing would be the death of her. Even when her heart was beating in a deadly, life-threatening rhythm, I had to find the pink pick and place it in the inner pocket of her purse before she left for the hospital.

Every Wednesday at 11:00 a.m. was the all-important hair day. Momma never missed that hair appointment and that pink hair pick was a constant accessory in her purse.

When my mother's lung doctor diagnosed her with sleep apnea, he instructed her to wear, in her own words, "that #@*! thing on her face." Well, the apparatus was short-lived. It messed up her hair.

I tried to explain to Momma that since her heart could use all the help it could get, the machine might give her a longer life. Without it she might die in her sleep. Her response was, "That's just fine. Johnny Stuhr [Stuhrs Funeral Home] will think my hair looks nice."

My daddy once said that he knew his funeral would be planned around Momma's hair appointment. I'm taking the Fifth Amendment on that issue.

During one hospital stay, Momma's hemoglobin dropped to 5.8. She was under the care of Dr. Theodore Gourdin, a wonderful gastroenterologist. When he came to see her he said, "You're the best looking 5.8 hemoglobin I've seen in a long time."

She assumed that was a compliment. She smiled, puffed her hair with her hand and said, "Oh, thank you so much!"

Dr. Gourdin laughed, puffed his hair with his hand, and said, "You're welcome."

After that, every time I saw him in the halls of Roper Hospital, he always commented on my mother's reaction, then he puffed his hair. Our little joke. He loved my mother, said she was the consummate Southern lady. He wrote me a lovely note after she passed away that I treasure to this day.

The hair pick symbolized Momma's beauty—inside and out. She always dressed well, stylish from her head to her toes. Her inside beauty was ageless: she loved people, she had a forgiving heart, and she loved to laugh. Those are timeless beauty products we would all be wise to pick.

I Am Woman, Hear Me Snore

One day Momma exited the master bedroom and made this announcement, "I can't take it anymore. It's horrible. Something has to change."

No, she wasn't referring directly to her marriage, but then again, in a way she was.

Momma was talking about Daddy's snoring. It rattled the walls and practically shook the house. When Daddy came in at noon and sat in his chair, he fell asleep in a nanosecond. He had sleep apnea, no doubt.

Years later, my mother's lung specialist (Dr. Cootie) recommended that she go to a sleep lab and be tested for the same issue. She wasn't at all happy since the test was scheduled for a Thursday night. Thursday had replaced Wednesday as Momma's hairdo day with Rhea. Neither Hurricane Hugo, freak snowstorms, nor sickness kept her from sitting in Rhea's chair at 9:00 a.m. on Thursday.

Finally Momma agreed to go to the sleep center. The staff couldn't have been any nicer. Everything was okay until they stuck a sticky electrode thing in Momma's hair. I cannot repeat what she said, but I knew it was time for me to leave.

When I arrived to retrieve Momma the next morning I heard, "What do you mean I have sleep apnea? I didn't even sleep!"

I have to admit she was a trooper. She tried to adjust to "the machine"; she did give it a go. But then she made an executive decision that she could "not tolerate" the apparatus.

During one of Momma's many visits to Roper Hospital, Dr. Blunt Ellison sat at her bedside and asked, "Mrs. Jenkins, are you using the machine?"

Just as serious as one can answer, Momma replied, "Blunt, I cannot tolerate that CPAP smear up my nostrils."

The sophisticated and professional Dr. Blunt Ellison laughed so hard that he almost rolled off the bed. I reminded Momma that the machine was not called a CPAP smear but a CPAP machine and that Dr. Ellison was her cardiologist not her gynecologist.

CHAPTER 8

Our Inheritance

The Best Birthday Present, Ever

One year we decided to celebrate my birthday on Johns Island. I wondered if I had lost my mind—going to the Lowcountry, knowing all the changes that had taken place and all the sadness that's there now.

Sunday morning, the day of my birthday, we went to early church, and then I walked to my parents' graves. Next to their graves was my sister's headstone—it had just been added. Time does ease the grief; it wasn't quite so heart wrenching to walk in the church cemetery.

Our next stop was the Sea Island Health Care Center to see my second momma, Tootsie. No doubt it was going to be the more difficult visit. Three years previous, Tootsie had a massive stroke. Usually when we visited her, she lay in bed, trying to communicate. I always left that facility with tears running down my face. If she couldn't get any better, I prayed that the Lord would gently take her to her wonderful heavenly reward.

As we turned the corner that day, there sat Tootsie in a wheelchair. She was using her good arm to roll all over the room. She looked at me and said, "That's my baby."

I could hardly believe my eyes and ears.

"I raised this child," Tootsie said.

I just grabbed her and didn't want to let go. It was the best birthday gift I received.

We reminisced about the good times: the time I taught her how to drive Daddy's pick-up and she drove into the ditch; all the many times she made biscuits and the fact she always made me a baby biscuit; the time she fell off of the riding lawn mower and ran after me without me knowing what was going on; our fun slumber parties when Momma and Daddy went out of town.

Although Tootsie's speech wasn't perfect and some of her sentences were incomplete, we connected. It was a wonderful trip down memory lane with my precious second mother. She even popped me on the bottom as I left.

I asked one of the nurses what had made the difference in Tootsie. She said, "She is loved here and God is so good."

God gave me a beautiful gift that year during our Holy Season: being loved and loving others, knowing that God is good all the time.

I celebrated with Tootsie that day, but I also knew that, for her, another celebration was soon approaching. The best gift of all.

The Final Destination

With its large, red digital message—5:30 a.m.—the hotel clock shouted my wake-up call one Saturday morning. Not until later in the day did I realize the timing that only our Heavenly Father could arrange. My second mother, Ruth "Tootsie" Bligen, entered her eternal reward that morning. At 5:30 a.m.

Tootsie worked for my family just shy of fifty years. I can still see the large yellow Buick with my mother's silhouette behind the wheel. Tootsie sat next to her. River Road was their highway to heavenly places such as Piggly Wiggly and, in Tootsie's words, the drug sto'.

Just hours before her stroke, Tootsie had called to give me a good tongue-lashing. I had fallen off a ladder and torn a ligament in my foot. Her language was always poetic. She spoke in pure Lowcountry Gullah.

After Tootsie's funeral, I decided to stop by Walker Funeral Home and make a contribution toward her funeral expenses. Using the GPS on my cell phone to locate the funeral home, I wound down the two-lane highway through massive, moss-covered oaks and hairpin turns. When I arrived, I put my phone in my back pocket but didn't turn off the navigation. Several other cars were parked in the lot. The place was filled with folks, so I decided to wait in the hall out of respect for the family members who were making arrangements.

The son of the funeral home owner greeted me in the hallway and politely escorted me into another section of the building. "Do you mind sitting in this room until my father can speak with you?" asked the young man.

"Not at all," I replied. Thinking nothing of his request, I took a seat in the dimly lit room.

As soon as I sat down, the fluorescent lights overhead flickered on, making the room brighter. I suddenly realized why the young man had asked if I minded waiting in that particular room: I was sitting between two bodies. Since I'm a humorist, my first thought was, *This is a bad sign. It must be a really long wait.*

Suddenly my cell phone, which was in my back pocket, announced in that typical monotone voice, "You have reached your final destination." Once my pounding heart calmed down, I had a good laugh.

I knew Momma and Tootsie were looking down from heaven, laughing and reminding me of the power of a merry heart. Their message to me was clear: Serve the Lord. Laugh. Enjoy the ride to your final destination.

Eleanor's Sunday School Joke

Momma told me that she had planted funny notes and crazy things all over the house to make me laugh after she passed away. She didn't want me to grieve too long after she left this earth. She wanted to make sure I returned to having a merry heart and that I remembered all of the wonderful times we spent together.

After three years, I finally began cleaning out closets and drawers. One particular place I dreaded was her personal drawer.

I saw her birthday list, some special cards from family that she treasured, and a few reminders for unfulfilled doctor appointments. My eyes filled with tears. Then I saw the envelope in her handwriting, "Eleanor's Sunday School Joke." That was her way of warning me that it was *not* a Sunday school joke:

> *There was a woman getting on a bus wearing a very tight skirt. The woman couldn't lift her leg so she reached back and unzipped her skirt. She tried to lift her leg again with no success so she reached back and unzipped her skirt a little more. The line of people waiting made her nervous so she reached back and unzipped her skirt all the way down. All of a sudden she felt these strong hands on her waist lift her to the top of the stairs of the bus. "How dare you be so fresh!" she said to the man.*
> *"Me, fresh!" he said sternly. "You've unzipped my pants three times!"*

Momma's Gift

I accompanied my daughter, Caroline, to the South Carolina Farm Bureau Convention. It was unusual for me to be an audience member at a Farm Bureau function, but hearing Caroline speak on the main platform as the female youth ambassador would be such a treat.

While we were at the convention Caroline had to study for exams, so I decided to give her some quiet time. Because I needed

some gym clothes, I invited my friend Blanche to shop with me. Waiting on Blanche to arrive, I noticed a beautiful cross in a particular store. Maybe the cross caught my eye because Caroline and I had just been to see *The Blind Side*, the wonderful story of Michael Oher. The main character, played by Sandra Bullock, wore a cross during most of the movie. To me the cross she wore represented her faith in action.

I wandered through the store several times, but I kept returning to that cross. When Blanche arrived, I took her to the jewelry counter. The lovely cross also charmed Blanche. "Jane," she said, "this is a Christmas gift from your mother. I heard that when you lose someone you love, you should give yourself a gift from him or her. This'll be your first Christmas without her. I think your mother would want you to have it."

Bless the clerk's heart. Through promotions, coupons, and one-day-sales, the cross was extremely affordable.

As I write these words, the cross sits in front of me. Its craftsmanship reminds me of my relationship with my mother. I treasure the cross because I treasured Momma. It is both silver and gold, which reminds me of how easily we related to each other. We laughed together and cried together. We just got along.

When I wear it, I feel strength and comfort. I feel my mother's love. The cutout filigree work compliments clothing and changes with the different colors I wear. Momma and I experienced so many changes as her health declined, which brought new challenges and fears. In the center of the cross is a diamond. It represents her valuable sense of humor and unconditional love. I pray I will shine the same light in my own life.

Thank you, Momma. Merry Christmas.

Mama Jewell at the Pearly Gates

Ending a book is always a challenge. And like many writers, I struggled until May 17, 2012, around 3:30 p.m. At that moment, my mother-in-law, Jewell Holmes Herlong, entered into her

much-deserved eternal reward. It had been a ten-year journey that ended with the cruelty of Alzheimer's, appropriately described by Ronald Reagan as the "long goodbye."

Mama Jewell had a servant's heart. She loved unconditionally; she was a devoted wife, mother, grandmother, relative, and friend. I was proud to be her daughter-in-law. Knowing Mama Jewell, I imagine the first thing she did when she met Saint Peter was to ask if he liked hot chicken casserole. Armed with groceries, cleaning supplies, and her signature homemade halter top, Mama Jewell would have been ready to cook, clean, and fluff the clouds of heaven. I imagine my mother was having her hair fixed and nails painted. In her fun diva-ish voice she would have said, "Jewell, sit down."

Since Thomas and I had a whirlwind romance of seven days, you can imagine how Mama Jewell and her servant's heart felt about Thomas getting involved with another beauty queen. After dating two Miss Americas, he had given the reigning Miss South Carolina a diamond ring. Just before Thomas informed the family that he was engaged, Mama Jewell said, "Thomas, please stop dating those beauty queens."

The first time I stayed with the Herlong family, I woke up, put on my robe, and walked into the den wearing no makeup. Mama Jewell looked at me, broke into a huge smile and said, "Oh, Honey, you *are* like us." I think she was afraid I'd put on my crown, ring a bell, and request brunch.

Alzheimer's had robbed Mama Jewell of so many things she held dear. She had only three pearl phrases left: "Thank you. You are so special. I love you." Those were her final pearls. She wore them and shared them every day. The caregivers loved her, and they always commented on her sweet spirit.

As Mama Jewell entered her new life, free from her diseased condition, I wonder if our Lord changed his greeting just for Mama Jewell. Maybe He said, "My daughter, thank you. You are special and I love you."

May God help us all to wear our strand of pearls with appreciation, service, and love. Lord, remind us how valuable it is to receive those pearls through the help of the Holy Spirit. May we be examples for generations to come.

The Final Pearl

Saying goodbye to the people you love is hard. In less than two years, I lost my mother, my sister, my college roommate, Tootsie, and my mother-in-law, Jewell. They were all very influential women in my life and represented the formation of several pearls on my strand. The healthy direction for me to take is the one that celebrates the life lessons and cherished memories these women gave me. I'm thankful that I know the loving God who put these women in my path.

My personal collection of pearls reflects all of the experiences the Lord has allowed in my life: gathering the seed pearls, discovering the pearl of joy, and finding the value in the pain of the dark pearl.

Completing our strand of pearls is a process of developing the fruit of the Spirit: love, joy, peace, forbearance, kindness, goodness, faithfulness, gentleness and self-control. It takes time, perseverance, and patience.

We may never fully understand our jagged, dark, or irregular pearl collection until we meet the Lord face to face. One thing I do understand is that all things work together for those who love the Lord and are called to His purpose (Romans 8:28).

Wear your strand, whether it is one pearl or one hundred pearls. Remember how important it is to handle life's issues for your spiritual and mental health and to benefit the next generation. Celebrate each jewel. Never forget that the Lord's best for you and for me is a life of love, laughter, and abundant joy.

Bury me with my pearls, Lord. Give me wisdom and a sense of humor as I journey through this life. Help me share my strand of jewels and be a blessing to others. Amen.

Jane Jenkins Herlong
Helping Folks Laugh More and Live Healthier

To book Jane or order her products visit: www.janeherlong.com

Laugh with Jane as she journeys from
tomato fields to the runway of the
Miss America Pageant - Book

Jane's CD Humorous Speech-LIVE!

Jane Sings Classic Songs on CD

Twenty Life Lessons for Women of all ages-Book

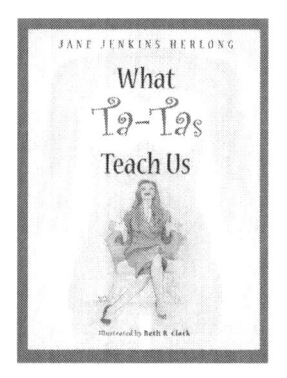

Jane's Humorous Speech on CD-LIVE

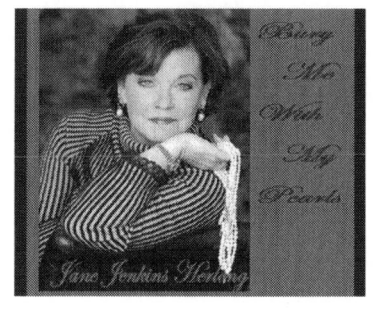

Jane's Comedy and singing CD- Sirius XM Radio

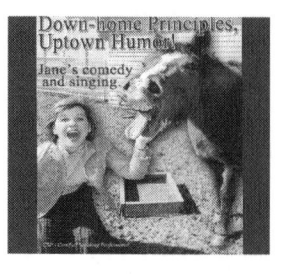

The Spirit of Christmas CD

Breast Cancer Tee Shirt

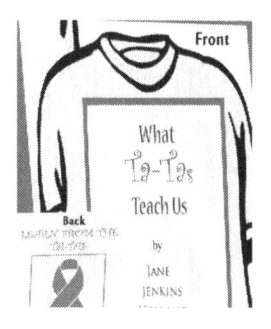

Made in the USA
San Bernardino, CA
10 January 2016

Callum MacDonald is a historian at the University of Warwick, England. He is also the author of *Korea: The War Before Vietnam*.

Picture Acknowledgements

Bundesarchivs, Koblenz: page 1 below, 8. Czechoslovak News Agency, Prague/Camera Press: pages 2, 3, 7, 9, 10 above, 11, 12, 13, 14, 15 below left and right, 16. Imperial War Museum, London: pages 1 above, 4, 5, 10 below. Private collection: pages 6, 15 above.